John Ruffini

Doctor Antonio

John Ruffini

Doctor Antonio

ISBN/EAN: 9783741165139

Manufactured in Europe, USA, Canada, Australia, Japa

Cover: Foto ©Andreas Hilbeck / pixelio.de

John Ruffini

Doctor Antonio

EACH VOLUME SOLD SEPARATELY.

COLLECTION
OF
BRITISH AUTHORS

TAUCHNITZ EDITION.

VOL. 553.

DOCTOR ANTONIO.

IN ONE VOLUME.

LEIPZIG: BERNHARD TAUCHNITZ.
PARIS: LIBRAIRIE C. REINWALD, 15, RUE DES SAINTS-PÈRES.
PARIS: THE GALIGNANI LIBRARY, 224, RUE DE RIVOLI,
AND AT NICE, 48, QUAI ST. JEAN BAPTISTE.

COLLECTION

OF

BRITISH AUTHORS.

VOL. 553.

DOCTOR ANTONIO. BY JOHN RUFFINI.

IN ONE VOLUME.

TAUCHNITZ EDITION.

By the same Author.

LAVINIA	2 vols.
LORENZO BENONI	1 vol.
VINCENZO	2 vols.
A QUIET NOOK	1 vol.
THE PARAGREENS	1 vol.
CARLINO	1 vol.

DOCTOR ANTONIO.

BY

JOHN RUFFINI.

COPYRIGHT EDITION.

LEIPZIG
BERNHARD TAUCHNITZ
1861.

CONTENTS.

			Page
CHAPTER	I.	Great and Small	7
—	II.	The Osteria	22
—	III.	Sir John Davenne	46
—	IV.	Skirmishes	55
—	V.	A pitched Battle	71
—	VI.	Little Occupations	92
—	VII.	Bits of Information	106
—	VIII.	Speranza	117
—	IX.	Lucy's Scheme	136
—	X.	In the Balcony	147
—	XI.	The 15th of May 1840	165
—	XII.	In the Garden	179
—	XIII.	In the Boat	190
—	XIV.	Sicily	200
—	XV.	Progress to the Sanctuary	220
—	XVI.	New Characters and Incidents	240
—	XVII.	The Theatre	257
—	XVIII.	Antonio pledges himself	268
—	XIX.	The Idyl at a Close	277

		Page
Chapter XX.	Absence	293
— XXI.	Eight Years after	299
— XXII.	Naples	319
— XXIII.	The 15th of May 1848	335
— XXIV.	Tidings	348
— XXV.	Væ Victis	359
— XXVI.	Continuation	372
— XXVII.	Ischia	386

DOCTOR ANTONIO.

CHAPTER I.
Great and Small.

On a fine sunny afternoon of early April, in the year 1840, an elegant travelling carriage was rattling, at the full speed of four post-horses, over the road, famous among tourists as the Cornice Road, and which runs along the western Riviera of Genoa, from that city to Nice.

Few of the public highways of Europe are more favoured than this—few, at any rate, combine in themselves three such elements of natural beauty as the Mediterranean on one side, the Apennines on the other, and overhead the splendours of an Italian sky. The industry of man has done what it could, if not to vie with, at least not to disparage Nature. Numerous towns and villages, some gracefully seated on the shore, bathing their feet in the silvery wave, some stretching up the mountain sides like a flock of sheep, or thrown picturesquely astride a lofty ridge, with here and there a solitary sanctuary perched high on a sea-washed cliff, or half lost in a forest of verdure at the head of some glen; marble palaces and painted villas emerging from sunny vineyards, gaily flowering gardens, or groves of orange and lemon trees; myriads of white *casini* with green jalousies scattered all over hills, once sterile, but now, their scanty soil propped up by terrace shelving above terrace, clothed to the top with olive-trees,—all and everything, in short, of man's handiwork, betokens the activity and ingenuity of a tasteful and richly-endowed race.

The road, in its obedience to the capricious indentations of the coast, is irregular and serpent-like; at one time on a level with the sea, it passes between hedges of tamarisk, aloes, and oleander, at another winds up some steep mountain side, through dark pine forests, rising to such a height that the eye recoils terrified from looking into the abyss below; here it disappears into galleries cut in the living rock, there comes out upon a wide expanse of earth, sky, and water; now turns inland, with a seeming determination to force a passage across the mountain, anon shoots abruptly in an opposite direction, as if bent upon rushing headlong into the sea. The variety of prospect resulting from this continual shifting of the point of view is as endless as that offered by the everchanging combinations of a kaleidoscope. Could we but give this sketch a little of the colouring,—real colouring, of the country, what a picture we should make of it! But we cannot. It is past the power of words to shadow out the brilliant transparency of this atmosphere, the tender azure of this sky, the deep blue of this sea, the soft gradations of tone tinting these wavy mountains, as they lap one over the other. The palette of a Stanfield, or a D'Azeglio, would scarcely be equal to the task.

Amid such scenery the carriage just introduced to the reader's notice rolled briskly on. It was as fine a piece of workmanship as ever issued from the hands of a first-rate London coach-maker, light, elegant, well balanced, capacious, comfortable-looking, and wanting in none of the appendages that bespeak rank and wealth, from the (scarcely visible on the dark well-varnished panels) miniature coat-of-arms, with numerous quarterings, surmounted by the bloody hand, that fixed the position held by the travellers, on the social ladder of Great Britain, to the smart lady's-maid and somewhat portly man out of livery, who showed their appreciation of the fine Nature around, by slumbering placidly in the rumble.

The two occupants of the inside, an elderly gentleman and a young lady, evidently father and daughter, seemed, if

one might judge from appearances, as insensible as their
servants to the various beauties soliciting their admiration.
White sails, gliding, like huge swans, over the heaving
waves, fruit trees, so laden with blossoms as to look less
like trees than overgrown nosegays, fields yellow with
daffodil, blue with anemone, white with long-stemmed Star
of Bethlehem, hoary rocks, armed at every crevice with the
lance-like leaves of gigantic aloes, passed in rapid succession
by our travellers, equally unnoticed or disregarded.

Half buried in a heap of cushions, pillows, and shawls,
the young lady lay at full length, trying hard to sleep; but
though her cheek was pale with fatigue, and a blue circle
round her eyes spoke sadly of want of rest, sleep refused to
come, as her incessant change of position, her jerks and
moans of childish impatience, clearly showed to her companion. A fair specimen she was of a type of beauty, not
rarely met with in England, especially among the higher
classes—a type uniting characteristics that would seem incompatible, a stamp of distinction akin to haughtiness, and
an almost ideal suavity of outline. The veil of languor
spread over her person, gave her loveliness a peculiar charm,
one irresistibly touching. Nature, who had made this girl
so beautiful, seemed to have written on her every feature
"fragile." The thin blue veins marbling her temples, the
soft azure of her eye, the maiden-blush clearness of the skin,
were but too suggestive of the transitory bloom and beauty
of some delicate flower. The hair, locks of which strayed
here and there out of their elegant prison of embroidered
gauze, had that rich golden hue with which the Italian
painters adorn the heads of cherubs. Altogether, hers was
as graceful and fairy-like a form as ever human eye rested
on, such as an angel would choose if condemned to assume
a mortal shape, just corporeal enough to attest humanity,
yet sufficiently transparent to let the celestial origin shine
through.

Sir John Davenne—for such was the name of the elderly
gentleman by the side of this fair creature—sat lost in a

brown study, one seemingly of no pleasant nature, and from which nothing had power to rouse him, but the sound, however stifled, of a short dry cough, which awakened all the solicitude of an affectionate parent. He would then turn to his young companion, ask, in a whisper full of tenderness, if she felt worse, mutter some words of endearment or cheering, and shake up or smooth the pillows.

The appearance of the father was at first sight prepossessing also in its way. The fresh complexion, almost feminine in its softness, the clear blue eye, the lofty brow, scarcely shaded by two scanty tufts of glossy gray hair, carefully brushed forward, the tall upright figure, that gave little evidence of the fifty-six or fifty-seven summers its possessor had numbered, all were calculated to produce an agreeable impression. A nearer inspection, a more prolonged gaze, revealed blots on this polished surface. The forehead, pure in colour and smooth as marble, was high but narrow, and sloping backwards, like the foreheads of George the Third and Charles the Tenth, an hereditary feature in the family from which this gentleman descended, and that kept the promise it gave, of an obstinacy which would not have discredited the crowned heads it has been likened to. The light-blue eye was too prominent and round, the nostrils of the thin arched nose were pinched, the small finely-cut lips had a pressure upwards, which, with the acute angle of the nostril, indicated an indulged habit of contemptuous pride. The general expression of this gentleman's countenance seemed to say, that the clay that other men were made of "did come between the wind and his nobility."

An uninterrupted series of explosions from the postilion's whip, and the stony pavement over which the carriage now clatters, loudly announce its having entered a town. A stentorian "ohe!" from the Automedon of the aristocratic vehicle, gives warning to the unseen occupant of a shabby two-wheeled *calessino*, standing in front of the post-house, to make room for its betters. Be it the effect of the bloody hand, that makes itself felt even at a distance, or be it simply that the owner of the gig had pressing business of his own, certain it is that the word of command was scarcely uttered before obeyed, and the dusty *calessino* started away at the full speed of its shaggy horse, leaving its ponderous competitor undisputed master of the field.

The lady's-maid and the man-servant get down from the rumble, and wait obsequiously at the carriage doors. The invalid asks for a glass of water. The water is obtained, and Sir John pours into it some drops from a phial, and holds it to the lips of the suffering girl. In the meantime, two professional beggars, a man and woman, in pictorial rags, begin a long litany of miseries, ending with an ever-repeated burden that the *Madonna Santissima e tutti i Santi del Paradiso* will repay any charity tenfold to the *buoni benefattori*. Miss Davenne looks for her purse, and puts some money into the woman's hand, who happens to be on her side of the carriage. Sir John throws some silver on the ground for the old man. Certainly, both father and daughter are actuated by an identically meritorious feeling, but how unlike is the manner in which it is expressed! Even the beggars feel the difference—the old woman drops a courtesy and a smile, while the old man picks up the money and turns away sullenly.

"What is the name of this place?" asks Miss Davenne. "San Remo," is the answer. Sir John Davenne does not approve of the name; at least one may argue as much from his pursed-up lips as he hears it. He looks up the street and down the street, and finally draws in his head. Had Sir John Davenne kept a note-book he would probably have made an entry of this sort,—"San Remo, a queer-looking place, narrow, ill-paved streets, high, irregular houses, ragged people, swarms of beggars," and so forth for a whole page. Fortunately for the public reputation of San Remo, Sir John kept no note-book.

By this time four horses were already put to the carriage, but the length of the next stage, and the hilly character of the road, required, according to the postmaster, an extra horse. This fifth horse, however, which was to be placed tandem-fashion, manifested a most determined disinclination for the post assigned him; kicking and plunging in fair alternation, he at last broke loose, and set off full gallop down the narrow street, pursued by all the men and boys apparently in the town, by whose combined efforts, after a keen chase, he was captured at last, triumphantly brought back, and fastened in front of the other four. The postilion jerked himself into his heavy saddle, waved his long whip round his head, first to the right and then to the left, a report like a pistol following each manœuvre, and the carriage was at length again set in motion, amid a perfect uproar of unintelligible vociferations.

In a short time it came in sight of the gig first noticed at San Remo, and now toiling up a long steep hill; a curious specimen, to be sure, of the conveyances of the country,— such a weather-beaten, discoloured, squeezed-in, almost shapeless thing,—it was a wonder how it held together or remained on its wheels. The distance between the two carriages diminished very perceptibly, the four wheels gaining on the two, much in the proportion of a big steamer in stern chase of a small boat. Now the thick layers of dust on the road deadened the sound of wheels and horses' feet, and made the usual warnings with the whip more necessary than ever. Still the postilion gave no sign of life. Most likely he took it for granted that the driver of the gig must be aware of the coming up of his magnificent neighbour, and would take proper care of himself, or maybe he was so engrossed by the mending of his lash as to forget his duty; however it was, it so turned out, that the English equipage, just as it reached the verge of the eminence, dashed unexpectedly at full speed past the unprepared humble vehicle. The shaggy little horse, frightened out of its wits, made such a sudden bolt to the left, that had the hand holding the reins been a whit less strong and experienced, gig, horse, and driver must have gone down into the sea.

The volley of expletives with which the single gentleman
of the gig saluted the sudden advent of his fellow-travellers,
(and from the angry tone in which they were uttered, there
was no mistaking them for blessings), sufficiently testified
his resentment of the postillon's unceremonious proceeding.
Fortunately Miss Davenne, though a tolerably good Italian
scholar, did not understand the patois of the Riviera, otherwise she would have had an odd and not particularly agreeable illustration of passionate local eloquence.

If the unexpected encounter had shaken the shaggy pony
and his master out of their equanimity, the famous extra
horse of Sir John's carriage proved not a bit more stoical.
Perhaps the alarm was contagious, or perhaps the creature
had a special antipathy to the process of going down hill,
which now began. Whatever was the cause, from the moment of passing the *calessino*, his progress became a chance
medley of galloping, plunging, and rearing. Sir John, who,
with his head out of the window, was following with mo-
mently increasing anxiety the strange evolutions of the
beast, would have at once called to the postilion, but from
the double fear of startling his daughter out of the half
slumber into which she seemed to have dropped after leaving San Remó, and of too suddenly checking the horses in
full career. But the carriage having reached the bottom of
the hill, which was not a long one, and Miss Davenne being
awake by this time, Sir John ordered the postilion to stop,
and in the same breath desired John, the companion of the
lady's-maid in the rumble, to get down and see what was
the matter. John got down; and there ensued a parley between the valet and the post-boy, unlikely to lead to any
satisfactory result, seeing that the postilion did not understand one syllable of John's questions or directions, expressed in the most imperfect of Italian, nor did John com-
prehend one syllable of the postilion's explanations, given
in the patois of the Riviera. Each party repeated his own
words over and over again, without conveying any idea to
the other; English John insisting on the restive horse being

put into the traces, and one of the quiet hind horses taking his place; while the postilion, with native fluency, persisted in asseverating that there was no danger, that the plunging and rearing of the leader was caused by the knocking of the splinter bar against his legs, and that he could put that to rights in no time.

At last the energetic pantomime of the Italian lad, for the postilion was not above twenty, gave John a glimpse of his interlocutor's meaning. The fact pointed out by the youth was so evidently one, though perhaps not the sole cause of the horse's restlessness, that John, glad to be spared any more arguing to so little purpose, and also at some cost to his dignity, readily accepted the explanation; and having reported to his master that there was only a trifle wrong with the harness, which would be remedied directly, climbed back gravely to his comfortable seat by Miss Hutchins.

The postilion had just begun to try shortening the chains of the bar, so that it should not strike against the horse, whistling loudly the while, when the gig, which had been left behind, came up and stopped by his side, without his having heard or seen it. "Hallo, Prospero!" said a voice, which made the young man simultaneously start, look up, and take off his hat with some precipitation, "what the devil is the matter with you to-day? Do you know, you stupid boy, that you have been within an ace of pitching me into the sea!"

"Pitching *Vossignoria* into the sea!" exclaimed Prospero, with an odd mixture of anger and distress in his voice. "*Vossignoria* knows I would rather be drowned myself a hundred times. But this is not the Signor's *calessino*, and how could I guess the Signor was in it?"

"And what had that to do with the matter?" retorted the voice of the so addressed "Signor" angrily. "What does it signify whether it was I or the Great Khan of Tartary? How dare you, sir, play with the life of any one? It is your business and duty to take care that the horses you drive be not the death of peaceable citizens. Do you hear?"

Prospero, now thoroughly humbled, said he was very sorry, and would do his best that the like should not happen again.

"Very well; but what horse is that you have got there?" continued the voice; and a hand stretched forth from under the hood of the *calessino* pointed to the extra horse.

"It is a new one, Signor; it came to the stables only yesterday. He's a fidgety beast."

"Fidgety you call him. *Bagatella!* he's as vicious an animal as I ever saw, and one your master ought not to put to any carriage with Christians inside. I have been watching your fidgety beast for the last quarter of an hour. Take good advice while it is yet time, Prospero; instead of fastening that buckle, undo it, and let the horse find its own way back to San Remo."

Had Prospero been a man of fifty, with an established character as a post-boy, the probabilities are that he might have accepted of good advice; but he was a mere lad, as we have said, full of courage and confidence in the strength of his own arms, and with an ardent desire to be known as a first-rate whip on the road. Now, to send back a horse, under the circumstances, was tantamount to the confession of his own inability to manage him—a confession that Prospero's self-love and ambition alike forbade. Postilions have their point of honour as well as the people they drive.

So Prospero replied, with some cunning, "Leave him on the road, Signor, you mean, for how would he ever find his way back, when we got him only yesterday, and that from inland? A pretty scrape I would be in with master, if I were to turn the horse loose here! But there is no danger," continued Prospero, recovering his good humour and politeness, "any beast would kick if he had a great piece of wood flapping against his legs every step he took. See here, Signor, if I let down the ropes a bit, and shorten up the chain, so as to keep the bar pretty stiff, he'll go as quiet as a lamb."

"Well, you ought to know best," answered the voice; "at all events, keep a sharp look-out on him, and try next time you come up with me, not to upset me, or give me a cold bath, if you can help it."

These last words were said good-humouredly; the postilion showed all his white teeth in the merry laugh with which he received the recommendation, and made a low bow as the gig drove off.

This dialogue, of course not understood by the English travellers, lasted scarcely two minutes; the manner of speaking of both interlocutors being rapid and incisive. The voice of the invisible one was remarkable for its richness of tone, and natural management of what it may be allowable to call the *chiaroscuro* of speech. When we say *invisible*, we mean with respect only to those within the carriage, who, the two vehicles standing one before the other in nearly the same line, could see nothing of the person in the hooded gig, but the hand with which he had pointed to the horse.

The lengthening of the ropes and the shortening of the chains being at last accomplished, it was not long before the great English carriage once more passed the democratic-looking *calessino*, but this time at a very gentle pace, and not till after every sort of whistle, cry, or call a throat could give forth, and every possible signal a whip is capable of, had been rung through the air by the repentant Prospero. Sir John Davenne gave a sigh of relief as they passed. Odd enough, the Baronet had condescended to take a personal dislike to the *calessino*, and he hoped that he had seen it now for the last time. Ah! Sir John Davenne, there is a legend or motto older than even the Crusades, "L'homme propose, Dieu dispose." The shy horse was behaving well for the time being, Miss Davenne was now fairly asleep, so all his causes for uneasiness or annoyance being at once removed, Sir John relapsed into his former reverie, which, in another few minutes, and in spite of one or two manful efforts, became a most flagrant doze.

A little after Sir John had closed his eyes, the road,

which for some time had been going up hill, began to descend. For a good mile it ran sloping zigzag round a barren reddish cliff that jutted into the sea, till, at a sharp turning to the right, there opened to view the last but most rapid part of the declivity, then a run of no more than two hundred paces on a level with the sea. Here the road began to rise again, and soon became bifurcated; the lesser branch climbing straight up a little promontory, that shut in the horizon to the west—a verdant smiling bit of land, with a steeple, and here and there housetops shining in the sun—the main branch skirting the rocky base to the left.

Now Prospero, whose sense of responsibility had been put on the *qui vive* by the warnings of the occupant of the gig, ventured down the slope with all possible care, and with an eye to the ticklish leader. But not all his vigilance or skill were sufficient to ward off a result inevitable under the circumstances, namely, that the strain kept on the traces of the front horse in ascending, being necessarily slackened in the descent, nay, at times entirely suspended, the bar by which the animal was fastened to the pole once more began to hit against his hind quarters. An occasional lash out of his heels gave warning of coming danger. Matters grew worse, as the declivity, gentle at first, just about the turning before mentioned became more abrupt, and the inconvenience arising from the splinter bar increased in direct ratio to the accelerated motion of the vehicle. The rage and terror of the goaded animal augmented with every step, while the efforts of the alarmed driver to quiet him, only served to frighten the other four. Feeling that the whole five were getting beyond his control, Prospero suddenly loosened the reins, and with a clack of his tongue launched them at full gallop, keeping a sharp look-out on the road, so as to avoid everything in the shape of an impediment, which, however small, at the fearful rate the carriage was going, must have endangered its equilibrium. He trusted, of course, to being able to pull in the horses so soon as they should feel the rise of the hill before them.

It was, indeed, the only chance of safety left, and in another minute the attempt would have succeeded, but Sir John all at once awoke. The real state of things had influenced his sleep, for he had been dreaming all this time of horses running away, and in a very natural bewilderment on first waking, he put his head out of the window, roaring to the postilion to stop. The noise awakened Miss Davenne, who, in her turn, greatly alarmed, began to scream. The call and the screams made the unlucky Prospero turn his head a little, and in so doing he lost sight of the road for a second;—even a second was too much at this critical conjuncture. One of the hind wheels jerked over a stone, the carriage gave a bound as if it were about to take wing, oscillated for a moment on the edge of the road, then tumbled over, horses and all. Bad as the case was, it might have been worse. The road was only a few feet above the shore, and, luckily, at that spot there was a thick bed of sand, which softened the fall. It was well that Sir John had not been sooner roused from his nap, or the upset might have proved too much even for a man of his consequence.

While Miss Hutchins, all in a flutter of spirits and garments, with her sudden flight through the air, picks herself up as fast as she can, astonished to find she is all in one piece—while John, as grim and dignified as ever, in spite of a very ugly somerset, and a long cut across the nose, which is bleeding profusely, pulls Sir John, who happens to be uppermost, and seems to have sustained no injury, through one of the windows—while all three uniting their efforts, try to extricate from the fallen carriage Miss Davenne's inanimate form—while Prospero, from the very excess of despair, stares vacantly first at one and then the other, leaving his horses to kick and struggle at their pleasure, looking as though he had fallen from the clouds instead of from off the road, the hated gig might have been seen, like a thunderbolt on wheels, rushing furiously down the hill. Has the shaggy little horse run away also, or does the person driving belong to that rare order of beings, upon whom the prospect of giving aid to fellow-creatures in distress, acts like an intoxicating draught, rendering them insensible to personal danger? We shall see by and by.

"Anybody hurt? any harm done?" cried the gentleman of the gig, as he drew up in front of where the accident had happened. "Can I be of any use? I am a medical man." At the same time there got out of the *calessino*, and made for the group standing round Miss Davenne, a tall, dark, black-bearded man, wearing a broad-brimmed conical hat —in short, just such a figure, as met by Sir John under any other circumstances, would have made him cock the two pistols he had invariably carried about him, since travelling in the classical land of banditti. As it was, the English baronet, who did not understand one word of the stranger's Italian, contented himself with staring at the new-comer half in amazement, half in displeasure, as much as to say, To what species does this creature belong? Nothing daunted by this stare, the stranger pushed past Sir John, knelt down by the side of the prostrate girl, and was trying to feel her pulse, when Sir John, not catching his meaning, made a dart forward, as if to thrust him away from his daughter.

"Are you mad?" bawled the stranger in Italian; then in French, "Je suis médecin, vous dis-je," adding rapidly this time in good plain English, as if in the Baronet's face he had seen the flag of Great Britain hoisted, "Did you not hear me say that I was a physician?" The sound of his native tongue at length conveys to Sir John's comprehension a clear and distinct conception, and a ray of consolation falls on his spirit. For, to have a doctor at hand in such a strait, and a doctor who speaks English, however his appearance may jar with all the Englishman's preconceived notions of medical gentlemen, Sir John allows to himself is something.

As if what he had said called for no further remark or question, the Doctor proceeded to feel the lady's pulse, took off her bonnet, and gently examined her head. No wound there, not even a bruise. The chest, too, was safe, for, though faint, her breathing was regular; "unless there be concussion of the brain," said the Doctor to himself. Just as he shook his head at this unpleasant conjecture, his eyes met those of Sir John Davenne. The keen anxiety of that countenance could not for a moment be mistaken. "You need not be uneasy about your daughter," said the Doctor, answering the unspoken question, and taking the relationship for granted, "this is a mere fainting fit, the young lady will soon recover;" and while still speaking, he pulled a case out of his coat pocket, from which he took a pair of large scissors. These he thrust into Miss Hutchins' trembling hands, saying, "You must manage to undo your lady's dress, while I run down to the sea for some water. Cut everything, mind, without moving her."

Waiting for no reply, the tall gentleman strides away, fills his hat with water, and returns in the twinkling of an eye. All his movements are quick but sedate, and though visibly excited, all he does and says, he does and says in a resolute, quiet, earnest way of his own, without hurry or fuss. As he comes back, the struggling horses and the petrified Prospero attract his attention, and he calls out in a voice that enforces immediate obedience, "Cut the ropes of those horses, do you hear? and do it at once," and keeps his eye on the postilion till he sees him twist his head round like Harlequin's pantomime of distress, and begin to fumble in one of his jacket pockets for a knife.

The Doctor sprinkled Miss Davenne's face and throat freely with water, laid a wet handkerchief across her forehead, while Hutchins held smelling-salts to her nose, and bathed her hands with Eau-de-Cologne. But in defiance of all efforts she continued insensible. It was becoming clear to a medical eye, that some more energetic remedies might be necessary to restore animation. The Doctor again drew out his case of instruments, and, to Sir John's great consternation, set about choosing a lancet. Happily, at this moment, Miss Davenne half opened her eyes, and faltered out "Papa." Sir John stooped fondly over her, "What is it, my darling?"

"Oh, my foot! such a dreadful pain in my foot!"

"Which foot?" asked the Italian.

She looked up at him in some amazement, then pointing to her right foot, said, "This one." The words were no sooner uttered than the Doctor seized his great scissors, and in a second had skilfully cut open the elegant boot and fine stocking, laying bare a little alabaster foot, just fit for a Cinderella's slipper, but shockingly sprained. Nor was this all. The leg was broken just above the ankle. This, with rapid medical intuition, he rather guessed than saw, and by a motion as quick as thought, he dropped a shawl over the wounded limb, so as to hide it from both father and daughter, saying, in a calm tone, "Ah, a sprained ankle! a rather painful, but not a serious thing. I must have all the handkerchiefs you can give me," he added, looking round. Handkerchiefs of all sizes and qualities came forth from the pockets of the bystanders. "Enough, enough," said he, smiling, as he looked at the unexpected shower. "These will answer in the meantime for a temporary bandage, which will alleviate the pain the young lady feels." He bound up the poor foot carefully, then said, "Now, madam, let me impress upon you the importance of remaining as quiet as possible. I must leave you for a little while, to fetch what is necessary to enable me to dress your foot properly, which must be done before you can be removed from your present uncomfortable position. Do you promise me not to stir while I am gone?"

"Yes," said Miss Davenne, with a feeble effort to smile her thanks.

The Doctor sprung lightly to his feet, and was hastening away, when suddenly turning to John, who was standing near him with a look of deep commiseration, almost comical to see on his black and blue face, he said, "Suppose you were to hold an umbrella over the lady's head, the sun is full upon her;" then continuing his way, he jumped into his gig, and pushed the shaggy horse to a gallop.

CHAPTER II.
The Osteria.

"So that gentleman is a doctor, papa," said Lucy, this being the simple christian name given to the daughter of the haughty Baronet.

"At least he gives himself out for one, my dear," said Sir John.

"How very lucky for me!" remarked the young lady.

"Very," replied Sir John, "though he is an odd-looking figure for a physician."

"Yes, in England we should think so," answered Lucy; "but abroad, you know, people are less particular about dress, and there is something gentlemanlike about him after all. Did you observe his hands, papa? I am sure they are like a gentleman's."

"May be so, may be so," said Sir John, doubtingly.

"I wonder whether he is English, papa; he speaks very good English."

"Yes, but there is a strong smack of the foreigner in his accent," returned her father.

Lucy was silent, and, leaning her head on her hand, seemed little disposed to continue the dialogue. Sir John thus left to himself, all at once remembered the postilion, and as he remembered, all the anger forgotten in his anxiety for Lucy returned, rose to fury and overflowed his lips. He began to abuse the unlucky lad in very Doric English, interspersed now and then with a word intended for Italian. "Look at the cold-blooded villain," stormed Sir John, pointing to Prospero, who, as he stood mechanically holding the bridles of the horses, and staring vacantly, did look as if the storm of words rattling about his ears for the last five minutes did not concern him; but this apathy was not indifference nor callousness, nor cold-bloodedness, on the contrary, it was the stoniness of despair. This immobility irritating Sir John more and more every instant, brought him at last to swear, that, since he could not remain on the spot long enough to prosecute the rascal for deliberate intent to murder, he would write to the postmaster and have the lad dismissed. The post-boy never winced. No, he would do better—he would apply to the English Envoy at Turin; he, Sir John Davenne, was determined to make an example of the wretch for the benefit of future travellers and post-boys. Still Prospero stood as unmoved as if part of the rock by his side. He, Sir John Davenne, would never rest, no, never, till the good-for-nothing Italian ruffian had been summarily punished, though he should have recourse to the King of Sardinia himself. The doomed Prospero heard the sound of the Baronet's angry voice, but without its ever disturbing his agreeable contemplation of the postmaster's fury *in posse*, and the dread *in esse*, of having done some mortal injury to the *bella Signorina*. This outburst of ire had one use, at least, it was a diversion of its kind, which helped Sir John to wait for the Italian doctor's promised return with more patience than he would otherwise have done.

Miss Davenne felt thankful when she saw the poor old gig once more. "Now, then," said the Doctor's cheerful voice, "we must all make ourselves useful. Ah! this umbrella is in my way here, will you have the goodness, sir," turning to Sir John, "to hold it yourself, and screen your daughter from the sun? Excuse me, but you will do it more effectually if you sit down by her, thus," and he placed Sir John at his daughter's head.

"You, too," he continued, addressing the servants, "will seat yourselves at the young lady's feet, and attend closely to what I say to you. My place is here in the middle;" and he knelt down on one knee with his back turned to Sir John and the patient, so as to entirely preclude their seeing anything of what was going to pass.

"I shall not keep you long, nor hurt you much," he added,

turning his head for an instant towards Miss Davenne. So saying, he undid the handkerchiefs, and bade Hutchins and John support the foot.

Lucy remained as quiet and passive in his hands, with even a look of faith in him shining in her eyes, as if, instead of chance having brought them together on a high road in Italy, he had been her medical attendant since her infancy. Indeed, all present, even Sir John, seemed under the spell of the combination of simplicity and force that breathed in the man.

A pull—a crackling as if of bones clasping together—a suppressed groan. "There, it is over!" cried the Doctor, shaking off, with a jerk of his head, the large drops of perspiration breaking over his broad forehead. "You feel less pain already, do you?" he asked, bending towards Lucy. Poor girl, she was so bewildered she could scarcely tell how she felt. The foot had to be bound up, an operation which required great care, and took some time. At last it was finished. Two thin flat pieces of something which were among the rollers the doctor had fetched, (two slips of wood, we suspect, wrapped up in linen beforehand to conceal their real nature from the bystanders,) were fastened on each side of the foot, over the bandage, so as to secure it and keep all in its place, and there was an end of it.

By this time, four strong sunburnt peasant women had brought a very primitive kind of litter with mattresses on it, and were waiting at a little distance from the principal group.

"Bring one of the mattresses here," cried the Doctor, directing them to place it close to Miss Davenne's side. He then opened a sheet, saying to her, "We are going to slip this sheet under you, to lift you up gently and place you on the mattress, which we can then raise into the litter without fear of shaking or hurting your foot. All I beg of you is, to remain perfectly passive in our hands, and even guard against any involuntary movement meant to help yourself or us."

"This is the second time you have so earnestly warned me. I am then very dangerously hurt?" asked the young lady with some alarm.

"Not in the least," replied the Italian; "you are not to take fright at the cautions I impose on you," and bending again towards her, he added, in an undertone, "you can understand that many unpleasant consequences may follow an accident without entailing any danger to life. For instance, to cure your leg—for, properly speaking, it is your leg that is hurt and not your foot—is an easy task, one depending more on time and patience than on any surgical skill; but to make sure, that, when it is cured, it shall be absolutely as it was before the injury, not the eighth of an inch longer or shorter," (Lucy changed colour as she heard this,) "is a very different affair, and will require the utmost care and nicety. Now, then, do you see why I impress on you the danger of disobedience to your Doctor," added he with a smile of encouragement; "any imprudence or neglect on your side may render every attention on his part useless."

Seeing by the look which answered his that he had said enough to insure his patient's docility, the Doctor, with Hutchins' help, passed the sheet under Miss Davenne, then beckoning forward three of the women, he and they took each a corner, raised her, balanced as if in a hammock, and laid her first on the mattress by her side, then carefully transferred that to the litter. He covered her with a shawl, put a cushion under her head, and gave the signal of departure; but the litter was scarcely in motion when he called to the bearers to stop and turn it round, so that her head being foremost the poor girl could see her father, who was a little behind. "It will be a comfort to the young lady," explained the Doctor to the women carrying her, "to be able to see the dear and well-known face of her father."

Any one of experience must often have noticed and admired the quick perception and delicacy of many a poor peasant in all connected with the affections. More especially is the strength of the social bonds felt by the olive-skinned passionate children of Italy. The four pair of black eyes glistened with tears that made them look like black diamonds, while the stout matrons uttered, with that peculiar intonation of their country, so expressive, so indescribable, the usual appeal to the Virgin.

Lucy did not need to hear the explanation to guess the intention of the change thus ordered, and with a slight inclination of the head, or rather of her eyelids, accompanied by a smile, made the Doctor sensible of her having understood it. The look and smile brought a pleasant glow to the face and heart of the physician. This incident established a sympathetic communication, something like a magnetic current, according to modern parlance, between the young people—the Doctor was under thirty. What a kind-hearted man, thought Lucy. The gentle, grateful heart, thought the Doctor. Thus each had had a glimpse into the nature of the other.

The Italian was walking slowly behind the litter, when the Baronet, coming up to his side, said, somewhat abruptly, "I think it right to introduce myself to you;—Sir, I am Sir John Davenne, of Davenne Hall, in ... shire."

The younger gentleman, thus startled out of his reflections, took off his hat, and, with a bow sufficiently graceful, replied—

"And I, sir, am Doctor Antonio, the parish doctor of Bordighera;" and there was a twinkle in his eye, as if he relished something in his own reply excessively.

Sir John contracted his nostrils and pursed up his mouth, just the play of muscles of one whose sense of smell is offended, an habitual grimace of the Baronet's when either provoked or displeased.

"May I ask you," continued he, addressing his interlocutor, with a manner too provokingly ceremonious not to betray an intense pique, most likely at his not having been consulted in all the arrangements about his daughter, "may I ask you where we are going?"

"Excuse me, my dear sir," (confound his impudence!

said Sir John, mentally,) "in my hurry and anxiety for the lady I have forgotten to tell you. We are going to that red house yonder, half hidden by trees," answered the Doctor, pointing to a shabby, two-storied, rather dismantled-looking building to the left of the road, about half-way between the spot where they were and the bright-green little headland already mentioned; "it is a mere roadside inn," he continued, "kept by poor but respectable and kind people. You will find there, I am sorry to say, scanty accommodation, but all proper care and attention, and," added he significantly, "the thing of most importance in this moment, a bed for your daughter."

To judge from the play of the muscles about the nose, Sir John would have willingly dispensed with a good deal of the vaunted care and attention in favour of a little more personal comfort, but he said nothing of the sort, and replied,—

"Well, well, the accommodation is of little consequence, for, as soon as my daughter has had some repose, we shall resume our journey to Nice."

"You are surely not in earnest," cried the Italian, stopping short in his amazement; but immediately checking himself, he added, in a quiet and conciliatory manner, "I fear, nay, I am sure, that Miss Davenne will not be able to resume her journey for some"—(a pause of hesitation).

"Hours?" suggested the Baronet.

"Days, perhaps weeks," concluded the Doctor, gently.

"Weeks!" gasped Sir John, standing still in his turn. "Weeks!" repeated he, this time with a burst of indignation. "Impossible! I have engagements that I cannot postpone. I must be in London within ten days."

"For your daughter, I regret to say, that is entirely out of the question."

"Out of the question!—out of the question!" grumbled Sir John, "Why out of the question?"

The tone in which this query was put was so peremptory and trenchant, that the Doctor began to chafe.

"Because," said he, warmly, "since you must have it, your daughter's case—it is not my wish to alarm you, but—your daughter's case is not—." He was going to add, "what I stated at first," with God knows what else; but at sight of the anxious look of the already alarmed father, the young physician had not the heart to go on, and wound up, instead, with, "is not one to be trifled with."

There, thought Sir John, recovering his self-possession and anger, I see what it is; this man is bent on frightening me to make the most of a good job—a reflection little calculated to sweeten his temper.

"Well, well," said he, impatiently, "I know, everybody knows what a sprain is. An odd pretension this, to keep us prisoners for an indefinite period of time, on the plea of a sprain!"

"Pretension to keep you prisoner!" exclaimed the Italian, with a wonderful contraction of the temples. "Nobody keeps you prisoner, my dear sir." (That second "my dear sir," the innocent translation of the common form of address in Italy, the "Caro Signor mio," one entirely of courtesy and not of familiarity, acted on all Sir John's aristocratic fibres as the grating of a file upon marble acts on the nerves of most sensitive people.) "You are not among Moorish pirates, there are other medical men in the neighbourhood whom you can consult, there are English physicians at Nice whose advice you can ask."

"I will ask the advice of nobody," retorted the Baronet, testily, "I want none. All I want is to be off, and off I will be!"

"You will do as you please," rejoined the Italian, "but I have a duty to perform, and perform it I will, and must. Miss Davenne, I declare most solemnly, cannot be removed with safety, for, at least, 'forty days.'" And having said this, the young man moved on, leaving his interlocutor to his own cogitations.

"Forty days!" gasped forth Sir John, standing stock

still. "Forty days!" and this time he changed his first tone of dismay into angry cachinnation. "That's a good joke!" and deliberately turning back, he waved to John, who was standing near the carriage, and desired him to have it brought up immediately to the red house, and ascertain what amount of injury it had sustained. This done, the Baronet followed the little caravan with slow and sullen steps.

The procession was not long in reaching its destination. "Here we are," said the Doctor, approaching Miss Davenne, as, leaving the high road, they turned down a wide lane in the direction of the beach, went through a gate on the left, over which hung a branch of pine-tree, and entered a garden, wherein stood the brick-coloured house. The litter was carried up a steep flight of outside stairs, and through a large room and a smaller one, to a little chamber, where Lucy and the mattresses were deposited upon a bedstead.

The Doctor dismissed the four women, and turning to his charge, who looked sad and pale, said,—

"Though everything is very homely here, you may rest satisfied that the bed and linen are clean: I saw to that before bringing you here."

"You are very kind," said Lucy, in a very low voice.

"The bare walls and want of furniture strike you disagreeably, I daresay," went on the Doctor; "we shall soon try and make the room a little more cheerful. Shall I introduce your landlady, Rosa, and her daughter Speranza, to you? Pretty names, are they not?" added he, as he noticed a smile on Lucy's face; "they sound like a good omen. Both are very desirous of making themselves useful, and you will make them very happy by accepting their services."

Lucy nodded to the women he pointed out to her, and who were standing at the door, one an elderly woman, the other a pale, black-eyed girl. They came forward at a sign from Doctor Antonio, and kissed the hand of the beautiful young lady with a mixture of enthusiastic tenderness and reverence. The fair skin, blue eyes, and golden hair, made Lucy seem to them more of an angel than one of the same species as themselves.

The Doctor, satisfied with the good feeling he saw already established between the guest and her hostesses, said to Lucy, "I must tell you what are the best arrangements I have been able to make for you. The four rooms of which this floor consists, the only decent ones in the house, are given up for your use; this for yourself, the one next it for your maid, and on the other side of the large entrance-room or lobby we came through, a bed-chamber for your father. Your man-servant will have a room down stairs."

"That will do nicely," said poor Lucy, trying to look cheerful. "I hope papa will be as well satisfied as I am." The Italian ventured no reply to this extravagant hope, but asked, "Have you any appetite? do you wish for anything to eat?"

"No, I thank you, I am not in the least hungry."

"So much the better. I should not advise your taking any solid food for the present. I shall now leave you, and I hope you will be able to sleep. At all events, remain quiet, and make no attempt at moving, remember. I will send you a mixture of which you may take a spoonful, from time to time, if you are thirsty."

"But I shall see you again, soon?" said Lucy, rather dismayed at hearing that her new friend was going away.

"In an hour or two," returned the Doctor, quietly, "and then we shall see what can be done to make this room a little more comfortable. I speak, of course, only of relative comfort. Everything here below is relative, *non è vero?*"

There seemed as though a sigh struggled with the smile with which the question was put.

"Use your scissors freely in undressing your young lady," said he to Miss Hutchins, on leaving the room. "Miss Davenne must not move, *must* not,—you understand?" and then he repeated the same caution in Italian to Rosa and Speranza.

As he issued from the chamber, on the threshold he met Sir John, who had lingered awhile below to catch sight of the carriage. The Baronet intimating by neither act nor word any wish for communication, Doctor Antonio walked on in silence. Reflecting, however, that the Baronet might have something to say after seeing his daughter, he loitered a few minutes in the lobby; (thus we shall call henceforward the entrance-room.) But the Englishman came forth, and conducted by the girl, Speranza, crossed the room towards his own without noticing in any way the presence of the Italian, who, perceiving that he was not wanted, left the house.

Sir John, when ushered into the room destined for him, threw himself doggedly on a chair, and darted an angry glance around. "A charming place, indeed, to spend forty days in!" sneered the Baronet. "Why not six months?" and he laughed aloud. The room, to say the truth, fully verified, if it did not surpass, the account of the inn given by the Doctor. The once white walls, now grown yellow from age, with not even a series of wretched prints of the *Via Crucis*, or a wretched bit of a glass to break their barren uniformity; the undraped window; the old deal table; the hard cane-bottomed chairs, two in number; the long coffin-like "*cassapanca*" (locker) at the foot of the uncurtained bed, made the room look more like the cell of an anchorite, than the bedchamber of a Protestant Baronet.

"We must get out of this hole at all events," murmured Sir John, rising and walking fretfully up and down, till the sound of approaching steps caused him to stop. It was John, who came as bidden, to report casualties. John brought good news. Save the glasses that had been smashed, and some scratches on the panels, there was nothing in the state of the carriage to prevent their going on to Nice.

"Very well," said Sir John, "have the glasses immediately replaced." Unfortunately that could not be done. John had already made inquiries on the subject, and the result was that panes of the required size were not to be found at the neighbouring town. Sir John pished and pshawed at this intelligence, and declared, in the bitterest of tones, that he should have much wondered, indeed, if it had been otherwise. John proceeded to state that he had not been able to bring the carriage to the door, on account of the garden gate being too narrow to permit of its passage; and then there was no coach-house there, added John. What was to be done?

Sir John made no reply, but led the way down to the garden gate, and after a short survey of the spot, a look at the carriage, one at the sky, and some further hesitation, bade John have the carriage removed a little to one side, where it might stand for the night, *if necessary*. "For," explained Sir John, with an angry sigh, "the nights are still fresh, and unless we can start in an hour or two, which is not sure, those damned glasses will detain us for the night. But to-morrow," continued the Baronet resolutely, "to-morrow, glasses or no glasses, we shall be off to Nice."

"Please, sir," observed John, hesitating, "will it be safe to leave the carriage and luggage all night in the lane?"

"Certainly not," returned the master. "Let me see,—in case we are detained you had better keep watch in the carriage with a brace of pistols."

Having thus settled the matter, whether much to John's personal satisfaction we cannot say, Sir John mounted the stone steps leading to the second story, his present quarters, and walked towards Lucy's room, but was met half-way by Miss Hutchins on tiptoe, with a report that her mistress felt very faint indeed, and had just closed her eyes to try and sleep. Whereupon Sir John, much grieved at the news, which confirmed but too well his fear of being kept where he was for the night, betook himself to his own room. However, he had not stayed there for a quarter of an hour when out he went again, and down the steps, and took to walking to and fro in front of the house, pushing on now and then to the outer gate, to cast a melancholy look at the carriage and up and down the lane. A second attempt to see his daughter having been foiled by the identical circumstances that had foiled the first, the unhappy Baronet took some dozen turns up and down the lobby, and repaired to his own room, sank into a chair, and said aloud, as he consulted his watch, "Why, time stands still in this confounded country!"

Yet time had moved on and brought with it a fresh addition to this poor gentleman's already superabundant stock of spleen and discomfort. Alas for the frailty of all flesh, even for that of the proudest man in England! Sir John was hungry, very hungry, and ashamed of being so, and provoked at being so, and terror-stricken at the dire necessity—a necessity which made itself more felt at every passing moment—of having to ask for food. Ask for food in *that* house!—sit down to dinner under *that* roof! It was tantamount to laying down arms in the face of the enemy; it was giving up at a blow all the heroic of his situation. Fancy Attilius Regulus, the first thing on his return to Carthage, asking for a beefsteak! Sir John felt all this. Sir John struggled bravely for a time, but at last surrendered. He instinctively put out his hand for a bell, of which there was no vestige whatever, and to his mortification had to go to the top of the stairs and call for John. "Go and see what there is in the larder," said Sir John, languidly, "supposing that there is anything like a larder in this—in this place; however, find out if anything fit to eat can be procured."

The sacrifice being consummated, Sir John went to see his daughter. Poor Lucy! she had all the heroism to herself. She was suffering acutely. "Where, my child?"—"Oh, papa, everywhere. I feel bruised all over. I have such an odd and disagreeable sensation at my foot, just as if it were swelled into a mountain of cork."

"But, my dear, you know that can be only fancy. Try and sleep."

"Dear papa, I have tried, and I cannot."

Poor thing, she was fainting with fatigue, and yet could not get a wink of sleep. Sir John did his best to soothe her, and, as he fondly stroked the stray curls that lay on her hot cheek, promised that she should go to Nice the next day, where, if she were forced to remain, she would have every comfort. But his words failed of their intended effect. Lucy felt no courage for the journey to Nice on the morrow, she did not care for the comfortable apartments which her father was sure their courier must easily have found for them, in a place so much the resort of the English, "and first-rate English physicians, my child," he added, by way of something better than all.

"As to that," said Lucy, "I am quite satisfied with this Italian doctor; he is kinder, and more considerate than any of the doctors I ever had—and you know, papa, I have had plenty."

Sir John puckered up his nose; he made no answer, however. "Don't you think so too, papa?" asked Lucy, with the obstinacy of an indulged child.

"Why, Lucy, I cannot say, I have seen so little of the gentleman, and I am not given to take hasty likings." A silence ensued, for pretty Lucy did not like being answered in this way.

In about half an hour there was a tap at the open door, and John's voice formally announced that dinner was on the table. "You must try and eat something," said her father, rising; "I will send you in the wing of a chicken, or an egg—that can be had here, at least. It will do you good, and raise your spirits."

"No, papa!" said Lucy, with marked determination, "the Doctor said I was not to eat."

"Well, my dear, follow his directions for to-day," replied Sir John, as obstinate in his feeling as the young lady; "to-morrow, I hope, you will have better advice to go by;" so saying, he left the room.

The cloth was laid in the lobby. The dinner, much to Sir John's surprise, and a little to his annoyance, though very simple, was excellent. Fish, a roast fowl, vegetables, an omelet, cheese, preserved fruit, oranges, and a bottle of the wine of the country, not to be despised even by the most fastidious palate of a connoisseur. Sir John ate and grumbled, but though he grumbled, he ate very heartily all the time. John, a large black patch across his wounded nose, a napkin, not of Flemish damask, but of good white home-spun linen under his arm; John, in white cravat and suit of sables, waited on his master as solemn and erect as on a gala-day at Davenne.

The Baronet was in the moody enjoyment of his second orange, fresh plucked from the bough, when Doctor Antonio, a large bundle under his arm, made his appearance at the top of the steps. The Doctor, with a bow to Sir John, passed on to the left—Sir John's room was on the side opposite—and was ushered by Hutchins into Miss Davenne's chamber.

"How long you have been!" said Lucy, with all the impatience of sickness, as soon as she caught sight of him.

"I am very glad to hear you say so," he replied; "it is a good sign when the patient longs for the presence of the physician; it implies confidence in him, and that is half the battle. I have been detained against my will. But tell me how you are." Doctor Antonio listened to his patient's account of herself with that interest which is so consoling to any one suffering, then said, "I wish I could relieve you, but I confess, that, for the present, at least, I do not think I can. You have gone through much agitation and much pain, and nature so disturbed requires a little time to recover its equilibrium. All that we doctors can do is to help, we cannot force nature. Drink freely of the mixture I sent you; perhaps it will make you sleep in a little while."

Lucy shook her head, as if she were quite sure she should never sleep again, but only said, "What have you got there?" pointing to the bundle.

"Some curtains for your window. All these rooms are to the south, and we must try and guard you from the intrusion of our Italian sun." So saying, suiting the action to the word, he got on a chair, and began driving in some nails as gently as he could. "One learns to be a little of everything in these small country places," he said, looking at her from his not very heroic elevation, and with one of the curtains on his arm; "we are differently off from you dwellers in large cities; we are poor folks, who can offer no inducement to tradesmen to come and settle amongst us. Every one hereabouts is his own gardener, carpenter, and upholsterer, as you see in this moment. Indeed, very often, to save the small fee, a man is his own doctor."

"You say 'we' in speaking of this neighbourhood," observed Miss Davenne; "you do not mean to say that you really belong to this place?"

"And what makes you suppose that I do not?" asked the Doctor, somewhat amused.

"I don't know exactly," answered the young lady, "but there is something about you which makes me fancy that you have not lived all your life here."

"In plain words, you mean to say that I do not look quite like the boor you would expect to find in the doctor of a village. You are an acute observer for your age, young lady."

"And how old do you think I am?" inquired Lucy, amused in her turn.

"Sixteen or seventeen at most."

"Much older, I am very nearly twenty."

"Ah! indeed? then you look younger than your age. Well, I must do homage to your penetration, and own that you are right, so far, in guessing that I do not belong to the Riviera. I am a native of Sicily; I was born in Catania."

"Will you forgive my being so full of curiosity, but have you not lived in England?"

"No, I have never been there," answered the Doctor. "My English puzzles you also, does it? I will tell you at once how I learnt to speak it. My mother's eldest sister married, in 1810, a British officer of one of the regiments quartered at that time in Sicily. My aunt's children were brought up in every respect like English children, and, having English nurses, talked English from their cradle. Now, as I was educated with my cousins, I naturally learnt the language also, which became almost as familiar to me as that of my own country."

Thus, alternately talking and hammering, the busy Doctor entertained the sick girl, and managed to put up the curtains. He contemplated for a moment, and with an air of great satisfaction, what his talents in the upholstery line had accomplished, then glancing round the room, he said, "Ah! more work for me. I see a split in that door behind your bed. Nothing is more treacherous than a draught, the smaller it is the worse." Away went the Doctor, but was back again in an instant, a long slip of paper in one hand, and an egg-shell in the other.

"Did you ever see a more economical or expeditious way of making paste?" asked he, showing Lucy the pinch of flour and drop of water contained in his egg-shell.

She laughed and wondered at his activity and ingenuity. Then no one could help being struck by the noble simplicity with which he did things gentlemen, in general, think beneath them, even putting himself into postures that would make most people ridiculous, without ever losing, for a moment, that comely manliness of appearance which would not have let him pass unnoticed even in a crowd.

Sir John came in just as Antonio was stooping down to paste the paper over the chink. The Baronet followed each of the Doctor's movements, at first with a look of uneasiness, as if he suspected him of being mad, and then, as he perceived the nature of the stranger's occupation, Sir John's features relaxed into a smile, expressive at once of the most intense disgust and contempt. Sir John's *beau idéal* of a gentleman was himself: now, not to save the world from ruin would Sir John have condescended to what he considered a menial act; and the man who would paste paper over a chink in the door, do the work of a carpenter, or paper-hanger, be it even for a Davenne, lost all right to respect and consideration in his eyes.

While Sir John was wasting a great deal of thought on the Doctor, who never thought of him at all, Speranza, the landlady's daughter, brought in a large nosegay, chiefly of wild flowers, and handed it to Dr. Antonio, who, apparently as contented with his success in pasting paper as in hanging curtains, began at once to examine and arrange the bouquet. Lucy, observing that he placed only some of the flowers in a vase, and threw others out of the window, inquired why he threw away some of the prettiest.

"Because the scent of those you call the prettiest may be injurious to you. I intend you to have a nosegay to gladden your eyes, and not one to perfume your room. It is wrong to put scented flowers into a sleeping apartment at any time, and *a fortiori*, they are still more out of their place in a sick-chamber. Nor do I mean to leave even these here," and walking into the adjoining room, he set the vase on a table, where Miss Davenne could see them from her bed.

"Now, what next?" said he, rubbing his forehead with his forefinger, as if trying to recollect something. "Ah! that is it;" and turning to Lucy,—"Are you in the habit of having a light in your room at night?" On her saying "yes," he continued,—"Then we must try and contrive one safe for you." He called to Speranza to bring a cork and a bit of the wick used in their oil-lamps, out of which materials he made a night-lamp, that answered as well as one of Child's patent. After once more looking to the bandages on Miss Davenne's foot, he said,—

"It is getting late, so I must wish you good evening. If, during the night, you should feel worse, which I hope and think will not be the case,—mind I say this solely in reference to you and not to myself—send at once over to Bordighera for me. The people of the house will find a messenger; and then everybody knows where Doctor Antonio lives."

"And pray how far is this—Burdigore, or whatever you

call it?" inquired Sir John, speaking for the first time since he came into the room.

"About ten minutes' walk," answered Antonio. "If you come to this window you can see it. There, on the top of the hill to our right."

"Thank you; and may I beg you to tell me whether there is a magistrate to be found in this neighbourhood?"

"We have a justice of the peace at Bordighera," replied the Doctor.

"Ha! that will do very well. I shall find time to see him to-morrow early, for I don't intend to let that scoundrel of a postilion escape so easily."

"If that is the case, you must have a little patience," rejoined the Doctor; "Prospero could not obey any summons just now. He is ill in bed, not from any bodily injury, but from the moral shock he has received. I had to bleed him before coming here this afternoon."

"I am sorry to hear it," said Sir John, mollified. "At the same time you must agree with me, sir, that it is a duty I owe to all travellers not to overlook the flagrant misconduct of a drunken fellow, and"—

"Excuse my interrupting you, sir. I have no wish to screen Prospero from blame, but, believe me, intoxication had nothing to do with the unhappy event of to-day. Prospero was never drunk in his life. I can affirm this positively, as I have known him for three years. The vice of drunkenness is very rare in these parts, and our postilions, especially, are looked upon as patterns of sobriety. Ask all the guards of the mail-coaches that go daily from Genoa to Nice, and *vice versa*, and they will tell you, as they have told me many a time, that if so few accidents occur on this road, in spite of its almost unbroken series of ascents and descents, and not a few sharp turnings, it is owing to the care and proverbial soberness of the postilions."

Sir John did not reply to this defence, so the Doctor, with a bow, took his leave.

"I hope you will not prosecute that poor young man, papa," said Lucy.

"It would be useless for the present, my dear, as you have just heard, and ere the fellow is about again, we shall be a good way off."

"Ah, papa," returned Lucy, "I fear I shall not be able to bear the fatigue of a journey for some time, I feel so weak and shattered. I am very sorry on your account, dear papa."

"Don't vex yourself about me, my dear girl," said Sir John, patting her cheek. "First of all, you don't know yourself what a night of sound sleep may do for you; and then, at the worst," added the Baronet, grown more magnanimous since his dinner, "so that you get well, I shall not care about a little discomfort for a few days." Lucy caught his hand and kissed it gratefully.

"Do you know, papa," said the invalid, after a short pause, "that I have found out what countryman he is?"

"Who?—the postilion?" asked Sir John, rousing himself from not very pleasant reflections.

"Papa, papa, how can you?—the Doctor. He is a Sicilian."

"Indeed; I have been told that Sicily is a very fine country," answered the Baronet, rather coldly.

"I am sure there is some mystery about him," continued Lucy. "I don't believe—Do you, papa?—that he was ever born to be a doctor. I should not wonder if he turned out to be one of the noblemen who have been banished. I remember hearing at Rome about political refugees. He is just like one of those heads by Vandyck we saw at Genoa. Don't you think him very handsome, papa?"

"Yes, he is a fine man, and would make a capital *chasseur*, with his long beard," said Sir John, drily.

"Oh, papa, that is too bad—how can you say so of a person so evidently a gentleman, and who has been so very kind to us?"

"My dear Lucy, your gratitude is not very logical. This person having been of use to us, is no reason for my at once believing him to be a prince in disguise. However, my dear Lucy, I don't object to your romancing about this black-bearded Esculapius, only I suspect he will prefer the mode I shall take of showing my sense of the obligations we are under to him."

Lucy fixed her eyes with some anxiety on her father's face. "Don't be afraid, Lucy, the fee I offer to your hero shall be in proportion to his presumptive rather than to his apparent rank." As Lucy still looked uneasy, the Baronet continued, "You foolish child, do you think this Doctor has given himself all this trouble for the love of your pretty face?"

Lucy sighed, for she had a very strong idea of her own that the Doctor had given himself all that trouble out of pure kindness; perhaps she was romantic in thinking thus. However, she said nothing more, as the sigh was followed by an attack of cough which left her in a state of exhaustion.

Sir John, when she was again quiet, thought it best to leave her alone, in the faint hope that she might fall asleep. As he stooped to kiss her, his eye was attracted by something strange at the head of her bed, which he had not noticed before. On looking closer, he found slightly fixed to the wall a little leaden crucifix, a plaster cast of the holy Virgin, with a small vessel of holy water incrusted underneath, and a palm branch, which, in fact, had been blessed. Any one who has ever travelled in Italy must have seen such things daily, either for sale in the streets, or in the bedrooms of the poorer houses. Sir John, as exclusive in matters of external worship as in everything else, lost his little remaining patience at finding what he considered idolatrous emblems over his daughter's head, and peremptorily ordered Hutchins to carry away all that trash, and to take care that he never saw such in any of the rooms again. He waited to see his order obeyed, and then, in no very charitable frame of mind, took a candle, and retired to his own apartment.

Lucy's discouragement as to moving next day, and the

state of complete prostration in which he had left her, caused Sir John, once more alone, to recur with sad misgivings to Doctor Antonio's alarming declaration as to the impossibility of his daughter's removal, and as he thought on it, the firm determination hitherto nourished to pay that declaration no attention, began to waver. Evidently a reaction was taking place in Sir John's mind. For the first time, since entering the Osteria, the proud gentleman felt as if the terrible award of "forty days" in that wilderness might be fulfilled. An admission, it is true, no sooner made than recalled, nay, put at nought by a mental rejoinder, to the effect, that will and money to execute that will, could not fail, after all, to conquer all difficulties. If a mattress were placed across the seats of the carriage, thought Sir John, and the horses made to go at a walk, why, Lucy would lie there as safe and comfortable as in her own bed. An excellent arrangement, to be sure, but —there were still "buts" in the way. Alas! do what he would to see it not, reality, stern reality, stared the unhappy Baronet in the face.

Amid such conflicting thoughts he prepared to lie down on his bed with a heavy sigh,—a sigh not merely called up by the appearance of the miserable couch and the prospect of an uncomfortable night; other grounds for disquietude now awoke out of old recollections in the Baronet's mind. That he was in a strange land, amid foreigners, none of his countrymen within reach, was in itself enough; but that he was among Italians was more than enough to occasion and authorize all sorts of fears. There was in a cell of his brains a tapestry of notions about Italy, on which stilettos, banditti, and vendette, figured in juxtaposition with solitary inns, or gaunt houses by the seashore, where travellers were enticed, murdered, and plundered. "Devilish disagreeable country!" sighed forth Sir John, "and where your village doctors must needs look like Rinaldo Rinaldini." The bells of the churches at Bordighera tolling the *De Profundis*, marking the first hour of night; the voices of the fishermen hailing each other in the distance; the very sound of the sea breaking lazily on the beach, had something sinister to the Baronet's ear. He stole quietly out of his room, went to the lady's-maid's door, and calling to her, bade her, in a cautious whisper, lock and bolt her door, then returning to his own chamber he barred himself in, and went to bed in as happy a disposition of mind as if he had fallen in with a tribe of Red Indians.

We must render this justice to Sir John. Had he known and believed that the accident met with by his daughter was of the serious nature it really was, uneasiness about his darling would have prevented all such paltry misgivings and fears from raising their hydra heads; whereas, indulging the belief that there was nothing worse the matter than a sprained ankle, and seeing in that no cause for apprehension, Sir John was sufficiently at ease to be able to brood to his heart's content, not only over the real annoyances, but over what he was pleased to fancy the dangers of his situation. But how could he, in the face of many a suspicious circumstance, and after Antonio's transparent hints, still labour under such a delusion? The answer is obvious. Sir John was misled by a preconceived idea, the idea that Doctor Antonio had every interest in rather exaggerating than diminishing the seriousness of the injury sustained by Miss Davenne. And as to his ever supposing that an utter stranger, a village doctor, and an Italian to boot, could, out of regard for his, Sir John's feelings, have kept back the worse feature of his daughter's case, such an absurdity could never enter his mind. The haughty Baronet might as well have supposed that—that the Davenne family was not one of the first families in all the United Kingdom.

While Sir John bolted himself in, and his humble namesake, in a state of intense nervousness, kept watch in the carriage, Rosa and Speranza, their services being no longer required by their guests above, had betaken themselves to their intended sleeping-place — a small dark back-kitchen, and in which a little store of charcoal and wood was habitually kept. A straw mattress, and a blanket between the two, were to be their bed and covering; it was all these poor, simple, hard-working creatures had thought of reserving for themselves. Between compassion for the young lady and awe of Sir John, and his man John, they had given up for their use not only that part of the house destined to the few humble chance travellers who sometimes passed the night there, but also their own room, and all they possessed in shape of bedsteads, mattresses, linen pillows, &c. Far from regretting the sacrifice of their usual little comforts, mother and daughter were entirely engrossed by how they could add to those of their unexpected inmates.—"How fortunate," said Speranza, "that these gentlefolks should travel with their own plate! But for that, what should we have done with our four silver spoons and forks? For only think, mother, the old gentleman must have clean forks and spoons with every dish." And the two women fell to reviewing in their minds the households of their wealthier neighbours, and weighing the chances they had of having such and such articles of furniture lent to them on the morrow. But, after all, what was the use of their racking their brains, when there was Doctor Antonio? Doctor Antonio would manage to get all that was wanting—Doctor Antonio would set everything to rights. To hear the two women anybody might have supposed that this country doctor was one of the genii in the "Arabian Nights," who had only to stamp his foot to make the earth bring forth a palace, with all its appurtenances.

"There is one thing, mother," said the girl, "we must do at once, and that is to take down the pine branch from over the gate. I know the old gentleman cannot bear the sight of it, he made such a face when he passed it."—"Then it shall come down," replied the mother; "perhaps we had better take the benches and tables out of the garden. To-morrow is Sunday, and the folks from Bordighera will be coming here after Vespers, and I am sure the gentleman won't like to see so many people about the garden. We can give those who choose their bottle of wine in the parlour, and those who don't must go elsewhere. It won't do to have smoking and singing going on under the windows of the

Signorina."—"That's true," said the daughter; "Doctor Antonio, of all things, said she was to be kept quiet. Oh, mother, did you ever see such a sweet face? she looks like the Madonna over the altar."—"Ay, she does indeed," agreed Rosa. "God bless her!"—"God bless her!" echoed Speranza; and with that blessing on their lips mother and daughter fell asleep.

Having for the present disposed of all our personages save the principal one—the one at least who ought to be so, according to our title-page—we may as well take a peep at him.

Doctor Antonio's dwelling at Bordighera consists of one tolerably large room, which answers at once for drawing-room, consulting room, and library, and within which opens a small bed-chamber; one side of the sitting-room is entirely covered with well-filled book-shelves, half a dozen chairs and a middle-sized table complete the furniture. On the wall opposite to the book-shelves hang a flute, a guitar, two foils, some fencing-gloves and masks; below these is a map of Sicily. Books are lying on the chairs, on the ground, everywhere; and there is a mountain of them on the table, before which sits our hero, caressing his beard, and poring over a volume, which absorbs all his attention. Between the printed leaves there are coloured engravings of legs in all stages of dilapidation, and of every variety of mode of dressing and bandaging them. Now and then Doctor Antonio rises and walks up and down the room, in deep meditation, goes to the book-shelves, takes down a large folio, and seems to be comparing notes. Hours are going swiftly by, and he is still reading and stroking his beard. Presently he looks at his watch, exclaims aloud in astonishment at how time has passed, lifts his lamp as if about to go to his bed in the next room, then stops suddenly, puts down the light again, and once more goes to the book-shelves. There is yet one point on which he is not quite clear, there is a complication which may arise, and which he has not yet found mentioned.

The dawn shining through the windows found him still reading. At length he closed the book, extinguished his now useless lamp, and, all dressed as he was, threw himself on the bed.

CHAPTER III.
Sir John Davenne.

SIR JOHN DAVENNE, the fifth Baronet of that name, had inherited with his paternal acres, what was to the full as much a family possession, and one as carefully transmitted from generation to generation—the *tic* of overweening and most exaggerated pride; pride of pedigree, of every person that could, in the remotest degree, claim kindred with the Davennes, of everything belonging or having belonged to them, and a corresponding contempt of every thing or creature less favoured in a line of ancestry, and historical recollections.

The Davennes of Davenne, in the county of—, professed to be descended from the Norman Squire of the name of D'Avesne, mentioned in sundry chronicles as having attended a De Vere at the Battle of Hastings. Sir John asserted, as his father and his father's father had done before him, that the Davennes had always shared in the glories and dangers of the warlike De Veres, who, history tells us, were among the hosts of Cœur de Lion's crusaders. Emerging from the borrowed light of these nobles, a Davenne won his golden spurs about that period, and from that time their family history became incorporated with that of their country. The Davennes took their share in the wars of the Roses; one was killed at Bosworth, another went with Essex to Ireland; a Davenne, after manfully fighting at Marston Moor and Naseby, was among the few who accompanied Charles in his flight to the Scots, and remained near his unfortunate master to the last—one of the most obstinate and undaunted of the cavaliers. When the power of

Cromwell became supreme and established, Davenne, whose property had been confiscated, fled with his family to join the Court of the young Charles in Holland. His loyalty and devotion to the Royal cause met with a more favourable *dénouement* at the Restoration than that of many other cavaliers as loyal and devoted. He not only received back his own estate, but, the tables being turned, got that of his neighbour to boot, who was, in the language of the times, a crop-eared Roundhead. It was at this epoch, also, that the Davenne of that day was created a Baronet, a title that the two Baronets, the father and grandfather of our Sir John, had refused to have converted into a higher one; the late Sir Aubrey saying, he liked better to be at the head of the baronets than at the tail of the lords.

From the Restoration to the Revolution of 1688, the Davennes seem to have thought more of attending to the hereditary paternal acres, than of intermeddling with the quarrels of Kings and Parliaments. It is certain that the family remained at Davenne when James the Second took refuge at St. Germains. Probably the Sir John of that day had youthful recollections, which counselled him to shrug his shoulders at the wickedness of the times, and to content himself with damning, in his own halls, the refractory Bishops and Commons. The only evidence he gave of his adherence to the Stuart dynasty was in refraining himself and all his family from appearing at the Court of William and Mary.

The warlike spirit of the old Davennes suddenly blazed out again in the eldest son of this prudent father. He fought and distinguished himself under Marlborough, and attained to the rank of General. His successor, Sir Aubrey, paid tribute to the military exigencies of his sire, by serving during the war of the American Independence. Keeping in mind the professional feeling of Sir Aubrey, and his high Tory principles handed down for centuries from Davenne to Davenne, it is easy to imagine the bitterness with which he viewed the success of the Americans, and the acknowledgment of their autonomy. But one must have lived in those days, or received from the lips of those who were then actors on the scene, a description of the English citizen, and of the country gentleman in particular, to be able to conceive the virulence, hatred, and horror that took possession of Sir Aubrey when the Revolution of 1789 broke out in France. His feelings at moments were worked up almost to frenzy, when in the daily papers he read speeches of English orators, which, to the angry Tory, seemed to express, in the very Parliament of Great Britain, sentiments little better than those of the French Republicans.

The reigning Sir John, born in 1783, had consequently been educated and had grown up to manhood amid all the violent feelings roused on this side of the Channel, by the state of affairs in France, and twenty years of incessant war. From the day when a child, he stood by his father's chair, and gave the daily toast of "Confound the French!" up to the present moment, Sir John's opinions, likings, and dislikings, all partook of the colouring of the passionate medium through which they had passed, and in which they had been developed. An unbounded and exclusive admiration for all that was, and an utter abhorrence of all that was not English, enclosed his mind and perceptions as within a Chinese wall.

Sir John had married in 1811, two years after his father's demise, the daughter of Viscount Deloraine, and granddaughter by the mother's side of the Duke of—. It was a happy chance that this marriage united safety to the "sangre azul" of his line, and satisfaction to his own inclinations, for Sir John was not the man to have done violence to his affections, for a twofold reason; first, because he hated contradiction in any shape; secondly, because he believed the lustre of his family to be such, as to make up for all deficiencies of escutcheon in his intended bride, had his choice fallen even on the daughter of a cobbler. In the spring of the year following this union, his son and heir was born, and became the point on which his pride and affections centred, it not being till 1820, when the little Aubrey was in his eighth year, that a girl came to put in a claim for her share of interest and love.

In 1815, when the Continent was thrown open to British travellers, Sir John, prevented in his youth from making the grand tour, thought it befitting a man of his quality to make up, though rather late, for this deficiency in an aristocratical education, and, with his wife and little son, spent some months in visiting France, Germany, and Italy. It is scarcely necessary to say, that Sir John's sojourn abroad left undisturbed the spider's web of prejudice spread over his intellect, which kept safe all the dead flies of his youthful notions. Intercourse with foreign people and manners, such intercourse at least as fastidious *morgue* and a perpetual fear of "*déroger*" would allow of, rather strengthened than otherwise what Sir John considered his patriotism; that sort of patriotism which shut up all honour, all good, all worth, within the narrow circle in which he himself was born and lived and moved.

Shortly after this foreign tour, a vacancy having taken place in the representation of—shire, where Davenne was situated, Sir John was urged to stand for the county, but declined that honour, as, indeed, he had constantly declined being returned for the family borough. Sir John had good sense enough to know that he was neither born to shine as an orator nor a statesman, and too much pride to figure only among the silent "yes and noes" of the House. But the ambition which he had not for himself, Sir John cherished, and thought himself amply justified in cherishing, for his son. Aubrey was a fine Hercules of a boy, full of the sportiveness and arrogance of the unchecked childhood of the rich. His high animal spirits, vivacious boldness, and dauntless repartees, were, in his father's eyes, so many tokens of precocious genius. Far cleverer men than Sir John are blinded by parental partiality and pride of authorship. Aubrey, then, evidently destined to become a great man, was devoted to Parliament and statesmanship while still in petticoats, and, scarcely out of them, placed in the hands of a tutor, who was to drive him full gallop to the first stage of the journey, Oxford. But the little William Pitt in the bud, opposed to all scientific and literary inoculation a *vis inertiæ* worthy of a better cause; which being perceived in the long-run even by the infatuated father, he sent his son to Eton, where, in fact, the young gentleman soon distinguished himself, not in classical learning, but in the native arts of boxing and single-stick.

At seventeen, Aubrey, at once a *petit-maître* and a bold young scamp, took leave of Eton and school-boy life. He had already all the appearance of a man, his physical development being in the inverse ratio to the intellectual. When informed by his father that he was to go to Oxford, and that he was vowed from his childhood to the priesthood of Downing Street, Aubrey begged distinctly to state that he hated politics, thought books in general a bore, and, as sure as he went to Oxford, he should be rusticated, if not expelled; that he had long made up his mind to serve no other god or goddess but Mars; and that the best thing his father could do was to purchase him at once the right of defending his Majesty's colours. All this was said with a fluent flippancy that struck to the earth the father's cherished ambition. Sir John tried reasoning, coaxing, expostulating, and at last threatening: but Aubrey was his father's own son; he tossed his handsome head, damned the family borough and the House of Commons; and gave it as his ultimatum, that if his father did not consent to let him enter the army as a gentleman, he would enlist as a common soldier.

Sir John's hair rose on his head as he listened to young Wilful's declaration, and as he listened the conviction flashed upon his mind that the boy would be as good as his word. Sir John knew something of the Davenne blood, and had sundry recollections of Master Aubrey's early obstinacy. The struggle was kept up for some time, but ended, of course, by Aubrey's being victorious; for, under the dignified coating, which made of Sir John Davenne a somewhat remarkable person, there lurked, as we have hinted, a host of weaknesses,—the most natural among them paternal over-indulgence. Now Aubrey, with his manly swagger and great good looks, was born to be the successful opponent, nay, tyrant of his father. In the Baronet's eyes, the arrogance which was the base of his son's character—an arrogance so intense that it seemed as if all the pride of the buried Davennes ran liquid in his veins, was a grace the more. Even all Aubrey's boyish scrapes at Eton, which, as recounted by himself, showed they took their origin from an unwarrantable assumption on his own part, had but endeared him the more to Sir John, who saw in this spirit which brooked uneasily an equal, only the proper pride befitting the representative of the Davennes. Thus it came about, that within six months after leaving Eton, Aubrey was gazetted cornet in a dragoon regiment, and within the year sailed with the—for India; he having brought his father not only to consent to his entering the army, but—more difficult still, for here his idolatry of his son militated against the son's wishes—to negotiate an exchange for him into a regiment under orders for Calcutta. Aubrey's waking and sleeping dreams had long been on tiger and elephant hunts, and India his land of Canaan. Thus the realization of the son's aspirations had crushed those of the parent.

While smarting under this severe disappointment, the first of any importance in his hitherto unchequered life, Sir John, looking round him in search of consolation, perceived, for the first time, that he had at hand a balm for his heart-sore in the pale lovely cherub who lifted up to him her tiny arms, and seemed to ask for her share in his affections, a share that was soon all hers. The wound that Aubrey's egotistical wilfulness had inflicted was scarcely skinned over, when the decease of Lady Davenne again threw a deep gloom over the Baronet's home. Lady Davenne's health had long been declining, and more rapidly so ever since her son's departure. The blow was none the less felt for being anticipated. Sir John's grief was extreme, though silent and subdued; for the haughty Baronet considered all outward demonstration of strong feeling inconsistent with his dignity. He had another also, and better reason, for controlling his emotions, viz., the fear of adding, by his own, to his daughter's violent affliction.

Sir John retired to his home in the country, and lived there in comparative seclusion, entirely engrossed by his daughter, who had now become his one occupation—his one pleasure. Lucy was a weakly, sensitive, intelligent child, truly needing all a parent's fostering care, one of those lovely fragile blossoms which equally call forth fond hope and tender anxiety. Country air, however, regular hours, and a prudent alternation of exercise and repose, of study and amusement, under the management of a sensible governess, so successfully strengthened her health, that at seventeen Miss Davenne, though still somewhat delicate, was grown into a tall, blooming, cheerful girl, and passing beautiful withal.

The life of a London belle was now before her. Sir John never dreamed of her departing from the habits of her caste. She was to be presented at Court; and the closed shutters of the house in—Square were once more opened, and such sun and light as is to be found in the metropolis of Great Britain shone in on the stately rooms. To town, then, Sir John and his daughter went in the spring of 1837; and Lucy, once launched into the current of London gaiety, was soon whirling giddily in its eddies. The end of her first season found her with pale cheeks and exhausted spirits; but the qualm that Sir John had felt was easily forgotten, when he saw that some months of comparative quiet at Davenne seemed to set her to rights again. Youth is a potent auxiliary to recovery; so when spring came round, it found father and daughter again in London. But party giving and party going, heated rooms and late hours, were not long in counteracting Nature's beneficial effects. Lucy's head drooped before the height of the season was reached; the alarmed father heard again the dry short cough—the signal of an enemy he had not forgotten.

Poor Sir John called in first one physician and then another; one advocated country air and milk diet; a second, cold ablutions and horse exercise; a third, sea-bathing and port-wine,—but all agreed in the necessity of an entire abstinence from every kind of excitement or gaiety. All was tried, but not any or all the remedies were able to banish the fits of teasing cough that thrilled through the heart of the terrified father, nothing could vanquish the morbid languor which seemed about to arrest the current of his daughter's life. Lucy continued thus for some months, until the physicians gave that advice, which to experienced ears sounds like the passing bell: "Try a change of climate; let Miss Davenne spend next winter at Rome," was the fiat issued. In spite of an old grudge he had against Rome,—"the dullest place in Christendom," Sir John was used to call it, and at the cost of the newly restored delights of clubs and coterie, the Baronet had not a moment's hesitation. The house in London again exhibited closed shutters—that dreary mark of desertion; the housekeeper at Davenne had a month's work in dressing up all the furniture; and Sir John and his daughter went to Rome.

The sacrifice was repaid. The winter of 1839-40 proved one of the finest and mildest ever recorded at Rome, and six months' breathing of the soft congenial air had a most restorative effect on Lucy's constitution. Sir John was so happy at this result, that, with the approbation of an English physician of some renown, he determined to prolong his stay until the hot weather set in, travel in Switzerland during the summer, and return again to Piazza di Spagna for another winter. Just as he had made all his arrangements there came a letter from Aubrey, now Captain Davenne, dated from Madras, announcing his intended return by the next mail, on a furlough of three years. This necessitated a change, or rather modification of Sir John's plan. They must leave Rome earlier than he had purposed, and England would have to take the place of Switzerland in their itinerary. The only embargo laid by the Doctor, when consulted again, was that the journey should be made by sea and not by land, to spare the newly convalescent Lucy all possible fatigue.

In compliance with this advice, Sir John and his daughter, towards the middle of March, embarked at Civita Vecchia on board a Government steamer, bound for Marseilles. The sea was like a lake when they sailed, but the fine weather lasted only a few hours. One of those furious gales, frequent in the Mediterranean at that time of the year, suddenly came on. The vessel, with both paddles disabled, lay at the mercy of the winds and waves for a night and day, and it was not till after a narrow escape of being wrecked in the Gulf of Spezia, that the passengers were landed at the town of that name, which lies to the east of Genoa. The protracted terror and sea-sickness had so completely worn out Lucy that she was unable to move or even stand; she had to be carried ashore in this pitiable state, and more than a week's rest was required ere she could recover sufficient strength to resume the journey,—this time by land, and by easy stages, the courier being sent forward every morning to provide the best possible accommodation for the night. Exhaustion was unluckily not the only result of the combined fright and sea-sickness. Some of the old symptoms, which had vanished during the sojourn at Rome, reappeared, to Sir John's great alarm.

It was on the fourth day since their leaving Spezia, when, having slept at Oneglia, they expected to be at Nice by the evening, that our story found the father and daughter; the latter, as we described, tossing restlessly in search of ease and sleep, the former, divided between newly awakened anxiety for one child and the mental delivery of sundry speeches to the other, all intended to persuade him to leave the army and take to statesmanship.

CHAPTER IV.
Skirmishes.

RATHER thoughtful, but with his usual air of self-possession, at a good steady pace, but without hurry, Doctor Antonio, early the next morning, might have been seen coming down the hill of Bordighera in the direction of the roadside inn, where his young charge lay. Doctor Antonio was not handsome, at least not handsome as heroes of novels generally are. He had a large mouth, a nose of a cut neither Greek nor Roman, rather high cheek-bones, in short, a cast of features altogether irregular and somewhat leonine,—all that could be said in its favour being, that it was highly expressive and intellectual. There was power of will and thought in his round prominent temples, which he could contract wonderfully at times. His smile, occasionally tinged with a shade of quiet irony, was habitually sweet and winning. The appearance of the man, on the whole, was remarkable, with more in it, perhaps, of what commands respect than attracts sympathy.

Our Doctor, then, early in the morning, made his way to the Osteria *del Mattone*, such being the name of the humble roadside inn; whether so called from its red brick colour, or from standing upon a ground once occupied by a brick-kiln, we have no data to go by. That it had a wretched as well as a quaint appearance, no one with eyes in his head could venture to deny. The fact was, that, when first built, the house had been intended to have its front to the north, that is, to face the road, but in course of time, probably to escape from the dust, the original windows and entrance had been blocked up with stones and plaster, and new ones broken out on the opposite side, viz., on the side that faced the south. The consequence of this was a twisted and distorted, and somewhat unnatural look, most ludicrous to behold. To replace the stairs which formerly had led from the ground floor to that above, and which the present arrangement rendered useless, a double flight of massive stone steps, connected at the top by a wide landing-place or balcony, had been added on the outside, and went up from the garden as high as the middle window of the upper story, cut down to answer as a glass-door. These comparatively enormous steps and balcony being sadly out of proportion with the diminutive house against which they rested, increased the oddity of its physiognomy, and suggested the idea of a grown man's coat put on the back of a boy ten years old.

Doctor Antonio found his patient in a state far from satisfactory. Lucy had scarcely closed her eyes all night; complained of headache and constant thirst; her lips were parched; her pulse bad—she was in a high fever. "I wish I had bled you yesterday," said the Doctor after feeling her pulse; "have you any objection to being bled?"

"None in the least, if you say it is necessary," replied Lucy; "but you had better speak to papa first."

"Very well; will you be so good, then, as to send your maid and tell Sir John Davenne that I wish to see him?"

Hutchins, with a glance at her mistress, moved to go. "Wait a moment in your own room, Hutchins, before you go to papa," said Lucy; "I want to ask Dr. Antonio something."

As soon as they were alone, Lucy opening wide her eyes, bright with fever, fixed them earnestly on the rather astonished Doctor, and then said, "Am I in danger?"

The Doctor laughed outright.

"No more than I am," he answered; "what put such a notion into your head?"

"Pray," said Lucy, "don't try to cheat me; don't treat me like a child. I am not afraid to die, and if I am dying I ought to be told, and I must, and will know."

"You have a brave heart, I am sure," replied the Doctor, with some emotion, "but I can assure you that your present situation calls for none of your fortitude. Believe me, you are no more likely to die just now than I am."

"*Parola?*" asked Lucy, putting out her little thin hand.

"*Parola*," answered Antonio, grasping it with his own.

"Thank you," said Lucy; "I will tell you now what made me think that I was in danger. Early this morning the first thing I saw was the girl you called Speranza. I suppose I had been half-asleep, for I did not see her come into the room. She was seated in a chair watching me intently. Her eyes, so expressive at any time, were so full of pity and sadness when they met mine, that a thrill of fear shot through my heart. Tears, big tears, were actually rolling down her cheeks. Methought that a girl would not have been so distressed about a stranger, except something very wrong was the matter with me, and as I felt very ill I could only fancy"—

"Very absurd things," interrupted the Doctor. "Speranza is a foolish girl, full of feeling, which she cannot help showing, in and out of season. We Italians are noted as a silly demonstrative people, you know," added he, smiling. "Besides, I do not wonder that a warm-hearted girl, such as I know Speranza to be, should be moved to tears to see one so young and so"—(here Antonio stopped and hesitated, but not more than a second,) "and so lovely, suffering so much. Will you allow me now to see your father?"

"Oh yes," and raising her voice a little, Lucy bade Hutchins go and deliver Doctor Antonio's message.

Sir John had got up very early in the deplorable frame of mind of one who had passed a deplorable night, and had some hints of the gout into the bargain. Sir John had already seen Hutchins, and received from her an unfavourable report of his daughter's state, and consequently lost all hope of leaving that day. Sir John had called for John to bring him his razors, and heard that John was not in the house. This string of annoyances had told in a forcible manner on the nerves of the absolute Baronet, who waited impatiently for the return of his servant to pour out on his large round head all the amount of crossness—crossness, not wrath, is the word—that was pent up in his breast. "Everything goes wrong in this cursed country!" exclaimed the Baronet, by way of relief.

Sir John had few but very decided notions about Italy and Italians. Italy, Sir John allowed, was a fine country, but scarcely habitable: a furnace in summer, a glacier in winter. Rome was a place worth seeing, but dull! dull! dull! The Italians he pronounced to be a rapacious, shabby-looking, oily-tongued people, who never went out without a rosary in one pocket and a stiletto in the other. Every second man met with in the street was either a singer, or a bandit, or a ruined noble who lived by his wits; a catalogue of the constituent elements of the Italian social body, enriched of late by the fresh addition of the bloodthirsty republican conspirator, plotting for ever against his lawful sovereign—a new variety of the species Italian, of which Sir John had heard much during his late stay at Rome, from a young Roman prince, the nephew of a Cardinal, and who greatly affected English society. For, the better to study Italian character, habits, and manners, Sir John frequented only English families; had an English physician, English servants, even an English cook; ate English dinners, drank *soi-disant* English wines, and bought from English shops—in short, Sir John had realized at Rome a little London of his own.

When John, on his return, presented himself before his master, his face had on it such a lively expression of despair, that even in his present mood the Baronet changed the meditated storm of invective into the question of,—

"What the devil is the matter now?"

"I have been at Bordighera, sir," replied John, "and there is neither beef, nor tea, nor fresh butter to be had! What are we to do?" asked John in so piteous a tone that three parts of a smile extended Sir John's lips.

Just at this interesting moment there came a rap at the door, and Miss Hutchins with the message. Sir John, a little alarmed, went at once to the lobby, where he found the Doctor. Sir John begged the Doctor to be seated.

"I find Miss Davenne this morning," began the Doctor, as he took a chair, "with a good deal of fever. It is only what I expected. I think she would be relieved by a little bleeding."

Sir John, one of whose favourite crotchets it was that all Italian doctors bled *all* their patients to death, on hearing this proposal gave a bound on his chair, and said, with great warmth,—"Bleeding! no bleeding whatever, on any account. I will have no bleeding!"

Doctor Antonio coloured up to the white of his eyes,— and who knows what he was going to reply?—but checking the ready rejoinder by a strong effort, he said, slowly and calmly, "Not even if I assure you that it is absolutely necessary?"

"I do not admit the necessity," replied Sir John, doggedly; "and I make no bleeding the *sine qua non* of your attendance on my daughter."

"It is so, is it?" said the Doctor; and without further parley he drew out his memorandum-book and wrote down some names on a fly-leaf, handing which to Sir John, he continued,—"These are the names and addresses of the two nearest medical practitioners; the young lady will be safe with either of them. I shall not withdraw till one of the gentlemen is here." So saying, he rose, with a bow, went to the balcony, and stood against the railing with folded arms, in the attitude of a sentinel waiting to be relieved.

Face to face with the resolve so suddenly acted upon by the Italian, Sir John, like most people who have been hurried on by passion, began to regret having gone so far. Like Alp on Alp, one difficulty after another shewed its rugged head. Suppose neither of the other two doctors spoke English,—not very probable they would; suppose Lucy, who had taken a fancy to this Antonio, refused to see them; suppose this man was right, and suppose her life should be endangered by his opposition. There is nothing for it, thought Sir John, but a little conciliation with this most disagreeable of Italians—the man, of course, waits but for a word; and making a prodigious effort, he called out in a querulous tone, "Why do you wish to bleed?"

"Because," replied Antonio, turning towards the Baronet, as he uttered the words, and then resuming his former position, "because, as I have already stated, I think it indispensable."

A dead pause ensued.

"Italian practice everywhere the same," broke out Sir John, soliloquizing aloud; "nothing but the lancet—the same quacks all through the country. No, no, it can't be; how can I authorize bleeding?"

Antonio heard, but made no reply.

"Doctor Antonio, you are then determined to bleed?" exclaimed the Baronet, walking about the room in exasperation.

"You mistake," retorted the young man, with some haughtiness; "I am determined to do no more in this case but resign the young lady into better hands. I shall wait the arrival of my successor below," and he moved towards the steps. Sir John came to the glass-door, and in utter desperation said,—

"Perhaps I have been too hasty; but you can understand my feelings, sir,—the feelings of a father for an only daughter."

There was real distress in the voice, real distress in the working of the Baronet's features, as perceived by the Doctor, who had faced round upon him.

"The proof that I understand and respect your feelings," said Antonio, "is, that instead of resenting your taunts on my profession and country, which I would have done with anybody else, I adjure you once more to let me do for my patient what I consider necessary."

The words were spoken so simply, yet so earnestly, there was such a stamp of dignity about the whole man, as he stood on the threshold in the attitude of one giving a solemn warning, so much reserve yet courtesy in his voice, that Sir John, provoked as he was, could not help being struck by the *ensemble*, and said, with marked hesitation,—

"If I were to consent to your bleeding my daughter, I

should be going against the express caution of every physician who has ever attended her."

"I should myself have given you similar advice," said Antonio; "but there are certain conditions which must modify the most salutary rules, and Miss Davenne's state is a case in point."

"Well," said Sir John, "situated as I am, I have no alternative but to let you do what you think proper; only remember, that in bleeding Miss Davenne you act entirely on your own responsibility."

"A thing I have never shrunk from, and I accept it willingly," replied Antonio, brightening, and without any further delay he returned to Lucy's room.

Sir John had no sooner given this ungracious consent than he was angry with himself for giving it, and walked back to his room with the feeling of one sorely aggrieved. At the end of a quarter of an hour, this feeling, duly nursed and fondled, had grown up, expanded, and ripened, into a clear and decided conviction that he had been unfairly got the better of, a discovery immediately followed by intense commiseration for himself, the victim, and a burst of fresh hot indignation against Antonio, the victimizer. "And so here I am at the mercy of this man!" said Sir John to himself. All the Davennes' proud blood tingled in his veins at the idea. He angrily strode to the glass-door and called to John, who was pacing the garden in low spirits, to order post-horses for the carriage at once, and to come up to him afterwards. Then opening his desk with a violent jerk, the Baronet began to write, not with his usual pompous composure, but much in the approved stage mode, making dashes right and left, fit to tear the paper to the heart, accompanied by a scratching and spluttering of the pen, sufficient to set on edge the teeth of any but a man in a passion.

Sir John had finished and sealed his angry missive, when his servant brought in the consoling intelligence that the horses would come up immediately. "Put them to the minute they come," said the Baronet, "and go to Nice as fast as you can with this letter to the British Consul there, and deliver it into his own hands. I have asked him to give you the name and address of the first physician,—English physician I mean, of the town. Find him out and bring him here at any cost, and with the least possible delay. No stoppages on the road; you must be back here to-morrow."

John bowed, and in ten minutes more Sir John had the consolation of hearing the carriage roll off.

One word is due to the messenger. John Ducket was the lineal descendant of a generation of servitors of the Davenne family, all like himself born and reared on the estate of Davenne, and succeeding one another as butlers with a regularity that had finished by making the office hereditary in their family. John, born while his master was still in petticoats, had been named by Sir Aubrey after his heir, in recognition of the faithful services of the Duckets. As Time used his scythe, John succeeded his father and grandfather, and was now Sir John's confidential valet,—a man in whom the Baronet put infinite trust, and less to his master's credit, often his *souffre-douleur*. John had been drilled to passive obedience from his youth upwards, and continued to walk in that way,—an obedience far from onerous, for if there was a man in the world who thought more highly of the Davenne family than Sir John himself, that man was John Ducket. He worshipped the very name; every word that fell from Sir John's lips had all the authority of an oracle with his man. Had Sir John ordered him to go to Nice and bring him back the first person he met in the town instead of the first physician, John would have set out with the same determination to obey literally, and believed Sir John to be perfectly in the right.

While John, lolling at his ease inside his master's carriage, plays the Baronet, and looks down superciliously on the pedestrian wayfarers, who take him for a great personage, and touch their hats to him as they get out of the way —while Sir John counts the passing hours, and savours in spirit revenge, that fruit so sweet in anticipation, so bitter in the tasting, Doctor Antonio awaits with disguised anxiety the effect of the morning's bleeding. He has already called four times in the course of a few hours, and Hutchins continues to give the same answer, which he continues to receive with the same look of intense satisfaction: "Miss Davenne is quiet, and appears to sleep." As no one is to be permitted to enter her room for fear of disturbing a rest so longed for and so necessary to the poor girl, Hutchins, who watches her through the door left open between the rooms, from time to time goes on tiptoe to Sir John and gives him a similar bulletin. The house, thanks to Rosa and her daughter's attentive care, is so quiet that one might fancy it uninhabited. The Sunday customers from Bordighera are pitilessly sent away. Towards evening Lucy calls her maid, and asks if the Doctor is come. He has been sitting alone in the balcony for the last hour, and goes to her at once. Lucy feels better, even thinks she has slept. Antonio places his fingers on her pulse, desires her not to speak, holds a glass containing a bland soporific to her lips, and wishes her a good night. No doubt of it; the timely bleeding has dissipated the complication that he apprehended; you see in his face that a great weight is taken off his mind. His step, as he walks homewards, is more springy than in the morning, and he hums a tune as he goes.

Lucy slept, and soundly; indeed did not awake till ten the next morning, and then so refreshed and composed that she felt quite another creature. "I was beginning to think you meant to dismiss me altogether," said Antonio, cheerfully, as he was ushered in by Miss Hutchins. "I have called twice already this morning, and each time found closed doors."

"I really have slept unconscionably late," said Miss Davenne, in a little confusion.

"All right," replied the Doctor; "you have to make up for much lost time. And how do you feel? your countenance is a herald of good news."

"What does it say?" asked Lucy; "let me hear if it speaks the truth."

"It says," Antonio went on, "first, that you have got rid of fever; secondly, that you are wishing for some breakfast. Have I guessed aright?"

"Like a second Daniel," answered Lucy, smiling; "I was really just longing for a cup of tea and some fresh butter."

"Hum," said the Doctor, "for the cup of tea we are all safe. I was so sure that an English young lady would be sighing for her tea, that, see, I put some in my pocket for you."

"How kind of you!" said Lucy. "Do you, as an Italian gentleman, disapprove of tea?" asked she, with some return of archness.

"Quite the contrary,—I am a great devotee of 'the cup that cheers but not inebriates;' I always take tea for breakfast myself. As to fresh butter, that is a very different affair. I believe if I were to offer its weight in gold, I could not find any for you in this neighbourhood."

"Don't people eat butter here!" exclaimed Lucy; "or do you mean to say that no one here knows how to make it?"

"They are not quite so behindhand," answered the Italian; "but I will tell you all about it presently. As you have been such an amiable patient, doing me such credit, I must contrive to reward you. I shall make you some butter myself."

"You!" cried Lucy, "you churn butter!"

"You will see," he answered, almost laughing at her genuine surprise; and went out of the room, and returned in a quarter of an hour, carrying a large bottle three-parts full of milk.

He now seated himself near the bed, and with all the gravity in the world began shaking the bottle with a violence and perseverance that soon made him as red as fire. Lucy tried in vain not to laugh. "You are laughing at my churn," he said, very calmly; "it is a primitive one, to be sure, but it will do its work very well;" and up and down went the bottle again. "Look," he said—and he held it before the large pair of eyes that were fixed upon him with such a mixed gaze of merriment and wonder—"do you see those little balls? That's the beginning of your pat of butter."

"But you forget," said Lucy, "that you have not told me why you are obliged to make the butter yourself;" and as she spoke, the thought crossed her, What would papa think if he saw the Doctor now!

"In the first place," explained the Doctor, "the soil is too dry here to afford good pasture, and that is the reason why our farmers do not keep more than one or two cows. Now the milk of one or two cows does not give cream enough to make it worth while to churn every second day, you know."

"No, I don't know anything about it," said the still laughing girl; "but go on."

"The consequence is," he resumed, "that they wait till they have a week's cream before they make any butter, and as by that time most of the cream is rancid, the butter it makes is detestable stuff, that burns your throat, and half chokes you. Yet, it might be very good, for, owing to the aromatic plants that grow about in abundance, the milk, though not rich, is very sweet. But the truth is, there is no demand for butter."

"No demand!" repeated Lucy. "How do all the people in the neighbourhood, I mean the gentlemen's families, manage?"

The Doctor smiled. "We are not in England, signora, and we find our oil an excellent substitute."

"Oh!" said Lucy, "I have such a horror of oil."

"One of your English prejudices," he answered. A short silence ensued, while Lucy considered the manly intelligent face and commanding figure of the Doctor, so at odds with his occupation.

At last, after an earnest searching gaze into his bottle, the Doctor exclaimed, "*Eccolo, oh caro,* here's your pat of butter;" and with a little triumphant air, he added, "Now,

I must see to the washing and pressing of my microscopic production, lest it should melt away during the process." Hutchins' countenance during the whole of the performance would have been a good study for a painter; incredulity, derision, and at last wonder, being admirably expressed in every feature of her face.

"As I cannot come and churn for you every day," said the Doctor, returning, "I think the best way to have fresh butter for you and your household daily, is to hire a couple of cows for your use. Speranza will manage the matter for you, if you like, and milk them herself, she said, to be sure that the article is genuine. And since we are on the subject of eatables, let me give you one or two hints which may be useful, as you will not be able to leave this poor place for some little time to come."

"What will papa do, then?" asked Lucy, anxiously; "he is so impatient to go to London."

"My dear young lady," answered Doctor Antonio, soothingly, "depend upon it, Sir John cares for nothing so much as for your recovery; so now listen to what I was going to say. Two mail-coaches are daily passing this, one from Genoa to Nice, and one from Nice to Genoa, and you can by their means be regularly supplied from the markets of either place with anything you may require, only you must have some one at Genoa or Nice to purchase for you, and have the things brought to the coach-office. I have friends in both places who will undertake all this for you, if you like."

"Thank you very much," said Lucy, "but we have our courier at Nice who can do all that for us without troubling your friends."

"So much the better," replied Antonio. Hutchins at this moment entered with the breakfast, and Miss Lucy attacked the toast and butter with an alacrity of good omen, pronouncing the butter to be the very best she had ever tasted. "Now that I think of it," said Miss Davenne, "what has become of Speranza? I have not seen her since yesterday morning."

"Speranza," answered the Doctor, "has had a good scolding, and is ashamed to show herself."

"Ah! so you have been scolding; why did you scold her?"

"For frightening a certain young lady with her nonsensical scared looks," returned Antonio; "I should never have guessed her to be such a simpleton."

"How?" asked the young lady.

"I suppose I shall do no harm by telling you of her foolishness. You must know," continued the Doctor, "that when the girl heard that you had sent away the crucifix and the Madonna hanging by your bed"—

"She took offence, did she?" suggested Lucy.

"No, no! but she at once jumped to the hasty conclusion, that you were not a Christian, and she felt so sorry, so sorry, as she told me, to think that you never could go to Paradise, that when she next saw you, she could not help crying about it."

"Dear kind soul!" exclaimed Lucy; "she must not be allowed to believe that I am not a Christian. Pray, Doctor Antonio, go and fetch her."

He went at once, and presently returned drawing in after him the reluctant Italian girl, looking prettier than ever, her cheeks as red as cherries with the glow of shame. "I beg your pardon, signora," she faltered to Lucy, "I did not mean to offend you, indeed I didn't."

"I am not offended, *cara mia*," said Lucy prettily, in Italian, though with a little embarrassment on her side also, which brought a faint blush on her pale face: the two girls made a nice picture. "Truly, I am grateful to you for taking so much interest in an utter stranger. If I were not a Christian, I should indeed be an object for the pity of every one. But I am, my good Speranza, and I worship and pray to the same Father in heaven whom you worship and pray to."

Speranza took the young lady's hand, and was about to

carry it to her lips, when Lucy drew her hastily forward, and kissed her on the cheek.

"That will do now," interfered the Doctor, who did not want his patient to grow excited; "you must not forget that some of my butter is still on your plate."

Sir John came into the room a little after this scene, and while the actors in it, still under its impression, were looking very pleased. For, though not new, it is nevertheless a consoling truth, and one worthy of being recorded, that nothing is so wholesome, nothing does so much for people's looks, as a little interchange of the small coin of benevolence. Sir John was in a mood that allowed of his taking the infection of the good humour he saw in the others. Unlike the first night, Sir John had slept very well—is it not wonderful and mortifying to think how much the colour of one's mental perspective depends upon the sort of night that one has passed? —Sir John, then, had slept very well; had shaved to his heart's content; had received a good account of his daughter; had had a cup of excellent tea—the Doctor's own tea, and altogether felt in good spirits.

"You see, Sir John," said Doctor Antonio, good-humouredly, after the morning's salutations had been exchanged, "you see that even so terrible an extremity as bleeding may be attended with satisfactory results. Here is your daughter to witness to the fact."

"No one rejoices more sincerely than I do at the success of your remedy; and Miss Davenne and myself are much indebted to you," replied Sir John, with no little embarrassment, as the thought came upon him all at once of the possibility of the English physician arriving while the Italian was still there. But just as the apprehension of such a collision presented itself before him, Doctor Antonio took his hat, saying, that he was afraid he should not be able to call again before the evening.

"Are you going to desert me, now that I am better?" asked Miss Davenne, with a cloud on her brow.

"Not for the world," replied the Doctor earnestly; "but

I have a visit to make at a place some miles off, which I have delayed for the last two days, and can do so no longer."

"One moment, Doctor Antonio," said Sir John, so much relieved that his good humour waxed active, and with an instinctive wish, so common in human nature, to do something to please the man for whom he had prepared a rod of mortification; "can you give me any news of that unlucky post-boy?"

"Of Prospero?" replied the no little surprised Doctor, "he is poorly enough; he has an intermittent fever."

"Is it dangerous?" asked Lucy.

"Not dangerous," was the answer, "but likely to nail him to his bed for weeks;—a very sad prospect, Miss Davenne, for people who have nothing to trust to for their bread but the labour of their hands, and who, besides, have others dependent upon them."

"Is Prospero married?" inquired the young lady.

"Not yet, but he has an old mother and a younger brother whom he supports, for poor Prospero is a better son and brother than postilion. But I really must leave you, so goodbye, and *a rivederla.*"

"Papa," said Lucy, when the sound of the Doctor's steps had died away, "you have no objection, have you, to my sending some money to that poor man? Doctor Antonio gives him such a good character."

Sir John checked an exclamation of satisfaction that rose to his lips at a proposal which gratified at once his parental pride in the warm feelings of his child, and reconciled the promptings of his really kind heart with those extravagant notions of dignity, before whose tribunal all soft impulse was a weakness. The fact is, that Sir John, to his praise be it said, on hearing of poor Prospero's case, had instantly begun to think how he could manage to send him a little money without committing himself. Now, Lucy's proposal was just what he could have wished. Prospero would have the money, and it would be her doing, not his; so he answered, with a studied carelessness, "You may do so if you wish it, my dear, though no thanks to him that we did not break our necks; however, that's no reason why the mother should suffer. Send the money to the poor old woman, who certainly deserves to be pitied for having such a harebrained son."

"I think, papa, I had better talk to Doctor Antonio about it, he will tell us what is best to be done."

"As you like, my dear," said Sir John; then, to change the subject, he remarked what a beautiful day it was.

"Is it not?" said Lucy; "and the air is so sweet. Go and take a walk, papa, it will do you good."

"I have half a mind to do so; but you will be lonely, perhaps. Would you like Hutchins to read to you while I am out?"

"I asked the Doctor if she might do so, papa, but he said it would not do yet."

"Your Doctor Antonio, my dear," said Sir John, fretfully, "is a dreadfully slow man."

"You know the Italians have a proverb that says, '*chi va piano va sano, chi va sano va lontano,*'" replied Miss Davenne, playfully. "I will be quiet and think. A pleasant walk to you, papa."

The sea, the sky, the mountains, everything was smiling around, and a soft breeze tempered the ardour of the noon-day sun. As, fanned by the genial air, Sir John walked on leisurely towards Bordighera, a sense of physical comfort stole over him, and under its influence all the better feelings of his nature awoke. Indeed, so softened was his heart, that had he been called on to specify his grievances against Doctor Antonio,—windmills which yesterday he had mistaken for giants,—he would have just now been sorely at a loss how to do so. We may even go so far as to aver that there was a moment in which Sir John wished, actually wished, that he either had not sent John to Nice, or that John might return alone.

But this good humour was short-lived. Exactly because Sir John was a very proud, he was also a very sensitive per-

son, and likely to be ruffled by finding a doubled rose-leaf
on his couch of grandeur. The doubled rose-leaf came to
disturb him this time in the bodily shape of a lusty villager,
with a frank good-humoured countenance. Sir John had already met several people, all of whom had lifted their caps
as they passed, which he felt was only just as it ought to be.
The news of the accident which had befallen the English
gentleman and his daughter, the description given by Rosa
and Speranza of the surpassing beauty and gentleness of
the latter, had spread both far and wide, and had naturally
created a warm sympathy for the strangers. This feeling
the good-natured people met with by Sir John had expressed on this morning, as we said, by taking their caps
off to the gentleman; but the stout labourer just mentioned
was not to be satisfied with silent pantomime. He accosted
the Baronet, and addressed him at some length, winding up
with an attempt to shake hands; a familiarity hateful to Sir
John at elections and public rejoicings in England, and one
he was little inclined to tolerate on a road in Italy. The
burly peasant, whose professions of interest and good-will
were expressed in a patois utterly unintelligible to his
listener, was far from dreaming of the offence he had given
when he saw the embarrassed Englishman suddenly turn his
back upon him, and retrace his steps to the Osteria, where
he arrived in a very different temper from that which had
graced the beginning of his walk.

CHAPTER V.

A pitched Battle.

SIR JOHN had not been long home, when the sound of
fast-approaching wheels made him spring to his feet and
hurry to the balcony, from whence he perceived his own
carriage standing at the garden gate, and his own man John,
who, after assisting a short, plump, middle-aged gentleman

to alight, conducted him across the garden. Sir John
hastened to close the door between Hutchins' room and the
lobby, and returned to his observatory in time to see the
new-comer stop at the foot of the steps, take off his hat,
draw forth a snow-white handkerchief, and while slowly
wiping his large bald head, shining in the sun like a golden
ball, take a hasty survey of all that he could see of his own
person; then after first stamping one foot and then the
other, to shake away some small particles of dust that
dimmed the brilliancy of his polished patent-leather boots,
mount the stairs with a deliberate step. "Something like a
physician," murmured the Baronet, as he caught a nearer
view of the broad, honest, English face, close-shaved chin,
and rigorous professional black costume, to which the irre-
proachable white neckcloth and finely-plaited wide shirt-frill
gave an exquisite finish. Sir John's heart expanded as a
flower bitten by the first frost expands under the cheering
rays of an October sun.

Sir John's reception of the stranger was as cordial as Sir
John's nature and habits permitted: he put out the index
and medium of his right hand in sign of welcome, and positively made a slight apology for the trouble he had given.
The English doctor received with due deference between
his own thumb and index the two fingers held out, giving
them a gentle professional pressure, as if he were feeling
their pulse. This done, Doctor Yorke—for such was the
name of the new doctor, such a contrast to the other—with
the self-possession of a man long habituated to deal with
all classes of all nations, and to detect at a glance the besetting foible as well as the besetting malady, proceeded to
beg Sir John not to speak of trouble. His services were,
as they ought to be, at the behest of sufferers in general; it
was his duty to be prepared for all emergencies. In the
present case, any little personal inconvenience was more
than compensated for by the honour of making the acquaintance of Sir John Davenne, (here both gentlemen
bowed,) and by, as he fondly hoped, the satisfaction of

being of use to Miss Davenne, of whose unfortunate accident he had heard from the servant.

This was all according to Sir John's ideas of propriety; and the sense of relief he felt in listening to Doctor Yorke, was something only to be compared to what a man feels who escapes from suffocation. While the stout little doctor paused to take breath, Sir John had time to bless his good fortune that had sent him a man so well bred. At last, all the preliminaries being over, the two Englishmen sat down, and Sir John entered at length on the tale of his misadventures,—the embarking at Civita Vecchia, the horrors of the storm, the landing at Spezia, (what a hole that Spezia! beds as hard as stone, and too short by a foot,) and the journey by land up to the climax of the overturn. To hear Sir John, one would have thought that the storm in the Mediterranean, and the short beds at Spezia, were both contrived for his personal annoyance; but he made no specific charge until he came to the unlucky wight of a postilion, when, forgetful of the morning's mercy, the Baronet declared his belief that the overturn was a deliberate act, nothing less than a clear attempt at murder. "Ask me not his motives," pursued Sir John, waxing warm—for Sir John wanted to be angry, and was trying all he could to lash himself into a passion—"his motives? do I know what may have been his motives?—But that there was premeditation, cool premeditation, sir, I have an unanswerable proof in the scoundrel's indifference after the mischief was done. Did he so much as lift his little finger to render assistance? No, sir, he stood as unconcerned as his horses—No, I am wrong, the poor beasts shook with terror."

Sir John next described Doctor Antonio bursting on them like a Congreve rocket. "The queerest-looking figure for a medical man I ever met with," said the Baronet, "with a beard like a French pioneer, and a sugar-loaf hat just like a captain of banditti in a melodrama." Doctor Yorke's polite attention redoubled at this point, and in the left corner of his mouth there quivered an arch smile, either in

compliment to Sir John's graphic powers, or in enjoyment
of some odd conceit of his own. "This Doctor Antonio, if
that be really his name, says he is a physician, and without
the smallest ceremony pounces upon my daughter, sets
about examining her foot, declares there is nothing the
matter but a sprained ankle, and with not so much as 'by
your leave,' takes upon himself to order her to be carried
here. Well, sir,' proceeded Sir John, with angry and
significant emphasis, "that is not all. I naturally enough
express my intention of continuing my journey to Nice after
a few hours' rest. 'Hours!' cries the man, staring at me;
'rather weeks.' Weeks! and on my remonstrating at the
mention of such a monstrous period, the oracle pronounces
his award, that my daughter cannot be removed for at least
forty days. Forty days! very easy for him to say, but not
so easy for me to get through in such a place as this; to say
nothing of my only son, Captain Davenne, being expected
in London at the end of this month, after an absence of ten
years."

"Very provoking, indeed," remarked Doctor Yorke.

"Not that this circumstance can alter the case in point,"
added Sir John, condescendingly; "but I put the question to
you, Doctor—"

"Yorke," suggested the Doctor.

"I put the question to you, Doctor Yorke, speaking to
you as to a distinguished member of the medical profession
—(Doctor Yorke bows)—Is it likely that a mere sprain
would prevent any one from travelling in an easy carriage
for the enormous length of time of forty days?"

Doctor Yorke thus directly appealed to, drew a massive
gold snuff-box with an inscription on it out of his waistcoat
pocket, gave it the three consecrated taps, held it to Sir
John, who declined, took a pinch himself, and after a second
of self-indulgence and meditation, said that the query put
to him was not so easily answered as might seem on a
prima facie view. Generally speaking, a simple sprain cured
in a week or two, though he must add that he had met, in

the course of his practice, with accidents of that description attended by such aggravated symptoms, as to necessitate absolute repose for even a longer period than that mentioned by the Baronet. In which category was Miss Davenne's sprain to be placed? that was the point at issue, and which nothing, resumed Doctor Yorke, could decide but a careful examination of the foot.

"Exactly so," chimed in Sir John, "a careful examination by a gentleman of your standing and experience is all I can wish for. I shall willingly bow to your authority."

"Then, Sir John, the less time we lose the better," observed Doctor Yorke. "Is the Italian gentleman here?"

Sir John replied in the negative.

"I beg you will send for him immediately, as his presence is indispensable."

"I am sorry to hear it, Doctor Yorke," answered the Baronet rather shyly; "for when Doctor Antonio paid his visit this morning, he mentioned that he had a call to make at some distance, and was not likely to return before the evening."

"Very strange!" exclaimed Doctor Yorke, "when he knew you had sent to Nice for a consulting physician."

Sir John, with increasing embarrassment, was here obliged to confess that he had not mentioned the circumstance to Doctor Antonio.

"God bless my heart, this is very awkward!" said the little gentleman, beginning to look very blank. "Do you not know, my dear Sir John, that it is a rule, a canonical rule among us medical men, never to examine another man's patient except in his presence?" A fine mess we are in, added he mentally to himself.

"But, Doctor Yorke, under the present circumstances, cannot you dispense with a mere formality?" observed Sir John, in a persuasive tone; "we are in Italy, you know, not in England."

"The rule holds good here as well as there," quietly returned the English practitioner; "it is not the mere formality it appears in your eyes, nor a mere act of courtesy either. It has been accepted as a law amongst us, with a view to prevent abuses, most likely to arise if there were no restrictions. You know the vulgar adage, Too many cooks—Ah! there you are," continued the Doctor, in quite a different key; "how lucky! we were just regretting your absence."

These last words were addressed to Doctor Antonio, whose tall figure here darkened the outer door. Doctor Antonio had returned sooner than he expected, and as he rode past the Osteria, a sort of misgiving had seized him that the toast and butter of the morning might have proved hard of digestion, so to clear this doubt, he had alighted and called.

Antonio's round, salient temples worked fearfully, and a flash of anger darted from his eyes—but it was only for a second, and as he entered the room his countenance was restored to its usual serenity and placid smile. Doctor Yorke rose with extended hand to meet his brother in medicine. Sir John now became disagreeably aware that the two physicians were acquainted, and to all seeming on excellent terms, which in fact they were. They had become known to each other at the time the cholera was raging at Nice and in the environs, and had met for many a consultation on that sad occasion, and stood side by side at many a deathbed.

"How do you do, my dear sir?" said Antonio, cheerfully, "how glad I am to shake hands with you! Come down to see the young lady, eh? we will go to her presently."

"You see me here," said Doctor Yorke, desirous of divesting his position of all ambiguity, "at Sir John Davenne's express invitation, to consult about Miss Davenne with Miss Davenne's physician, who, I am glad to find, is yourself. I am sure when the patient is in such good hands there is no need of me; however, if you have no objection"—

"None in the world," said Doctor Antonio, not allowing

his colleague to finish the sentence; "to submit the measures I have employed to so kind and competent a judge, is at all times an honour for me"—Doctor Yorke waved his fat white hand deprecatingly—"yes, an honour, and, allow me to add, a gratification," wound up Antonio. "But enough spoken between old friends; I fear I have already detained you too long. Had Sir John Davenne been so good as to let me know this morning that he expected you," pursued the Italian, with meaning in his voice, and facing round upon the Baronet, "you should not have found me out of the way—"

Sir John's conscience lent weight to the words, and he held his tongue, glad that he had not found time to mention the bleeding, the second count in the indictment against Antonio. "I am now at your service, Doctor Yorke, but I think there is a point to be considered before we go to Miss Davenne, that is, if she be unprepared also—"

"Quite so," said Sir John.

"Well, then," went on the Italian, "Miss Davenne may, perhaps, take fright, be alarmed I mean, as sick people are apt to be, by the unexpected sight of two doctors at her bedside"—("And enough, too," said the English physician, in a stage-aside)—"she may very naturally suppose," continued Antonio, gravely, "that something very serious is the matter with her."

"Ah, true! very right, very thoughtful indeed," smiled Doctor Yorke; "an old head on young shoulders, Sir John."

Sir John wished Doctor Yorke would not be so facetious.

"It would be prudent, therefore," resumed the Italian, "to introduce Doctor Yorke as a friend of mine."

"No lie that," put in Doctor Yorke.

"A friend of mine, met with by chance on his way back to Nice, and of whose advice I was glad to avail myself."

This proposal being agreed to, Sir John went to his daughter to tell her of the intended visit.

As soon as Sir John had left the two doctors alone, Antonio said, "I must profit by this moment to warn you that the case in question is of a serious nature, nothing less than a fractured leg, and a foot severely sprained."

Doctor Yorke drew in his lips, ejaculating, "Tut, tut, very bad, very bad!"

"Yes, indeed," pursued Antonio, "a most disagreeable complication. Unwilling to alarm my patient, who is a delicate, excitable young creature, I termed it a sprained ankle." —("A good notion that," struck in the Englishman.)—"And as I was about to state to the father the real nature of the case, the old man looked so scared that my heart failed me; the more so as I knew that he was condemned to remain in this out-of-the-way place, and among strangers. Now I think it over," continued Antonio, "perhaps I was wrong; and if you consider it more advisable to make him acquainted with the truth "—

"By no means, by no means," interrupted the short gentleman, hurriedly. "What could be the use of doing so? You have acted like a fine fellow as you are;" and seizing Antonio's hand the little doctor gave it a warm squeeze. Hutchins made the English doctor put a bridle on his sensibility, by announcing that her young lady was ready to receive the gentlemen, who followed, and entered Miss Davenne's room arm in arm, to satisfy any demur on her part as to their friendship. The Italian formally introduced the Englishman as his colleague and intimate friend. Doctor Yorke followed the lead, and said a multitude of little prettinesses to the young lady, whose reception of the new doctor, if polite, was very cool. The inspection of the foot scarcely lasted a minute. After a few questions from Doctor Yorke, for form's sake, and the expression of his gratification at the prospect of her speedy recovery, the two doctors withdrew, and so did Sir John.

They found the cloth laid in the lobby, and a succulent refection served—thanks to provident John, who had taken advantage of his trip to Nice to bring back a supply of beef, tea, and fresh butter, likely to suffice for six months, and stuffed every spare inch of the carriage with all the delicacies

of the table he could lay hands on, both in the way of eating
and drinking. Sir John and the English doctor sat down to
lunch, Doctor Antonio declining the Baronet's invitation to
join them. Antonio placed himself in a manner to face both
Sir John and the doctor, and after a little silence addressed
himself to the latter.

"As I have some engagements," said he, "that rather
press on my time, I beg leave to enter at once on the matter
which brought us together. Sir John Davenne's presence is
also material to me." Sir John's nostrils curled ominously
at the announcement. "To put you in possession of the
case," continued Antonio, "I will briefly recapitulate its
circumstances from the beginning, then submit the course"—

"My dear Doctor Antonio, that is quite unnecessary,"
interrupted Doctor Yorke, with polite haste; "the very satisfactory state of your patient bears more than sufficient testimony to the masterly course you have pursued."

"Thank you," said Doctor Antonio; "but I have my
reasons for wishing to proceed in this matter as regularly
and methodically as possible. Will you oblige me by allowing me to have my own way?"

"Certainly, certainly," replied Doctor Yorke, prescient
of a storm in the air.

"When I first saw the young lady," began the Italian,
"which was immediately after the accident, I found her
lying on the beach in a deep fainting fit. The usual restora-
tives proving unsuccessful, yet there being no external
injury visible to account for the protracted swoon, I apprehended a concussion of the brain, and I was about making
preparations to bleed her, when she revived, and by her ex-
clamations directed my attention to her right foot. Upon
examination I found that she had sprained her ankle in
the peculiar way I mentioned to you before you saw
her."

Doctor Yorke here nodded most significantly.

"I bound up the foot as well as I could with handkerchiefs, and drove home for a proper bandage. You have

seen the dressing of the foot; does it meet with your approbation?"

"Most entirely," said Doctor Yorke; "it would do no discredit to a first-rate surgeon,—a rare aptitude, which it would be well if more of us physicians possessed."

Doctor Antonio bowed slightly, and went on.

"I then had the lady placed on a sort of litter—the only conveyance she could bear, and conveyed to this house, cautioning her repeatedly against attempting the slightest movement, for fear of unpleasant consequences. Is it your opinion that I was too particular?"

"No, no, my dear fellow," said Doctor Yorke, his wish growing stronger with every detail to prevent the bursting of the storm-cloud; "caution is never *de trop*, and you are not the man to make a fuss about nothing. The foot is a very delicate member," continued he, turning to Sir John, "so full of ligaments, tendons, and—a—in short, a monstrous ticklish matter. To manage a foot is like walking upon eggs."

"Sir John Davenne," continued Antonio, "being naturally anxious to pursue his journey, I felt in duty bound to tell him at once, that for forty days at least the lady could not possibly travel. Do you think that I overrated the time?"

"I wish I could say 'yes,'—I wish I could," blurted out the English doctor, "but I can't; I am forced to agree with you that she cannot stir from hence for many a day to come."

Sir John heaved a sigh, and the faint sunshine on his face vanished.

"All this," went on Antonio, "was taking place on Saturday afternoon. Early on Sunday morning I found my patient very far from well, restless, thirsty, with parched lips, no sleep, a good deal of excitement, and a pulse up to 120. I did not hesitate for a moment, and"—

"You bled her, of course," suggested Doctor Yorke.

Sir John hated his fellow-countryman at that instant.

"Yes, I bled her," rejoined Antonio. "Would you have done so?"

"Necessarily—the symptoms were imperative."

"By six o'clock in the evening the fever had abated, and this morning, after a good night's rest, entirely disappeared. The patient, as you say, is going on as satisfactorily as can be expected. I have nothing more to add touching the case," concluded the Italian.

"And I," said Doctor Yorke, with an animation intended to satisfy Doctor Antonio's legitimate anger, and to bring Sir John to a sense of the necessity of some acknowledgment of the services rendered, "and I have only to say—Go on, and prosper as you have begun."

"I thank you," said Doctor Antonio, with some reserve. Then turning to Sir John, he added, "I hope you are satisfied, sir." The Baronet, rather at a loss what to say, bowed as graciously as he could.

"And now," resumed Doctor Antonio, rising, "it only remains for me to say that I resign my patient into abler hands than mine, and to wish you good-morning."

"You don't mean what you say, my good fellow," said Doctor Yorke, who felt that it was all over with them; and so perturbed was the good man, that his fork, with a slice of ham on it, remained suspended between his plate and mouth, while his extended eyes wandered from the Baronet to the dark-visaged Italian.

"Excuse me, Doctor Yorke, but I do fully mean what I say. I have reasons that are peremptory with me for acting as I do. A medical man, to enable him to fulfil his trust, must have his will unfettered, and mine is not; he must possess the confidence, not only of his patient—and in that here I am fortunate, but also of those in authority round his patient. Now, this too is wanting. Sir John Davenne has no confidence in me."

Doctor Yorke made an attempt to speak.

"Grant me one moment more," said Antonio, with a kindly smile to him, "and I have done. Sir John Davenne, I repeat, has no confidence in me. I simply point out the fact; I do not complain of it. And the best proof of this want of confidence is your presence here, the presence of a medical gentleman without any previous intimation to me. My course in this state of affairs, the only one consistent with what I owe to my patient, with what I owe to myself, and to the dignity of our profession, is to withdraw; and this I do without any ill-will, on the contrary, in the best possible humour with everybody." And hastily shaking the hand Doctor Yorke had held out to detain him, the Italian bowed to Sir John, and walked away, neither humbled nor elated, rather sad. Doctor Yorke ran to the balcony, which he reached just in time to see his retreating friend disappear through the garden-gate.

"Fine mess we are in!" muttered Doctor Yorke, as he resumed his seat at the table, with the face—such as probably he had caused many of his patients to make—of one who has just swallowed a very disagreeable medicine. There ensued an awkward silence, broken at last by Doctor Yorke saying, "It is a pity you had not mentioned to Doctor Antonio your intention of sending for me."

"I did not see the necessity," replied Sir John, curtly; "Doctor Antonio's attendance upon my daughter arose from a chance, of which he cleverly availed himself, with the view of making a good thing of it."

Though a worldly man, exclusively bent on making his own fortune, and generally disposed, as such, to humour the whims of his clients, especially if wealthy, Doctor Yorke had feelings, and in spite of all his systematic efforts to keep them down as a nuisance, these feelings, like spirited horses in harness, would now and then kick, and plunge, and run away with him, as now when he felt that Sir John was an ungrateful old English baronet indeed. So, uttering an "oh!" that sounded like a groan, Doctor Yorke took a pinch of snuff, *ab irato*, and said, with some warmth, "Allow me to say, that in this you are entirely mistaken. Doctor Antonio is the last man to be influenced by sordid motives."

"Is he?" returned the Baronet, letting loose at once all the spleen heaped up during the last half-hour. "I am glad to hear it. I am ready to give him credit for being a pattern of disinterestedness. But what if I am sick of his overbearing manner, and will not endure any longer his airs of superiority. Am I not at liberty to choose my own physician? Now, will you oblige me, sir, with dropping the subject?"

"As you please," returned the doctor coolly, and with an imperceptible toss of his head, as much as to say—of what use is reasoning?—"but just allow me a last question in reference to it. Is it your opinion, then, that Miss Davenne can do without medical attendance?"

"I rely upon yours," replied Sir John.

"Certainly," said Doctor Yorke, with marked hesitation, "as far as directions by letter, and a call now and then—say once a week, can do, I am at your service."

"Cannot you remain with us," said Sir John, with a beginning of dismay, "and undertake my daughter's case? The remuneration," he went on haughtily—

"Do not mention a word of the kind," interrupted the little gentleman with quickness. "I wish with all my heart that I could stay here, or that you were nearer to Nice, so that I could get you out of your difficult predicament. It so happens, however, that my staying here, were it only for a day, is a matter of absolute impossibility just now. I have a set of sick people at Nice whom I cannot leave; Lord B—, with a severe fit of gout, a patient of twenty years' standing —not to be deserted, you see; then there is little Viscount F— with the measles,—his mother, a poor nervous creature, dotes on him, takes fright at everything and nothing, wants to be assured every two hours that the child is doing well— keeps me constantly on the trot. I cannot leave these patients, quite impossible; you see yourself."

Though disappointed beyond expression, Sir John did not for one moment question the validity of the plea, and the two aristocratic names fell like two drops of oil on the wound inflicted by Doctor Yorke's refusal. Would the

Baronet have been so patient, had the people concerned been plain Mr. Smith or Mr. Brown?

"This being the case, can you recommend any good practitioner near this?" asked Sir John, after a second's reflection. The Doctor rubbed his forehead violently, turned his eyes to the ground, as if studying a map spread there, then answered,—

"Why, within a circuit of ten miles, indeed, I may say in all the Riviera, there is no one to be compared to Doctor Antonio."

"Doctor Antonio again!" broke in the Baronet, angrily; "name any one but him."

Doctor Yorke recurred again to his snuff-box for counsel. "I wish I could," said he; "but men like this—Italian doctor do not grow on every bush by the way-side. He might be an Englishman: see how he speaks English. Yes, he ought to be an Englishman. Certainly his appearance and manners are so foreign that I do not wonder at your being startled. I quite understand that; still—the young lady, our first consideration in all this, seems satisfied with him."

As Doctor Yorke stopped purposely here, as if expecting an answer, Sir John was obliged to give a reluctant bow of acquiescence.

"Important point," resumed the doctor; "a patient satisfied—mind kept unruffled—very capital consideration this, Sir John, and well worth the sacrifice of any little unpleasant first impressions. In short," wound up the doctor, after taking breath, "the best course, in my opinion, would be to make up matters with this—Italian doctor, and get him to resume his visits."

"Resume his visits!" exclaimed the Englishman, within a hairbreadth of losing his temper, but recollecting in time, that it would never do for a man like him to get into a vulgar passion with a man like Doctor Yorke, who could revenge himself by showing him up to his patients at Nice. "Ask him to return after what has passed, expose myself to the humiliation of a refusal!—lower my dignity with this—a —confounded touchy foreigner!"

"Come, come," said Doctor Yorke, in a soothing manner, "who talks of humiliations, who speaks of your asking anything? Am I the man to advise Sir John Davenne to any step derogatory to his character and position in society? What if I can arrange this business to the satisfaction of all parties, while you remain neuter and quiet here? what if I guarantee that the proposal I have suggested shall be accepted with—with gratitude?"

The word "gratitude," no sooner dropped in the heat of argument than mentally recalled, did more for the success of Doctor Yorke's diplomacy than all his eloquence, which was not little. Sir John felt replaced, as if by magic, on his pedestal or hobby-horse; his own superiority, the honour conferred by his notice, were both openly confessed, and the inferiority of his adversary was implied, if not acknowledged. Doctor Yorke saw and urged his advantage with great nicety of tact. Sir John, after a decent show of resistance, relented, and empowered his countryman to negotiate Antonio's return, with but one stipulation: Doctor Yorke was to promise that he had taken upon himself to declare on behalf of the Italian, that Doctor Antonio had intended no offence. Upon this understanding, the medical plenipotentiary, after one hesitating glance at the sun, armed himself with an umbrella, and sallied forth in search of Doctor Antonio.

Doctor Antonio had retired to his tent, in other words, had taken himself home, where, the door remaining wide open, his brother physician found him desperately fencing with some imaginary enemy, represented for the time being by one of the walls of his sitting-room. "An excellent way of getting rid of one's spleen," gasped forth the little man, "though rather hard work in this hot weather."

"Hot weather!" said Antonio, "but it is most pleasantly cool."

"Ouf! allow me to close that window, if you please, I

am in a perfect bath of perspiration. Thank you.—Fine mess we are in!" added he to himself, as, after one look at Antonio, he fell rather than sat down on a chair.

"Very good of you to venture so far in the sun, you who have such detestation of it," said Antonio; "what will you take? a glass of old sherry, or rosolio, or, as you are so hot, some warm negus?"

"No, no wine—some lemonade, if you please. Ouf! these chairs are none of—the softest, my good friend," said Doctor Yorke, fanning himself with his handkerchief.

"Not comfortable, eh?" said Antonio, smiling. "How did you leave Miss Davenne?" asked he, squeezing a fresh lemon into a glass.

"I am not made of stone like you," answered Doctor Yorke, beginning his attack, "so I did not see her before coming here. I had not the heart to go and tell her that you had forsaken her."

"Poor little dove!" said Antonio, with a feeling that did not proceed from stone, "as gentle as a lamb, and so sensible withal."

"Yes," said Doctor Yorke, coolly, "you had time to find all that out."

"She will regret me, I am sure."

"No doubt she will," said the little man, delightedly; "and that poor Sir John! one cannot help feeling for him also. I never in my life saw a man half so puzzled."

"What about?" asked the Italian, stirring the sugar into the glass of lemonade.

"None so blind as those who don't choose to see. You abandon him, and I cannot stay. So what's to become of his daughter, sweet, pretty creature?"

"You cannot stay?"

"Impossible! I must return to Nice this afternoon, I have so many ill there."

"Very provoking!" sighed Antonio, "very—unfortunate! I am very sorry, very sorry on account of the poor young lady. As for that stiff, old incarnation of pride, her father, he has only got what he deserves. I never saw such a hard, self-conceited, stubborn, arrogant, unfeeling old mummy."

Doctor Yorke put up his shoulders to shelter himself from this pelting of epithets.

"If his daughter had been my own sister," continued Antonio, "I could not have done more for her; and what has been the return I have met with at this worthy gentleman's hands? Nothing from the first but opposition, distrust, contradiction, insolence, and Heaven knows what not."

"You must make allowance for him, my dear fellow," interposed Doctor Yorke, soothingly—"force of habit—people of rank, you know—one of the first families in England."

"Zounds!" exclaimed Antonio, all in a blaze, "what's that to me? Let all England worship his rank and his family then; I don't choose to do so; I am made in God's image as well as he, and won't be trampled on were he twenty times as rich or as great as he is. You English are a proud race—so much the better—I am proud myself, and like people to know their worth. But is a noble pride, such as is founded on the consciousness of one's value, to exclude a proper regard for the dignity of others?"

"Certainly not," remarked Dr. Yorke, with his hands clasped over the respectable bulk of his waistcoat, twirling his thumbs first one way, then another.

"Methinks a little courtesy," resumed the Italian, "such as even perfect strangers accord to one another, was the least I was entitled to, had that man had an atom of sense or feeling, considering the relation in which we stood to one another. For, after all, was he or I the obliged party? Had he rendered me a service, or I him? I see a carriage overturned; I hasten to give assistance; I—but now that I think of it, perhaps that was an intrusion. Yes, yes, to be sure! Fool that I was, not to read it at once in the old man's face! Yes, he was right; what business had I to meddle with the lady's foot, or to bandage it, or to do anything that I did, without first asking permission of this English potentate!

When you see him again, pray offer him my unfeigned apologies, and tell him that I shall never sin in that way again. I will be d—— if I do! Henceforward all English ladies may break their legs, and arms, and necks, without any fear of my proffering assistance in a hurry."

Have you ever seen a skilful angler with a large salmon on his hook, ever watched how he lets the infuriated fish run all the line off the reel without the slightest check, nay, yields rod and line to the utmost of his power, encouraging the captive to spend his energies, how he waits the moment when it shall have exhausted itself by some vigorous leap, and then, with one dexterous jerk, throws his prey panting and helpless on the bank? By an identical process did acute Doctor Yorke let his young friend go on uninterruptedly with his philippic, giving his wrath plenty of line, and watching all the while for the favourable moment to wind up, and land him high and dry.

"But the young lady," said Doctor Yorke, seizing the first pause, "you don't mention the young lady. Did she behave ill too?"

"Bless her," said Antonio, in a suddenly softened voice, "no; from the very beginning she was grateful and kind."

"Why, then, in the name of wonder," cried the little doctor, turning sharply round on Antonio, "should you visit the sins of the father on his unoffending child?"

Antonio was silent.

"Very well," said Doctor Yorke; "I understand your silence. The question with me now is," (tightening the line,) "who is to attend Miss Davenne? You will not, and I cannot."

"No lack of doctors," replied Antonio, with a grim smile; "there is one at Ventimiglia, another at San Remo. I have already given Sir John Davenne the names and addresses of both."

"Very considerate of you; but you know very well that neither of them will do. Yes; stare at me as long as you please—but you know very well that Miss Davenne's case requires a degree of manual skill that neither of the gentlemen you mentioned possess, and an unremitting care and attention that only a person on the spot can give. Now, then," continued the Doctor, giving a great pull, "what if this innocent young lady—such a lovely girl too!—should be lame for life, and all for want of proper care?"

"God forbid!" ejaculated Antonio fervently.

"Come, now," pursued Doctor Yorke, "say a word, and help an old friend out of this scrape, will you?"

"What scrape?" asked the astonished Italian, who expected quite a different request.

"Why," said the Englishman, landing his salmon, "you must feel that, whatever my engagements at Nice may be,—and they are really of consequence, even at a certain risk to my practice, I cannot decently leave father and daughter in such a dilemma, alone in a strange land."

"Am I to understand," inquired Antonio, after a short silence, "that you come from Sir John?"

"Of course I do," was the answer.

"And that Sir John is willing"—

"Willing is not the word," interrupted the delighted little gentleman; "happy, my dear sir, happy to receive you back on your own terms. You are to be absolute monarch in the sick-room."

"Well, let it be so," said Antonio, vanquished. "I will return, and again take upon myself the care of his daughter; but bear in mind, that if I do so, it is for your sake and that of the young lady."

"Thank you, thank you," said Doctor Yorke, with real feeling; "you are a noble fellow, and worth a dozen Sir Johns. Thank you," he repeated again, cordially shaking Antonio's two hands. The Italian put on his hat, the very conical hat that had so scared and shocked Sir John at their first meeting, and the two doctors, side by side, directed their steps towards the Osteria *del Mattone*. Doctor Yorke avoided the mention of the "no offence" declaration, which according to Sir John's instructions, was to be the *sine qua non* preliminary of all negotiation. He did not choose to risk the success of his diplomacy by any such complication. He knew Antonio's warm and generous nature too well not to be certain that any hint on the subject from the Baronet would be met more than half-way by the Italian, and responded to in a kindly spirit.

Sir John had all this time been pacing to and fro the lobby, in a state of considerable perplexity, every now and then stepping out into the balcony, which formed the limit of his perambulation on one side, to look up the road to Bordighera. During one of these halts the Baronet descried the two gentlemen coming down the hill, arm in arm—a sight which, far from seeming palatable, made his nostrils suddenly contract, as though every orange and lemon tree perfuming the air in the garden, exhaled baneful and nauseous vapours. However, by the time the two gentlemen entered the room there was no indication left of contending feelings on Sir John's smooth brow, and the reception he gave to both his visitors proved most gracious. He even condescended to address to Doctor Antonio a few polite but rather formal words, expressive of his regret for the misunderstanding that had taken place, and which elicited from the Italian a declaration identical in substance, but far more satisfactory in tone. Doctor Yorke, whose anxiety during this transaction betrayed itself by sundry desperate appeals to his snuff-box, drew an enormous breath at last, and said inwardly,—"Fine mess I am out of."—"And now," said Sir John, turning to Doctor Yorke, "it only remains for me to tender my thanks, and, by releasing you at once, offer the best amends in my power for trespassing so long on your valuable time. Shall I order horses to the carriage at once?" The alacrity with which the offer was accepted shewed how welcome it was. "Well then, gentlemen," pursued the Baronet, "I must leave you to entertain one another, as I shall take this opportunity of sending some letters on business to Nice;" and, glad of an excuse to escape, he hurried from the room.

Sir John made good use of the time it took to procure horses; he wrote letter upon letter to his son Aubrey; addressed to the house in—Square, to his bankers, to his man of business in London, and to his head man in the country, (directions being given to the three last named to forward all his letters and papers to him at Bordighera,) added to which he penned a long list of articles which his courier was desired to forward without delay to the Osteria. John was also intrusted with a score of verbal instructions, all of which, letters, lists, instructions, and directions, implied that Sir John had made up his mind to a protracted stay in his present disagreeable quarters. It was so in fact; Sir John had at last realized his situation, and though much against the grain, sulkily submitted to its necessities. This, and this alone, was the result of the experience of the last few hours. Pique is a bad counsellor, and few men can afford to be just under the smart of a double defeat. We regret to say it, for in spite of his prejudices we confess to a foible for Lucy's father, but truth must be told, and the truth is, that the leaven of resentment was fermenting in Sir John's breast as fast as ever.

Sir John insisted on accompanying Doctor Yorke to the carriage, and seeing, with his own eyes, that everything was as it ought to be. This was the pretext which enabled him to lay on the seat, by Doctor Yorke's side, a folded paper, that the doctor chose not to see at the moment, but which, as soon as the carriage-door had been banged to by John, he carefully unfolded and examined, and, with manifest marks of satisfaction, deposited in his pocket-book. What with mental worry and bodily exertion, the English physician was so worn out, that after once more exclaiming, "Fine mess I have been in!" he stretched himself at length, and fell so soundly asleep that he never awoke till the carriage stopped at his own door at Nice.

CHAPTER VI.
Little Occupations.

"I HAVE a thousand questions to ask you," said Lucy, when Antonio made his appearance the next morning.

"Have you!" replied the Italian, good-humouredly; "very well, I am ready. You will be sooner tired of asking than I of answering. But first, will you tell me how you are, and allow me to feel your pulse?"

The medical inquiries being properly satisfied, "Now," said Lucy, "to begin, let me tell you that I wish to give Prospero some money. How much shall I send him?"

"Let me see," said Antonio, pondering. "Supposing that Prospero is unable to work for a fortnight, and it is more likely than not, fifteen days' work at thirty sous a day, his usual wages, come to twenty-two francs, fifty centimes. If you send him five-and-twenty francs there will be a little over to procure some better food during his recovery."

Lucy desired Hutchins to bring her her purse. Be it remarked once for all, that Hutchins was always at hand during the Italian's visits, either working by the side of her young mistress, or at a little table in her own room facing the open door between them. Lucy handed some money to the Doctor.

"Fifty francs!" said he, "that is double the sum I named."

"The additional five-and-twenty francs," observed Lucy, "will pay for Prospero's medicines."

"Prospero has neither doctor nor medicine to pay for. I am the doctor of the parish, and the parish pays me to attend the poor."

"But who provides them with medicines?"

"Myself. I have plenty of which I am only too glad to be rid. We must be very careful how we relieve the poor. A larger gift than positively necessary only encourages idleness, and is a doing of evil instead of good."

"That's just what papa always says," replied Lucy. "I shall not insist on having my own way this time, Doctor Antonio, if you promise me that, should Prospero require more help, or should you hear of any one in distress, you will let me know."

"Indeed, I am not sure that I shall make any promise of the kind," said Antonio, with a smile that softened the words; "had you your own way, as you call it, I fear that the poor but independent people of this country would be spoiled before long. Are your questions already at an end?"

"Scarcely begun. Tell me next why yesterday you brought that odious English doctor to see me?"

"Odious! in what way odious?" asked Antonio in his turn, and with surprise in his tone.

"Odious, because he is so sweet and oily. I hate honey-tongued people. I will have no other doctor but you, so you need not bring any one to see me."

"Thank you for the preference, which, if I guess right, I owe to my uncourtly manner. There is no fear of Doctor Yorke starting a competition with me: he is quietly at home in Nice by this time."

"I hope he will stay there then. But why did he come at all?" said Lucy, resolutely.

"He came at my request, as he told you. He chanced to pay me a visit on his way back to Nice, and I was glad to consult him about your foot. Now, as this could not be done without his examining it, I brought him to you. Independently of the weight I attach to his opinion, I thought also that, should our views of the case coincide, as I hoped, his advice would give mine an additional authority with Sir John."

"Why?" asked Lucy, as pertinacious as a child.

"It seems very natural to me, does it not to you, that an Englishman should have more confidence in an English than a foreign physician?"

"Have you and papa disagreed, then?"

"Disagreed! no. Sir John not being a doctor, could not be expected to view certain points as I did—that is all."

"And, pray," insisted Lucy, "what were those points?"

"You are cross-examining me, I believe," said Doctor Antonio, laughing.

"Yes, I am," resumed Lucy, gravely, "but not out of idle curiosity, as I daresay you think. I do not know exactly what it is that makes me suspect there has been some misunderstanding between you and papa about me, but I do suspect it," and she looked into Antonio's face; "and I want to know all about it, that I may do what I can to smooth it away."

"You are very good, but there is no occasion now for any mediation. Thanks to that 'odious' Doctor Yorke," said he, smiling, "Sir John has been made to see the necessity of a more prolonged stay in this poor place than he might have expected or wished. Now you know the point on which we were at variance."

"Ah! that is why papa was so silent and thoughtful all last evening. Shall we be able to leave this by the end of this month?"

"I fear not.'

"How provoking!" exclaimed Lucy.

"Are you then also so anxious to leave Italy?"

"Oh, no! I was only thinking of papa. Shall we be able to go away in a month from this day?"

"Yes, I think so, within a month or thereabouts."

"A month, I am afraid, will seem very long to papa. He is so dull here, with not even a horse to ride, he who used to take his ride every morning. Is there any saddle-horse to be hired in this neighbourhood?"

"Not the least chance of it."

"How provoking!" exclaimed Lucy again. "And when shall I be allowed to get up?"

"I am sorry that I cannot answer that question. Best put it *ad referendum*, as they say in the Swiss Diet."

"*Sine die*, you mean," said Lucy; "your Latin may be classical, but it is little pleasant."

"Cannot you make an effort, and fancy for a while that you have no feet at all?" said Antonio, gravely. Lucy had a great mind to laugh, but said instead, that it was a shame, and all nonsense, and that she had never seen such a cross doctor in her life; for Lucy, though nearly twenty, had preserved much of the freshness, the charm, and even the pouting ways of childhood.

"I assure you," said the Italian, in answer to this *boutade*, "that I shall not keep you in bed an hour longer than indispensable."

"Very much obliged to you," said Lucy, pettishly.

The Doctor did not speak.

"Do you know, Doctor Antonio," continued Lucy, after a while, "that I long to get up to see again that little sunshiny hill that was right before us, just when we were overturned? I should like to see it quietly, not passing by at full gallop."

"You mean the Cape of Bordighera?" said Antonio.

"Yes, I suppose so. I had been half asleep, when papa, calling to the postilion, startled me, and on opening my eyes, I had a glimpse of something so green, so fresh, so beautiful; only a glimpse, but comprehensive of such loveliness, that the recollection haunts me like the vision of a fairy land."

"Do not let your fancy have too much play," was the answer, "or you will lose the benefits of reality."

"How do you mean?"

"I mean that reality, my dear young lady, be it ever so charming, rarely keeps pace with the promises of imagination."

"I don't know much about the charms of fancy," said Lucy, "but I do know that reality is often disagreeable."

"As when one is obliged to keep in bed," said the Doctor, slyly.

"Exactly so. But tell me, pray, did I imagine or really see big palm-trees on the hill of Bordighera?"

"You saw them. Bordighera is famous for its palm-trees."

Lucy having apparently exhausted her stock of queries, Antonio was taking leave of her, when she detained him, saying, "One more question, and then you may go; it is about Speranza. She interests me very much; at times she looks so very unhappy. Do you know what is the matter with her?"

"Speranza has trials of her own," said Antonio; "hers is a simple but affecting story, which would lose all its effect if told by me. I am glad that you feel an interest in that girl. There is much primitive nobility in her nature. Do not disdain to seek her acquaintance, and try to win her confidence. The moral world, dear lady, is just like the physical one. We have only to stoop to find in the humble spheres much to notice and sympathize with."

The Doctor remarked, not without some surprise, that from that day Miss Davenne never complained again of having to stay in bed, or so much as hinted at the possibility of getting up.

On the morrow Lucy was permitted to read in moderation, and Doctor Antonio brought her a volume of Shakespeare, and Manzoni's *Promessi Sposi*. In a day or two she was allowed to sit up in bed. According to the Doctor's directions, the bed was taken out of its corner and moved near to the window, which, the Osteria standing on rising ground, commanded a full view of the Mediterranean.

"Have you ever lived by the sea?" inquired the Doctor.

"Never. When I was sent to Brighton for sea-bathing, the doctors forbade my being in any of the houses near the beach."

"So much the better," answered Antonio; "our sea, then, will have all the charms of novelty for you. It is a sight always new, a book that never tires. It will afford you unceasing occupation and matter for wonder, to watch the changeableness and richness of its colours, varying from the pure white of snow to the deep black of ink. Then ask it the secret of its thousand sounds, from the low plaintive murmur, so like a sigh or a kiss, to the thunderlike roaring that makes the earth quake. All poets have sung of the sea, but none more powerfully than the Hebrew king." And taking up an English Bible that was lying on the table near Lucy, he sought out in the Psalms, and read these verses: —"'They that go down to the sea in ships, that do business in great waters; these see the works of the Lord, and His wonders in the deep. For He commandeth, and raiseth the stormy wind, which lifteth up the waves thereof. They mount up to the heaven, they go down again to the depths: their soul is melted because of trouble. They reel to and fro, and stagger like a drunken man, and are at their wit's end.' No matching that, Miss Davenne, for simplicity, truth, and grandeur."

Lucy looked and listened to him as certainly she had never listened to or looked at any one before; then she said, "How strange! you seem to know the Bible well!"

"And does that astonish you?"

"Yes; I thought that Roman Catholics never read the Bible."

"That is a common error with Protestants. If you were acquainted with our Church services, you would be aware that portions of the Scriptures form their chief part, and are read and chanted daily in our churches, both morning and evening; in Latin, it is true, but a translation is to be found in all our prayer-books. In fact, the whole Bible, translated into Italian, is open to all readers, with only two conditions: first, that it be the translation of the Scriptures commonly called the *Vulgate*, collated and completed by St. Jerome; and, secondly, that the Latin text be printed opposite the Italian. If the Bible is not so generally diffused in Italy as might be wished, I think the fact depends partly upon the want of popular instruction, and chiefly upon the little encouragement given by the clergy to its perusal. However,

I can assure you, that many among the educated class in Italy know the Bible thoroughly, and read it both in the authorized and unauthorized translation."

Lucy was grateful, and enjoyed both the reading of her books and the contemplation of the sea, as he had hoped she would; she even gave the Doctor a full and vivid description of a charge of cavalry, in which the waves, furiously dashing and breaking against each other, and plunging and rearing like maddened horses, were the actors. But by degrees both the sea and her reading lost some of their power to interest; and Antonio, who watched his patient with a solicitude that had something motherly in it, became aware that it was time to find her some new occupation. First, he proposed that she should read to him a chapter of Manzoni every day; then he was sure it would improve his accent, if she could bear to hear him read a scene or two from Shakespeare. With these readings came now and then those little laughs, tinkling like silver bells, that sounded so sweet in Antonio's ears, and in which, though at the expense of his not faultless pronunciation, he joined so heartily.

His visits were now very frequent—he called three or four times a day; indeed, every moment he could spare from his duties found him by the couch of the fair invalid. And he rarely came empty-handed, bringing almost always something with him that he thought would amuse or interest her. It was at first an album of views and costumes of Sicily, a small collection of ancient coins, a few specimens of lava—all his scanty stock of curiosities. This exhausted, it was a flower, a rare plant, a curious insect; a scarabæus in an armour of jet, a green locust with a head like a horse, a butterfly with wings of gold or silver, or one of those canary-coloured hairy caterpillars with regular black stripes round its body. Hours went by unnoticed, while the Doctor explained to her, in clear and brief sentences, their habits and peculiarities, and even the use of many of them. "That little creature, whose shining green coat you admire so much," he would say, "will sadly fall in your estimation, I am afraid, when you know its name and the use that is made of it. Do you not guess now what it is?"

"No," replied Lucy, "I do not think I ever saw one before, at least I never noticed it."

"That is a specimen of the genus *cantharides,* or Spanish fly, of which blisters are made, and a sly wee thing it is, for as soon as you touch it, it emits a nauseous smell, and counterfeits death. Is it not wonderful how every living being, however small or ugly, has its special purpose, and is provided with some means of self-defence! Now, look at this many-legged thing, which runs so nimbly about; see, it rolls itself up into a ball. That is its defence against impending danger. This slow, ill-favoured little fellow, whom you scarcely deign to notice in the bright day-light, has often, I daresay, attracted your admiration in an evening walk."

"Is that the glow-worm, then?" asked Lucy.

"Yes; he also makes believe that he is dead when his liberty is about to be interfered with, though he is extremely tenacious of life. I once made an experiment with one of them. He bore first the imprisonment of a week under a glass, and afterwards a three hours' stay at the bottom of a vase full of water, and nevertheless came out of it alive, so I thought it but fair to set him free."

Doctor Antonio succeeded perfectly in his object, to make the hours of her confinement less long and dreary for Lucy. She was never tired of asking questions, which Antonio answered with a good humour highly creditable to his patience as an instructor.

One day, after just such another conversation, Lucy lay back as if in deep thought, which Doctor Antonio, by his own silence, seemed to respect. What was Lucy thinking of? or was she thinking at all? No, she was enjoying one of those rare moments when the mere sense of existence is happiness; when the blue sky, the rippling sea, the soft air, all seem bluer, brighter, sweeter, than ever known before. Doctor Antonio's eyes, from the sea on which they had been fixed, wandered to, and settled on the thoughtful countenance of his companion. A moment more and she looked at him. "Have I wearied you?" he asked.

"Oh, no!" said Lucy, in a very reassuring manner.

During the question and answer, the evening breeze came floating by, laden with the rich odour of the orange and lemon trees, that grew in the plot of ground below the window. "What a delicious fragrance!" exclaimed Lucy.

"Delicious indeed," echoed Antonio; "are you fond of flowers?"

"Very, very fond," said she. "I had plenty of them at Davenne, but none that ever smelt half so sweet as the plants in this garden."

"If I were a young lady," said Antonio, "I am sure that a garden would be one of my chief amusements."

"So you think, because you are a man," said Lucy; "you do not know anything about young ladies, you have no idea how much they are made to learn—to find out afterwards, as I have done," added she, slightly colouring, "that they know nothing."

"As to that," answered Antonio, laughing, "I am sure most young men can say as much for themselves."

There was another moment of silence, then Lucy returned to the point from which she had started. "I always fancy," said she, "that the orange flowers smell sweetest in the evening."

"It is not fancy," replied the Doctor; "orange and all strongly-scented flowers do really give out more perfume towards the close of day, and during the first hours after sundown. There are even some, like the Indian jessamine, which, scentless in the day, are very sweet at night."

"Then what does make flowers smell; do you know?"

"I will show you to-morrow," he said, "it is too late this evening.—I greatly rejoice," he went on kindly, "at the interest you take in these subjects, it helps you well through this wearisome confinement. It is incredible, is it not, what a rich mine for observation and wonder we may find, if we choose, close to us in an insect, a plant, even a blade of grass?"

The colour rose in Lucy's face as the Italian spoke, and holding out her hand, she said, "How much I owe you!" Antonio laughed outright at the strange notion, and bid good-bye in great haste. Left to herself, she gazed long out upon the sea, the distant tremulous lines of which, illumined, during the last minutes of Antonio's visit, by the golden glories of the sky, were fast vanishing in the dying light of the horizon: and as she watched, she seemed to listen, as though the inarticulate language of that immense creation, soft as a sigh this evening, was answering the silent questionings of her heart. Sky, and sea, and garden, had lost all colour, motion, and form, still Lucy remained looking into the darkness.

"Why, Lucy, my darling," exclaimed Sir John, opening the door, with a light in his hand, "all in the dark, and alone!"

"Yes, papa, after Doctor Antonio went away, I sent poor Hutchins to take a walk."

Sir John advanced close to the bed, still holding the light. "See, Lucy, I have taken quite a fancy to this odd-shaped lamp. The woman of the house told John that they were to be had at Genoa, in silver. I must have some to take home with us;"—and Sir John showed Lucy the object of his admiration, one of the common lamps used throughout Italy,—a brass globe for the oil, with three beaks on a very slender shaft, that, passing through the centre, was terminated at the top in a handle, from under which hung the chain, that held an extinguisher, and a pin for quickening the light.

"It is very pretty, papa." Sir John's eye fell on his daughter's face, as she turned it towards the lamp, and he exclaimed, "How well you look to-night, Lucy! I have not heard you cough to-day."

"Oh! I have lost my cough for these last two days," answered Lucy; "the air of this place does me so much good."

"I think it does," observed the father in a pleased manner; "we must not have too much of a good thing, however," added he, closing the window.

On the following morning, Doctor Antonio brought Lucy a sprig of orange flowers, its pure white blossoms nestling among the glossy dark green leaves. "Here, I present you," he said, "with what may be called the crown of our shores."

"You beautiful thing!" apostrophized Lucy, as he gave it into her hand; then inhaling the odour eagerly, "Now, where does such a fragrance come from?"

Antonio detached from the flower one of its thick white petals, and bade her hold it up between her and the light. "Do you see those transparent dots in its texture?" he asked.

"Yes."

"Now then," he added, "you see where the smell comes from. Each of those diaphanous dots is a diminutive essence-bottle; it holds a particle of the essential oil, which perfumes the flower, as you might scent your wardrobe with a *cassolette* of *attar* of roses."

"How strange!" cried the delighted girl; "how glad I am to know this!"

He then cut a bit of the rind of an orange, and shewed her that it was full of the same kind of little vessels for oil. "So it is," said Lucy; "and are all flowers scented in the same way?"

"Yes, and many green leaves; those of the myrtle, for instance, have receptacles of the same sort."

"I always thought," said Lucy, "that the smell was in these small powder puffs;" and she pointed to the anthers.

"They have quite a different destination," answered he; and he told her the names and uses of the different parts of the flower. "I shall never remember all that," said Lucy, with a sad shake of her head.

"I will write them down for you, if you really wish to remember them," said Antonio.

"Oh do, Doctor Antonio, and I will repeat my lesson to

you to-morrow." The bright animation of the fair speaker's countenance made Antonio say, "You have a taste for botany, you see."

"Botany!" exclaimed Lucy, "oh, no! I cannot bear the very name of botany and its hard scientific words; but I like to hear you talk of flowers."

"Well," said Antonio, smiling, "we will busy ourselves about flowers, and only about your favourite flowers. I suppose you will not object if I bring you some more rare than usual, to read about them, because I warn you my knowledge on the subject does not extend very far."

"Far enough to tell me all I wish to know," said Lucy; "but if you get tired of teaching me, then I suppose I must have one of your terrible wise books."

From that day flowers became Miss Davenne's favourite occupation, and Antonio's most useful auxiliaries in his task of kindness. Delightful to her were those long conversations, in which he told her Nature's mysterious processes and the all-wise distribution of qualities allotted to the vegetable in relation to the animal creation, the similitude and dissimilitude existing between the two kingdoms, and the link connecting them into one great whole.

Antonio happened to call one afternoon during a violent shower. "See," said he, pushing Lucy's bed nearer to the window, that she might have a peep of the trees at the further end of the garden, "see what a banquet for trees and plants, how the leaves stand up and drink every drop that falls!"

"How odd it is," said Lucy, "to hear you talk of plants as if they were living beings, breathing, drinking, and—what next?—eating, perhaps," and she laughed.

"Why not?" observed Antonio, with one of his quiet half sarcastic smiles. "It seems that of all the flowers that adorn the earth, you wish to keep for young ladies the exclusive privilege of eating oysters and underdone beefsteaks. But let me tell you that some of your rivals of the garden actually do consume solid food."

"O Doctor Antonio!" was the laughing exclamation, "what do you mean?"

"I am in earnest," he said. "The Dionœa, commonly called 'Venus's fly-trap,' has leaves armed with small hairy spines. When an insect touches the leaf, the leaf closes, clenching its bristles together like locked fingers, holds fast its prey, and never opens until the insect has wasted away. More than that, the experiment has been tried of feeding the Dionœa with small bits of raw meat."

"Raw meat!" repeated the young lady, with disgust.

"Yes, indeed, raw meat! and the leaves closed in the same way, and when they opened again the meat was gone —eaten up."

"Horrid Dionœa!" cried Lucy, "I will never have another in my garden. A flower to eat raw meat! It might as well be a cannibal."

Doctor Antonio's aim had been at first not that of instructing, but simply of providing his bedridden young patient with such little diversions as he could place within her reach. Her quick perception of his meaning, and eagerness to learn, ended, however, by drawing him on farther than he had thought of, and at last he found himself regularly giving her lessons in botany, and frequently writing down a résumé of their conversations for the grateful pupil. In this way Lucy soon commanded a little stock of knowledge on botany, acquired without effort, and almost unconsciously. So when the Doctor put one of the wise-looking books before her, she found that much of its contents was already familiar to her, and when he told her to try and classify such and such plant by herself, and she succeeded, it would have been hard to say which was the greater, her gratification or wonder. And Lucy looked up to her instructor as a marvellous lamp of science, and probably thought him the cleverest man in the world.

One morning, Lucy heard, to her infinite surprise, some one singing to the guitar in Hutchins' room. It must be Doctor Antonio, it could be no one else. "Bravo!" she cried; "will not the mysterious troubadour show his face?"

"Now, Miss Davenne," said Antonio, entering the room, a guitar slung across his shoulders, "you will never again think me deficient in gallantry." She looked very much astonished. "Oh! do not deny it, you know you have been expecting a serenade every evening past. It would be too bad that a young lady in Italy should neither meet with banditti nor be serenaded. Now, you have had a serenade, and one in broad daylight too, which adds to its zest."

"Confess, Doctor Antonio, that you think young ladies very foolish creatures," said Lucy, laughingly.

"Why so?" said he, laughing also.

"Because you suppose they must be always expecting something silly or extravagant, as if they were so different from you."

"By no means. Are there not such things as banditti and serenades, and is not the love of adventure natural to youth? For my part, when I was your age I would have given anything for a moving accident by flood or field, and Mrs. Radcliffe's romances are nothing compared to those I created in my own fancy."

"What! you who look so grave!"

"Yes, indeed, my own sedate self. But in the meantime you say nothing of my song."

"I was just going to tell you how much I liked it, it is so simple and full of pathos."

"That's right, it is one of my favourite Sicilian airs. I have come to-day with the intention of teaching it to you."

"But I cannot play the guitar."

"But you can learn; no time so good as the present. Are you in the humour to take your first lesson now?"

Lucy was all impatience to begin. Antonio showed her how to hold the instrument, and the motion of the fingers of the one hand on the frets, and of the other on the strings. After the lesson, at Lucy's request, he finished the song he had only begun, and a pretty one it was, and well she liked it.

CHAPTER VII.
Bits of Information.

"WILL you allow me," said Lucy, one evening, "to ask you a question?"

"A mighty ticklish one, I daresay," replied Antonio, "if it needs so ceremonious a preamble."

"The question relates to you, Doctor Antonio, and I do not quite feel as if I ought to ask it."

"Never mind," said Antonio, "I here give you full permission to put whatever questions you please, whether they concern me or not."

"Thank you. I wish to know, then, how a superior man like you"—

Antonio fell to laughing outright.

"Ah! very well," said Lucy, stopping short, "you may laugh as much as you please, but you are a superior man, you know you are."

"If a decent average of education and good breeding constitute what you are pleased to call a superior man, then I may be proud of my country indeed."

"Do you mean to say that there are many like you in your country?"

"Are you serious?" asked Antonio. "You look upon Italy, then, as a kingdom of the blind, where the one-eyed is king. Believe me, my dear lady, you may find many far superior to me, who both live comparatively useless, and die unknown.—You have no idea," pursued he, "what an amount of intelligence, strength, and noble aspirations wastes away, for want of space and air, in this huge pneumatic machine, marked on the map of Europe as Italy."

A cloud of unspeakable sadness overshadowed his usually serene countenance. Lucy felt for him, and was silent.

"Well," said Antonio, with a graceful movement of the head to one side, as if shaking off some weight, "will you go on? You were wondering how a superior man like me—did you mean, could condescend to play the guitar?"

"Oh, no, no!—could live in a small country village like this, among rude peasants"—

"Rude peasants!" repeated the Italian; "I beg your pardon for again interrupting you, but I cannot bear to hear the mildest race on earth so grossly misrepresented. Call them ignorant, superstitious, anything but rude. What caused you to think them so?"

"Why," said Lucy, a little abashed, "papa told me that more than once he has been stopped in his walks, and rudely spoken to."

"That Sir John, who does not know their language, should be annoyed at being addressed by the country people, I can understand; but how he can mistake their cordiality for disrespect, and accuse them of rudeness, that, I confess, passes my comprehension."

"Still, Doctor Antonio, you have not answered my question."

"You consider my lot, then, as a mean one?"

"Not mean, but unworthy of you."

"What if I have no choice?" said Antonio.

"But you know that such is not the case," retorted Lucy, with some warmth; "you know that you have only to speak one word to change your present position for one far superior."

"I see how it is," replied Antonio, smiling; "you have been making friends with Speranza, and she has told you fairy tales of the grandeur that awaits my acceptance. Let me warn you against such suspicious channels of information as Speranza and her mother, in all that relates to me."

"Yet you told me that Speranza was a sensible person."

"So she is, and so is her mother; but their imagination gets the better of their sense whenever I am concerned. I am their hobby-horse, and were they told that a throne was in store for me somewhere, they could believe it."

"If they are attached to you, and I know they are—they have good reasons for being so."

"Imaginary, or, at least, highly exaggerated reasons. Women, I am told, are apt to run into extremes. Nothing will ever put it out of Rosa's head that I saved her daughter's life in her last illness, which is not the fact; and as to Speranza, she thinks she owes me an enormous debt of gratitude, for some efforts I made in a matter she had much at heart, efforts, I must say, which utterly failed."

"How ingenious you are in trying to undervalue yourself!"

"Not in the least, Miss Davenne; I beg you to believe that I have a tolerably good opinion of myself, but I cannot bear to be overrated. Should you like to know in what consisted those great prospects boasted of by Speranza?"

"To be sure I should," said Lucy.

"They will cut a sorry figure when reduced to their natural proportions. Last year—but to be clearer, perhaps, I had better tell you first what chain of circumstances brought me to this place."

"Pray, do so," said Lucy, eagerly.

"It is a story for which few words will suffice. That a native of Sicily, or of any part of this peninsula, who asked but to live and die in his home, should have been suddenly and forcibly cast out from it, a flaming sword behind, and all the wide world before him, is a matter of too common occurrence in this land of anomalies, to require any explanation. To think, or only to be suspected of thinking with liberality, is enough to expose any Italian to such a chance. But what must seem, and is in fact more strange, considering the close partnership in oppression, into which all the governments of Italy have entered, is how a man, driven out of Sicily, could find a refuge, and be tolerated in the Sardinian States. [The reader is requested to remember that Doctor Antonio is speaking in 1840.] Now this is how it happened. The day that the soil of Catania became too hot for me—it is unnecessary for our present purpose to enter into the cause, political, of course, that made it so—that day, I was fortunate enough to obtain a passage on board a Genoese merchant vessel going to Genoa. When we arrived there my passport was demanded, and as naturally I had none, I was refused permission to land. Fortunately, my uncle—the English officer whom I already mentioned to you as the husband of my mother's eldest sister—when I took leave of him, had had the lucky thought of giving me a letter of introduction to an old friend and comrade of his, the British Consul at Genoa. I sent my letter to that gentleman, and through his kind offices, I obtained leave not only to land, but to remain in the town a week. I was sorely at a loss, as you may imagine, what to do, and where to go at the expiration of that time, when one morning I saw a paragraph in the local official paper that put an end to my irresolution. I ought to have told you that at the time I allude to, the year 1837, the Asiatic cholera was raging throughout this Riviera. The paragraph I read was an address to medical men in general, especially to young physicians, urging them to place themselves at the disposal of the Proto Medicato, a sort of board of public health, by whom this appeal was issued. Some pecuniary emolument was offered to those who should volunteer their services. A motive of humanity prompted me to do so, and a more selfish motive decided me. I felt as though a plank had been thrown to me, on which, if I could place my foot, I should be saved from complete shipwreck; for to have left Italy would have been utter despair to me. If successful I should be sure of gaining my bread honestly, and at no charge to my family. So I went to the Board of Health, and stated, as was the fact, that I had some experience in the treatment of cholera, which had broken out in Sicily a few months previous. I was very well received; but, on showing my diploma, which, with a few other papers, I had brought with me from Catania, I was told that, being a foreigner—yes, a man born in the south was called a foreigner in the north of Italy!—my services could not be accepted, unless, through a petition to the king, I obtained an exemption. At first, the notion of sending in a petition to be allowed the privilege of exposing my life in the service of my fellow-creatures, proved very unpalatable. However, these gentlemen were so very earnest in begging me to comply with what was, they said, but a formality; they offered, with such a good grace, to transmit the petition themselves, and support it in the proper quarters; the British Consul, on the other hand, combated my reluctance so strenuously, that at length I yielded. So I sent the petition—horrid stuff, to be sure—and at the end of another week, my permit of residence having extended so far, I was informed that my request was granted. The Board of Health at once despatched me to San Remo, where I arrived on the 23d of April.

"My birthday!" exclaimed Lucy, in girlish glee. "What a strange chance!"

"Say happy as well as strange," observed Antonio, touched by her innocent elation at the coincidence. "So you will be twenty in two days. I am glad you have told me now, for though in a strange land you shall hear friendly voices giving you hearty good wishes."

"Do not forget," said Lucy, playfully; "but now you must go on and tell me how you came to remain here."

"I have little more to say. When I arrived at San Remo, the cholera was at its height. I did my best, though with little success. What can man's skill and energy avail against an impalpable foe, which seems to mock and set at nought all human calculation, and defy all remedies? All I can say in my own favour is, that I did not spare myself."

"That I am sure you did not," said Lucy, warmly.

"And I have been more than repaid by the affection and gratitude of the people all about this part. After several months of hard struggle and hard work, the fearful visitation diminished, and then disappeared of its own accord. Shortly after, the parish doctor of Bordighera, a very old man, died, and the town-council offered me the appointment. I liked the little town, which I had visited many a time. I liked the good people, most of whom I knew, and so I accepted the offer. But the Government refused to ratify my election, again on the plea of my being a foreigner, and having taken my degree in a foreign university. Bordighera, however, had it at heart that I should be the doctor, and a deputation, composed of the mayor and one or two of the council-men, actually went to Turin to try what could be done. The Commandant of San Remo, with whom I had become very friendly, backed the deputation, and wrote in my favour. My services were pompously set forth and pleaded, and at last my nomination—a state affair—received the official seal and signature. That is how I came to settle in this country place as physician and parish doctor."

"What a sad destiny to be thus driven from one's birthplace, from one's home, far from those one loves best!" exclaimed Lucy, with tears in her eyes. "What you have just been saying gives me a glimpse of a state of things I never dreamed of before. You will be shocked at my ignorance —but pray, how many separate States are there in Italy?"

"So many," replied Antonio, "that unless I reckon them on my fingers I am not sure of the number myself. Let me see,—there is Naples (including Sicily), Rome, Sardinia, Tuscany, Parma, Lucca,* and Modena; the Lombardo-Venetian, under Austrian rule, makes the eighth."

"And are the governments all alike?"

"All alike, each and all of them working on the grinding principle."

"And the Pope,—is his as bad as the rest?"

"Fully, nay, if possible, still worse. I daresay it did not strike you as being so."

"To tell the truth," said Lucy, with some little embarrassment, "I did not think about the matter."

---

* A clause in the Treaty of Vienna provided, that after the death of Maria Louisa of Austria, reigning Duchess of Parma, the Duke of Lucca should be restored to his paternal States of Parma, and that Lucca should be incorporated with Tuscany. These changes took place in 1847, at the demise of Maria Louisa, and consequently the number of the petty States of Italy was diminished by one, that of Lucca.

"No great wonder, at your age. A young lady who goes to Rome in search of health and amusement is not likely to trouble herself much about the character of the government. Did you know many Roman families?"

"Scarcely any, except that of Prince Sofronia. We visited exclusively among the English."

"That is almost universally the case with strangers. They come to Italy as they would to a convenient hostelry; and when a man goes to an hotel it is certainly not with the intention of interesting himself about the people of the house."

"What should I do, then, to get some knowledge of men and things when I next go to Rome?"

"There is only one way," said Antonio; "to mix with *all* classes of society, and to keep eyes and ears wide open. But this, of course, a young lady cannot and ought not to do."

"I wish I were not a young lady," said Lucy, with child-like impatience, "if being so is always to hamper me at every turn. But, at all events, I can try to obtain information."

"Of course," replied Antonio; "and as you say you are to return to Rome, let me give you a timely warning. Never, under any pretext or persuasion, lend one of your Protestant Bibles to a Roman."

"Why not? You told me the other day that many Italians read the Bible."

"Very true; but I told you at the same time that only one translation was allowed. Were you to be found infringing the prohibition against disseminating any other version, you might learn to your cost what sort of leniency and toleration graces the sway of the Vicar of Jesus Christ. As to those among my countrymen who take upon themselves to read unauthorized translations, they do so at their own risk and peril. But I think we have had enough of politics. I must now tell you of my great prospects."

"Ah, yes! do," said Lucy.

"I had been here two years, when I was offered a similar appointment in a distant part of Piedmont proper. The sole advantage over the one I hold here was pecuniary, the emoluments being fully double. On the other hand, the little town to which I was invited was situated in a narrow valley, hemmed in by mountains, damp at all seasons, and very cold in winter. Was I, who had none dependent on me, to leave my kind and grateful neighbours, each of whom I knew by sight and name?—was I to give up this vast extent of glorious nature, which gladdens my eyes and lightens my heart whenever I look at it, and all for a little paltry money? I could not do it. I am a spoilt child of the south. I want air, light, warmth, colour. I dote on this sky,—on this sea. I cannot do without them; they are my life."

"It does my heart good," said Lucy, "to see you can be enthusiastic for once."

"Put me on the chapter of this nature at any time," retorted Antonio, smiling, "and you will see."

"So you sent a refusal," said Lucy.

"To be sure, and without the least hesitation."

"It was just like you," pronounced Lucy, whose interest and respect for the narrator rose with every particular which placed in stronger light the noble simplicity of his mind.

"My second grand opening in life," continued the Italian, "was of so misty a nature that I am at a loss how to explain it. It was the chance of a supplementary chair of anatomy at the University of Turin. There was to be a competition for it. The actual head professor, somewhat a friend of mine, advised me to come forward as one of the competitors. To have my name admitted on the list of candidates would have required me to send in a petition again, to be exempted from one of the requisite conditions, viz., that of Sardinian nationality. Now, I had petitioned once, and that was more than enough for me, so I thanked my friend, and there the affair ended."

"That was too bad," said Lucy, in a tone of reproof.

"You say so, because you don't know what petitioning

means in this country," replied Antonio. "One is compelled to use an express formulary, a most abject one, and of which the language is less that of man to man than of a slave to his driver. The very name of the thing, a supplication, (*supplica,*) is sickening to me. No, not to save my life shall I ever write another petition."

Two days after this conversation was the 23d of April. When Antonio called he found three immense bouquets, at least twenty inches in diameter, arranged according to the Genoese fashion, and fastened to sticks two feet long, standing by Lucy's bed. Rosa and Speranza, not satisfied with preparing their own, had furnished Sir John with one to present to his daughter. "Look,—look! Doctor Antonio," cried Lucy, as he entered the room, pointing to her magnificent flower show.

"Many happy returns of this day!" began the Italian. "I knew I had no chance of vying with Rosa and Speranza, so I brought you no nosegay, but a single flower multiplied by itself;"—and so saying he tendered to Lucy a branch of peach-tree in full blossom, that he had hid behind him.

"Oh! this is best of all—how glorious!" cried Lucy, clasping her hands in delight.

"Yes, is it not splendid?" said Antonio. "Can you conceive anything more elegant than this corolla? anything richer than the tints of these petals, fading from this royal purple into the most delicate blush of the rose? The corolla, as you see, is polypetalous"—

"No technicality, no analyzing," interrupted Lucy; "let me enjoy unmixed admiration to the full."

"You are right," answered Antonio; "if by analyzing we add to our stock of knowledge, it is rare that we do not interfere with our enjoyment. That this is one of Nature's wonders, a *chef-d'œuvre*, is all we require to know about it."

"It makes me think," said Lucy, "of what is written of the lilies of the field,—'And yet I say unto you, that Solomon in all his glory was not arrayed like one of these.'"

"To my eyes," resumed Antonio, "this peach-branch

bespeaks the hand of a supreme Artificer as conclusively in its way as all the glories of the firmament."

"It does, indeed," returned Lucy. "How unaccountable it seems that there should be people who see nothing in all the marvels of the universe but the working of matter and the result of a blind chance!"

Antonio said nothing, but gazed on the fair speaker with intense sympathy. She remained pensive, with her face upturned towards the heavens,

> "And looks commercing with the skies,
> Her rapt soul sitting in her eyes."

No words so aptly as these of Milton can describe our sweet Lucy at this moment. Neither of the young people spoke for some time, but their hearts had never before been in such close communion as during this pause. Antonio was the first to speak.

"Have you ever read Picciola?"

"No. Is it a novel?" asked Lucy.

"Yes, it is a novel, by a celebrated French author, Monsieur Saintine. What you said just now brought it to my recollection."

"What is it about?"

"A flower," answered Antonio. "The heroine of the novel is a flower."

"How strange!—a flower!"

"Nothing more nor less," said Antonio; "and performing the most glorious part ever allotted to a heroine."

"You excite my curiosity," said Lucy. "Do tell me a little about this Picciola."

"The groundwork of the tale is simply this. The hero, just such a sceptic as you have been alluding to, is a young nobleman, implicated in some conspiracy against Napoleon I., and for that cause imprisoned in the Fortress of Fenestrelle. Shut up between the four bare walls of his cell, deprived of books, pen, and ink, and of all human intercourse, save with his jailer, the poor prisoner is allowed no other recreation but that of an hour's exercise in an inner court of the fortress,

In one of these daily walks up and down the dull yard, his eye lights by chance upon a diminutive green shoot, trying to force its way between two stones. At first the sight is perfectly indifferent to the prisoner; but as on each returning day he views the gradual development of the plant, and its hard struggle for existence, his interest is gradually aroused, and increases every day, till it grows into a passion. The mysterious wonders of vegetation strike upon the mind and heart of the materialist, and the humble little flower becomes the ladder upon which he elevates himself to the conception of a first cause. Picciola, or little one—such is the name he has given to the plant—is, in short, the missionary which converts the sceptical *blasé* man of the world into a believer."

"That is really a beautiful story," said Lucy; "I must get the book, if you will write down the title for me. And what plant was it that worked such a miracle?"

"The hero of the tale, it is said, could never discover the botanical name of his wonder-working flower."

"What a pity!" said Lucy. "One might have wished that it had been a violet or a forget-me-not,—or—By the by, Doctor Antonio, among all the flowers you have brought me there have never been any forget-me-nots. Do they not grow in Italy?"

"Yes, in quantities."

"And you have never brought me any!" said Lucy reproachfully. "Why have you never done so?"

"Why, I don't know," said Antonio, smiling, but with a shade of embarrassment; "perhaps I thought that seeing me so often, you did not need any to remind you of me."

"A presumptuous, bad reason," answered Lucy, tartly; "I would not advise you to rely too much on it."

The next time he called, the Doctor brought his young patient a large bunch of these pretty little blue flowers. She put them into a glass on the table near her, and said, pointing to them, half seriously, half playfully, "You don't know yet that I am very forgetful; as long as I have these, I shall not forget you."

If Antonio had been a commonly vain man, he might have thought that she meant more than she expressed; but he only gave her credit for wishing to atone for her rather sharp speech of the day before.

CHAPTER VIII.
Speranza.

WHAT with reading, watching the sea, lessons in botany, lessons on the guitar, and chatting with Doctor Antonio, Lucy had reached the twentieth day of her stay in bed in tolerable spirits, and without complaining of time hanging heavily on her hands. The necessity of this tedious confinement was, in fact, the only serious inconvenience still entailed on Miss Davenne by her late accident. The fits of pain that would now and then shoot through her injured limb, especially the foot, during the first days, had gradually subsided, and then completely vanished; so had that sense of restlessness which interfered with her sleep; and, on the whole, Lucy's health was rather improved than otherwise from what it had been for some time previous to the unlucky casualty that had brought her to the Osteria.

On that twentieth morning, then, Antonio paid his visit earlier than usual, and said, "I have come to wish you good-bye till to-morrow; I am called away to a place some hours distant, and I shall have to sleep there."

This piece of news made Lucy's heart contract painfully. "It will be a long day for me," she answered, and could not resist adding, "But you will be sure to be back to-morrow?"

"Without fail," replied Antonio; "I shall bid Speranza come and keep you company. Her stories may amuse you. Now, tell me, do not you think I had better see Sir John Davenne, to let him know that I shall be absent for the next four-and-twenty hours?"

"Yes, pray do so," said Lucy, thankfully; for Lucy had not been without remarking, that there existed a certain restraint in the manner of the gentlemen towards each other, and hailed anything in the shape of an advance from the Doctor, as possibly conducive to a better understanding. So Hutchins was sent, as usual, to see where Sir John was, and Antonio taking leave of Lucy followed Iris to the presence of the British Jupiter.

As it is not our intention to give our hero credit for more generosity than he had in his nature, we shall at once state that the proffer he had just made to Miss Davenne, was not a sign of any growing kindness, but neither more nor less than a stroke of policy. Antonio had a little plan to propose to Sir John, which he rather preferred that Miss Davenne should know nothing about for the present. Now, to see Sir John unknown to Lucy being difficult, he was glad of having a specious pretext for an official *tête-à-tête* with the stiff-necked, stiff-backed papa of his patient.

Ever since Doctor Yorke's memorable visit and Antonio's decisive victory, Sir John, by one of the strangest among the strange delusions of mental optics, had eyed the Italian in the light of the author of all his woes. Sir John was not quite sure whether Antonio, with his nonsensical chattering to Prospero on the road, had not been the primary cause of the overturn of the carriage; but as to the Italian's having in some way or other managed to bring about the present unpleasant state of things, of this Sir John felt not the slightest doubt; and his resentment was proportionate to the injury he had received. Now, well-bred gentlemen, as everybody knows, have a thousand ingenious ways of their own to make it perfectly understood, that they wish you at the deuce, without deviating the eighth of an inch from the strictest propriety in word or manner. Least of all, was this inheritor of a yard long of pedigree, this quintessence of gentlemanliness, deficient in the talent of making himself disagreeable in a polite way if he chose. This is a peculiar branch of diplomacy much studied and practised in fashionable drawing-rooms, and among the higher circles. In this school are acquired the ceremonious bow, that throws you to a greater distance than would the wrong end of any telescope; the bland smile that proves so charmingly provoking; the frigid "hope you are well," that sounds like a *memento mori*, and a variety of other such choice ways of being superlatively annoying in the most engaging manner; —all of which our polished Englishman applied with distinguished ingenuity in the present emergency. But where he came out with unparalleled excellence, was in the daily expression of regret and reiteration of apologies for the trouble the Doctor was put to. One would have sworn to seeing sharp needles issue from his mouth at every word. Antonio, after several unsuccessful attempts at conciliation, took the hint, and repaid the Baronet in his own coin; returned his bows at precisely the same angle of inclination at which they were made; inquired for Sir John's health in the same icy tone in which the state of his own had been investigated; conducting himself in all other respects as if no Sir John existed, and going in and out of the Osteria with an ease and equanimity, that left his English foe in a pleasant doubt as to whether or not his tactics were understood.

Strangely enough, this uncomfortable state of things had lasted on, even when the causes producing it had partly ceased to exist, viz., when the old gentleman's feelings of irritation towards the younger one had considerably subsided, —a result chiefly brought about by that best of all peacemakers, time, and various other almost imperceptible agencies, whose workings on the human mind are as positive as undefinable. The Osteria, which at first had been like Frederic the Great's kingdom, "all sting," though not positively transformed into a land of peace flowing with milk and honey, was nevertheless no longer the bed of nettles it had been. Sir John was, on the whole, tolerably comfortable, he received the *Times* regularly every morning, and was well supplied with those savoury literary entremets, English periodicals. An avalanche of arm-chairs, couches, looking-glasses, curtains, lamps, crockery, &c., &c., had come from

Nice to minister to his ease, and so had a cook—fancy, the cook of the late bishop of Albenga, the greatest gastronome in the Riviera. By the mail from Nice to Genoa, his courier managed to supply his table with everything in season. Two cows at a neighbouring farm had been appropriated to the service of the family, and very passable butter figured at the Baronet's breakfast and tea. His walks were free from all molestation, it being now well known that the *Milordo Inglese* did not like to be spoken to. Sir John was a kind of walking notification of "no trespass allowed." The mayor, and the majority of the town-council of Bordighera, had waited on him in state, and so had an elderly nobleman, called, by antonomasia, "the Count," who lived in retirement in his palazzino, just on the other side of the hill of Bordighera. These visits, punctiliously returned of course, had agreeably tickled the Baronet's self-love and importance. After all, he saw he was among people who knew their betters. Find, if you can, a member of the baronetage of Great Britain, who acknowledges or believes that an Italian nobleman, whose name, perhaps, figures in history before the Plantagenets were heard of, can be his equal! Sir John, in a word, felt nearly as comfortable as he had done anywhere since he left his native shores, and was therefore considerably mollified towards Italian mankind in general, and in particular towards that sample of it, which went under the name of Doctor Antonio. The never-ending anthem of praise Lucy sang of all that the Doctor did and devised to amuse her, and what Sir John had himself witnessed of it, had probably not been without some effect on the father's heart. Unhappily, Sir John was too proud to give any outward sign of his altered sentiments which might be regarde d as an advance on his part, and continued, from false shame, if not so biting as of old, at least as formal, as distant, and frigid as ever.

This premised, we shall understand how Sir John, on emerging from his room, apologized most ceremoniously to Doctor Antonio for having kept him waiting so long—just half a minute—and how Doctor Antonio in return offered a rather verbose excuse for having disturbed Sir John at such an unseasonable hour. Hearing which, the Baronet made a declaration to the purpose, that he was always at Doctor Antonio's service, and begged him to be seated. Here came a flourish of bows, followed by a skirmish as to who should or should not be seated first, a difficulty which was settled by both the gentlemen sitting down at the same time.

"It is my pleasant duty," began the Doctor in a somewhat oratorical tone, "to communicate excellent news of our interesting invalid. Miss Davenne is uncommonly well this morning."

"I rejoice to hear you say so," replied Sir John, with great condescension, "though I could scarcely expect less, considering all the skill and attention you have shown in your treatment of Miss Davenne."

Antonio would have said something to beg a truce to compliments. "No, no!" pursued Sir John, "you must allow me to say so. I know the extent of my obligations and the value of your time, and I shall do my best to show my sense of both."

Does this Don Magnifico mean to pay me for my conversations on botany and my lessons on the guitar? thought Antonio, and at the thought, he knitted his brows portentously, and said dryly, "You overrate both the extent of your obligations and the value of my time; especially at this season of the year, when, I am happy to say, there are so few ill in the parish, my time is worth very little. Perhaps, to avoid any future misunderstanding, I had better at once distinctly inform you, that nine out of ten of my visits are not professional, and consequently exclude any question of fees."

Sir John made a very wry face, and his nostrils contracted as if there were a bad smell in the wind. Antonio went on saying, "My motive for troubling you this morning, is on a matter relating to Miss Davenne. Miss Davenne, I must render her this justice, has borne her confinement in bed with admirable patience and sweetness; still the trial is heavy, and will become more so as she advances in her recovery, and I have been thinking much of late whether we could not contrive some means of alleviating it. Supposing we could manage to have her carried every day to that balcony, so that she might enjoy a more extended view of the country around, have more fresh air, amuse herself with drawing, and even receive visits, if she chose,—I think this would prove a great relief to her."

"A great relief, certainly," echoed Sir John.

"Now," resumed Antonio, "what would be quite out of the question with ninety-nine out of a hundred persons in her case, seems to me worth while trying, and even likely to succeed with a lady of Miss Davenne's sense, and discretion, and earnestness in obeying directions."

"Could we not," said Sir John, "have a sofa placed on the balcony, and have her carried there every day?"

"A sofa would not be safe," answered the Doctor. "We must guard Miss Davenne against the chance of doing herself harm, even by an involuntary movement, and I think I have hit on a means which meets even that danger. Here is the plan of a seat," continued Antonio, handing Sir John a paper with a rough sketch on it, "which is something, as you see, between the body of a carriage and an arm-chair, on which Miss Davenne could lie at length. This padded hollow in front is meant to keep the foot steady, and guarded from any motion, even independent of the will. The whole could be put on wheels made to move at the pleasure of any one sitting on it. If you approve of my plan, I can have it executed immediately by a most skilful cabinet-maker, a friend of mine, (Sir John winced visibly at this last announcement,) and whom I shall see this very day at a place to which I am going for four-and-twenty hours."

"Your idea is excellent," said the Baronet. "But are you sure that the man you speak of is capable of executing your orders perfectly?"

"I have no doubt of it," said the Italian; "the person I

mean is a genius in his way, and I even rely on him for suggesting any improvements that can be made, and which he will see at a glance. By the by," added he, "I have mentioned nothing of this to Miss Davenne, lest the scheme should fail from some cause or other, and"—

"Quite right," interrupted Sir John, "I shall not breathe a word about it."

"Thank you—and now that I have your sanction," wound up Antonio, rising, "I will not trespass longer on your time."

"Pray, sir," said Sir John, rising also, "receive my very best thanks; very considerate of you, I am sure—very—kind. I am infinitely obliged to you."

Sir John was really in earnest in his thanks, and these last words were pronounced in a tone to which he had little accustomed Antonio's ears. The Italian's unvarying independence and disinterestedness both piqued and pleased the haughty Baronet. Of all qualities in a man, that which Sir John could best appreciate and valued the most, was pride. After all, said he to himself as he bent his steps towards Lucy's room, there is a dash of the gentleman in that Italian. After all, said Doctor Antonio to himself, as he crossed the garden, there is a touch of feeling in that old ogre. Thus both gentlemen had separated more kindly disposed towards each other than they had felt hitherto.

Lucy did her best to beguile the hours, but with little success. Everything which had so lively an interest for her so long as Antonio was there, had none now that he was absent. The very sky was not so brilliant, the sea not so blue. She put aside her books and flowers, and fell to musing. Never had such a feeling of loneliness fallen on her before, and as it is the privilege of a present sadness to awaken those of the past, so did there come to her, strangely distinct from out a mass of confused thoughts and images, the recollection of her mother, making the girl clasp her hands, while a pang of sorrow stung her to the quick, as if for the first time she had known, that never more had she a mother's heart to lean on. Then memory carried her back to her childhood. Her old nurse, her playthings, the lawn, the garden, all old familiar faces and scenes came before her, and hot tears rolled over her cheeks. Lucy was very sad, and wondered why it was that she was so sad, and why it was that she felt so lonely; why there was such a blank around her. Her eyes drooped, and she began to wish that Speranza would come to keep her company, as Antonio had said she would. Speranza was the only society that would have suited Lucy this morning,—Speranza who seemed to her, and really was, so very different from Hutchins, to whom Miss Davenne never could have looked as a resource.

Speranza at last made her appearance, and went quietly to take her usual seat by the foot of the bed. Lucy, on looking at her, saw traces of tears in her eyes, and said, "You have been crying, Speranza—tell me what is the matter." Speranza attempted a faint denial with her hand,—her heart, poor thing, was so full, that any effort at speaking would have made it overflow—and bent her head lower over her distaff.

"Come and speak to me," said Lucy, and drawing her gently down towards herself, she asked in her sweetest tone, "What ails you, my poor girl?" Lucy's tender voice went straight to the poor peasant's heart, who, unable to control herself any longer, hid her face in Lucy's bosom, and burst into a passion of tears and sobs. "Pray, tell me what is the matter, perhaps I can help you," insisted Lucy, kissing Speranza's head, and crying herself by way of comforting her.

"Thank you, madam," sobbed the girl, "God will reward you for your pity—for me—but my sorrow—is past help;" and saying so she drew a letter out of her pocket, put it into Lucy's hand, then seating herself again on her stool, covered her head with her apron, and began rocking herself to and fro, with little moans expressive of intense anguish. The letter, written in a neat clear hand, was dated "Genoa," and signed "Battista," in huge, rather primitive characters. It ran thus:—

"My good Speranza,—My case was brought yesterday before the Council of Revision, and I gave in my certificates, I mean the Mayor of Bordighera's letter, and the one you sent me from the Curé. The officer who read the letters, and had the talk all to himself, said they were stuff and nonsense, and that I might thank the Council for not declaring me contumacious—I think that's the word—and punishing me as such. Then they wrote down my name in what is called the Roll-book. So it is all over with me now, I am regularly entered for four years as a sailor in the king's service. If I had come fairly by it I should not mind. I might say to you, 'You are young, and so am I. Four years come to an end some day;—wait for me.' But I have been hardly used, and not a bit of justice in it, and so they shall find me a bad bargain, I can tell them. I'll give his Majesty the slip the very first opportunity, and try my fortune in some better country, where there is justice for the poor as well as rich; so you need not think of me any more, unless you choose to think of me as a departed friend, for such I am and shall be to the last. If I were to tell you that my heart is fairly broken, it would serve no purpose but to make your sorrow greater, so I sha'n't say anything of the kind, only good-bye on this side of the grave. I have tried hard to be a good son, and live in the fear of God and of the Madonna Santissima. What good has it done me? I have more than a mind to take to swearing, and drinking, and fighting, like most of my messmates, who seem never the worse for it, but rather the better. It's of no use writing any more,—so God bless you, as I do from my innermost heart; and do not forget me in your prayers, and think sometimes of your unfortunate—BATTISTA.

"*P.S.*—My duty to dear, dear mother Rosa, and to kind Doctor Antonio. I meant to have sent you the lock of hair you gave me on the evening before my first voyage to Marseilles, and the ring we exchanged in the chapel of the Madonna of Lampedusa. But I can't part with them,—really I can't."

Lucy wiped her eyes as she gave back the letter to Speranza, who had never ceased her moans, and swaying to and fro.

Now, though explicit enough in the main, Battista's epistle left many minor points obscure, which the warm-hearted English girl, with a true woman's interest in a love story, wished to have explained. This desire led to a string of questions from the one and answers from the other, these last interspersed by sobs and tears, which, though adding to their pathos, rather interfered with their clearness. It is out of these answers, only put in some better order, that we are going to extract Speranza's little story, leaving it, however, entirely in her own mouth, lest by telling it ourselves we should do what Antonio was afraid of doing, and would not do—that is, spoil its simplicity.

"Battista," began Speranza, "was the only son of a poor woman, who was always called 'Widow Susan,' though her man was still alive; but he had deserted her when Battista was only two years old, and had gone to France, and settled there. As Widow Susan lived next door to us—that was long before we kept this Osteria—Battista and I were almost as much together as if we had been brother and sister, and when we were neither of us as high as that"—and the girl pointed to a table—"he never called me by any name but 'little wife,' and I always called him 'my little man.' Every Sunday, after vespers, Battista would wait for me at the church door to go home with me, and never spoke to any girl but me, though he was spoken to often enough—for, though I say it, it is true, madam, he was the handsomest boy in the parish. When I grew older, and began to go to the wood, Battista was sure to come and meet me half-way, and carry my bundle for me. And so it came about that it was as good as settled, and everybody in Bordighera, and we most of all, took it for granted, that, as soon as we were old enough, we should be married; though neither father, nor mother, nor Widow Susan, had ever said a word about the matter. Battista had a great liking for the sea, and would fain have gone to see the world, and make some money for me, but he was too good a son to think of leaving his poor dear mother, who had no support but him, and so he stayed at home, and turned fisherman; and it was a real pride, madam,"—and Speranza's cheek flushed,—"to see how he managed his boat. He was the smartest and best of all our boatmen, and everybody said so.

"Year after year passed, bringing no change, till this house was set up for sale, and my father, who had long taken a fancy to it, agreed for the purchase, and we came to live here. My father, whose health was failing fast, had it in his mind that the air of this place, not so sharp as at Bordighera, would do him a deal of good. So we settled here, and father one evening—I remember it as if it was yesterday—said to Battista, 'As this house is to be yours one day, I mean when you and Speranza are man and wife, I expect you to lend a hand towards paying the price of it; for I must tell you that all my little savings have gone at once in the first instalment, and there are three more of them owing, one each year for three years running, and we cannot expect to get the money for these payments, and enough to keep us too, out of the produce of the land and the custom of the house. So, my lad, go to work, with God's blessing, as hard as you can, and make money. Widow Susan shall come and live with us while you are away; so your mind may be at rest about her.'

"Battista was quite overjoyed at this arrangement and at my father's talking to him in this way, because it made him quite sure of being one day his son. He made no delay, but set off at once to Nice, where he engaged himself on board a trading vessel bound to Genoa, went from thence to Leghorn and then to Marseilles, and as far away as Cette, and to many other places; and whenever he came home, which he did three or four times in the first two years that he spent at sea, he always brought some little comfort for his mother, and something curious or fine for me, and a little money for father; but it was very little, because Battista's wages were very scanty.

"One day my father said to Battista, 'At this rate it will take us ten years to pay for this place. I had to borrow money for the second payment, and now the third is almost due. How am I to manage?' Battista said, that if it hadn't been for the Conscription, which bound a man hand and foot, he knew of a place where he could go and be sure of getting money, and he named it,—a far, far off place, in a country called Tipodes, that the schoolmaster said was on the other side of the earth, below our feet. But Battista, who has been there since, says it is all nonsense; for if it was so, how could people stand on their feet? and yet they do." And Speranza looked up at Lucy as if she had uttered an unanswerable argument.

"That is not quite a proof," said Lucy, smiling; "but we will talk of that another time. Go on with your story now."

"Well, then," pursued Speranza—"'But,' said father to Battista, 'you can't be taken, you know, because you are all the same as the only son of a widow.'"

"'So I am,' said Battista; 'still I must attend and draw out a number, as it seems, at least I was told that such was the law, when I went for my papers at Genoa.'"

"'Ah!' says father, 'they are always plaguing poor folks with their law. Well, never mind, it's only three months to wait; who knows, you may draw a good number, and that will set it all right.'"

"'Please God it be so,'" said Battista.

"God was good to us, madam, for, when the time came, Battista's number was one of the highest, and he had not to be marched away. He was not present at the drawing, which took place at Nice; but that did not signify, the gentlemen of the board drew for the young men who were absent. As soon as his good luck was known at Bordighera, the mayor wrote him a letter to Genoa, where Battista had gone a trip,—a beautiful letter it was,—to give him the happy news; and with this letter in hand, Battista got leave to go where he pleased, and all the papers he wanted, and he sailed away for that far, far off place.

"From that day we had nothing but misfortunes. Widow Susan fell ill of a fever, and, in spite of Doctor Antonio's care, died within a month. I was so broken-hearted at this unexpected loss, and at having to break the sad news to Battista,—he had made me promise to let him know anything, good or bad, that might happen to his mother,—and withal so worn out with sitting up night after night with Widow Susan, that I fell ill myself next, and was in bed for six weeks, and should never have got up again but for Doctor Antonio. I was just beginning to crawl about when, one morning, the mayor called here, and said that Battista's case was not so clear as he had thought at first, and that Battista must go and pass before that Council of Revision, which has taken him now, and that if he did not go he would be breaking the law. In a few days more a paper was posted up at the town-hall, and another at our house, where Battista's poor mother had lived last, summoning him to appear at a short notice. Now, there was no sense in this, for had not the mayor himself put it as plain as pen, ink, and paper could make it, that Battista could not be taken! and then how could he answer the summons, when he was a three months' voyage off, as everybody knew?

"Oh no!" continued Speranza, in a voice full of indignation, "all this was done to throw the blame of having disobeyed the law upon the poor lad; and who could have an interest in making him appear in the wrong, but the Commandant of San Remo?"

"How the Commandant of San Remo?" asked Lucy, in surprise.

"You must know," went on Speranza, "that this Commandant had an old spite at Battista, and this is how it was. Once the Commandant sent to desire Battista to get him some fine fish, as he was going to give a grand dinner to the Governor of Nice. Battista caught a beautiful San Pietro,

(John Dory,) and took it to the Commandant's palazzo, expecting to be praised, and to have a good price for it. But he was offered just half its worth, and that put him in a passion after all the trouble he had taken, and he said he would rather throw it back into the sea than give it for less than its value; and so he did, and the grand dinner turned out all wrong, because of there being no fish. When the Commandant heard the reason, he was terribly angry, and swore that sooner or later he would make Battista pay for it. We could not help feeling for Battista, but all the same—we scolded him well for getting into such a scrape. Just fancy a poor fisherman presuming to stand against the greatest man in the province—a military man, too, used to have his own way and to make everybody tremble. Every one said that the Commandant would be as good as his word, and so it proved.

"Time went by, and very hard time it was, and we had no tidings of Battista. What we earned by keeping the inn was very little indeed. Father was going fast, and his temper waxed sourer every day, and he never ceased moaning and complaining about his health, and at no news from Battista, and worrying about his debts, and this and that, till the customers grew weary of him, and fell off one by one. The little we made went in soup, and good meat, and wine for the poor old man, who was ill of a bird in the stomach—"

"Of what?" exclaimed Lucy.

"A bird, madam, which ate everything he swallowed; ask Doctor Antonio, madam, he will tell you what I mean. We were so poor now, that often I had to go twice a day to the wood, and after all, I earned only enough to pay for a bit of meat, or a bottle of wine for father. If it had not been for Doctor Antonio, who helped us in many a way, and was like a guardian angel hovering over us, I don't think we could have got on at all. At last, after sixteen months of this life, a letter came from Battista. It was sad, for, poor fellow! he knew, by the time it was written, of his mother's death, but to us it came like a message from heaven, to bid us keep up our courage. This letter was the first that reached us, but not the first that he had sent. He said that he was well, and had put by already a good round sum of money, and was sure of doubling it in six months more; but after that he should come home, and we should all be happy together. We wept for joy as we read it. Father, who was in bed in a very low way, joined his hands and said, 'Now, my God, take me when it is thy will; I am ready to go, for my child will not be left destitute.' A week after," continued Speranza, wiping her eyes, "we carried the dear old man to the burying-ground.

"Ah! madam, we reckoned the days as a man condemned to death counts the hours he has to live. Six months went by, then seven, eight, nine, ten, and no Battista. It was one stormy evening last March; mother and I were sitting sorrowfully in the dark, to spare oil—our little provision was almost gone, and we had no money to buy any—the wind was howling, and the sea roaring like a wild beast, and I was thinking of poor sailors at sea, when all at once I heard a step crossing the garden—my heart jumped up to my throat, and I rushed half crazy to the door. It was he—I knew his step, I was in his arms once more. Oh! the blessed moment! All my troubles were forgotten, all my misery was gone, for he had come back, he was there,—he, Battista. Oh! why did God give me this little look of heaven to make me feel the loss of it more bitterly. Mother and I were mad with joy, but it did not last long. As soon as the lamp was lighted we saw a world of sorrow in poor Battista's face, he was so worn and pale; his eyes were sunken, his cheeks quite hollow. He had his right arm tied up in a handkerchief. 'What is the matter?' asked I, all in a shake. 'We have been shipwrecked,' he said, 'all hands drowned, poor fellows, except another and myself, and everything I had on earth gone!' and as he spoke these words, he fell a crying. I thought, I did indeed, that my heart was going to split in two. I undid the handkerchief; there was a great gash across the hand. Mother went to fetch Doctor Antonio—I was too sick to move—and brought him back with her. As soon as I heard the Doctor's voice I felt comforted, for I said to myself, He will help us. The voice of a friend is very sweet in sorrow, dear lady," said the poor creature, trying hard to keep down her tears. "Doctor Antonio dressed the wound, and began at once to cheer us by saying, that we ought to be thankful for the good left us—what if Battista had been drowned with the others?—that money, after all, was not happiness; that Battista and I were young and strong; and that, as he had lost his money, we must work the harder, and bless God that we were spared to one another. And as I listened to these good words the sickness left my heart. The Doctor sat down with us, and then Battista told us all about the shipwreck; how the vessel had struck on a sunken rock close in to the coast of Corsica—almost in sight of home!—and gone down in a minute; how he and one of his shipmates had been picked up by a French ship going to Marseilles, and he had made his way on foot from thence to Bordighera. We sat long, and talked and talked over the past, and of poor dear father, and poor dear Widow Susan, and made plans for the future; and when we separated, we did so with light hearts—for, after all, was he not spared to me, and I to him? As it was now long after midnight, and Battista would find no house open at that hour, Doctor Antonio took him home to his lodgings for that night.

"Next morning, I made sure that Battista would be down with us early, so that I wondered very much when eight o'clock came, and still no Battista. But I never supposed that anything was wrong until I saw Doctor Antonio coming alone. As soon as ever he was near enough, I knew by his face that he had bad news for me. The Doctor told me at once that Battista had been summoned to San Remo on that business of the Conscription, and that I must not distress myself, but make ready and go with him and mother to San Remo. He would, he said, see the Commandant, and do his best to right Battista. The Doctor did not tell us then, what we knew very soon afterwards, that two carabineers had been sent from San Remo to fetch Battista; that they had arrested him in the street, put handcuffs on him, and thus paraded him about the town as if he had been a thief or a murderer, and then taken him away in a boat. They said it was law. I don't think there's much justice in such laws," said Speranza, very sharply.

"So the Doctor and mother and I went as fast as we could to San Remo, and made first of all for the jail, but as we had no pass, were refused admittance. We next went to the Commandant's, who was busy, we were told, and could see no one. Doctor Antonio insisting, however, he was introduced, but he could obtain nothing—not even the permission for us to see Battista—only the answer that it was the law, and that the law must be obeyed. After being kept a week in the jail at San Remo—God knows for what reason!—Battista was marched off, under an escort of carabineers, to Genoa, and taken to the dockyard there, out of which he was never allowed to go. Doctor Antonio wrote in his behalf to all his friends at Genoa, even to the British Consul there. The curé gave us a letter, saying how Battista was all the same as fatherless, for his father had deserted him when only two years of age; but nothing availed."

"And what difference," asked Lucy, "would it have made if his father had really been dead?"

"Oh, madam, he would not have been taken in the Conscription. The only son of a widow is exempted from the service. So far the law is merciful to one whose father is dead; and why should it not be so to one whose father is all the same to him as if he was in the churchyard? But what's the use of reasoning about it? the law is too strong for the poor—Battista, as you know, is condemned, and"—(Speranza made a desperate effort to conquer her emotion, and continued slowly and composedly)—"Well, let it be so; I can bear it all without complaining. Everybody is not born to be happy. I am willing to offer up my hopes in this world as a sacrifice to the Blessed Virgin, holy mother of sorrows. If it is ordained that I am not to be—Battista's wife, well, I can give him—up on this side of the grave. But I cannot, no"—(she went on with a burst of passion, that made her eyes actually rain tears)—"I cannot bear that he should turn to wickedness; that he who has been such a pattern of goodness should take to breaking God's commandments, and that we should be separated in all eternity. That is what wrings my heart and drives me mad. Oh, no, no! that is what God will not let come to pass."

This was the first view that Lucy had ever had into an aching heart—this was the first time that such things as want, hardship, and anguish, hitherto vague abstractions with her rather than stern realities, had stood up in a living shape, and told their sad tale, and moaned and writhed within her sight and hearing. We leave the reader to imagine how all the holy springs of sympathy and pity heaved in Lucy's gentle bosom, and gushed forth in soothing words and caresses, and earnest promises of assistance.

"Perhaps you know the king?" said Speranza, all at once raising her head with a flash of hope in her eyes.

"No," said Lucy; "why do you ask?"

"Because," said Speranza, "if you could have told him Battista's story, I am sure he would be merciful to us. Oh! if the king could only know, he would be sorry for us. Why should he, so great on his throne, wish poor folks to be wretched?"

"If we cannot speak to the king," said Lucy, "we can write to him,—I mean, we can send him a memorial on behalf of Battista."

"That would be of no use," replied the girl, dejectedly. "Memorials sent by poor people never reach the king; the bad counsellors stop them."

"But, perhaps," insisted Lucy, "we can find somebody who will promise to put the memorial into the king's own hands."

Speranza shook her head despondingly. It was plain

that she had as bad an opinion of memorials as Doctor Antonio.

"We shall find some way, depend upon it," continued Lucy; "I will ask Doctor Antonio what to do." Both girls brightened up at this. Evidently Speranza's faith was greater in Doctor Antonio than in the memorial.

Lucy thought long over Speranza's story, wishing that the morrow were come, that she might ask the Doctor how best to help her protégée; and then she fell to musing with particular complacency on the part he had played in the little drama. Nor, it must be confessed, did she consider the Italian girl's enthusiastic expression of his having been like a guardian angel, either exaggerated or misplaced. The man seemed born to do good. For, had she not heard, did she not know from her own experience, that wherever there was sickness or sorrow, tears to dry, or sinking hearts to raise, *there* he was to be found, cheering, sustaining, ministering in many a way? And now a glimmering light dawned on Lucy's understanding, by which she began to perceive how a superior man like Doctor Antonio might be reconciled to his present lot; nay, she even felt disposed to think highly of that humble sphere into which fate had jostled him,—a sphere, she saw, teeming with misery, oppression, and injustice, and therefore calculated to draw forth all the energy and chivalrous kindness of his nature.

Lucy very soon lost herself in an inextricable labyrinth of speculation and argument, into which we need not follow her, but which interested her far more than Manzoni or the guitar, and brought her on to the end of the day less disagreeably than she had expected. Sir John, also, when he came to see her in the evening, looked more serene and cheerful than he had done since they had taken up their abode in the Osteria,—a serenity and cheerfulness partly attributed by Lucy to the Doctor's considerate step in the morning; but as Sir John was very loud in his praises of the Bishop of Albenga's former cook, we are inclined to believe that the dinner he had eaten had more to do with his present optimism than Doctor Antonio.

CHAPTER IX.
Lucy's Scheme.

WHEN Lucy awoke next morning, she discovered that all was right again with the sky and the sea, and that the birds' song was wondrously sweet. The breakfast tray had just been removed, when the well-known step, so quick yet so firm, the step that she could have singled out from among ten thousand others, made itself heard. Lucy wondered why her heart gave just such a bound as Speranza had spoken of, when describing her recognition of Battista's footstep in the garden.

Another moment and here was Doctor Antonio, erect, and gentle, and smiling, as was his wont, radiating benevolence, so to say, from every pore. Here he was, all covered with dust, and looking none the worse for it in Lucy's eyes, for that dust betokened some impatience and eagerness to see her again.

"A prize patient," he began, "who has slept soundly, for she looks well—see, I have worked hard for you this morning," and he showered down a quantity of aromatic wild plants; "here's thyme, lavender, and rosemary, and sweetbriar, enough to put the best perfumer's shop to the blush. You ought to tell Hutchins to make *sachets* of them. There's no *patchoulis* or musk can compete with these."

"Thank you, thank you," said Lucy; "how fresh they smell! they make me think of green hillsides."

"If you do as I advise you," said Antonio, "they will serve some day, when you are far, far away, to make you think of our poor Riviera."

"Do not talk to me about going away, Doctor Antonio. I have grown so fond of this ugly old house, that I shall try and persuade papa to buy it, and make it into a beautiful cottage. Should you be sorry to have us for neighbours?" The arch look in her face softened into a smile, that Doctor Antonio's eye met rather gravely, yet lingered on.

"Now, Doctor Antonio, come and sit down by me, and do not expect to get away for two hours, at least. I have so many things to tell you, so many things to ask you."

Antonio complied, and Lucy then, with a somewhat important air, began: "Speranza told me yesterday everything about herself and Battista."

"I know she did, and I am glad of it. You have raised her spirits, and she looks less unhappy already. I have this moment read poor Battista's letter."

"We must help them," said Lucy, eagerly; "and you must advise me what to do. All Speranza told me is true, is it not, and Battista is really a good man?"

"Yes," said Antonio, "he is an excellent lad, what we Italians call *di buona pasta*, quiet and simple, insomuch that I have sometimes wondered how such a lively and clever girl as Speranza, became so strongly attached to him; folly, after all, to wonder at such things. Suffice to say, that all Bordighera is unanimous in speaking well of the unlucky fellow,—and praising one's neighbour, you know, is not the distinguishing virtue of small places. As to the accuracy of Speranza's statements, of that I am not quite so sure. Not that I mean that Speranza deceived you wilfully—she is incapable of that; but she and Rosa, and Battista himself, and indeed, I may say, nine-tenths of the inhabitants of Bordighera, entertain certain false notions of their own on this case, which nothing you can say will ever put out of their heads; and naturally, Speranza cannot but have given you her own erroneous impressions. An article of faith with them all is, first, that Battista's mother, owing to her having been deserted by her husband, was to be considered a widow —in fact, they always called her Widow Susan—and Battista consequently a widow's son. Now this may be to a certain extent in the spirit, but does not come at all within the letter of the law. Secondly, they all believe that the Mayor of

Bordighera's letter, purporting that Battista was not to march, constitutes in Battista's favour an official title, in right of which he ought at all events to be exempted from the service. And in this also they are mistaken. The Mayor's letter was nothing but the expression of an individual opinion, an act of kindness, and of no legal value whatever. Battista's case stands thus. He drew a number, or to speak more correctly, a number was drawn for him, sufficiently high, it was thought, to insure his not being drafted away, but which ultimately proved not so."

Lucy looked as if she did not understand.

"Suppose," exclaimed Antonio, "that the province to which Bordighera belongs, be called upon to furnish ten young men for the navy—very well—the lad who draws number 'twenty' is considered to be, and in all probability is safe. It nevertheless occasionally happens, that out of the ten who have drawn low numbers, say from 1 to 10, and are consequently those who by right would have to serve, one or two are not of the regulation size, one or two more have settled abroad, and are not forthcoming, some others are able to prove that they are among the exceptions recognised by the law, and so on. What is the natural consequence?—for, when the Government says, I want ten men, ten men must be found one way or the other—the natural consequence is, that those who have high numbers are substituted for the ineligible, or missing low numbers. This was poor Battista's case; and though at first no one doubted but that his high number would secure him from being taken, yet from the unprecedented exemptions and exclusions that took place in the class to which he belonged, it turned out that every one, the Mayor among others, was mistaken."

"I see it all now," said Lucy, "and judging from what you have just said, I fancy that the charge Speranza brings against the Commandant of San Remo, of having, out of revenge, caused Battista's misfortune, has no ground but in her imagination."

"I am inclined to think so," answered Antonio; "that much partiality and injustice is shown, in general, by worthy Commandants in this matter of the Conscription, as in most others, is a fact of notoriety beyond all doubt, and which explains the preconceptions entertained on this head by Speranza and Co. The Commandants are too often disposed to abuse their power. But nothing in the particular case of which we are speaking, has come to my knowledge which entitles me to say that Battista's difficulties are in any way to be laid at the door of the Commandant of San Remo. Let us try and be just even to our adversaries."

"Is this Commandant hostile to you?" asked Lucy, in some little alarm.

"Oh, not at all! though I may be dubious as to his private sentiments being over-friendly, we are to all appearance on excellent terms. I will tell you one day to what I am indebted for this show of good-will. When I called him my adversary, I meant in a political point of view. He is of course a most violent partisan of pure depotism, indeed one of the fiercest I ever met with. He foams at the mouth when he speaks of the Liberals; he would willingly hang the last of them with his own hands."

"What a monster!" exclaimed Lucy.

"But if I acquit him," pursued Antonio, "on the ground of conspiracy against Battista, I have no words to express my indignation at the gratuitously harsh, nay barbarous manner, and for that I hold him responsible, with which he had the law enforced—a law pressing hard enough upon the poor without need of aggravation. What reason could there be for keeping the poor fellow a week in the jail of San Remo, denying him even the comfort of seeing those two poor women, and sending him with a guard of carabineers to Genoa, like a malefactor, unless it was to gratify an old grudge?"

"How very cruel!" said Lucy, with flashing eyes. "Surely if such conduct were made public, or the people of the town were to petition the Goverment, he would be at once removed."

"You forget that we are in Italy," said Antonio, with a sad smile. "Such conduct is public. The Commandants, my dear Miss Davenne, are but the expression of the spirit of the Government, and, as such, supported and backed by it to the utmost. What do you imagine would be the result of such a petition as you suggest? Why, it would be sent back to the Commandant himself, and then the petitioners might look to themselves."

"Why, what could he do to them?" asked Lucy.

"Ask rather what he could not. He could do anything he chose. We are all at his mercy. He can arbitrarily summon any one to his presence, load him with abuse, consign him to prison, or march him away to a fortress, without trial or legal form of any kind;—he can order the shop of one tradesman to be closed, the license of another to be withdrawn;—he can, by sending two lines to Turin, have me dismissed from the appointment I hold, and expelled from the kingdom;—he can stick a hat on a pole, and Gessler-like, command every one that passes to bow to it. If he does not do this, it is not that he lacks the power, but that the idea does not come into his head."

"But you describe a state of things quite intolerable," said Lucy.

"Intolerable is the word," went on Antonio, "at least for thinking people. The unthinking, who constitute the majority everywhere, feel it less. The obscurity of the greater number screens them, to some extent, from annoyance, and *res angusta domi*, with the cares it entails, engrosses most of them too much to allow of time or disposition to think of anything but their individual concerns; then the priests assert that it is all right. But we are wandering far from Battista."

"Yes, indeed," smiled Lucy, "we were quite forgetting him. Now, give me your advice, or rather tell me how I can best help him."

"Alas!" said Antonio, "I see no way but one."

"And what is that?" inquired Lucy, finding Doctor Antonio stop short.

"To provide a substitute for him," said he.

"You mean paying some one to serve in Battista's place?"

"Just so; but that is quite out of the question."

"Why out of the question? Will it cost so very much? I will do it if I can," said the eager girl. "Now, Doctor Antonio, what have I said to make you open your eyes so wide, and look so astonished?"

"I confess that your kindness and generosity take me a little by surprise."

"O Doctor Antonio, Doctor Antonio, what a bad compliment!" said Lucy, shaking her head. "Have we not often agreed that it is the duty of the rich to help the poor?"

"So it is," said Antonio, recovering his sedateness. "Thank Heaven, there exists a better order of beings, for whom doing good is a necessity of their nature."

"That is just what I thought of you many a time, and I have a right to think so," said Lucy, with a playfulness that struggled with the tears that would start into her eyes; "and you have *no* right to say me nay. Do you think," she went on quickly, "that it would be difficult to find this substitute?"

"I cannot be sure; but I hope not. I heard a short while ago of a seaman of Spedaletti, a village close by, whose time had expired, and who was said to be anxious to re-enter the service."

"Would he require a large sum to take Battista's place?"

"I should say from fifteen to eighteen hundred francs."

"And how much is that in English money?"

"From sixty to seventy-two pounds."

"That is not so very much," said Lucy; "I do not think that I have it actually in my purse; but I can afford the sum."

Hutchins was desired to bring Miss Davenne's desk; and upon examination of the state of the exchequer, the balance was found to be thirty pounds, seventeen shillings, and some pence. "I will ask papa for the rest," said the young lady; "the whole sum shall be ready to-morrow. Will you set about this matter directly, so as not to lose another day?"

"Most willingly," was Antonio's answer. "My first step shall be to find out the man that was mentioned to me. If he be really willing to re-enter the service, we will despatch him immediately to Genoa, with fifty francs for his travelling expenses. The rest of the sum we agree to give can be deposited in the hands of some person at Genoa, the British Consul for instance, to be paid over when the exchange is effected. You must make up your mind to some delay ere this can take place. There are hosts of formalities to be complied with in this as in any other affair. But not a word to Speranza; we must have a care how we raise her hopes, for were our scheme to fail, we should have only prepared too bitter a disappointment for her."

"Then you think there is a chance of our not succeeding?" inquired Lucy, with a blank face.

"Yes," replied Antonio; "should the Commandant get scent of our plan, and take it into his head to oppose us, we should infallibly be defeated. We have therefore to act with the greatest caution."

How sweet to Lucy's ears sounded the words *our* scheme, *we* must do this or that! How pleasant it was to have an interest in common with that kindest of doctors!

"When the right time comes, I shall have to lecture both Battista and the substitute on the danger of any imprudent talking," said Antonio; "in the meanwhile, I must write a word of encouragement to the lad. I will do so this very day."

"Thank you," said Lucy; and seeing that the Doctor was about to rise, she added, "I have not done yet, Doctor Antonio; I want to know what was that far, far off place to which Battista went?"

"Sydney," said the Doctor, "*in the country of Tipodes;*" and he laughed outright.

"And of what complaint did Speranza's father die?"

"Of a complaint of which you never would remember the hard scientific name; one that prevents the stomach from assimilating any nutriment. As sufferers from this disease are always craving for food, and yet grow thinner every day, the good folks of these parts have settled it, that it is a beast or bird in their stomach that devours all they eat. Did not Speranza tell you as much?"

"She did, in fact; and, pray," continued Lucy, "what does 'going to the wood' mean? Speranza spoke of it so often."

"Almost all our parishes," explained Antonio, "possess some woods of their own, which are a great help to poor families, who draw from them not only the fuel and fodder they require for their use, but realize a little money, by supplying these two necessaries to their more affluent neighbours. This hard work of going to the wood devolves exclusively on women; it is, however, the only severe labour to which they are subjected. It is usual for the wives and daughters of poor peasants to start as early as one or two in the morning for the wood, which is often a two or three hours' walk from where they live, so as to be back by ten o'clock, in time to prepare the family dinner, after earning fivepence or sixpence—a pittance equal to the wages paid for a woman's whole day's out-of-door work. There are some girls—and these are always pointed out with admiration—who manage to go to the wood twice a day. This, and the gathering of olives in the season, constitute the chief occupation and resource of the women here; and it is to the want of sleep, and excessive fatigue consequent on this going to the wood, that I ascribe the fact of many of them looking so worn and old before their time."

"And," asked Lucy, "this Madonna of Lampedusa alluded to in Battista's letter?"

"It is a sanctuary," answered Antonio, "held in high veneration, and much resorted to by our simple people on account of an image of our Lady enshrined there, and which, as the story goes, was miraculously brought to these shores from Lampedusa, a little island to the south of Sicily. It is a place worth visiting: the chapel is built on a projecting rock, half-way up a steep mountain, and the view from it is magnificent."

"I should like to see it," said Lucy.

"Nothing easier, when you are able to go out; the distance is not great, four hours would take you there. Several rooms are attached to the establishment for the accommodation of visitors and invalids, who are often sent to benefit by the air, which has a reputation for particular salubrity."

"Have you ever been there yourself?"

"Many a time. It is only an hour's walk from Taggia— a curious small town about two miles inland, three hours' drive from this, and where I was yesterday. By the by, I made a sketch of it for you. Where is it now? I put it somewhere—ah! here it is in my hat."

"How well it is done!" exclaimed Lucy; "I was sure you could draw, from the way you spoke of scenery. What a pretty place this Taggia must be, stretching so gracefully up the side of the hill!"

"I am glad you admire it—the place, I mean, not the sketch. I hope to see you do it more justice yourself—some day. But I must go now, or I shall be too late to send off a letter to Battista. *A revoir.*"

In crossing the garden Antonio met Sir John, and stopped to tell him that the arm-chair he had planned would be ready in a few days, and that the person who was to make it had pronounced that it would answer the purpose. Sir John reiterated his thanks, and then condescended to inquire after the postboy—an inquiry always made when Sir John wished to be particularly civil to Doctor Antonio. Prospero was a sort of neutral ground, on which the belligerent powers met in courteous truce. Prospero, said Antonio, had just crawled out of bed, but was as yet unfit for work in any shape. Would Doctor Antonio be so obliging, requested Sir John, as to inform that unlucky person, that, in consideration of the good.

character given him by Doctor Antonio, he, Sir John, had made up his mind to take no further notice of the deplorable affair in which the postboy had played so conspicuous a part? Antonio did his best to acknowledge the compliment to himself couched in Sir John's words, and said how glad he was to be intrusted with so kind and cheering a message for his patient. Upon which the two gentlemen separated, much satisfied with each other.

In the evening Lucy gave her father an outline of poor Battista's story, telling of his present sad plight, and winding up with a demand of some money to help him. The demand was immediately acceded to, Sir John being really as generous as he was rich; indeed, he seldom grudged money to anybody, least of all to this pet daughter. The grant of money was not all that Lucy received from her excellent father— it came accompanied by a large amount of advice, the essence of which was, that she ought to make further investigations into the man's real character in order to ascertain that he deserved her kindness; for who knew, said Sir John, that he might not be one of those bloodthirsty Republicans, never content but when in open defiance of all lawful authority, of whom they had heard so much when at Rome! How on earth came Sir John, *apropos* of Battista, to start off upon the scent of Republicanism! The fault was Lucy's, who, in her hot haste to vindicate her new protégé, had ventured on dangerous ground, and stumbled against some of the steel traps that beset her father's intellectual premises. Some of his pretty Lucy's assertions hit the Commandant of San Remo rather hard, and even seemed to glance at higher quarters. Sir John, knowing himself as most people do know themselves, thought himself a liberal-minded man, and always open to conviction; but the truth was, that he could not hear any, the slightest animadversion thrown upon any constituted order of Government, or indeed upon any Government officer, without bristling like a porcupine, and setting up the whole array of fretful quills that guarded his understanding from the intrusion of novelty in any shape. His daughter's innuendos startled him the more, as he was unaccustomed to see her take any interest in politics, and he began to think that the whole transaction smacked of disaffection. It was accordingly in a tone of voice a pitch higher than he was in the habit of using when speaking to his darling, that he wound up his discourse by saying, "As to those absurd strictures on Government with which you have favoured me, my dear Lucy, let me tell you, and you may tell Doctor Antonio, from whom, I suppose, you gleaned them, that a people in possession of a good municipal system, such as I see in action here, have no one to blame but themselves, if such occasional grievances, as all communities are liable to, are not redressed in good time."

This was one out of a little store of favourite sentences which Sir John kept for effect, and delivered when in a vein of wisdom. What ground he had for believing that the municipal system at work in Bordighera was good, we are at a loss to discover, considering that he had taken no earthly pains to know anything about the matter, unless, indeed, he took it for granted that a system represented by such jolly-looking fellows as the mayor, and some of the councilmen, whom he knew by sight, could be nothing else than wholesome.

Lucy had winced several times during the evening's conversation; she, however, remained, after the last speech, humbly silent, a better means perhaps of allaying the irritable susceptibility of her father's feelings, than any answer, even in the soft, low voice she possessed. Neither did she think it necessary to repeat to Doctor Antonio any of Sir John's last evening's harangue, when he came, brisk and cheerful, the next morning, to give her the news she was longing for, that the man he had spoken of was found, and for fourteen hundred francs had agreed to go in the place of Battista, and was positively to set out the following day for Genoa. Lucy's eyes said many more pleasant and grateful things than her words, as she gave into his hand the money, which they decided should be sent to the British Consul at Genoa. They were both very happy, talking over the happiness they were preparing for others, and even Sir John might be satisfied for that day: the Government, indeed all Governments and municipal systems, were mercifully forgotten.

CHAPTER X.
In the Balcony.

THE easy-chair of Antonio's devising at length arrived, and was duly tried by Sir John, who pronounced it to be the paragon of easy-chairs. Sundry other minor preparations connected with the event in contemplation, and among which figured a huge box of drawing materials, supplied from Nice, being completed, on the first day of May about noon, Doctor Antonio entered Miss Davenne's room, and said, "Prepare yourself for a great surprise."

"What can that be?" asked Lucy; then looking up at him, she seemed to read his face, for her colour rose, and she said, "Am I to get up?"

"*Brava!*" shouted Antonio, "guessed right at first. *La lingua batte dove il dente duole.* Yes, you are to get up, but on condition of submitting to a quantity of tiresome warnings, directions, and restrictions. You are not allowed to walk, not so much as to put your foot on the ground; it requires another fortnight of absolute repose. You only get up to lie down quietly on that long chair that Rosa and Speranza are bringing in, and are expressly requested to give yourself up passively to them, and to Miss Hutchins, who will dress you. You are not disappointed after all?" he asked anxiously, as he marked the bloom in the fair cheek die away, and the corners of the expressive mouth begin to droop. "I wish that I could let you do more, but I *dare* not."

Lucy must have had a harder heart than she had, could

she have been proof against the earnest and feeling tone and look of the Italian. The little cloud of annoyance melted into a sunny smile,—"I am very ungrateful," she said, "forgive me;" and she held out her hand to him—such a charming little hand, that he felt a terrible inclination to kiss it; he contented himself, however, with holding it for a second within his own. An hour after, Sir John giving a helping hand in great glee, Lucy was wheeled through the glass-door of the lobby to the balcony we have so often mentioned in this our true story, where an awning had been put up to protect her from the sun.

"How beautiful! how passing beautiful!" exclaimed the girl, her eyes dilating as she looked around. "How could you ever fear, or for a moment think," turning to the Doctor, "that my fancy could go beyond such reality as this? No fancy, not even a poet's, could conjure up, in wildest daydream, this wondrous beauty."

"Truth to say," he answered, "I was only a very little afraid of your being disappointed. Sicilian as I am, and an enthusiast also in my admiration of my native island, yet I own that the scene before us is second to none of the most celebrated in Sicily."

"What an Eastern look those waving palms give the hill of Bordighera! One might believe one's-self in Asia Minor," said Lucy.

It was indeed a beauteous scene. In front lay the immensity of sea, smooth as glass, and rich with all the hues of a dove's neck, the bright green, the dark purple, the soft ultramarine, the deep blue of a blade of burnished steel,— there glancing in the sun like diamonds, here rippling into a lace-like net of snowy foam. In strong relief against this bright background, stands a group of red-capped, red-belted fishermen, drawing their nets to the shore, and accompanying each pull with a plaintive burden, that the echo of the mountain sends softened back. On the right, to the westward, the silvery track of the road undulating amid thinly scattered houses, or clusters of orange and palm trees, leads the eye to the promontory of Bordighera, a huge emerald mound which shuts out the horizon, much in the shape of a leviathan couchant, his broad muzzle buried in the waters. Here you have in a small compass, refreshing to behold, every shade of green that can gladden the eye, from the pale grey olive to the dark foliaged cypress, of which one, ever and anon, an isolated sentinel, shoots forth high above the rest. Turfs of feathery palms, their heads tipped by the sun, the lower part in shade, spread their broad branches, like warriors' crests on the top, where the slender *silhouette* of the towering church spire cuts sharply against the spotless sky.

The coast to the east recedes inland with a graceful curve, then with a gentle bend to the south is lost by degrees in the far, far sea. Three headlands arise from this crescent, which so lovingly receives to its embrace a wide expanse of the weary waters; three headlands of differing aspect and colour, lying one behind the other. The nearest is a bare red rock, so fiery in the sun the eye dares scarcely fix on it; the second, richly wooded, wears on its loftiest ridge a long hamlet, like to a mural crown; the third looks a mere blue mist in the distance, save one white speck. Two bright sails are rounding this last cape. The whole, flooded as it is with light, except where some projecting crag casts its transparent grey shadow, is seen again reversed, and in more faint loveliness, in the watery mirror below. Earth, sea, and sky mingle their different tones, and from their varieties, as from the notes of a rich, full chord, rises one great harmony. Golden atoms are floating in the translucent air, and a halo of mother-of-pearl colour hangs over the sharp outlines of the mountains.

"There is ample food for your pencil," said Antonio. "A fortnight hence, when you have become intimately acquainted with, and so to say, made your own the various beauties you are now viewing with such restless eyes, you will enjoy them to the full."

"But I do so already, I assure you," affirmed Lucy.

"But will do so better in a little while," persisted Antonio. "The perception of the beautiful is gradual, and not a lightning revelation; it requires not only time, but some study. It is with a landscape such as this as with a piece of music, say a symphony. Many a beauty of detail we can make out on a first hearing, but the connecting links between the various passages, their reference to each other, and to the whole, what, in short, constitutes the *ensemble* of the performance, does not seize upon us till after we have heard it repeatedly and attentively."

"I daresay you are right," said Lucy, who generally thought Antonio right. "I wonder," she went on, "why anything Eastern-looking always takes such a hold on one's fancy. I cannot take my eyes from those palm-trees, they make me think of crusades and knights all mixed up with Scripture stories."

"Fancy borrows much from memory," said Antonio; "and so looks back to the past. Stories first heard standing at a mother's knee, are never wholly forgotten,—a little spring that never quite dries up in our journey through scorching years."

"I love this Bordighera!" said Lucy, after a little pause.

"Beautiful as it is," remarked Antonio, "it robs you of a most extensive and magnificent view of the coast of France."

"I do not regret it at all," answered Lucy; "a wide-spread landscape puzzles my attention, and then I never can keep my eye from straining to the horizon. The sea and the heavens are the only large spaces one really enjoys."

"Very true," said Antonio; "you have the soul of an artist."

"I wish it were so," said Lucy, slightly colouring.

"Now for my duty of cicerone," said the Doctor, good-humouredly. "You see that small village at the foot of the craggy mountain, it is called Spedaletti, and gives its name to the gulf."

"What an odd name, *Spedaletti!* it means little hospitals, does it not?"

"Yes. A friend of mine, who prides himself on being somewhat of an antiquarian, pretends to have ascertained the origin of the name. He says, that a ship belonging to the Knights of Rhodes, (some of those you were thinking of just now,) while on a cruise in the Mediterranean, I forget the century, landed some men sick of the plague here, where barracks were erected for their reception; and these same buildings, according to my friend, served as the first nucleus of the present village, which he avers has naturally retained the name of their first destination. To give some weight to my friend's opinion, there are at a little distance the ruins of a chapel called the 'Ruota,' which may or may not be a corruption of Rodi (Rhodes.)"

"And are there still hospitals there?" Lucy inquired.

"No; Spedaletti in the present day is exclusively inhabited by the healthy families of very industrious fishermen, who never want for occupation. Nature, which made this bay so lovely, made it equally safe and trustworthy. Sheltered on the west by the Cape of Bordighera, and on the east by those three headlands, let the sea be ever so high without, within it is comparatively calm, and the fishermen of Spedaletti are out in all weathers."

"And what is the name of that village perched so boldly on the brow of the second mountain, just above Spedaletti? Has that a story also?"

"It is appropriately called La Colla (the hill). I doubt whether you will think it interesting to know, of course I do, that while the cholera was raging fearfully at San Remo, which lies at the foot of the other side of the mountain, not one case was heard of at La Colla."

"Such a thing must have appeared very like a miracle to the inhabitants," observed Lucy.

"That there was plenty of nonsense talked on the subject, I have not the least doubt. The extremely elevated situation of La Colla accounts very well for its escape. But a more striking and really inexplicable fact is, that the fatal scourge did not get round that second cape, the Cape of

San Remo, but leaped at once to Nice, sparing all the intermediate tract of country.—Confess," pursued Antonio, smiling, "that La Colla seems very matter of fact to you in comparison with Spedaletti. Knights and the plague take precedence, do they not, of the cholera and doctors?"

"I will answer you," said Lucy, "in the Irish fashion, by asking another question. Is that white speck gleaming out so brightly on that far away promontory, a convent?"

"That is another sanctuary, the Madonna *della Guardia*, a would-be rival of that of Lampedusa, but beaten hollow by the latter."

"Are all sanctuaries then dedicated to the Madonna?"

"Almost all. The Madonna is the great passion of our people. To me, I openly avow, there is something extremely touching in this, call it superstition if you like, which deifies woman, and makes of her the channel through which compassion and mercy from on high flow to suffering mortals here below. It is the highest compliment paid to your better nature."

"Do you truly think that women are better than men?"

"My instinctive feeling is that they are," replied Antonio; "but, to speak candidly, I cannot boast of sufficient experience of women, or indeed of men, to be able to decide the point *ex cathedra*. This I do know, that of all my fellow-creatures with whom it has yet been my lot to come in close contact, the one I have found far superior to all, is a woman."

Why such a statement, calculated one would have thought to please her woman's pride, should have chilled Lucy, and made her silent, we do not pretend to guess. Sure it is that it did so, and that she sat, long after the Doctor was gone, unmindful of sea or landscape, of books or pencil, lost in what seemed a melancholy reverie. Poor little Lucy! she was startled from her thoughts by Sir John coming to her with a letter in his hand. It was from Aubrey, to say that he had been obliged to postpone his departure on account of regimental business, and that he knew not, under the circumstances, when he should be able to get away, not for four months, certainly, but that he would write again to let his father know. Lucy bore this piece of news very philosophically.

"After all, papa, it is only four months, and one comfort is, we need not be in such a hurry to leave this."

"Well," replied Sir John, "as it turns out, perhaps we may call this delay lucky;—yes, after all, this news takes a weight off my mind;—it would have been a dreary welcome for my boy to find none but servants in his home. We can travel slowly, and stop a short time in Paris"—

"Oh, papa!" said Lucy, "I do not care a bit about Paris; let us stay in this beautiful Italy as long as we can."

"But, my dear," replied rather fretfully the Baronet, who did not like so many scotches put to his plans, "I wish you to know something of Paris, it is right and proper. We went through it so hurriedly last year, and you were so ill at the time, that you could scarcely form an idea of it." And after a little inward cogitation, as if discussing some point with himself, he added, "Though vastly inferior to London, still Paris is a place to spend a few weeks in rather agreeably; there are some things worth seeing in Paris; the Champs Elysées, for instance, although not to be compared to Hyde Park"—

But this first of May was destined to be a red letter day with Sir John, the result of whose summing up of the comparative merits of the two great cities was never made public, in consequence of an interruption from his man John, who announced that there was a man below who wanted to see Sir John. Where did he come from? The man had mentioned Doctor Antonio's name, and John thought he looked like a horse-dealer. "A horse-dealer!" cried the Baronet; and he ran down the steps with an alacrity that would have done honour to more juvenile legs than his were.

Any one in Sir John's predicament, any one, we mean, who, being accustomed to a daily ride, had been cut off from his favourite exercise for nearly a month, will easily understand how the very mention of a horse-dealer sounded as welcome in Sir John's ears as the rushing of water in the ears of a thirsty wayfarer. He had had two horses sent him successively from Nice, the first of which was soon discovered to be lame, the second so vicious as to be perfectly unmanageable; and the upshot was, that he had given up riding in despair.

The man turned out to be really a horse-dealer on his way to Genoa with horses for sale, first-rate animals, *bestie magnifiche*, as he said. The conversation was kept up in a sort of *lingua Franca*, by which, however, Babel-like, the principals managed to understand one another. Of course, it was "il Dottore" who had said the "Signor Milordo Inglese" would like to see the horses; they were at so short a distance that "Sua Eccellenza" could almost see the stables; and the cunning fellow stood on his toes, and pointed somewhere or nowhere. However, he carried away Sir John in triumph, accompanied by John, who passed with his master for being a thorough connoisseur in horseflesh; and in a couple of hours after, to Lucy's utter astonishment and delight, her father made his re-appearance under her balcony, mounted on a square-made, handsome-looking bay cob, warranted quiet as a lamb, which he properly was, as he numbered a good third more of years than the dealer had sworn to.

"I hope he really is quiet," cried out Lucy, rather alarmed at her father's gay manœuvring.

"A baby might ride him," answered Sir John, who had for a year or two felt the necessity of avoiding caracoling spirited steeds. "See what a mouth he has, Lucy, he obeys the least touch;" and suiting the action to the word, the enchanted Baronet turned and returned the cob, till Lucy called out "Papa, papa, you will make yourself and the poor beast quite giddy."

While this was going on, a lad in a post-boy's jacket and hat in hand came stealthily through the little garden gate, and after a moment's hesitation, went up to Sir John, who immediately reined in his steed. This was Prospero, who, in his humble way, was about to contribute his mite towards the Baronet's gratification on this memorable day. Though Prospero's heartfelt thanks were delivered in a jargon which had no meaning for Sir John's ears, there was that in the poor lad's voice and look which conveyed to the English gentleman's mind as clear a perception of what the Italian said and meant, as if he had spoken English like John. The pale countenance and emaciated form were an emphatic accompaniment to his simple eloquence. Sir John was moved, and to hide that he was moved, he immediately began in a blustering tone to read the boy a lecture on the duties of post-boys to travellers in general, and to travellers of a certain sort in particular. This harangue being denuded of all that expressive pantomime of look and gesture, which would have made patent to any understanding the lad's address, fell heavily on the uncomprehending ears of Prospero, who, twirling his hat, and with eyes fixed to the ground, looked very like the criminal Sir John was carefully describing him to be.

In this crisis, just when the Baronet, still on the back of his cob, was beginning to be puzzled how to conclude the scene with dignity, his eye lighted on Doctor Antonio, who had walked up to the Osteria to see the purchase, of which by this time all the parish had heard. "My dear Doctor," cried out Sir John in a hearty voice, "I am very glad to see you; I am under infinite obligations to you." Doctor Antonio to be called "my dear Doctor," in that bluff, sincere way by Sir John Davenne! It was the first time, so no wonder Antonio pondered on the words. He begged Sir John not to talk of obligations, and congratulated him warmly on the lucky chance that had secured him such a capital beast. John came up at this point, and announced to his master that the stable wherein he used to keep the former two horses, for some reason or other, could not be had for a week, at least,—an intelligence which marred not a little the good old gentleman's satisfaction. Seeing which, the kind Doctor took the repentant-looking Prospero aside, and after a minute's parley with him, turned to the

Baronet and said, that at the house where the lad lived, there was a tolerably good stable, and that, perhaps, it would be a convenience to Sir John, and most certainly an act of charity on his part, to intrust the care of the horse to Prospero, who, when able to resume his duty as post-boy, had a younger brother to act as groom in his place. The Baronet caught at once at the proposal, and Prospero, not a little elated at this piece of good fortune, helped to dismount his new "Signor Padrone," who delivered the cob to his care, with special directions to be every morning by seven o'clock at the Osteria, to receive daily orders.

Lucy, who from the balcony could hear and see all that was passing below, had followed all the incidents of this little episode with an intensity of interest, which, to an indifferent observer, could not but have appeared unwarranted by the occasion; and when Sir John had called Antonio "my dear Doctor," a flush of complacency had overspread her white cheek, and her smile had become sweeter and sweeter. After all, it was but natural, that, kind-hearted as she was, the better understanding which was evidently growing up between her father and her doctor should give her pleasure.

"How kind of you!" said Lucy to Antonio, as he went up to her, and took a seat by her side.

"Kind! how do you mean?" asked Antonio, his eyebrows bristling up like a hedgehog who puts himself on the defensive.

"To think about the horse," explained Lucy.

"Ha! ha! ha!" and the Italian forthwith opened his safety-valve against charges of kindness, that is,—he laughed his own peculiar laugh, a clear, merry laugh, with something still in it of boyhood's ring. "But suppose I have not been thinking about it, what then?"

Lucy's eyes looked incredulous.

"When some time ago you expressed a wish that your father could have a horse, I mentioned the subject in a letter I was writing at the moment, and then, I am afraid, I forgot all about the matter; so you see, you have only to be grateful to a lucky chance."

"And did this easy-chair and awning for a foolish girl, who showed her gratitude by being cross and impatient, come here by chance too?"

"There again," said Antonio, throwing back his head with a movement usual with him when annoyed, "as if such common courtesies were worth making a fuss about. At this rate, if I sneeze, and a neighbour says, 'God bless you,' I am bound to him for life."

Lucy could not help laughing at the oddity of the illustration, and asked, "May I, without giving offence, express my admiration of the beautiful workmanship of this chair, and of the bright yellow wood of which it is made?"

"Yes, you may," replied Antonio, smiling; "it always does me good to hear the people or things of this country praised. The chair is of olive wood, and is the work of a very clever fellow. If we ever go to Taggia together, I will show you pieces of furniture of the same wood, and by the same hand, that I daresay would not be out of place even in Davenne Hall."

"Such a clever workman," said Lucy, "ought to go to London, he would be sure of making a fortune there."

"Very likely," answered Antonio, "but he does not seem to feel the necessity of making one. The people of the Riviera are extremely attached to their birthplace, and stick to their homes and quiet habits, seldom going abroad unless compelled by want. Besides, our chairmaker is something more than a skilful workman, he is an artist."

"I can understand any one being reluctant to leave this," said Lucy, "much more any one with an artist's eye and feelings. Where could he find a nature like this?" and her own eyes gleamed with deep rapture. Antonio was watching her; for all answer he said, "The open air has done you good already, you look more—lively than this morning."

"Do I? I feel so well and happy; and it is said, you know, that happiness does a great deal for one's looks."

Antonio threw up those black eyes of his into Lucy's soft blue ones, but made no remark. The look and the silence embarrassed Lucy, she knew not why, but she felt as if called upon for some explanation, which rather disappointed Antonio when it came.

"My brother cannot be home for four months, and so now papa will not fret about our staying here; and then I am so glad about the horse, and that I am able to sit here and enjoy this beautiful view. Have I not a right to feel happy?"

"To be sure," said Antonio, rather gravely, and stroking his beard, "to be sure." What had he missed in the enumeration of Lucy's causes of happiness?

A short pause ensued, during which Doctor and patient seemed anything but at their ease. "By the by," said the Italian, rousing himself, "I have not seen your drawing; will you show it me?"

"It is all in a mess," said Lucy, with a little blush. "I can make nothing of it; I am ashamed of myself, and utterly disheartened."

"I guess how it has been," replied Antonio; "you have been too greedy. Shall I give you a little advice? You see that half-ruined tower, shaded by palm-trees, on the Cape of Bordighera?—try that first, or that piece of wall with its drapery of bitter sweet, standing forward so well from the background of dark blue sea. Do not bewilder yourself with too many objects at once; and, take my word for it, it will not be long before you master strong foregrounds and soft distances. But beware of ambition."

"'Vaulting ambition, which o'erleaps itself and falls,'" said Lucy, laughing.

"That is from your Shakespeare," said Antonio. "I think all English people know him by heart. I never met one of your countrymen or women, however ignorant in other respects, who did not some time or other give out a line from Shakespeare. What a man he must have been, who could thus embody, and 'give a local habitation and a name' to the feelings of a whole nation for centuries to come!"

"You seem as much at home with Shakespeare as with your own poets," said Lucy.

"He *is* one of my poets. Shakespeare is not the poet of any age or country, but of mankind. He, like the sun, spreads light and warmth over the whole world of intelligence.—Can you draw figures?" went on the Doctor, pointing to the beach. "What a group those fishermen would make, with that woman on the donkey stopping to speak to them!"

"But I cannot draw figures the least bit in the world," said Lucy, in a despairing voice.

"Well, you can learn. Figures are so picturesque in Italy, it is almost a matter of duty to copy them."

"Yes, but one must know how. I am sure I have not an idea how to begin, whether with the hat or the shoes; and who is there here to teach me?"

"If you really wish for a master, I will find you one."

"Can you, indeed? then I do wish it."

"I will introduce you to a master to-morrow. You have often said that you would like to read Dante's poem with some one who could explain and annotate upon it; now, if you continue in that mind, I know of a fit person."

"You seem to have the gift of finding everything I want or wish for," said Lucy, turning a pair of grateful eyes to him.

"You were so uncomplaining in your submission to my severe orders," answered Antonio, "that I feel bound, now that you are able to leave your bed, to give you the benefit of all that our neighbourhood affords, to amuse you; and I assure you we have more resources than at first might be thought possible. Among all classes in this country there exists a singular aptitude to learn, and much natural taste. For instance, we have a tolerably good band of musicians, most of them self-taught, and an excellent organist, who never had any master but himself."

"Wonderful!" said Lucy; "and are they as good as they are clever?"

"To say the least, they have many good points," returned Antonio; "they are sober, independent, and warm-hearted; there is a native mildness in their blood; and when they quarrel—for where is it that men are always at peace with one another?—the quarrel rarely ends in blows. You look as if you scarcely believed me."

Lucy's colour rose, for she felt what Antonio was saying to be the very reverse of the character she was in the habit of hearing ascribed to Italians.

"Forget preconceived notions, or rather," continued Antonio, "remember all, and compare hearsay evidence with what comes under your own observation. Facts are stubborn things, Miss Davenne, and observation of facts will show you that amongst us there is scarcely an example of wives and daughters bearing the marks of the brutality of their husbands and fathers; that drunkenness is a very rare thing, and so is crime; that there are whole provinces—that of San Remo is one—in which no murder has been committed within the memory of man. Property is so divided, that the two extremes of great riches and great poverty are almost unknown, and so, fortunately, are most of the evils arising out of them,—beggary for instance. I am not speaking of the great towns of course, but of the country districts, in which nearly every man owns his little bit of land, which he cultivates as well as he can. The small proprietor who has time to spare, hires his services to the neighbour, who, possessing more land, requires more hands, but both employer and employed deal and converse with each other on a footing of perfect equality. The hired labourer no more considers himself the inferior of his employer because he takes money from him, than the employer thinks himself the labourer's surperior for paying it."

"You are describing a real Arcadia," said Lucy.

"I wish it were so," continued Antonio, shaking his head; "but there are deep shades to the picture. The baneful action of despotism makes itself felt here as everywhere else in Italy. The state of utter ignorance in which the populations I am speaking of are left by a Government systematically hostile to all sorts of instruction—the worship of the dead letter in lieu of the spirit that vivifies, in which they are nursed and kept by their priests—the habit of dissembling grievances, for which there is no possible redress, and which it would be dangerous to resent;—all these deleterious influences combine to keep the standard of morality rather low. The man who would not for the world eat a morsel of meat on Friday, or miss hearing mass on a saint's day, will not scruple to cheat his master of an hour's work, or to say the thing that is not, to obtain an abatement in the rent he pays to his landlord."

"That is too bad," said Lucy; "and do the priests know of such doings, and not try to prevent or put a stop to them?"

"Certainly they do not use their authority to the extent necessary to cure the evil. They fear to lose their influence if they deal, I will not say severely, but firmly with their flock. There seems to be a tacit agreement between sheep and shepherds. Give us everything in point of form, say the latter. We will, answer the former, but on condition that you do not exact too much in point of substance. Thus the letter kills the spirit. Provided the churches be well attended, the confessionals besieged, the alms plentiful, the communion tickets numerous, our *Reverendi* seem to care little whether morality remains stationary or even slides backwards. The Curé, who is in many respects what I believe you call vicar in England, preaches from the pulpit that lying is a sinful habit, and that a hired labourer owes a fair day's work for a fair day's wages, but to little purpose. And why is there no amendment? Because the confessors do not practically support what is preached; they are too lenient, and dare not, textually dare not, refuse absolution to those of their penitents who are in a state of backsliding. They dare not, because they say, 'we do not choose to lose our penitents,' and such to a certainty would be the case, were they to show a proper degree of severity. The aim and ambition of confessors, you must understand, is to have a great number of penitents, and they vie with each other who shall be most run after. The country folks know this weakness and profit by it. It has happened to me more than once to hear it said, 'If my confessor will not give me absolution, I shall go to such and such a one who has "larger sleeves,"' meaning by that, who is more indulgent."

"These are, indeed, ugly shades to your pretty picture," sighed Lucy.

"Very ugly," echoed Antonio. "The great business of our *Reverendi*—there are, of course, many honourable exceptions—is the embellishment of their respective churches; and for this purpose they take advantage of the taste for the beautiful, which is innate in our people. Offerings or contributions flow in plentifully for the purchase of a new organ, a set of silver lamps, for pictures, for the adornment of the shrine of the Madonna. At the same time the town is dirty, not lighted at night, the pavement all holes, the roads are detestable, and bridges absent where bridges are most needed. But what does it matter so long as the church looks splendid, and outshines this or that church in the neighbourhood?"

"And how do you fare with these *Reverendi*, as you call them?" asked Lucy.

"Why, so so, they are not over friendly to me, I believe, the Curé especially, who cannot forgive my regularly refusing the ticket that he as regularly sends me every Easter."

"What is it for?"

"A most vexatious botheration. At Easter, the Curés take upon themselves to send to every one of their parishioners what is called a communion ticket, and they require of every person, after communicating, to leave this ticket in the vestry as a proof of having done so. You can conceive that this species of coercion is very humiliating,—at least I feel it so. Very willing as I am to fulfil my religious duties, still I choose to do so freely, and like a man who judges for himself, not like a boy, on compulsion. So I always send back the ticket."

"And the Curé is angry with you," said Lucy, with a little grave face.

"Yes, but he keeps his anger to himself. He and his reverend brethren give me credit for being a tolerable physician—as good, at least, as can be hoped for hereabouts; but it is not their confidence in my medical skill alone that keeps them civil to me. Public opinion runs high in my favour, and even here, and in spite of all, public opinion has its weight. And then my beard," continued Antonio, stroking it playfully; "is not that one of the strongest possible proofs of my favour with our three-tailed Pacha, the Commandant of San Remo?"

"How so?" asked Lucy.

"It may seem strange, but nevertheless it is true, Miss Davenne, that one of the strictest duties, as well as one of the most agreeable sports of Commandants, is to suffer no chin to be unshorn; and mine, I believe, is the only one in all the Riviera which can boast of anything like a beard on it. The truth is, when I first came to San Remo, I was so occupied by day and night, that I literally lacked the time to shave. This reason I pleaded to our Gessler, who accepted it, and little by little, and by dint of habit, my beard came to be tolerated."

"You seem to care very much about your beard," observed Miss Davenne, smiling at Antonio's grave way of speaking about it.

"I confess I rather do," he answered, smiling also. "Without speaking of the time it saves, and other disagreeables, I think that since Nature, who does nothing without a purpose, bestowed a beard on man, she meant it as ornamental or useful. Altogether, it seems to me that every man, but an Italian in particular, with his olive complexion, looks better with than without a beard. You are laughing at me, but tell me which do you prefer, which looks best, one of Vandyck's heads with its beard, or a modern close-shaven portrait? I suspect the advantage lies with the former."

"Yes," said Lucy, with a little blush, and a little hesitation, as her own remark to her father on first seeing Doctor Antonio started to her memory, "when living men are like Vandyck portraits."

"No reservations," cried Antonio, "or I shall think you share in the prejudice I have heard exists in England against beards."

"Oh no, I don't!" said Lucy; "but most English people dislike them."

"Well, let them shave, there's no accounting for tastes," observed Antonio, with an air of resignation.

"You promised once to tell me what made you such a favourite with this Commandant. By the by, does he command all the Riviera?"

"No such thing. Every province of this kingdom wears a like jewel on its head."

"And in what originated your favour with this one?"

"In a most absurd notion of his. I have often told you that, when I came to San Remo, the cholera was at its height. I found the Commandant panic-stricken, and labouring under a fixed idea that he must take the disease. I saw at once the necessity of setting his imagination to work the contrary way, so I gave him a small phial of camphorated vinegar, with directions to smell it a certain number of times a day, assuring him that it was an infallible specific against cholera. And he believes it to this day," went on Antonio, with a hearty laugh. "The phial is now empty, and should the cholera re-appear, he knows of no one to whom he could apply for a fresh supply of this wonderful antidote but myself; so he is very civil to me, and—to my beard."

Lucy enjoyed the joke, and laughed so heartily that Antonio joined her till the tears stood in his eyes.

CHAPTER XL
The 15th of May 1840.

A FORTNIGHT has slipped away, during which Lucy's health and other matters have been steadily progressing at the Osteria; new habits have been formed, new occupations and pursuits entered upon—in short, every consecutive day has brought to our little colony its fresh supply of pleasurable excitement, and increased good-will.

The weather, to begin with, has been splendid, and Sir John has not once missed his morning ride, and is enchanted with Buffy, (thus Lucy had christened the plump bay cob,) whose temper and paces, Sir John declares, improve wonderfully with every ride;—an assertion to which the Count, who is now a daily visitor to the Osteria, nods enthusiastic assent, observing that really his English friend has had the animal for nothing. By what mysterious process these two gentlemen understand one another, considering that the stock of spoken signs they have in common, is limited to a score or so of French words on either side, is a matter of wonder to everybody, most of all, perhaps, to themselves. But that they do understand one another, is a fact beyond dispute, inasmuch as Sir John professes himself highly indebted to his noble friend, for the primary idea of a project, which engrosses most of Sir John's time and thoughts, and in the realization of which he is greatly assisted by the Count and Doctor Antonio. The project is no other than to make a collection of the finest young orange and palm plants to be found in the neighbourhood, and transplant them to the seigneurial seat of all the Davennes. "Yes, I shall build an orangery," says Sir John, "but that's nothing, I shall build a palmary; Lucy, a palmary!" and exultant Sir John rubs his hands. "You see, my dear, I shall not only create the thing, but the very name of it." The Baronet follows up his scheme with unabated ardour; is in communication with all the owners of palm-trees in Bordighera—Bordighera that stands unrivalled for palm-trees; rides over to San Remo, where the orange-trees are said to have distanced all competitors; is for ever receiving, and, with Lucy acting as a secretary, answering letters connected with his plan,—in short, Sir John gallops both cob and hobby-horse to his heart's content, and to that of all about him.

A *post-diem* celebration of Miss Davenne's twentieth birthday, which, as you remember, she had actually spent in her bed, has been the grand event of the fortnight. Wonderful the doings, and great the bustle at the Osteria, which is beginning to forget its ugliness, and to fancy, like many other plain old things, that very fine feathers make very fine birds; and it cannot be denied that Sir John has done his best about the new plumage. Ay, a dinner—hybrid, perhaps, between a public and private entertainment, and for which Sir John managed to send out printed cards of invitation—has been given to the Count, and some other notables, among whom figured Doctor Antonio, the Mayor, several Councilmen, the Justice of Peace of Bordighera; and in the evening minor luminaries, one of them Lucy's drawing-master. The dinner was on a splendid scale, the late Bishop of Albenga's cook surpassed himself; John could only prove equal to himself. Sir John did the honours the more charmingly that he did not do them in state, but in an *incog.* unpretending way, as one may suppose other magnates do, when they drop their crowns and make believe to be only Counts or Countesses. Probably, Sir John felt as he was accustomed to do, when presiding at the annual dinner he gave his tenants at Davenne.

In Italy, as elsewhere, toasts are a prevalent fashion, but speeches of dubious eloquence are superseded by the rattle of glass touching glass in general sympathetic clatter. The Count proposed a bumper to the health of their distinguished host, and of his accomplished daughter, and the sentiment was drunk with universal enthusiasm. The Mayor, two Councilmen, and the Justice of Peace followed in the same track, showing much ingenuity in devising variations on the same theme. Sir John felt himself called upon to return thanks for himself and his daughter, which he did in a rather lengthy speech; and Doctor Antonio, after transmitting to the guests in Italian the Baronet's effusion, conveyed to him in a few neatly-turned English phrases, the gratified feelings of the company.

During the evening, Lucy made her first appearance, wheeled in upon her rolling-chair, and we need scarcely say that her beauty and grace created quite a sensation among the proverbially enthusiastic Italians. Antonio sang some of his most spirited Sicilian songs, which were heartily applauded and encored; and the drawing-master, who is something of an Improvvisatore, extemporized a sonnet to Miss Davenne, in which he compared her to a lily, and to a palm-tree, and to Minerva into the bargain, all which was received with loud bravos by those present, with the exception of the Count, who (it being a notorious matter that the Count and the drawing-master were at daggers drawn) was observed to make, while the sonnet was being delivered, sundry wry faces, intended to convey and express a considerable amount of doubt as to the *bona fide impromptu* nature of the performance. Except this trifling incident, which escaped the notice of both the Baronet and his daughter, and the marked coolness with which tea was received by the majority —a damp soon counteracted by Sir John ordering in a fresh supply of black bottles for the dissenters—everything went on capitally, and entirely to the satisfaction of all concerned; so much so, that Antonio, after a rather long colloquy with the Baronet in the balcony, came forth and announced *séance tenante* in the Amphitryon's name, that should a little conversation and a little music prove a sufficient inducement to give him their company, Sir John Davenne would be delighted to receive all present on every successive Wednesday and Saturday, at eight o'clock in the evening.

There is a circumstance connected with this entertainment too important to be overlooked, and it is, that Doctor Antonio achieved the conquest of Sir John on the occasion. Was it his rigorous professional costume, and white cravat —was it his gentlemanly manner, or his speechifying powers, or all the three causes combined, that won Sir John's British heart? We cannot say, but to this we must testify, that Sir John's heart was won. Sir John treated Doctor Antonio all dinner-time, and throughout the evening, with marked distinction, addressing him publicly as "my honourable friend," and privately and confidentially as "my dear friend;" he even went so far as to declare emphatically to Lucy, after every one was gone, that "could that man be brought to shave, he would not be out of place at the table of a king." From that day forward, the Doctor was promoted to the honour of shaking hands with the Baronet; and let Antonio say what he would, John was despatched daily to the Doctor's dwelling with Sir John Davenne's compliments, and the newspaper of the previous day.

Already have two brilliant "*soirées musicales*," as Sir John calls them, been held in the course of the last week at the Osteria, and the expected third is creating great anxiety in the neighbourhood; the English *Milordo's* concerts are the talk of the country for ten miles round. Visitors from so far off as Ventimiglia and San Remo have left cards for Sir John and Miss Davenne, and many are making interest with the Count and the Doctor for invitations. The management of the music devolves entirely on Doctor Antonio, under whose superintendence quartettos are executed. The performers, a bassoon, a violin, a violoncello, are all *dilettanti* from Bordighera; Antonio makes the fourth, playing by turns the guitar or the flute. Hutchins' little room is transformed on Wednesdays and Saturdays into a refreshment room, the buffet in which is most regularly attended. To see Sir John on these evenings is to see a man thoroughly on good terms with himself—step, voice, and look express, "I am monarch of all I survey;" and let wise folks theorize as they may, the upshot of the matter will always be, that mankind, including womankind, do like occasionally to be "the glass of fashion, and the mould of form, the observed of all observers"—were it only at Bordighera. On all other evenings of the week Sir John's society is limited to the Count and Doctor Antonio, to which privileged circle Sir John, while sipping his tea, imparts little glimpses of London life—fashionable life of course—interspersed with hints that, like flashes of lightning, reveal something of the splendours of Davenne Hall, and of the greatness and mightiness of the Davennes, or "the family," as Sir John fondly calls his race. As ten strikes, he regularly sits down to chess with Doctor Antonio (this is the signal for Lucy to withdraw, and for the Count to begin to doze), and invariably wins two games out of three, Antonio having discovered that Sir John cannot lose games without losing his temper also, and when cross, Lucy's father is unbearable.

Almost the whole of Lucy's time during this fortnight has been spent in the balcony. Ever since she has been able to pass the day in the open air, her health has strengthened considerably. She exceedingly enjoys the "*soirées musicales*," greatly for the sake of the music—Lucy is really fond of music—but a little, too, for the sake of the effect she herself produces. Curious enough! Lucy never seems to have surmised before that she was lovely, or if she had surmised it, only begins now to care about being so. Every one, she observes, is so well bred, so respectful to her, so full of attention. Lucy is, in truth, a little queen with a little Court. She is making visible progress in drawing, particularly in figures, to which she has taken a great fancy, so much so, that she has sketched Speranza twenty times over—Speranza, who sits to her with angelic patience for hours, no longer wan and dejected, but brightened by some mysterious presentiment that a happy change is at hand for her; besides, there are the practisings on the guitar, and Doctor Antonio's visits, so Lucy's hours are pretty full. The drawing-master, too, amuses her to a degree,—such a fiery, violent little man, so good-natured withal and so clever! Dante, Lucy tells the Doctor, is rather too deep a well for her, but she perseveres in drawing up all she can. She openly confesses that she does more fully enjoy the prospect from the balcony now than on the first days; to use her own expression, it seems as if all its separate beauties had melted into one great beauty.

Doctor Antonio does not look elated by high favour with Sir John: he takes it meekly, maybe like a man who felt himself entitled to it all along; nor have his successes as conductor of the orchestra, and guitar and flute-player, turned his head. Doctor Antonio continues exactly the same serene, unassuming, serviceable, good-humoured creature he was fifteen days ago. If there be any change in him, it is a change for the better in his personal appearance, so slight, however, that the eye must be scrutinizing indeed—the eye of a woman probably—to find it out. His coat is perhaps a thought more carefully brushed, his hair and beard more carefully trimmed, his cravat less loosely twisted round his throat than it used to be. Nor does the management of the musical department at all interfere with his attendance on Miss Davenne, which is as assiduous as ever; and though he has evidently plenty to do elsewhere, he finds time to make himself useful and agreeable at the Osteria. For instance, on hearing Lucy observe one day, that the musquitoes were beginning to become troublesome at night, he fell to work immediately, fastened up poles to her bed, and to Sir John's, and upon these poles hung musquito nets; then on a complaint from the same quarter, of flies being intolerable, he caused large bundles of a common viscous plant, (Erigeron Viscosum, *Lin.*,) dipped in milk, to be hung up in all the rooms and the balcony, which attracted all the flies, and freed her at once from one of the plagues of Italy. Lucy had one thought very carefully hidden in the inmost folds of her heart, and that thought was, that surely there never was any one in the world like this Doctor Antonio.

Such was, on the whole, the rather satisfactory state of

things and parties in the Osteria *del Mattone* on this blessed day, the 15th of May 1840.

It was ten in the morning, as lovely a morning as poets and birds can sing. Miss Davenne, in a light-blue gown, sat in the balcony busy with her pencils. Was the choice of a blue dress quite accidental on her part, or was it in any way connected with Antonio having mentioned the evening before, that, of all the colours, he liked blue the best? Who can tell? Antonio was also seated on the balcony, a little behind Lucy, and pulling his beard violently, a sign of troubled weather. Hutchins within was arranging in a vase a large bunch of roses just brought by the Doctor. He rarely came empty-handed; and yet his horror of anything like thanks remaining unabated, Lucy had learnt to acknowledge his little presents only with a smile. Contrary to custom, the two had little to say to one another, and conversation flagged. Maybe that Lucy was engrossed with her drawing, maybe that she was otherwise absorbed. Antonio was most palpably so, and his wonted equanimity had deserted him this morning. It is the first time since we made his acquaintance, that he betrays strong symptoms of a malady which might have been supposed utterly unknown to him—irresolution. A word or a phrase trembled on his lips which he was afraid to utter. He occasionally bent forward as if about to rise, then fell back on his seat again. At last he made an heroic effort, bounded up from his chair, and said resolutely—

"Suppose, Miss Davenne, you were to try and walk?"

A welcome summons to Lucy, whose pale cheek, paler even than usual on this morning, is suddenly suffused with crimson. As Miss Lucy has declared some time ago that she will rather die in her chair than use crutches, Hutchins is called, and desired to support her young lady on one side, while Doctor Antonio does as much on the other. Lucy rises, leans on the two proffered arms, and moves. Antonio's heart beats loud and strong as the piston of a steam-engine.

"Do you feel pain anywhere?" asks the Doctor in a whisper.

"Not any," declares Lucy, but her ankle is a little stiff.

"And," pursues Antonio, in a queer thick voice, "do you think you could walk alone?"

"I think I could," says Lucy, turning her smiling face up to his.

"Well, try."

The Doctor and Hutchins gently let go their hold of Lucy; Antonio stands in front of her with outstretched arms, ready to catch her, much in the attitude of a mother who watches the first steps of a dear babe. Lucy walks on unsupported,—one, two, three, four steps—only four; but more than enough for Antonio's quick, experienced eye to feel sure, that there is no cause for any apprehension of impaired gait.

"*Vittoria!*" shouts Antonio, clapping his hands so loudly that Lucy and Hutchins are both startled by the report; "*Vittoria!*" he shouts again, then suddenly checks himself, lest his joy should betray the extent of his fears, and occasion Lucy a retrospective shock. But tears are in his eyes as he and Hutchins once more take hold of their precious charge; "for," continues the Doctor, pretending to composure, yet still all in a flurry, "she must not overfatigue herself; she must lean well on his arm, so—and now lie quietly on the sofa—there, all's right again." To see his countenance now all in a glow with noble and sweet emotion, to hear his voice, to listen to his laugh, must have made the conquest of the most morose of human kind. Lucy does listen, but silently; she never for a moment removes her eyes from him; they follow him as he strides into the balcony, as he comes back with her little table, as he first stoops to slip a bit of paper under one of its legs, and then arranges her pencils and colours just where they ought to be. Lucy does not speak, does not even say "thank you;" for Lucy feels that she could not say it without doing something else she is striving against. She does not even dare to extend her hand to him, as her heart, full to the brim, prompts her to do, lest she should give way; but those clear soft eyes that rest on him speak volumes.

After half an hour's rest, Lucy had another walk from the sofa back to the balcony, and was to have a third within another half hour from the balcony to the sofa, and no more till Antonio called again—an injunction that will not be infringed, judging from the manner with which it was received. While the third, and for the time being, last trip was in progress, Sir John came in; and we leave the reader to imagine if the good humour that shone in his eyes was likely to be spoiled by the sight of Lucy on her feet again, and actually walking. He hastened to withdraw her arm from Hutchins, and put it under his own, delighted to take just five steps with his darling, and replace her on the sofa. And three happier faces than these three, we lay a wager on it, the lobby of the Osteria had never beheld.

When the present excitement produced by this incident had subsided, Sir John began recounting with great glee his morning's excursion. Sir John had ridden over early to San Remo, to inspect a garden recommended to his notice by Doctor Antonio, and in that garden had found a treasure —a real treasure, as he emphatically declared, "orange-trees of the Bergamot species, flowers of the size of those (pointing to the roses on the table), and a fragrance, a fragrance!" Sir John was as happy at this discovery as if the Bergamot species were of his own making. The owner of the garden had himself shown Sir John over the grounds, and placed all the plants at the Baronet's disposal. "A most gentlemanlike person," Sir John asserted, (what a pity, Sir John, you do not keep a note-book now!) "a most gentlemanlike person, to whom, by the by, I have given an invitation for to-morrow's *soirée musicale*." Having thus far vented his enthusiasm, and fondly kissed Lucy, and patted her cheek, and observed to the Doctor how well she looked—an assertion the Doctor allowed to pass uncontradicted—Sir John sat down to his letters and papers. Antonio said good-bye, and was already at the glass-door, when he met with a sudden obstruction in the shape of Speranza, closely followed by her mother, who both dashed past him, rushing into the room like thunder-bolts.'

Both the women are in tears, and half choke with sobs, yet theirs are not the looks or gestures of people under the pressure of painful feelings. Speranza, on her knees by the side of the sofa, clings passionately to Lucy, covering her hands and feet with kisses and tears. Rosa, less violently agitated, has stopped short in the middle of the room, where, alternately wiping her eyes with the corner of her apron, and clasping and unclasping her hands, she ejaculates all the time, "*Oh caro! oh Madonna Santissima!*—Oh, that I should have lived to see this day, *ohimé, ohimé!*" Presently it is the Doctor's turn to have his hands kissed and bathed, which is no sooner done than Sir John has to go through the same ordeal. "The girl is mad," cries the astounded Baronet, getting very red in the face, and violently repossessing himself of his own hand. "Yes," says Antonio, "mad with joy. Battista is come, I suppose, is he not, you silly girl?" The silly girl's smiling assent sparkles through a fresh shower; she takes Antonio's hands, and gently draws him towards the balcony, where Speranza and he, and Rosa after them, vanish from sight.

"What sadly demonstrative creatures these Italians are!" observed Sir John, in a dissatisfied, grumbling tone, by way of entering a protest against his momentary emotion.

"It is their nature to feel strongly, and to express strongly what they feel," answered Lucy.

"There's no denying the last part of your statement, my dear," said her father; "the more's the pity."

"Why so, papa?" asked Lucy.

"Because," replied Sir John dryly, "any such exhibition of sensibility is highly derogatory to human dignity, and carries with it a presumption of shallowness. Deep feelings, like deep rivers, Lucy, so I have heard, are rarely noisy."

"But in this case, papa, nobody can doubt the reality of poor Speranza's feelings, and you must have been struck by that yourself, for I saw the tears in your eyes."

"Tears in my eyes!" growled Sir John, in a scornful tone, "nonsense!" and, taking up the *Times* newspaper, he raised it as a barrier between himself and Lucy's investigating glance.

Antonio, after a little while, came back and said, that, as in duty bound, Battista craved the honour of being admitted to the presence of his kind benefactor and benefactress. "Oh yes, by all means!" cried Lucy eagerly, "let him come in at once." Young ladies of twenty, whatever their station, are apt to feel some curiosity about the hero of a love-story, let him wear a ducal mantle, or only a seaman's blue jacket.

"Yes, let us get it over at once; but on condition," interposed Sir John, "that we have no fresh supply of tears or hand-kissing."

"I think there is no fear of that," said Antonio; "the women are now more composed, and, as far as I can judge, Battista is not much addicted to the melting mood."

"So much the better for him and for us," grumbled Sir John; "I have had enough of that sort of thing to-day to serve me for the rest of my life."

And now the hero of the day, a comely, middle-sized, strong-built, chocolate-complexioned young man of two-and-twenty, led by Speranza, and pushed on by Rosa in the rear, makes his anything but triumphal entry, and with slow, reluctant steps approaches the sofa where Lucy rests. The young lady, feeling for his confusion, kindly, and in a low voice, addresses some words of welcome to him. Battista looks up, utters a half cry, and stands for a second amazed; and, with averted eyes, would then have taken to his heels, but for Rosa and Speranza, who catch and bring him back. He turns his eyes to the right and to the left, plunges them into the depths of the red woollen pouch he is twisting in his trembling hands, looks anywhere but at Lucy—verily, Battista would rather face a hurricane on a furious ocean than those blue eyes. "Are you crazy?" says Antonio, perplexed; "why, man, have you nothing to say to this lady, who has been a second Providence to you?" Battista makes ineffectual attempts to speak; at last the inarticulate sounds become a muttered whisper of—"It is the Madonna," and down he drops on his knees, and crosses himself most vigorously. Sir John may say what he chooses, but we question whether homage in better taste was ever paid to earthly purity and loveliness. Antonio saw the expediency of cutting short a scene which, from the very intensity of the poor lad's feelings, was becoming embarrassing to all parties; so stepping up to him, he raised him up, saying, "That will do, my lad, the lady understands all you wish to express—come away now, we will put off your thanks to another time;" and patting him good-humouredly on the shoulder, the Doctor towed the abashed boy out of the room, the two bewildered women following in the rear.

We beg the reader to believe that this is no picture drawn from fancy, but a real sketch from nature. Had not such a scene as we have described, with all the particulars related, come to pass under our own eyes, we should never have ventured to put it on paper. We ourselves can understand very well how a simple, ignorant, but imaginative Italian youth, whose notion of all that is beautiful and graceful is from earliest infancy embodied in the image of the Madonna, that is, in a lovely figure with flowing, fair curls, clothed in blue,—we can understand, we repeat, how such a youth, put suddenly face to face with such a *suave* specimen of womankind as this young English girl, should identify her with his long-worshipped type of loveliness and gentleness.

Battista's infatuation held good for some time, in spite of Antonio's lectures and Speranza's scoldings, who was quite ashamed, she declared, of seeing him make such a goose of himself. Battista had but one argument, but with that he parried and overruled all objections; he had seen *her* before, he was sure of that, and she had spoken to him, and told him that she was the Madonna. It was, according to Battista, one night, a tremendous night at sea, when, tired with long working at the pumps, he had thrown himself on a locker and fallen asleep. And the Madonna appeared to him in his sleep, and said, with flashing eyes, "Is this thy devotion to me, that thou goest to thy rest without saying a 'salve regina' in my honour?" With that Battista awoke, got up, said his prayers reciting as usual a "salve regina," and then once more fell asleep. When, lo! the Madonna came to him again, this time with most benignant eyes, and said, in sweet tones, "Battista, thou art a good boy; as long as thou puttest thy trust in me no evil shall befall thee; be of good cheer, thou shalt see Bordighera again." Now, whether they believed it or not, Battista did not care—Battista was growing dogged with these continual reasonings—but the voice he had heard, the eyes, the hair, the figure he had seen in the up-stairs room of the Osteria on that blessed morning of the 15th of May, were the voice, hair, eyes, and figure of Battista's nocturnal visitor at sea. Battista could swear to it all, and to the blue gown into the bargain.

"We must help them to marry," said Lucy in the afternoon, when alone with the Doctor. "Must we?" answered Antonio, with a merry laugh; "I thought all that would come of itself soon enough, even without our help."

"I have a great mind to call you a *slow* doctor, as papa once did," said Lucy, with a pout of impatience; "you know very well what I mean. Did you not tell me yourself that Rosa's affairs were in a bad state? and is it not a fact that Battista has lost all he had in the world? Now, is it not *very* plain that they do want our assistance to be able to marry?"

"Do not say *our* assistance," said Antonio, "for as to me, I have nothing to give but good wishes."

"Not at all," said Lucy, quickly; "you *must* give a great deal more,—time, and trouble, and all sorts of things; you must find out about their debts and difficulties, and calculate what sum will be necessary to set them afloat."

"A large sum," replied Antonio, gravely, shaking his head at the eager speaker, "a large sum."

"Never mind," said Miss Lucy, "papa will give it, whatever it is, to please me—he must; I shall tell him that we might as well have left Battista on board his ship, if we do nothing more for him, and for Speranza."

Antonio only smiled, but his heart was pouring blessings on her, though the blessings never reached Lucy's ear.

A day begun under such happy auspices—a day so rich in deep and gentle emotions to most of our personages, came to a close, we are glad to say, in a manner worthy of itself. Towards midnight, all the echoes of the garden were awakened by the sounds of sweet music. The *dilettanti* of Bordighera in full force, we need not say by whom inspired, assembled below the balcony to give a grand serenade to Miss Davenne. Sir John, who had not yet gone to bed, went down to the garden to acknowledge the compliment, and was received by loud "*vivas!*" Trays with wine and glasses were soon circulating among the company, by the united exertions of Rosa, Speranza, and the no little astonished John, whose raised eyebrows, in spite of his rigid silence, had more than once betrayed of late the series of surprises through which his master was making him pass. When we speak of the company, we mean not only the musicians, but also a great number of *amateurs* who had followed in their wake, and filled the garden.

Lucy, from behind her blind, enjoyed the serenade exceedingly. The music was unquestionably good; but that which gave her far more pleasure than the well-played overtures to "La Gazza Ladra,". and "Semiramide," was a villanella for three voices, one of them a rich, sweet bass, dear to her ears and heart. These villanellas, somewhat of the fashion of the serenade in Don Pasquale, are the popular songs of the Riviera. The melody, of the simplest kind, is taken up in succession by one or other of the voices, with no other accompaniment than a few syncopated notes from the other two. Altogether an effective sort of performance when the voices are true, which is commonly the case in Italy—and one full of melancholy. So much so, at least, in the present instance, that Lucy forthwith began to do freely what she had so determinately resisted doing in the morning, and made her way back to her bed crying heartily. Her tears, however, did not interfere with her sleep, which was sound and refreshing.

CHAPTER XII.
In the Garden.

"SEE what a beautiful carpet Nature has spread out for you!" said Antonio, a few days after, as he handed Miss Davenne into the garden. The night had been windy, and there was on the ground a thick silvery layer of orange and lemon blossoms, out of which came forth in strong relief a profusion of violently red wild poppies. "Will you have such in store for me when I come to Davenne?"

"Not so rich and gaudy as this," answered Lucy; "still," continued she, with some pride, "you will find at Davenne, at all seasons, what my country alone can produce—real English turf, as green as only itself ever is, and as soft as velvet."

"I shall admire it very much," said Antonio; "indeed I feel inclined beforehand to admire everything that is English."

"Do you!" was the reply, in a little joyous, triumphant tone. "Oh, then, come to England soon, and I shall be your cicerone there!"

"In that case I must not go for a long time," said the Italian, jokingly; "or have you forgotten that you are to stay here, and build a cottage out of spite to somebody or other?"

"I wish it were true; I could stay here willingly all my life," said Lucy, simply.

"Could you, indeed!" exclaimed Antonio with a thrill in his voice, while a column of blood rushed to his face.

She looked up to him.

"But you can't," he added gravely, nay, with a touch of despondency, "you know you cannot. What would the world say," he went on with an awkward attempt to laugh, "if the daughter of Sir John Davenne were to desert her place in society, and bury herself in an obscure Italian village!"

He paused slightly, it might be for an answer, then continued,—"Rank and riches are chains of gold, but still chains. It was Seneca, was it not, who said that a great fortune was a great servitude?"

"I fear so," answered Lucy, with a sigh that would not be kept down.

The couple moved on in silence. It was a treat to see them walk leisurely along—he measuring his steps to hers, and supporting her with such gentle care—she leaning on his arm so confidingly, so complacently. Both young, elegant, and graceful—both bearing about them that cast of distinction which characterizes refined natures; yet with so much in common, how different in type! Lucy all golden hues and softness, Antonio all dark shades and energy;—her little cherub's head bending gracefully forwards as if in search of a stay, his so resolutely set upon his shoulders;—her step so light and childlike, his so manly and steady, as if at every stride he took possession, in right of some unknown power, of every bit of ground he walked upon. Such a contrast, and yet such a harmony—strength and weakness blended together! Every characteristic feature of the one setting forth to advantage and giving zest to that of the other—the fiery black diamond casting lustre over the oriental pearl, the oriental pearl in return lending softness to the black diamond!

While Doctor Antonio and Miss Davenne were, notwithstanding sighs and little misgivings, enjoying this first morning's saunter together, they were inflicting real suffering on an unsuspected witness of their *tête-à-tête*. Battista, of course, was every day, and all day, at the Osteria, most of the time in the garden, where he used to smoke his pipe, and have a peep at Miss Davenne from some convenient place, probably with the design of getting clear of his perplexities about her.

Sir John having complained of the unwonted odour of tobacco infesting his apartments, Battista had renounced his pipe, but not his observations, which he carried on most perseveringly, comforting himself with chewing the fragrant weed the while. Now, Lucy never having ventured out of the house before, her presence close to his daily post came quite unawares upon Speranza's lover, who hastened to take himself and his confusion as far from the young lady and her companion as the limits of the little enclosure would allow, in the hope of being able to make his exit when they should have turned towards the house again. But to his great mortification, instead of turning, they continued their walk directly towards him, and thus cut off his meditated retreat through the garden gate, leaving him no alternative but to confront them, which he would not do, or of ignobly hiding behind the trunks of some trees, which he did, and where the Doctor's keen glance was not long in detecting him.

"Look at your devotee," said Antonio; "see how he is skulking behind those trees to avoid your presence. Shall we march straight upon him, and force him to extremities?"

"No," replied Lucy, thoughtfully.

"Are you tired? should you like to sit down?" asked Antonio.

"No, not yet, thank you, I would rather walk a little longer," and on they walked, Lucy still musing.

"Suppose," said she all at once, "you were to go to London and settle there?"

Antonio looked at her with unfeigned surprise, then answered, "Well, suppose I did, what great good would be obtained then?"

"Why," said Lucy, "with your talents and medical skill, and papa's interest, you would soon get a large practice, and make a fortune."

"Did we not agree," retorted Antonio, with a smile, "that fortune might be a drawback?"

"True," replied Lucy, rather abashed, "yet it seems

so natural—does it not?—to try and better one's condition."

"Well, but will a fortune better my condition?" said Antonio, doubtingly—"that is the question. Let us take it for granted that the practical difficulties of the plan you recommend are overcome; let us assume that my fortune is made. I am rich then, but to what purpose? and mark first at what cost: at the cost of a complete exile from my country, at that of all my inclinations and habits, of much that cheers my heart and eyes, of the familiar tongue, of my dear warm sun and blue sea, of those orange groves, wafting to me perfumed recollections of my sweet Sicily. These things, light losses to many perhaps, would be heavy ones to me, yet to be borne, were the aim to be reached worth the sacrifice. But such an aim is exactly wanting for me. My mother, thank God, is tolerably provided for; my other relations well off. As for myself, I really should be at a loss to say what increase of comforts Fortune could bring to me."

Antonio paused, but as Lucy was silent, he continued—

"A fine mansion?—but I feel lodged like a prince in my little dwelling at Bordighera, larger, after all, than I require, and which, for situation and the prospect it commands, beats many a lordly château. To be sure I have no velvet carpets nor double green-baize doors. What use is there for such things in this genial climate, where the winters are so short and mild, that I scarcely think of having a fire lighted? A rich table?—but mine is the table of an epicure: no need here to be a man of capital, no need of forcing-houses to have the luxuries of the table at command. Equipages and horses?—have I not my *calessino* and shaggy little horse? Then I dislike riding and driving, and never feel so happy as when I can have a good walk, fanned by this wholesome, sweet-scented sea-breeze. So that, all things considered," wound up the Italian, as if his discourse must have brought conviction home to his patient listener, "you see that a fortune could do nothing for my real comforts."

As he stopped, he was struck by the pallor that had succeeded to the vivid blush on Lucy's cheek. "You are over-tired," he said, "let us go in at once."

Lucy's womanly instinct had been sharply roused by what Antonio had said, and left unsaid. The apparent indifference with which he had received and treated her proposal, without so much as alluding at least to one argument, whose mention seemed so naturally called for by the wish she had just been expressing, of remaining where she was for life; the sort of affectation with which he had dwelt upon his reasons for being content with his lot,—all this had affected her painfully. Lucy had no conception of that firm self-control which enables a man to rein in at once an involuntary emotion, and hold straight on along the highroad of common sense. Antonio, whatever his object, had purposely viewed the idea she had thrown out in an exclusively matter-of-fact way women can hardly bear, and are always hurt by, the more or the less depending on the relation in which they stand to the speaker. The one instinct awoke another, which bid her conceal her wounded feeling, and she saw no better means of doing so than going on resolutely with the subject.

"Be it all as you say," resumed Lucy, "yet you must, at all events, admit that in London your abilities and knowledge would be better appreciated than here; and there must be satisfaction in being properly valued. I suppose you are not insensible to fame?"

"Fame!" echoed Antonio, smiling; "have you forgotten Dante's definition of fame? '*Non è il romor mondan altro che un fiato—Di vento ch'or va quindi ed or va quinci.*"*

"It sounds so sad and unnatural," said Lucy, "to hear one so young talk as if he had not one spark of ambition left."

"I beg your pardon," retorted the Doctor, quickly; "I

---

* ". . . . . the noise
Of worldly fame is but a blast of wind,
That blows from divers points."—*Cary.*

have an ambition, and a great one, that of serving my country, and doing my best in her cause."

"What chance is there of your doing that cause more good here, situated as you are, than in London?"

"Very little, certainly; however, should any movement take place in Sicily, or in any other part of this peninsula, as sooner or later must be the case, think how much more speedily and easily I could join it from here than from London."

"You are fondly devoted to your country," said Lucy.

"Who is not?" replied Antonio.

"Are you sure that the cause you are engaged in is the rightful cause?"

"As sure as I am that there is a God in heaven," answered Antonio, solemnly; "what makes you ask?"

"You must make allowance for—for my prejudices, I suppose," said Lucy. "I have heard so many strictures passed on Italian character, not only by papa, but by many other of my countrymen,—I have heard so much said against the Liberal party in Italy, particularly while we were at Rome, that"—Lucy hesitated.

—"That you are rather inclined to think they must be in the wrong," said Antonio, finishing the sentence for her. "I do not wonder at it, nor do I wonder at the opinions you have heard expressed by Englishmen on these subjects. The sympathies of the strong and the powerful are seldom with the weak and the oppressed. Do you recollect how ingenious Job's friends were in proving that it was his fault if he lay covered with sores on the dunghill? Such is the common tendency of human selfishness in presence of suffering, in order to dispense with compassion and assistance. That our national character may be open to objections, (pray shew me the people whose character is not,) that busybodies, nay, evil, self-seeking spirits may be found in the ranks of the national party—where are they not?—I can readily admit. Far be it from me to hold out my country as a pattern of perfection. Italians are men like other men, with their share of man's greatness and man's weakness. Look through the world, study the history of mankind, and what is the lesson they teach?—one of reciprocal forbearance and indulgence. But," proceeded he with growing animation, "believe me, Miss Davenne, when I say, what I am ready to proclaim aloud, and to seal with my blood if necessary, that Italy is a noble, much trampled on, much wronged country, and her cause one as holy as truth and justice can make a cause. Excuse my warmth," continued Antonio, relapsing into his usual sedate manner; "but if you knew the hundredth part of the self-devotion and sacrifice spent in behalf of this ill-fated land, with no better meed from the world than sneering indifference, you would, I am sure, sympathize with my feelings."

A tear trembled in Lucy's eyes as she replied, "But I do sympathize with your feelings,—I wish so very much you would tell me all about your country."

"I will some day, at least about Sicily," said Antonio; "but now you really need some rest, and see, there comes your drawing-master."

Lucy's drawing-master, side by side with Sir John, was indeed hurrying across the garden, talking all the while in a thundering voice, and accompanying what he said with frantic gesticulations. Had it not been for Sir John, the big-headed little man would, notwithstanding Doctor Antonio's loud calls, have passed on without noticing Miss Davenne or her cavalier.

"What on earth has happened?" cried the Doctor.

"A piece of such rare impudence as passes imagination!" ejaculated the drawing-master, stopping short, and throwing his hat on the ground in a rage.—"*Cose incredibili, orrende, mostruose!* Can you believe that now, when the organ-builder is come from Nice to set up the organ, the Count after all his promises refuses to receive him, and flatly denies that he ever engaged to give him a room in his palazzo? Denies it, sir, with the minute of our proceeding of the 19th November 1839, every word of which I myself wrote down at

the time and place,—with that minute, I say, staring him in
the face, the mean, stingy fellow! I will make ten thousand
copies of that minute, and of that of this morning's meeting, and to every copy I will affix in red ink this verse of
Berchet,"—and he recited with immense emphasis the following four lines:—

> "Vile, un manto d'infamia hai tessuto
> L'hai voluto, sul dosso ti sta;
> Nè per pianger, o vil, che farai,
> Nessun mai dal tuo dosso il torrà."
>
> LITERAL TRANSLATION.
> Coward! thou hast woven a mantle of infamy,
> Thou hast chosen it, it hangs on thy back;
> Nor for tears that thou mayest shed,
> Will any one ever take it off thy back.

"Yes; I will spread and distribute these copies all over the
Riviera, and have this noble Count hissed in our streets and
highways, I will brand him, and hand him down to posterity
as the barefaced impostor he is."

Having made this passionate declaration, the incensed
little body stopped to take breath, picked up his hat, and
with quite a dramatic change of look and gesture, said gallantly to Miss Davenne—

"I rely on the Signorina's well-known goodness to excuse
me from giving her a lesson to-day. I am in no mood for it;
and I have arrangements to make with regard to this unpleasant affair, which render my presence in Bordighera imperative;"—then, turning to Antonio, he added, with a solemnity that more than bordered on the ludicrous,—

"Of one thing you may rest assured, my friend, the Confraternity of the Reds shall come out of this difficulty with
honour, though it be at the cost of all I possess in the
world;" so saying, he trotted out of the garden, first giving
his hat such a resolute thump on his head as to send it down
over his eyes.

"Had you not better follow him?" said kind Miss Lucy
to Doctor Antonio. "If he were to meet the Count while

he is in such a passion, I am afraid there would be some mischief."

"Do not make yourself uneasy as to that," replied Antonio, smiling; "with all his fury and blaze, our little friend is a most peaceful creature, he would not hurt a fly willingly. If he were to meet the Count just now, he would probably show his displeasure by a peculiarly stately bow, or at the worst by a volley of harmless verses, hurled *in petto* at his *pro tempore* foe."

"But what is all this fury about?" asked Lucy. "I could not find out what made him so angry."

"I must begin by telling you," said Antonio, "that the Count is *priore*, (president,) and your drawing-master *sotto-priore* (vice-president) of the Confraternity of the Reds. But you know nothing of the Reds or the Whites. Suppose, as you are to have no lesson, that I were to give you a lecture on Confraternities."

Before Lucy could answer, Sir John said, "Ay, pray do, Doctor Antonio; and instead of going to the balcony, let us have chairs out here, and listen to the Doctor's story under these orange-trees."

When they were all seated, Antonio began:—

"As I told you more than once before, the parish church, its embellishment, the splendour of the church services, and processions, are the great interest, indeed the only public excitement accessible to the mass of the laity here. The parish church, with its church-wardens, choristers, and officials of all sorts, affords scope, however, to the activity of only a limited number of persons. To remedy this inconvenience, there have arisen, under the wing of the parent establishment, brotherhoods of many colours, whose business it is to assemble in a place of worship of their own for prayer in common, to bury their dead, and under one pretext or another, continually muster in processions. There are here, as in every little town of the Riviera, Confraternities of the Reds, the Whites, and the Blacks, so named from the colour of the hooded robes worn by the brethern. Each of these associations, naturally not over-friendly the one to the other, has a numerous staff of dignitaries and functionaries—a prior and under-prior, a prioress and under-prioress, a chapter, or body of councillors, choristers, crucifix-bearers, standard-bearers, mace-bearers, lamp-bearers, and so on, whose annual election, especially that of the *priore* and *sotto-priore*, and chapter, set the brethren in a blaze. Thus, you see, every one of these societies becomes a small focus of petty ambitions, rivalries, intrigue, and gossip. What wonder, if, in the state of utter ignorance wherein the majority are kept, and which renders them incapable of intellectual enjoyments and pursuits—if in their exclusion from all participation, even in the management of their parish affairs, or of anything to do with those local interests, such as are confided in England to corporations,—what wonder, I say, if, in the absence of legitimate sources of excitement, as necessary to man as the very air he breathes, these good folks should fall back on futile and childish occupations?"

"Ah!" interrupted Sir John, knowingly, "an absolute government cannot help much of what you complain of, Doctor Antonio; change one thing, and all the rest tumble about your ears. But after all, you do not mean to say, that the different parishes do not elect their own town-councillors, out of whose number, I suppose, the mayor is chosen?"

"Elect their own town-councillors!" cried Antonio, "not even in a dream. A mad dog has not greater horror of water than our ruling powers of the elective principle. Municipal institutions are a dead letter here—a body without a soul, a mere mockery. Do you wish to know who chooses the mayor and town-councillors? The late mayor, (necessarily a creature of the government, or he wouldn't have been a mayor,) the Curé, and the officer of the Carabineers, these three make out a list, which is placed before the Commandant for approval and revision. The Commandant sends it duly revised and approved to the Intendente, (the chief civil magistrate of the province,) who in his turn forwards it to Turin, where it receives the official confirmation. As to your observation," continued Antonio, turning to Sir John, "that all I complain of is the unavoidable consequence of an absolute government, I can only ask, If any particular form of government avowedly works badly, why should it find defenders and upholders among those who would not submit to it in their own country?"

Sir John pursed up his lips most ominously, but did not speak.

"I now come to the kernel of the matter," said Antonio, without appearing to notice the cloud on the Baronet's brow. "The Chapter of the Reds, the Count presiding, as usual, some time ago voted a sum for the purchase of an organ for their own little church, or oratorio, as they call it—money is never wanting for such objects. At a later period, and when the organ in question was almost finished, the Chapter met again to consider the propriety of voting a further sum to defray the travelling expenses and the stay here of the organ-builder. It was on this occasion that the Count declared he would take all that upon himself, and receive the organ-builder at his own palazzo, whereupon there was a unanimous vote of thanks to the Count. This took place in that famous sitting of the 19th November 1839, to which the drawing-master just now referred. It would seem that the Count, who has the reputation of being a stingy man, wishes now to take back his word, and refuses to fulfil his promise. *Inde ira.*"

Sir John fumed a good deal on hearing this, and protested that there must be some gross mistake in the statement of the drawing-master. The Count a stingy man! Nonsense! He had put his Casino at his (Sir John's) disposal, twenty times over. A nobleman like the Count was incapable of such shabby tricks. He would see the Count himself, and have the whole matter cleared up.

Sir John was as good as his word. On the evening of that same day he had a long conversation with the Count, the upshot of which was, that on the morrow the organ-builder was installed in the Count's palazzo, to the infinite satisfaction of all parties.

CHAPTER XIII.
In the Boat.

ONE afternoon, as Lucy, arm-in-arm with her father, was strolling as usual about the garden, Antonio a few paces in front of them, the latter took the bar off the little gate that opened on the beach, and led the way down a gentle slope to the seaside. The path, as smooth and carefully swept as a gravelled garden walk, (we suspect Battista of having had some hand in this,) was bordered on either side by a quantity of yellow, white, and pink flowers, shooting out of the dry sand as brisk and vivacious as if planted in the richest soil. Lucy was so taken up observing, admiring, and picking them, and so intent on listening to Antonio's explanations about this particular genus of marine plants, that she did not notice Battista with another man, standing by a boat with a gaily-striped awning, its bow already in the water, till she came close to them.

"Oh, what a pretty boat!" exclaimed she.

"The boat and the crew are here for your service, if you feel inclined to make use of them," said Antonio to her.

"Thank you, I shall enjoy a row on this beautiful, beautiful sea so much!" exclaimed Lucy in high glee. "You have no objection, papa? But," added she with some timidity, "will it be safe to go with only two men?"

"You will be as safe as in your balcony," replied Antonio. "Battista is a first-rate boatman as well as sailor, no one more expert in the management of sail or oar. The countrymen of Columbus are well known as capital seamen, allowed to be so even by the English, who are proud, and justly so, of their superiority on the sea. An intelligent Government," continued Antonio, as he handed Lucy into the boat, "would work wonders with such elements; but—" and the complement of the sentence was a shrug and a sigh.

Lucy looked at the speaker, and said, "Now, we are none of us to think of Governments or politics; we are going to enjoy ourselves this afternoon." There was so much of the woman's kindness mixed with the girl's buoyancy in this, that the Italian did not feel sore at the remark. Lucy only liked to hear Antonio talk of the troubles of his country when Sir John was not present.

There was not a ripple on the sea, whose bright blue was only now and then chequered by broad white streaks—milky paths on the azure—some stretching forth in straight lines, others winding forward in graceful zig-zags. Battista and his comrade put forth the strength of their brawny arms, the former keeping his eyes carefully averted from Miss Davenne, who lay back on the cushioned seat, parting the water by the boat's side with her delicate fingers, deep in pleasant imaginings, it would seem, from the half smile on her lips. Swiftly they glided past the Cape of Bordighera, and then a new and splendid panorama opened out before them.

A glorious extent of hilly coast against a background of lofty mountains, stretched semicircularly from east to west, broken all along into capes and creeks, and studded with towns and villages, full of original character,—Ventimiglia, with its crown of dismantled mediæval castles,—Mentone, so gay on the sunny beach, well named Roccabruna, all sombre hues and frowns,—Turbia, and its Roman monument, a record of the greatest power on earth, covering with its shadow the lilliputian principality of Monaco below,— Villafranca and its lighthouse. Further on, running southward, loomed vaporous in the distance, the long, low strip of French shore, with Antibes at its extremity; and further still, in the west, the fanciful blue lines of the mountains of Provence. Here and there a snowy peak shot boldly above the rest; some hoary parent Alp, one might fancy, looking down to see that all went right among the younger branches.

Lucy's eyes and soul feasted in silence on this prospect,

over which the warm tints of the setting sun cast a magical splendour of unspeakable effect. As the sense of the beauties amid which she lived grew every day stronger upon our sweet English girl, she gradually found out how empty and inadequate to express what she felt were those everyday set forms of admiration, of which she had been so profuse at first. Sir John, on the contrary, though long familiar with this scene, was enthusiastic in his praises of it, ending with a lament that the Osteria was not on this side of the Cape of Bordighera.

But the Gulf of Spedaletti, and the three well-known head-lands to the east, found an eager advocate in Lucy, who insisted on their superiority. She allowed that the view towards the coast of France was the more varied and extensive of the two; but she declared that it wanted the harmonious unity and character of melancholy grandeur which marked the view from the Osteria. "A painter," said Lucy, "might prefer the former; but a poet, I am sure, would find the latter more suggestive of thoughts and images going home to the heart."

"Heyday!" laughed Sir John, looking fondly and proudly at the fair speaker, "is my pet going to turn poet herself?"

"Who knows?" retorted the smiling girl, with a guilty blush. Indeed, she felt as if she were.

Between two richly wooded hillocks, a little to the westward of Bordighera, appeared the white Palazzino of the Count, now all in a purple glow. "There's a glorious situation for you," exclaimed Sir John, pointing it out to his daughter.

"The Count is a man of taste," said Antonio, "he chose the site, and gave the plan of his casino himself."

"He is a cleverer fellow, then, than I thought," observed the Baronet; "it stands exactly where it ought."

"Does it not?" replied the Doctor. "Transport it in imagination anywhere else, and it will lose something by the change."

"What you say of the Count's casino, might be said, I

think, of all the numerous towns and villages that we see from here," said Lucy; "no one could wish them moved higher or lower, to the right or to the left, by way of making them look prettier or more picturesque. Even the most insignificant hamlet seems just where it looks best on its own account, and where it adds most to the effect of the whole. Do you not think so, Doctor Antonio?"

"To such an *impartial* admirer," answered Antonio, smiling on her, "I may venture to say, that the race which inhabits this country is a race of unconscious artists. They possess an uncultivated but decided appreciation of the beautiful, the workings of which are as clearly traceable in the choice of a situation, and the building of a town or village, as in the choice and arrangement of a flower in the women's hair. Perhaps Nature has so ordained it, that man's works should not be at odds with her own in this privileged land. If you observe the attitudes and gestures of these people, the way in which they mingle the colours, and the grace with which they wear their simple costume, you will at once detect an inborn nicety of taste, for which they are indebted to the medium in which they live. Take, for instance, the head-gear of the men, nothing but a red pouch lined with brown, or the coloured kerchief which the women tie round their heads; can anything be more simple! yet see in how many different ways, and all picturesque, they contrive to wear them. The peasant girl, who carries on her head or under her arm the bundle of grass for her cow, never forgets to hang at one of its ends a bunch of red poppies, or of blue corn-flowers, or any other flower of the season. How often I have seen originals of Leopold Robert's two famous pictures here!"

"Are the women generally handsome?" asked Lucy.

"Yes—that is, they have all the characteristics of a fine race," replied Antonio; "long, well-cut eyes, rich hair, fine necks, on which the head is well placed, small wrists, ankles, and feet. But many of these beauties are lost or spoiled by over-exertion, or neglect, their hair in particular. You have a good specimen of the women of this country in Speranza."

"Ah! she is really very beautiful!" exclaimed Lucy, with such enthusiasm, that Sir John stared, then said,—

"Is she? well, it is odd that I never found it out."

"That is because you have not looked enough at her, papa," retorted Lucy, laughing. "If you had tried to draw her picture twenty times, as I have done, you would have found out the exquisite purity and elegance of all the lines about her."

"Well done, Miss Lucy; where did you pick up all this fine artist's talk?" cried the somewhat amazed father. "I suppose, Doctor Antonio, the medium you are so fond of talking about is affecting my little English girl?"

"Probably," answered the Doctor, with one of his quiet smiles. "However, I agree with Miss Davenne. Speranza is a beauty; and I never see her washing her linen at the fountain, without thinking of Homer's description of Nausicaa. If the rest of her person were as faultless as her head and her bust, Rosa's daughter might sit for a Hebe. As it is, the going to the wood and carrying great weights, spoils the finest proportions."

"I must take a good look of this beauty when we reach home," said Sir John.

The boat, now on its way back, was just opposite Bordighera. "What is that on the height, a little way in front of the town," asked Lucy, "that looks like a bit of a ruin?"

"It is, or rather was, an open battery. By the by, there is a story in connexion with it, in which, as the English are concerned, you may take an interest."

"I hope it is not something against them," said Lucy.

"Judge for yourself," replied the Doctor.—"On a calm day of July 1812, an English brig-of-war came in sight of Bordighera, and, with or without a motive, ran so close in shore as to place herself under the battery of the town. Now, the officers in command of the batteries along the coast had precise orders to fire upon all English vessels chancing to come within reach of cannon shot. The Riviera in those times belonged, by right of the strongest, to France. The French lieutenant, who, at the head of a dozen men, happened to be in command of this battery on this particular day of 21st July, must have been, to all appearance, a sober-minded man, without a particle of "*furia Francese*" in his blood, for he saw the enemy's progress with perfect coolness, and without making any hostile preparation. But a conduct so philosophical was far from suiting the good folks of Bordighera, who had reckoned on something better. It was not every day that brought to the quiet and rather dull citizens of the little town such a good chance of sport and excitement as an English vessel to fire upon; and they were determined to make the most of it. So they came in numbers to the battery, and uproariously insisted that the officer should carry into effect the instructions he held, by at once firing upon the audacious brig. The lieutenant, not daring to take upon himself the responsibility of a refusal, yielded a grudging assent, but first, though every rope of the rigging was distinctly visible to the naked eye, he reconnoitred the enemy through an immense spyglass; and so long did the survey last, that it might have been suspected he was not without a secret hope that the vessel which had placed itself in his way, and in harm's way, would move off. However, it did not; there it lay, as idle 'as a painted ship upon a painted ocean.' There was nothing else for it, so the order was given to load and fire an old eight-pounder. The aim was pretty good, since part of the enemy's bowsprit was demolished. Again the Frenchman looked through his glass; there was a great bustle on board the brig, and then the boats were lowered, for an attack no doubt; and many were the curses that he launched at the blockheads who had brought him and themselves into such a scrape. When lo! instead of approaching the land, the boats were observed to be towing the brig as fast as they could out of the little bay. You may imagine the triumphant exultation of these Falstaffs of Bordighera; the huzzas with which they celebrated their bloodless victory must have been heard by those on board, though the projectiles with which they were accompanied fell short of their aim.

"One fine day, two months later, the same brig hove in sight, making for Bordighera in a very decided manner, but this time in company with a small frigate and another brig, which came up right and left, bringing their guns to bear so as to command the high road, and cut off any succour either from the side of Genoa or that of Nice. This done, the first brig fired a broadside, but evidently not intended to do much harm, since only one man was killed. At the same time, a hundred sailors and marines were landed, and marched straight on the battery. The struggle was neither long nor sanguinary; the old eight-pounder was spiked, and the lieutenant and his dozen men locked into the guard-room. It is said that only two out of the warlike citizens were to be discovered in the town—the mayor, Mr. Giribaldi, was one; the other a hero whose name is lost to history, who, at sight of the red uniforms, fired his gun at random, and ran away. The English carried the mayor on board the frigate, sentenced him to—an excellent dinner, and sent him back in the evening in a very jovial state, the key of the guard-room in his pocket. Thus terminated the war between Bordighera and Great Britain, for at sunrise the next morning, there was no trace of frigate or brigs."

As the Doctor finished his story, the latter part of which had tickled Sir John amazingly, the boat gently forcing its way through the sand, came to a full stop also. Antonio jumped out and offered his hand to Lucy; but Lucy playfully put it aside, and sprang on shore without assistance. Antonio uttered an exclamation of alarm.

"Well done, Lucy!" cried the Baronet, who had seen the whole transaction, and was highly amused by Antonio's rueful countenance. "Ha! ha! the patient is asserting her independence, and going to give her doctor the slip."

What was there in these words, spoken without any *malice prepense*, nay, most good-humouredly, to cast a gloom over Doctor Antonio's brow! He evidently attached to them a meaning they had not. All men, even those with healthy, well-balanced minds, have their hours of over-sensitiveness, and it is probable that our Doctor was in one of those pleasant hours. He made no reply to Sir John's vivacious sally, and walked on alone. Lucy, with that quick perceptiveness that affection gives, understood his silence, and, going up to his side, complained of being tired. Antonio immediately gave her his arm, and the three returned to the Osteria in unbroken silence. What party, large or small, and bent on a pleasure expedition, ever did return in the self-same mood in which they set out? Once at the house, Antonio took his leave, then suddenly coming back, said, with what was studied carelessness, "By the by, Sir John, I think this is your forty-eighth day of bondage." The colour fled from Lucy's cheek.

"Is it?" asked Sir John, in some surprise.

"Yes, and the day of your deliverance also," pursued Antonio, quickly. "It is my pleasant duty to tell you, that Miss Davenne is sufficiently recoverd to bear the fatigue of a journey without danger or inconvenience."

Wonder of wonders! Sir John does not leap for joy at this announcement, does not throw himself, in a transport of gratitude, on his deliverer's neck, or madly shake his hand, but lets him depart with an embarrassed "Ah! indeed —very well, thank you," and follows Lucy into the house without another word. How is it that Sir John receives this longed-for piece of news with such marked coolness? Is he not the same man who, but a few weeks ago, would have willingly purchased his release from the wretched Osteria with half his year's income? No, Sir John is not the same man—Sir John is altered, Sir John has grown lazy, has no energy to take a resolution, lacks the courage to say "tomorrow, next day, next week." The elderly gentleman has insensibly taken the colour of the medium in which he is living. The sky, the sea, the soft, sweet-scented air, have all told upon him also. Hannibal has found his Capua.

O Italy, fair Italy! thine is the imperishable spell to soften and subdue all natures, however rugged and rebellious: all on whom thy warm breath plays yield to thee. Many have come to thee in hatred and defiance, lance in rest, who, no sooner had they tasted the sweet milk of thy breast, than they laid down their arms, blessed thee, and called thee "Mother." Thy history is full of such conquests, O parent land of many beauties and sorrows!

Sir John sat down silently and moodily. Lucy's intent gaze seemed as if it would read his innermost thoughts; and it was with anxious trepidation that she awaited the result of his brown study. There was a frown on the Baronet's forehead—the frown of a man at a loss to see clearly into his own mind and feelings. Light dawned on him at last, and showed him the inconvenience of leaving Bordighera just then. His collection of plants for Davenne was not yet completed, and really Lucy's health was so improved, it would be a pity to go away without some pressing necessity; and since Aubrey could not be in London before the end of August at the soonest, it might be as well to let Lucy have as long as possible of the air which seemed to suit her. As he came to this conclusion, Sir John's features relaxed, and brightened like those of a man who had solved a riddle. "After all," said he, rising, "it is pleasant to know that we can go away whenever we like, though I see no reason for setting off at once, as Doctor Antonio proposes, unless my darling wishes to do so."

"Oh, no, papa! pray, let us stay a little longer," replied Lucy, eagerly—"we are so comfortable here."

"Oh! comfortable, comfortable!" muttered the Baronet, with a comic mixture of testiness and satisfaction; "for my part, I confess I do not see these great comforts, unless the prospect of being broiled alive in this furnace of a country, which will be the case in a few days, be one in your eyes. However, before it gets too hot, we shall luckily be gone."

Sir John involuntarily sighed, and, quite reconciled to

himself by this little tirade, he left the room, without any suspicion that his daughter had sighed also, and from the depths of her young innocent heart, at the thought of leaving the Osteria. Sir John was no exception to the rule, that all papas and mammas have exactly that sort of sight, which distinguishes objects at a distance clearly, while they need spectacles to see those under their very nose.

Thus it came to pass, that two hours later, as Sir John was arranging his pieces on the chess-board, (Lucy having retired for the night,) he said to the taciturn Doctor,—"So you really think, Doctor Antonio, that this climate agrees particularly well with my daughter?"

Antonio looked with some surprise at his interlocutor, even paused an instant before answering, "You have only to compare the Miss Davenne of to-day with the Miss Davenne of a few weeks ago, to be able to answer the question yourself; no more cough, colour good, sleep and appetite both excellent—"

"It is your opinion, then," persisted Sir John, "that a longer stay here may tend to strengthen her constitution?"

Antonio felt an almost irresistible impulse to knock over table and chess-board to give the unsuspecting Englishman a hearty hug,—fathers of lovely daughters have no idea of the perils they run,—but gloriously conquered himself, and answered with proper professional dignity, "I have no doubt of it. This climate is as healthy as any in the world; and regular, quiet habits, and the absence of all excitement, are the real panacea for such delicate persons as Miss Davenne. A course of sea-baths during the hot season would, I am sure, do her good."

"In that case," replied the Baronet, "I suppose we must manage to remain here a little longer; now for our game, it is your turn to begin."

They played three games that evening. Sir John was so kind as to be wonderfully surprised at winning them all three. Antonio all the way to Bordighera sang, "O bell' alma innamorata," with an energy and expression that did credit to his lungs and musical taste.

CHAPTER XIV.
Sicily.

LATE on a warm summer evening, Sir John, Lucy, and Antonio, sat on the balcony, listening to the nightingales and watching the progress of the slow sinking moon. As the bright disk, lingering for a while on the top of the hill of Bordighera, shot, through its thick screen of trees, streams of light that quivered like fire, Lucy uttered a little cry of delight.

"Is not that like a volcano?" asked she; "I never saw one, but I fancy it must be like that," and she pointed to the hill.

"You are right," said Antonio: "it is so similar that it seems as though I were looking on my old familiar Etna in miniature. It recalls to me many a happy night, when, seated on the terrace-roof of my home in Catania, I watched the solemn signs of an impending eruption, and dreamed bright waking dreams of the future. The present," he continued, with a sad smile, "bears as little likeness to my dreaming as the red-hot liquid to the cold lava, that the *lazzaroni* shape into fanciful ornaments to catch a few '*grani*' from strangers."

This led to many a question from Lucy, and answers from the Doctor, about Etna, Catania, and Sicily, in the course of which Antonio had more than once occasion to stigmatize, in strong terms, what he called the mismanagement of his unfortunate native Island. Sir John could not hear this without entering his protest. "Come, come, be just," remonstrated the Baronet; "are kings, in a question which is one of life and death to them, to be allowed no right of self-defence?"

"Put your question the other way, and you will be nearer

the mark," retorted Antonio; "Is a nation to be allowed no right of protecting and defending its liberties and independence?"

"Certainly," said the Baronet; "but you go too far, too far by a great deal; if kings are sometimes driven to extremities, whose fault is it but that of the party with whom there is no possible transaction, I mean the ultra-democratic party, that will be satisfied with nothing short of implanting republics on the ruins of every throne?"

"Ultra-democratic party! republics!" exclaimed Antonio, in unfeigned amazement. "Who ever dreamed of a republic in Sicily? If we ever come to that, and it may be the case some day, it will be the Bourbons' own doing. The Sicilians are an essentially monarchical people; their traditions, habits, and customs are deeply rooted in monarchy. We owe our free institutions to kings, and through a long line of kings was Sicily respected and happy. When the storm of 1789 swept the Bourbons of Naples from off their continental dominions, where did they find safe shelter, assistance of all kind and devoted hearts, but in faithful, loyal Sicily? For all which what return they made the world knows. And who helped us to consolidate our political edifice, I mean who assisted in the framing of our Constitution of 1812—that Constitution in the name and defence of which Sicilians have been struggling and dying for the last eight-and-twenty years—but monarchical Great Britain?"

"Have you, then, a Parliament like ours?" asked Lucy.

"We had," answered Antonio, sadly.

"And why has it been abolished?" inquired Lucy. "You promised to tell me all about Sicily some day—pray, do so now."

"That was a rash promise," said Antonio, with a half smile, "the fulfilment of which would amount to nothing less than giving you a summary of Sicilian history, and I scarcely think your patience, or Sir John's, would last out the trial." However, Lucy insisted, Sir John expressed his willingness, and Antonio yielded. (The reader who objects to history in a work of fiction, has only to slip over the rest of the present chapter.)

"Sicilian liberties," * said Antonio, "are contemporaneous with those of England. As early as in the eleventh century, Sicily, under the auspices of a Norman Prince, like England, settled the foundations of her freedom and independence. The national sovereignty resided, *de facto*, in the Parliament, who disposed of the crown of the island, and no prince ever considered his title good or his power secure, unless based on an election by Parliament. The great objection felt to the Princes of the House of Anjou, was on the score that they were imposed by the Pontiff, and not elected by the nation. This, and no other, was the origin of the irritation, which exploded in the Sicilian Vespers (1282). It was the Parliament who, of its own free will, called to the throne the line of Arragon, in the person of Peter, and at a later period the Castilian, in that of Ferdinand the Catholic. And it is not amiss to note, that, at the death of the latter, his successor, Charles the Fifth, was not immediately acknowledged; was not till 1518 that he received the investiture from the Parliament, and swore, like his predecessors, to maintain intact the immunities and free customs of Sicily. It may seem strange that the Sicilian Autonomy passed unscorched through the fire of three centuries of union with Spain, but our wonder will cease when we reflect that the bond between Spain and Sicily was rather nominal than real, and that during this whole period, the island preserved its own national representation, its own laws, its own administration, flag, coin, and army. At the war of succession, in the beginning of the last century, the throne of Sicily was disputed along with all the other dominions of the deceased Charles the Second of Spain. The Treaty of Utrecht gave Sicily to Victor Amadeus of Savoy, who, by a

---

* Mémoire Historique sur les Droits Politiques de la Sicile, par MM. Bonaccorsi et Lumia. La Sicile et les Bourbons, par M. Amari, Membre du Parlement Sicilien. Gli Ultimi Rivolgimenti Italiani, Memorie Storiche di F. A. Gualterio. Vol. IV.

special clause of that Treaty, was bound 'to approve, confirm, and ratify, all the privileges, immunities, customs, &c., enjoyed by the island.' Thus the liberties of Sicily came to form part of the public right of Europe. But the sway of Victor Amadeus was of short duration, for, a little more than twenty years after, Cardinal Alberoni succeeded in tricking the Duke of Savoy out of Sicily, which once more of its own free-will united itself to the fortunes of Spain. The Bourbons began their rule by a scrupulous observance of the fundamental compact, and the two kingdoms of Naples and Sicily continued to be as independent and distinct, the one from the other, as during the reign of Philip the Second. When Charles the Third received at Palermo, in 1735, the crown of Sicily, and the homage of the National Representation, he in his turn took the oath of fidelity to the Constitution. And so did his son and successor, Ferdinand, who assumed the style of Ferdinand the Third of Sicily and Fourth of Naples, in order that the distinction of the two kingdoms should be made clear to all the world.

"The first years of his reign, under the guidance of the enlightened Tannucci, (Ferdinand was eight years of age when placed on the throne,) gave general satisfaction as far as regards Sicily, and this explains how the storm of 1789 passed over the island without disturbing its tranquillity. Happy and secure in a Constitution, which gave her the power of reform by pacific means, when necessary, why should she take part in a struggle that could bring her nothing better than what she already possessed? Meanwhile the thrones of Continental Europe were shaken from their foundations, and none more so than the Neapolitan. Will it be believed that this was the moment chosen to aim a blow at our secular liberties, and thus estrange the faithful Sicilians from their Sovereign? The Neapolitan Government had joined the coalition against France, and set about raising money, that great sinew of war. Our Parliament was accordingly applied to for a monthly grant of twenty thousand ounces (ten thousand pounds sterling) for as long as might be required. The Sicilian Parliament was composed of three parts, *braccia* we call them, that is, three arms or branches of the State; the nobility, the clergy, and, thirdly, the tenants of the Crown. A majority of the whole was required for the validity of any measure. The clergy and nobility did not oppose the grant, but they objected to there being no period specified for its duration. The dependants of the Crown alone voted the supply without restriction. King Ferdinand, by an audacious stretch of power, ordered that the vote of his tenants should stand good for that of the whole Parliament. This first attack on our rights, however, fell to the ground of itself; for just as a fierce resistance was on the eve of breaking out, the defeat of the Austro-Neapolitan army, under General Mack, leaving Naples at the mercy of the French, compelled the Court and its adherents to take refuge on board the English ships of war then in the bay.

"After having escaped many dangers on land, the Royal fugitives had to encounter the perils of the sea. Two days after their embarkation a violent storm arose, during which one of the young princes expired; but at length the rest were safely landed at Palermo. 'Men of Palermo,' cried Queen Caroline, as she stepped on the pier, 'will you receive your Queen?' At that moment all past grievances were forgotten, a general enthusiasm prevailed, and Ferdinand and Caroline were conducted in a sort of triumph to the Royal Palace, where they were soon surrounded by all their accustomed luxury. The inhabitants of Palermo could not do enough for their Majesties,—horses, carriages, plate, and money were supplied in abundance. The Sicilians felt confident that this arrival among them was to cement a firmer union, and secure a more permanent good understanding between the nation and the Sovereign. They were speedily undeceived. But of this period of four years, from 1799 to 1802, when, at the Peace of Amiens, the Royal family were restored to the throne of Naples, I shall say nothing, as it would be only giving the same picture, but with subdued colours, which I shall have to paint hereafter.

"In the year 1806, Ferdinand and his family were obliged once more to fly to Sicily. Like to all the Bourbons, experience and misfortune preached in vain to this Royal pair. Holding, as they did, to the hope of reconquering Naples by the aid and resources of Sicily, it would have seemed but natural that they should carefully avoid, if only out of policy, hurting the feelings of the islanders. But quite the contrary. First of all, the Court laid violent hands on the *Monti di Pietà*, the patrimony of the poor. The money invested in the bank on Government security by private individuals was next seized; the property of absentees, whether that of friends or foes mattered nothing, was confiscated; and the sums thus collected went to fatten the Neapolitan *émigrés*, who swarmed at Court, and who, according to a grave historian, Colletta, were nothing better than 'rogues, cowards, the worst consciences of the kingdom.' Every post in the Administration, (and remember the Court was in Sicily,) every office, every charge, every honour was bestowed on Neapolitans, and Neapolitans alone. A system of political delation was organized. No public place, no drawing-room, but was infested by spies; the very privacy of families was not safe from their intrusion. The Government sniffed Jacobins everywhere. A person was imprisoned solely because he had often been seen to converse with a friend of his, who had been exiled on the charge of Jacobinism,—*pro crebris conversationibus*. A citizen was banished for having read a certain newspaper with pleasure,—*pro lecturâ Gazettarum cum delectatione*. There was no end to the petty vexations exercised against those who wore whiskers and pantaloons, both considered as the outward signs of Jacobinism.

"King Ferdinand was one of the weakest of the Spanish Bourbons: so that he could hunt or fish with his low associates, be the King of Nimrods, or Lazzaroni, he little cared who enacted the part of King of the Two Sicilies. His wife, the absolute, iron-willed, unscrupulous Caroline of Austria, ruled him completely. This ambitious woman could not make up her mind to the loss of the Neapolitan throne. The rapid and immense success and fortune of the Napoleon dynasty depriving her at last of all hope of regaining Naples by the sole help of the Sicilians, and of a few English vessels, she bethought herself of trying a new experiment. She entered into a secret negotiation with Napoleon himself, through the medium of her niece, Maria Louisa. Napoleon kept her at bay some time, holding out hopes that he would finally restore Naples to her, and give her the March of Ancona into the bargain, provided she managed to get rid of the English.

"If the Bourbons of Naples still wore a crown, it was, undoubtedly, thanks to the English, and it was not for those reaping the advantage to argue, whether there was more of self-interest than generosity in the opposition offered by England to France, wherever it was found possible. That an English fleet had saved the king and royal family in 1799; that English blood had been freely shed at Maida, and English gold freely spent for them, (from 1805 the king had received a yearly subsidy of three hundred and eighty thousand pounds, which was raised to four hundred thousand in 1809;) that from ten to fifteen thousand English soldiers were in the island for their protection—all these were notorious facts. It was natural to expect, at least, a candid policy from those accepting of these favours. But neither common gratitude nor common honesty were the distinguishing attributes of Ferdinand and his queen. The English did at last get scent of Caroline's machinations. The details are up to this day shrouded in mystery, but damning proofs of their reality exist among the papers in the Foreign Office at Paris.

"Up to 1810, England remained an attentive but passive looker-on of all that was passing in the island; that year, however, she roused herself to action. Lord Amherst was recalled, and Lord William Bentinck sent in his place as

Minister Plenipotentiary from Great Britain, and Commander-in-Chief of the British forces in the Mediterranean.

"The English Ambassador found Palermo in a high state of excitement, occasioned by a new outrage committed by the Court on the very eve of his arrival. The large sums voted by the Sicilian Parliament the year before being exhausted, the King, urged on by his Camarilla, resolved on obtaining fresh supplies without troubling the representatives of the country. For this end, the Council of State, composed, with one single exception, of Neapolitans, was convened, and from its deliberation emanated the three Decrees which threw Palermo into such a ferment. By the first, all the landed property of religious bodies and of parishes was arbitrarily declared to be Crown property; and in order more promptly to realize the value, a second decree organized a lottery, in which the lands aforesaid were to be the prizes. The third established a tax of one per cent. on all sales of whatever kind.

"The indignation at these measures was general, and Parliament acted as the mouthpiece of this indignation. Forty-three of the nobles of the Baronial branch signed an energetic protestation, and had it laid before the King. He did not make them wait long for an answer. In the night of the 5th July 1811, the Princes of Belmonte, Castelnuovo, Villa Franca, Aci, and the Duke d'Angio, considered as the ringleaders of the opposition, were arrested, and embarked for different prisons in the neighbouring islands.

"It was just at this crisis that Lord William Bentinck appeared, and his advent was hailed by the Sicilians as that of a saviour. While on one side he did his best to calm the popular effervescence, on the other he made energetic representations to the King and ministers, on the imprudence and folly of the course they had entered upon,—but in vain. 'That fat serjeant,' said the Queen, who had taken a hatred of him, 'was sent here by the Prince Regent to make his bow to the King, and not to lay down the law.' Unable to overcome this obstinacy, Lord William went back to England to explain to the Cabinet of Saint James's the actual state of affairs in Sicily. After a six weeks' absence he returned to Palermo, and this time with full powers to adopt any measures he deemed advisable. The Englishman was not one to let himself be made a fool of; so finding that the conferences, to which he was continually summoned by king, queen, and heir-apparent, led to no answers of the very categorical demands he had presented, he cut the matter short by very decided conduct on his own part. He began by suspending the supplies of money furnished by England to the royal family, established his head-quarters at Palermo, and brought thither some of the English troops from Messina. These steps producing no effect, he threatened to put himself at the head of his army, take Palermo, seize the King and Queen, and send them off to London. As Lord William was known to be a man to keep his word, the business was soon settled. The King had an official illness, and naming the Prince-Royal Vicar-General of the kingdom, he went for change of air to his Park of Ficuzza. The Queen also left Palermo; the command of the Sicilian army was given to Lord William; the five barons were set at liberty, and the illegal decrees annulled. At the same time, the three branches of the Legislature were called together for the avowed purpose of reforming the Constitution.

"The Prince-Vicar opened Parliament in person, and after a speech on the subject of the intended changes, proposed the Constitution of Great Britain as guide for that now contemplated for Sicily. The first meeting of Parliament, prolonged through the whole of the night, and even part of the next day, will always be marked in our annals as bearing witness to the patriotic devotion of all its members. The clergy, renouncing their privileges, agreed to unite themselves to the barons, so as to form one chamber of peers. The barons on their side gave up all those hereditary rights, of which, from time immemorial, they had shown themselves so jealous. On that night feudality ceased to exist in Sicily. Twelve articles, after long debates, were agreed to, as those on which to raise the new Constitution. As the Sovereign's sanction was necessary, the Parliament, unwilling to run the risk of future subterfuge, prayed the Prince-Vicar to obtain the King's approbation before affixing his own signature. The Prince wrote a letter to the King to that effect, and in the margin of this letter the King wrote with his own hand, 'This being in conformity to my intention, I authorize you to do it.'

"Notwithstanding this, the Court party was busy hatching a plot against the openly approved of reform. A day was fixed on for the King to go to the Church of St. Francis, to return thanks for his recovery; and under cover of this pretext, a demonstration against the Constitution was to be made. But the royal conspirators had forgotten to take Lord William Bentinck into their reckoning. Some artillery appeared in the streets, and there was a military parade,—significant hints that stifled the demonstration in its birth. The King gave up St. Francis, and contented himself with saying his prayers at home. But the lesson was lost upon him, or rather upon the incorrigible Caroline. Nothing daunted, she prepared another *coup-de-main*, for the execution of which she trusted to the Sicilian troops stationed at Trapani and Corleone. The object in contemplation was to get rid at once of the English and the Constitution. But Lord William was once more too much for her. All attempts at persuasion proving unavailing, coercive measures were resorted to. A regiment of cavalry, to begin with, surrounded the Royal dwelling during the night, and blockaded it completely. Then only, and not till after many a shift and evasion, did Ferdinand yield to stern necessity, and agree to Lord William's conditions, which were,—That the Queen should leave Sicily at once; that the Government should be once more confided to the Prince Royal; and that the *alter ego* conferred upon him should be without restriction.

"This victory over the Court party, together with the absence of the Queen, restored something like tranquillity to the country. During this calm, the Parliament continued its work of reform, and several important clauses were added to the Constitution,—among them one regulating the succession to the Crown, and establishing the independence of Sicily. The article is literally as follows:—'In the event of the King of Sicily recovering the throne of Naples, or indeed acquiring any other Crown, he shall be bound to put in his place, upon the throne of Sicily, his eldest son, or he shall leave his son in the island, and give it up to him, declaring, from the present date, Sicily independent of Naples and of all other kingdoms or governments.' In May 1813, the Constitution of 1812, as it was called, was promulgated, and Lord William Bentinck, believing his task finished in Sicily, went to Spain. His back, however, was scarcely turned, when the new political edifice was vigorously attacked. Though Queen Caroline was absent, her spirit still ruled at Court; and not only was every effort made to throw discredit on the Constitution, but everything was tried to excite the popular mind against the English. Lord William Bentinck returned in time to reconquer the ground lost in his absence, but he was soon ordered to Leghorn and Genoa. It was as though the good genius of Sicily had departed with him.

"I shall leave undescribed the hand-to-hand struggle for and against liberty that ensued between the nation and the king, and hasten to the catastrophe. After the fall of Napoleon, the English evacuated Sicily. Then followed the negotiations at Vienna, the surprise of the Emperor's return, the stir and tumult of the hundred days, and the final victory of the Allies. Murat's dethronement, decided on at Vienna, restored to the Bourbons their dominions on *terra firma*, and Ferdinand, leaving the heir-apparent at Palermo, went at once to Naples. The signing of the general Treaty of the Congress of Vienna took place in June 1815, and in December of the following year appeared those two famous edicts, which erased the name of Sicily, as an independent kingdom, from the map of Europe.

"By the first of these edicts, purporting to be based on the 104th article of the Treaty of Vienna, Ferdinand cancelled the separate titles under which he had reigned over Naples and Sicily, adopted the style of Ferdinand the First of the united kingdom of the Two Sicilies, and by uniting the two crowns annihilated at one blow the independence, the national flag, and coin of the island. By the second, with a strange want of logic, the Constitution was at once suppressed and maintained, for the king, while claiming as his royal prerogative the right of fixing the taxes, nevertheless engaged himself never to raise their amount beyond the figure decided on by the Parliament of 1813. 'No increase' (such were the words used) 'can take place without the consent of Parliament.'

"I said that the first decree purported to be based on an article (104th) of the Treaty of Vienna. I should have said pretended, for, after all, it was a quibble. The terms used in the Treaty were these:—'King Ferdinand the Fourth is re-established, himself, his heirs, and successors, on the throne of Naples, and hereby recognised by the Powers as King of the kingdom of the Two Sicilies.' Now this arrangement could neither in its form nor substance affect Sicily. The agents sent by Ferdinand to Vienna were sent to discuss an affair purely personal to himself—his restoration, namely, to his lost throne of Naples. The interests of Sicily were not mixed up in this matter—Sicily had nothing to do or to say to the Congress of Vienna—had not even a representative there. The King and the Chevalier Medici figured before it solely on account of the Neapolitan dominions. This is so true, that it was only as Ferdinand the Fourth of Naples, and not under the conjoined title of Ferdinand the Third of Sicily, that the king was named in the acts of the Congress. It is also to be presumed, that, if the Powers assembled at Vienna had really intended to merge the two countries into one, they would have declared such an intention clearly and without circumlocution, as they did when the annexation of Warsaw to Russia, Belgium to Holland,

and Genoa to Piedmont, was stipulated. It is to be supposed, that the conditions of such a union, as in the other cases, would have been specified. Nothing of this is to be found in the Art. 104th. It simply says, 'Ferdinand is recognised as King of the kingdom of the Two Sicilies.' Can it be seriously argued for a moment, that the form of the singular given to the word *kingdom* instead of the plural—a single letter more or less in a word—be sufficient grounds to go on to destroy a right founded on ages?

"So much for Sicilian independence. As for Sicilian liberties, Ferdinand had provided himself with a plausible pretext for getting rid of them in a treaty secretly concluded with Austria. By this treaty it was declared that 'His Majesty the King of the Two Sicilies, in resuming the government of his kingdom, shall not admit any innovation which can interfere in any way with the ancient monarchical institutions, or with the system and principles adopted by His Imperial and Royal Majesty in the internal government of his Italian (the Lombardo-Venetian) provinces.' Had this convention been aimed against the Sicilian Constitution, it would only have been one proof more of Ferdinand's perfidy and treachery, and could never have been considered as binding on Sicily. But the words of the Treaty prove that only Naples was and could be meant. The possession of the kingdom, and the changes to be or not to be effected, were spoken of in the future. Now, in the first place, Ferdinand had never lost anything in Sicily, the Prince-Vicar having administered the affairs of the island as his delegate; and secondly, the changes in Sicily had been consummated three years previous to the above convention; and far from being incompatible with monarchical institutions, they had been made with the view of re-establishing the monarchy in its former conditions, and of restoring to vigour laws which had been sworn to by thirty monarchs, one after the other. But of what avail is right without might? Those who had the power would not use it in our behalf. The English Cabinet haggled a little with the Neapolitan Ministers as to the more or less of nominal privileges to be left us, but on the main point, independence, we were abandoned to our fate"—

Sir John here made a movement as if about to speak, but the Italian resumed, with a smile—

"I am only repeating historical facts, Sir John. The fault of what happened, perhaps, lies less with individuals than with the circumstances of the time. Peace was the great desideratum of Europe, and to that desire Sicily was sacrificed. When I say *sacrificed*, I am only echoing opinions publicly held and expressed, both in and out of the British Parliament, by distinguished fellow-countrymen of your own. Lord William Bentinck, than whom no better authority on the subject, said, in June 1821,—'What I complain of is, that liberty was not given to a people to whom it was promised. In fact, I look on our national honour as pledged to see the promise fulfilled. As to the instructions sent from England, I must own that, had I framed them myself, even the deep interest I feel in the Sicilians, could have suggested nothing better. But what has been done to enforce these instructions? Nothing. Received with hope and joy by the Sicilians, by what were they followed? By the union of the two kingdoms. This Act of Union was not a mere violation, it was the complete overthrow of the Sicilian Constitution. It annihilated the rights of the nation, and made Sicily a province of Naples.' I cannot vouch for these being Lord William's exact words, as I am quoting from memory," continued the Doctor, "but I am positive as to their meaning. Sir James Mackintosh was another who took a similar view of the subject. But enough of this.

"Do I need to say that Parliament was never assembled, and that both the letter and the spirit of the so-called concession of 1816 were daily infringed? Public irritation increased with each passing hour, and an outbreak was at hand, when the Revolution of 1820 exploded at Naples, and was followed by the proclamation of the Constitution of Spain. The moment seemed favourable to the Sicilians for the securing of their ancient independence by peaceful means. A deplorable misunderstanding, however, brought on a collision between the people and the Neapolitan soldiers quartered in Palermo, in which the former were victors. A provisional Junta was formed, with full powers to decide on the best measures for re-establishing the independence of the island. This Junta sent a deputation to the King at Naples to demand an independent Government for Sicily, with the Prince-Royal at the head of it. These demands were not listened to. The Neapolitan Parliament claimed to absorb Sicily in the name of two very opposite principles:—1*st*, the divine right of the king, confirmed by the Treaty of Vienna; 2*dly*, the right of democracy, which could not allow so aristocratic a constitution as that of 1812 to subsist in Sicily. Unfortunately the island was divided against itself by the partisans of the Constitution of Sicily and of that of Spain. An army was sent from Naples, and in the month of September the siege of Palermo was commenced. After a fortnight of obstinate fighting, a capitulation was signed, which left to the Sicilian Parliament the solution of the question of independence. But the Parliament of Naples took upon itself to annul this capitulation, as one dishonouring the Neapolitan army; it retained, nevertheless, the arms and fortifications which had been given up in virtue of the agreement. While the two countries were thus quarrelling with each other, what was King Ferdinand doing? He was gone to Laibach and Troppau to solicit Austrian interference against that very Constitution to which he had so solemnly sworn in the month of July of 1820. What mattered one perjury more or less to the old King? A few months afterwards the Austrians occupied Naples and Sicily, and the two countries who had not been able to agree to live respectively free, now groaned under the yoke of a common slavery.

"Ferdinand died in 1825. He was succeeded by his son Francis, who, as Prince-Royal, had taken the oaths to the Constitution of 1812, in 1820 to that of Spain, who had even participated in the armed protestation against the foreign occupation of 1821. But in ascending the throne, Francis I. lost his memory, and followed without hesitation in the paternal footsteps. The whole five years this reign lasted, the Government was floundering in a bog. The spread of corruption, both at Naples and in Sicily, was incredible. Everything was to be bought, everything to be sold; offices, honours, titles, even justice itself, was in the market. Viglia, the King's valet, and Caterina'de Simone, the Queen's First Camerista, were the two most influential persons of the kingdom, and through them most of the infamous bargains were concluded. The King did not attempt to veil his cognizance of all that was going on; he was, on the contrary, profuse of his cynical witticisms on the subject. In 1828, the world had proof that he was to the full as cruel as he was despicable. An attempt at insurrection in the town of Cosenza and in the province of Salerno, was literally quenched in blood. By order of Del Carretto, the King's other self, the little town of Bosco was cannonaded till it was reduced to ruins, and then a column of infamy raised to shew where once it stood. The last days of Francis are said to have ben tormented by vain remorse. He died in 1830, leaving to Ferdinand, the reigning king, a degraded, impoverished, and highly irritated kingdom.

"Young Ferdinand's early measures (he was scarcely twenty) augured well. Most of the ministers, creatures, and favourites of the late King were gradually dismissed; Viglia was sent away; days of public audience were established; and a manifesto issued declaring it to be Ferdinand's determination to restore order to the dilapidated finances of the country. These were most popular measures. Nor was Sicily left without her quota of promises. It was the King's intention, as distinctly stated in his manifesto, 'to seek to heal the wounds inflicted on Sicily by his father and grandfather.' The dismissal of the Marquis della Favara, lieutenant-general of the island, a man universally detested, and the appointment in his stead of the Count of Syracuse, his

Majesty's own brother, made the good islanders believe that the new Sovereign was in earnest. Consequently, when in 1831 he visited Sicily, his reception was most enthusiastic. Unfortunately the sequel belied the commencement. What had appeared pure love of justice, was in truth mere kingcraft. The shock of the Revolution of the three days in France was still reverberating throughout Europe, and our King was wise enough to see the expediency of soothing and conciliating the people, still under the smart of the ignoble misgovernment of Francis.

"But as the danger diminished, so did the king resume his natural disposition. The first symptom of the reaction which was taking place in Ferdinand's mind, was the nomination of Del Carretto, the exterminator of Bosco, as minister of police. This fatal man, and Monsignor Cocle, the king's confessor, soon acquired a complete ascendency over the young monarch. Jesuitism[*] and the police became presently the two corner-stones of the State. Everything had been marketable in the preceding reign—matters were no better now—Monsignor Cocle and Del Carretto playing the part of the *ci-devant Cameriere* and *Camerista*. The punishment of flogging, which had been first known in the Two Sicilies during the Austrian occupation of 1821, was re-established under the present administration. It was not long ere all the new-born illusions of the Sicilians vanished. The Government seemed imbued with the desire of poisoning rather than healing old wounds. Our Parliament was no more spoken of than if such a thing had never existed—it was a crime only to name it; yet the taxes had risen far beyond the amount fixed by the Decree of December 1816, and in spite of the engagement entered into that they should not be augmented without the consent of Parliament. The

---

[*] The king's infatuation for this famous order went so far in subsequent years, as to appoint, by a Royal Rescript, its founder, St. Ignatius de Loyola, field-marshal of the army, with the pay and appurtenances attached to the rank. The money was actually paid to the Chief House of Jesuits at Naples. See *Gli ultimi Rivolgimenti Italiani*, *Memorie Storiche, di F. A. Gualterio.* Vol. IV. chap. XLIX. p. 75. *Florence, Felice Le Monnier*, 1852.

abrupt recall of the Count of Syracuse, in 1835, brought the popular discontent to a climax.

"In the summer of 1836, the cholera made its appearance at Naples. Up to that time, the quarantine regulations between Naples and Sicily had been extremely severe and vexatious. But when the terrible scourge was actually in Naples, the sanitary cordons so strictly maintained while it was still as far off as Russia, were all at once disregarded and neglected. This inconsistency gave rise to a very universal belief, that the King and his ministers were in league to send the cholera into Sicily. The epidemic reached Palermo but too soon, and no city, I believe, suffered more cruelly from its ravages. Out of a population of 170,000 inhabitants, 24,000 perished in a month. The general terror quickly lashed itself into a general delirium. The idea that the Government was poisoning the people by wholesale got abroad. An infant suspicion of this kind once born, soon becomes a full-grown certainty.

"Mario Adorno, one of those who had writhed most violently under the loss of Sicilian independence, took advantage of the prevailing excitement to bring about an insurrectionary movement in Syracuse, where he shortly after proclaimed the Constitution. Catania immediately followed the example, raised the Sicilian standard, tore down the statues of the Bourbons, and formed a Provisional Government. Partial risings took place also in the valley of Messina, and in the small towns adjacent to Palermo, where the belief in the poisoning plot was deeply rooted. Furnished with unlimited sovereign power, and accompanied by a strong body of troops, Del Carretto was sent to Sicily, less to conquer than to reap the fruits of victory; for, by the time he landed, all revolution was over. In fact, the news of his expedition having reached the Catanians, they, finding themselves unsupported, of their own accord effected a counter-revolution. All those most compromised sought safety in flight, with the exception of Mario Adorno, who was taken and shot. The absence of all resistance in no way induced the destroyer of Bosco to forego one cruelty in his power. Courts-martial were established everywhere, and citizens sent by thousands to prison. Several hundreds were condemned to death, and no less than a hundred underwent the penalty. At Bagheria a boy of fourteen years of age was shot. Executions took place to the sound of military music. Such, indeed, was the rage for killing, that once, after one of these direful exhibitions, when the corpses were counted over, one more than the appointed number was found.

"The noble conquest being achieved, and the noble conqueror rewarded with the insignia of San Gennaro, the real meaning of the bloody tragedy was speedily revealed by the official acts which followed. The King gladly seized on the pretext, which had been thus offered him, to do away at once with even the shadow of the last remaining Sicilian franchises. The substance had long ago vanished. The taxes were augmented, the administration was filled with Neapolitans, a thorough system of centralization in Naples adopted, all vestige of municipal liberty, of the liberty of the press, of association, of petition, was destroyed. To make a long story short, nothing was left to Sicily but eyes to weep, and the undying memory of her rights. This memory, and the consciousness of the righteousness of her cause, will support that noble and unfortunate country through all her trials until a day of reckoning comes for her, as come it surely will."

Antonio wiped the drops of perspiration from his brow —less the effect of heat than of deep emotion. Lucy was scarcely less moved, and it was almost in a whisper that she said, "You have not told us what obliged you to leave Catania."

"True," answered Antonio; "all recollection of my individual troubles was lost in that of our national catastrophe. Indeed, few will be able to credit that such a trivial incident as I have to mention could be sufficient in any country to force a man into exile. I had taken no share in the disturbances in my native town. Not that my Sicilian heart did not beat fast and loud at the sacred names of Independence and Liberty—not that I did not sympathize with, and approve of the struggle, in spite of the sad forebodings that filled my mind as to the issue of an insulated attempt; but my every hour was occupied by professional duties. The cholera, though less deadly than at Palermo, was nevertheless making sad havoc in Catania, and day and night I was in requisition. One evening in the month of March, I was called to the bedside of a dear friend, who had been suddenly taken ill. I had but just time to recognise the first symptoms of the prevalent malady, when a party of soldiers entered the room. An order for the arrest of my friend had been issued, and a serjeant at the head of half a dozen men were sent to seize his person. The poor sick creature was desired to get out of bed and prepare to accompany the soldiers. I interfered, and making known my name and profession, I said, that, to remove my friend in his actual state was equivalent to killing him, and I therefore cautioned the serjeant as to the heavy responsibility he was taking upon himself. The answer I received was, that precise orders had been given, and that, dead or alive, my friend must go; saying which, the serjeant drew the blankets off the bed. I lost all self-control at the brutal act. I do not know to this day what I did or said, but it ended by my being handcuffed, forced out of the house, and marched through the streets.

"We had not proceeded far when we were met by an officer, one of high rank, too, as far as I could judge in the growing darkness. He stopped my escort, and asked some questions of the serjeant. 'A physician!' I heard the stranger exclaim; 'this is surely not the time to arrest physicians, my good friend.' After a little more parley, I was freed of the manacles; the officer took me by the arm, and led me one way, while the serjeant and his men went the other. Being close to him, I now saw by his epaulettes that my companion was a general officer. 'Where do you wish to go?' he asked. I named the street where I lived. He saw me to my own door, and as he took leave of me, he said, 'These are difficult times, and a charge of rebellion is a very serious one. Had I any advice to give you, it would be to get out of the way as soon as possible;' and with these words he left me. This was the circumstance which led to my exile. Far less than I had said or done that day had cost many a man his life. My mother and uncle insisted on my following my unknown friend's counsel, and so I did. Since then I have become acquainted with his name, and with the fact that I am not the only one whose life he has succeeded in saving. God bless him! I am proud and happy to say that he is a Sicilian!"

"And your sick friend?" asked Lucy.

"Dead, young lady, dead, a few hours after I left him. I knew of his death before sailing. They had not dared to take him away, but had contented themselves with leaving a guard to watch his dying agonies."

CHAPTER XV.
Progress to the Sanctuary.

ALL difficulties in the way of Battista and Speranza's marriage being now removed by a splendid grant from Sir John of two hundred pounds, three-fifths of which were sufficient to cover all the debts of the family, and the remaining eighty pounds more than enough to make the Osteria a profitable, nay, brilliant business, it was settled that the two lovers should be married on the 25th of June, Speranza's birthday. Now, in every age and in every country, birth, marriage, and death have always been escorted by preliminaries and ceremonies of one kind or another. In the present case, a pilgrimage to the sanctuary of Lampedusa was deemed especially necessary, that our *Promessi sposi* might pay their devotions, and offer their thanks (in the shape of ex-votos) to the lady of that name, to whose intercession they owed such a bright change of fortune. For Rosa, and Speranza, and Battista, as, indeed, nearly the whole of the parish of Bordighera, held it as an article of faith, that the Madonna in general, and the Madonna of Lampedusa in particular, had brought Lucy, and all the blessings that had come with her, to the Osteria;—thus unconsciously laying that mischievous trick of the overturn of the carriage at the Madonna's door. Lucy's interest and curiosity being greatly excited by the idea of this pilgrimage, it came to be arranged that Sir John and his daughter should take the same time to visit the famous shrine, and breathe the fresh air of the mountain for a couple of days; that Doctor Antonio, of course, should be of the party, and that to him should be intrusted the care of all the preparations for the trip, and arrangements for the sojourn at Lampedusa.

On the 20th of June then, Sir John, his daughter, and Antonio—the betrothed were not to come up till next morning—left the Osteria in a smart boat, with a gaily striped red and white awning, commanded by Battista, and at which he had been hard at work for more than a week, cleaning, painting, and trimming, to do honour to the occasion. Under the combined action of a sail tolerably well puffed by a little breeze, and of three pair of vigorous oars, they were not long in doubling the second headland. San Remo —bright, verdant San Remo, rising up in the form of a triangle, and smiled upon by its seven hills, clad all over in most luxurious vegetation, then broke full in their view.

"Do palm-trees grow naturally in this part of the country?" asked Lucy, pointing to the plantations that covered the shore; "or are they cultivated for beauty's sake?"

"Their beauty, I believe, is their least merit in the eyes of their proprietors," answered Antonio. "Palms, you do not perhaps know, are a very profitable kind of property, and that is why they are cultivated. Cargoes of them are sent yearly to France and Holland. In all the Catholic countries the consumption of palms during Passion-week is very great; but throughout Italy, and especially at Rome, it is enormous. There is a family of San Remo, which has held for centuries, and still holds, the exclusive privilege of furnishing palms to what is called 'The Apostolic Palace,' that is, to the household of the Pope."

"Was the monopoly purchased?" inquired Sir John. "I need scarcely ask, however, for I have been told that everything is, ever was, and ever will be, sold at Rome."

"Contrary to the rule," replied the Doctor, "this privilege was given in acknowledgment of good service. The story, such as it is, may amuse you, and help to while away the time till we land. You have, I daresay, seen and admired in Rome the obelisk which stands in Piazza San Pietro, or Vaticano, and itself goes by the name of Vaticano. This obelisk in 1584, that is, during the first years of the Pontificate of Sixtus V., was still lying half-buried in the earth, not far from the ancient vestry of San Pietro. Many a Pope before Sixtus had formed plans for having it disinterred and removed to the Piazza San Pietro, but had always been deterred by the great difficulties and expenses of the undertaking. Pope Sixtus V., an ambitious and enterprising spirit, as everybody knows, made up his mind to realize that which his predecessors had only thought about. He confided the arduous task to Domenico Fontana, an architect of great renown, liberally furnishing him with all the necessary means for its success. The mechanics of that period were far behind those of the present day; and it was found no easy matter to free from the ground in which it was sunk, and transfer without injury to the place where it was intended to stand, a monolith of such portentous magnitude. These two preliminary acts, however, were successfully performed in the course of a year. But the final and most delicate operation, that of raising the stupendous bulk upright, still remained to be accomplished. All the preparations for this purpose being at last completed, Fontana went to the Pope and requested him to fix a day for the elevation. The Pope did so, and promised to honour with his presence a ceremony which could not fail to attract from all parts an immense concourse of people.

"'That is what most alarms me,' said the architect;

'should the noise of the crowd bewilder the workmen, and prevent my slightest direction from being attended to, I can answer for nothing.'

"'Never fear,' said Pope Sixtus, 'I will take good care of that;' and he instantly penned an edict, by which he made known, that whosoever uttered a sound during the erection of the column should suffer death. This proclamation, with the tremendous Papal seal affixed to it, was without delay placarded on the walls of Rome.

"On the day settled, Fontana, after having confessed, taking the sacrament, and received the Pope's benediction, mounted the high scaffolding from which he was to superintend the great work. His orders were to be signified by means of bells, and of divers coloured flags, so that the workmen out of hearing could understand and execute them. The Piazza Vaticano, crowded to suffocation, looked as if paved with heads; and a great and imposing sight it must have been to behold that countless multitude remain, by the will of one man, as motionless and silent, as if, instead of living people, it were composed of statues. Pope Sixtus, from the lofty seat prepared for him, looked down upon the assembled throng, standing thus spell-bound before him.

"At last the signal is given, the capstans begin to wind, the pulleys to revolve, the cables and ropes to stretch and strain, and creak. Up, up, slowly rises the granite monster. Fontana waves his flags, the Pope stoops eagerly forward, the thousands below hold their breath—a minute more and the huge monolith will be erect. All at once an ominous crack is heard, the obelisk is motionless for a second, then sinks some inches; the ropes no longer bear upon it. The Pope frowns,—all Rome turns pale. Fontana's presence of mind forsakes him. 'Water! water!' shouts a voice on a sudden; 'wet the ropes.' Fontana obeys the blessed prompting; water is thrown on the ropes, the slackened hemp contracts, once more the workmen bend to their work with a will. The majestic column is upreared, and stands before the admiring world, another glorious proof of man's daring and ingenuity.

"He whose timely interference had brought about this result, was the captain of a trading vessel, named Bresca, a native of San Remo; one who in his seafaring life had probably had some similar experience of the slackening of hempen ropes. In spite, however, of the undeniable service he had rendered, the Swiss Guards, who knew of no virtue but obedience, of no crime but disobedience to their master, seized on Bresca, and brought him before the Pope. The known severity of Sixtus V., a severity frequently amounting to wanton cruelty, left little hope of the captain's life being spared. Fortunately, the success of the undertaking he had had so much at heart, disposed the Pope to be lenient —we ought to say, to be just—towards the man who had so materially contributed to that success. His Holiness, then, contrary to general expectation, received Bresca courteously, and promised to grant any favour he might ask. The good captain, as a matter of course, begged first the Pope's holy blessing, and secondly, the privilege for him, and his descendants, of yearly furnishing the Apostolic Palace with palms. This request was immediately conceded by a Papal Brief, which further conferred on Bresca the title and grade of Captain in the Pontifical army, and the right of wearing the uniform, and of hoisting the Papal flag on his vessel. This Brief is still in the possession of the Bresca family, and the monopoly it bestowed lasts to this day."

"Still, I think, this Pope Sixtus must have been a hateful man," exclaimed Lucy.

"Certainly not an amiable one," observed Antonio. "One can scarcely help shrinking from the skilful surgeon who cuts deep into the human frame, although we know that the most humane motives arm his hand. The task of Sixtus V. was of a somewhat similar nature. When he came to be the head of Church and State, both were in so rotten a condition, that only heroic remedies, if any—the free use of knife and scalpel—could heal them; and these he applied unflinchingly, unsparingly. Men are but what circumstances make them—a truce to moralizing, for here we are at the end of our voyage," added the Doctor, looking around—"and there, just in front of us, between those two gently receding mountains, the little valley of Taggia stretches inland; and that river falling into the sea, a hundred paces a-head of us to the east, is the Argentina, the pride of the inhabitants of the dale, and now and then their scourge, as when chafed by mountain torrents it roars like a mad bull, and carries everything before it."

A walk of two minutes brought our party to a cross-way formed by the Taggia road, and the high road to Nice meeting at right angles, and where an open carriage was in waiting for them. Their drive was now through plantations of olive-trees, whose branches closing from either side of the way, made a green canopy over their heads.

"What capital studies for a painter these twisted gnarled trunks would make!" cried Lucy; "I never saw such a number of odd picturesque shapes."

"Whatever may be said," observed Antonio, "of the monotonous effect of olives seen in masses, we cannot deny the individual tree credit for variety and originality of form."

"Certainly not," said Lucy; "for my part, I confess to a foible for the olive-tree. It speaks to my heart and imagination. It recalls to my mind the branch-symbol of peace that the dove brought back to Noah; the moving forest of olive-boughs that welcomed our Saviour on His entry into Jerusalem; the garden where He prayed and suffered."—Really, Lucy, as these holy associations awoke in her mind, did look very like one of Guido's divine Madonnas, at least Antonio did not wonder at Battista's mistake any more.

"Pray, Doctor," said she, after a pause, "let me have one of those twigs that hang over head." Antonio having complied, Lucy examined the leaves, dark dead-green on one side, and silvery-grey on the other, then said,—"Are those little white balls hanging in bunches the fruit?"

"They are," answered Antonio; "and if the weather permits, by next January, those same small white things will be transformed into glossy black berries, which, ground in mills, furnish the well-known oil. After that, the crushed kernel, washed and dried, makes excellent fuel, while the dead leaves are used as manure. The olive-wood, as you already know, is much prized by cabinet-makers for their finest articles; so, you see, no part of the tree but has a value."

"How comes it, then," asked Sir John, "that with so rich a product at their very doors the people of this country are poor?"

"The apparent contradiction is easily explained," replied Antonio. "In the first place, you must understand that only once in three years there is a good crop, that is to say, only every third year are the trees well covered with the white balls you are now looking at, which, remember, are, after all, the promise, and nothing more, of a rich harvest. For these little balls have to remain on the tree from April or May when they form, until the following January when they are to be gathered, and as they are of a very delicate constitution, likely to be equally injured by extremes of any kind, whether of heat or cold, drought, rain, or wind, you may easily imagine the risks and losses they are liable to during so long an interval as that of eight or nine months. Add to this, that the cultivation of the olive is expensive, the tree needing, at least, every fourth year, plenty of a particular and very dear manure, consisting of woollen rags and the horns and hoofs of cattle; that at certain seasons the earth round each tree must be dug to give air to the roots; that the *muricciuoli*, or little walls of the terraces, which support the soil of our mountainous districts, are continually requiring repairs, while, as a climax, the cost of gathering the fruit, and making the oil, is calculated to be twenty-five per cent. of the net produce. Bearing all this in mind, you will, I think, cease to wonder at so rich a product affording only poor incomes."

Sir John, far from assenting to the Doctor's explanation, shook his head, as much as to say, there must be bad management somewhere; but as they had now come in sight of the two dark, ivy-festooned towers, which command the approach to the town, the conversation took a different turn.

"Many a fierce assault of the Saracens has been bravely met and repulsed here," observed the Doctor, as he assisted his companions to alight. "Down to a comparatively recent period, this Riviera has been infested by Barbary Corsairs, who took advantage of the unguarded state of the coast, and the want of easy communication between town and town, to pounce upon a given point, and accomplish their only object, plunder, before help from other parts could be procured. Yes, indeed," continued Antonio, answering the mute wonder expressed in Lucy's eyes; "there are persons still alive who recollect a descent of the kind, when a convent of friars was broken into, and most of the monks carried off. It was the policy of the most Serene Republic of Genoa, at all times, out of jealousy of her near neighbour, France, to prevent any carriage road being made between the capital and this part of her dominions; and but half a century ago a journey from Genoa here was considered, and really was a difficult and rather dangerous undertaking."

"Not much to boast of yet as to safety, Doctor; your Prospero was almost as bad as a Corsair," said Sir John, laughing.

"Ah, indeed!" retorted the Doctor in the same tone; "still I hope Bordighera has not been quite so bad as Algiers or Tunis."

"Not quite, not quite," returned Sir John, good-humouredly. "Then this fine road is a modern work," continued he.

"Entirely so," replied Antonio; "the actual Cornice road was only completed in 1828, and we owe it to the following accident:—Charles Felix, the then reigning Sovereign, was

extremely partial to Nice, where he often resided. His road
from Turin thither was naturally by the Col di Tenda. It so
happened, that during one of these visits to Nice, there was
a heavy fall of snow, rendering the return to Turin by the
usual route impossible. The only alternative was to go by
water to Genoa, from whence his Majesty could easily reach
his capital. He accordingly embarked, but the weather was
so boisterous, and the sea so heavy, he was obliged to put
back. The people of the Riviera, who had long been vainly
endeavouring to obtain permission to open a road along the
coast, seized the opportunity thus offered to them. I ought
to have said before, that the Government of Piedmont, along
with the ancient States of the Republic of Genoa, had inherited also its prejudices against a road towards France.
So the populations of all the towns and villages turned out
en masse, headed by the Mayors and Curés, gaps were filled,
and rocks removed, in an incredibly short space of time.
'Here, your Majesty, is a road at your service,' cried out
every voice, and his Majesty was graciously pleased to accept of the accommodation. Red-hot orders arrived from
Turin, commanding the Riviera to let alone road-making—a
day too late, however, for the road was made, and King and
courtiers had already sanctified it."

With this the Doctor led the way through the town, a
quaint-looking place, to be sure, with an intense middle-age
air and colour about it, full, both on the right and the left,
of dark vaults and mysterious archways, some of these last
opening unexpectedly on green, sunny vistas, refreshing to
behold. Miss Lucy wondered at the number of massy stone
bridges thrown overhead across the street from house to
house; and which, her cicerone explained, were meant as a
safeguard against a frequent unpleasant visitor—the earthquake. Another thing that puzzled the young English lady,
was to see, now and then, on the outer-door steps, plates
full of oranges, lemons, and vegetables, without any one to
watch them. She was surprised to hear that they were
there for sale; anybody who wanted such or such an article,

taking it *sans cérémonie* out of the plate, and leaving instead the price, one or two sous.

This novel method of trading highly amused Sir John, who remarked, "That though ingenious and economical, it was not of a kind to thrive much in many places."

Our trio now came to a street wider than the rest, where a great many persons of all classes, gentlemen, priests, labourers, and mechanics, were either assembled in groups, or loitering about under arcades extending on both sides. "This is the *Pantano*," said Doctor Antonio; "the Exchange and the Regent Street combined, of the good folks of Taggia. Here business is transacted, and here beaux and magnates exhibit their finery and importance to the world. That tall man in uniform is the quartermaster of the carabineers, one of the powers that be. If we stay here a few minutes longer, we shall see him set off to make an official report as to how Doctor Antonio of Bordighera was seen to traverse the *Pantano* at five minutes past four in the afternoon, in the company of a foreign lady and gentleman; an important event of which my friend the Commandant of San Remo will be informed before sunset."

"Are you in earnest!" cried Lucy. "I can scarcely believe that any one would trouble himself about such trifles."

"Trifles, indeed!" repeated Antonio with the utmost gravity; "might not Sir John be a French general in disguise, (he looks very like one, I am sure,) come to revolutionize his Sardinian Majesty's town of Taggia? Our police are for ever ready and willing to save the country from such risks."

Every hat was raised as our friends passed by, and many a nod and smile, and waving of hands, addressed in particular to the Doctor, gave evidence of his treading on familiar ground. He beckoned to a tall, thin, fair-haired young man, ("the maker of your easy-chair, Miss Davenne,") who came forward, and after saluting the company, shook hands with Antonio—an act of familiarity that called up on Sir John's countenance only half of his wonted grimace, for, making a strenuous effort, the Baronet so far overcame himself as to suppress the other half. This unpleasant impression was, however, soon obliterated by the quiet and deferential manner with which the young cabinet-maker introduced his visitors into his workshop, a large room with bare walls, and where they found a lad modelling a head in plaster.

"That youth," said the Doctor, "has a decided talent for sculpture; untaught he has already modelled heads and even full-length figures. He is about to go to Rome, where a rich and generous family of this country has volunteered to pay all his expenses while he studies there; and I am greatly mistaken if the name of Salvatore Revelli does not become, in a few years, one honoured in the Republic of Arts.* This tall fellow, too," continued Antonio, playfully pointing to the cabinet-maker, "but for his obstinacy in sticking to the *Pantano*, might have earned fame and money. —Now, out with your fine things, sir, if you please."

The number of fine things was not large—where was the use of adding to them when what was there already found no purchasers?—nevertheless, there was more than enough to prove the uncommon skill and taste of the workman. There were, indeed, only a few paper-knives and portfolios, richly ornamented with most delicate and fanciful carvings, or diminutive figures, and three tables of most exquisite workmanship. On one of these was delineated a series of figures representing the different costumes of the people of the Riviera, so admirably done that Lucy exclaimed— "This is not the work of a cabinet-maker, it is that of an artist, who not only draws beautifully, but is also a first-rate colourist!"

"My friend," said Antonio, "has all the merit of choice and arrangement, but there are no colours in these figures

---

* Antonio prophesied right. Revelli placed himself at once among the most promising young sculptors of the day by his first work exhibited in Genoa in 1849; a bas-relief representing an episode in the life of Columbus, and intended for the monument the Genoese are erecting to their great countryman.

except those bestowed by nature on the different bits of wood of which they are composed."

Lucy could scarcely believe this, and Sir John needed the joint testimony of eyes and glasses before he could admit the fact. He at once offered to purchase all that had been shown them, expressing his regret to the Doctor that the cabinet-maker's stock was not larger. After a cordial exchange of good wishes and thanks, Antonio and his friends took their leave, and winding their way through some more streets, all verdure and sunshine in the balconies and terraces above, all shades and gloom below, they arrived at a bridge which joined the two banks of the little valley.

On a lofty ridge opposite rose Castellaro, shimmering in golden light. "How bright and beautiful!" said Lucy; "that is the gayest village in the world; one might fancy that Castellaro feels the happiness of existence."

"Or," pursued Antonio, "that in a transport of joy it is about to fling itself into the arms of the valley."

"Just so," laughed the Baronet; "they must have stout hearts who live in those foremost houses; the mere idea makes me giddy."

About the middle of the bridge they came to a stone pillar, on which was a Madonna and a Latin inscription. "Here is another memorial of an earthquake," said Antonio, pointing to the inscription. "It is here stated, that in the month of June 1831, a dreadful visitation destroyed two arches of the bridge, the third and this one on which we are now standing. Two children, brother and sister, who were crossing at the very instant of the shock, were thrown down with this, the eleventh arch, and, wonderful to relate, sustained no injury; in acknowledgment of which miraculous escape the grateful father erected this pillar, with an inscription commemorative of the fact."

At the foot of a narrow steep path, a little past the bridge, the party found two mules and two men waiting for them. The Doctor preferred walking, he said. Sir John, once in the saddle, opened his umbrella and took the lead, closely followed by Lucy, a man at the head of each mule. "I never saw such a detestable break-neck road," cried out the Baronet, after a short time, "certainly the parish does not ruin itself by keeping the roads in order."

"It will improve as soon as we pass into the parish of Castellaro," said Doctor Antonio. "Castellaro has more than once pressed on Taggia the necessity of the latter having its part of the road repaired. You will never guess the answer always given:—It is not Taggia that wants to go to Castellaro, but Castellaro that wants to come to Taggia; so let Castellaro repair the road if it chooses, at its own expense. Such are the notions of political economy entertained hereabouts."

The elastic air of the mountain, strongly impregnated with the racy perfume of the rosemary and thyme growing plentifully about, began to act as a gentle stimulant on our travellers, whose spirits rose with every step. Sir John waxed so poetical, as to liken the enormous clusters of yellow furze scattered over the hill, to smiles irradiating a rugged old face. Lucy, with girlish buoyancy, fell to pelting Antonio with every flower supplied by the victim, who cried out treason, and, seemingly in mortal fear, would fall back, shriek, and hide behind rocks and trees, and play such childish tricks, as we, his historiographers, cannot take upon ourselves to relate. Lucy's merry peals of laughter at Antonio's odd ways, and at the grave face with which he warned her against peeping behind, and thus spoiling her pleasure, were most cheering to listen to. He presently came out of one of his hiding-places shouting and waving a huge bunch of flowers, so inconceivably gay, that they could only be met with, he declared, on the way to the gayest village in the world. From the centre of each of the large white blossoms he held in his hand, there sprung up a long elegant aigrette of deep lilac stamens. The ensemble, so rich and delicate, had a certain resemblance to the tail of a white peacock. "What can it be?" said Lucy. "It is the *capparis spinosa*," answered Antonio, "and these flowers you admire so much are but capers in full blossom, best known for culinary purposes." This piece of information did not cool Miss Davenne's admiration, who said she liked caper-sauce, and, seeing Antonio stick some of the flowers in his famous conical hat, wished to have some in her own, which looked pretty indeed. Sir John, laughingly, allowed himself to be adorned in the same way—the two guides had likewise their share, and thus caparisoned, the little troop traversed the village of Castellaro, rather stared at, but received with the same tokens of respect and sympathy which had accompanied them throughout the day. Now and then some villager would step up to the Doctor with a request that he would go to visit some sick person, which, the case not being urgent, was put off with a good-humoured smile for the morrow.

A broad, smooth road, in high order, what Sir John called a road fit for Christians, opened from the village northwards, and stretching over the side of the steep mountain in capricious zigzags, now concealed, now gave view to the front of the sanctuary, shaded by two oaks of enormous dimensions. "The Castellini who made this road 'in the sweat of their brows,'" said Antonio, "point it out with pride, and well they may. They tell you with infinite complacency how every one of the pebbles with which it is paved was brought from the sea-shore, those who had mules using them for that purpose, those who had none bringing up loads on their own backs; how every one, gentleman and peasant, young and old, women and boys, worked day and night, with no other inducement than the love of the Madonna. The Madonna of Lampedusa is their creed, their occupation, their pride, their *Carroccio*, their fixed idea."

"A strange infatuation," remarked Lucy; "I should like to hear the legend, for, of course, there is some tradition extant about it."

"All that relates to the miraculous image," answered

Antonio, "and the date and mode of its translation to Castellaro, is given at full length in two inscriptions, one in Latin, the other in bad Italian verses, which are to be seen in the interior of the little chapel of the sanctuary. Andrea Anfosso, a native of Castellaro, being the captain of a privateer, was one day attacked and defeated by the Turks, and carried to the Isle of Lampedusa. Here he succeeded in making his escape and hiding himself, until the Turkish vessel which had captured his left the island. Anfosso, being a man of expedients, set about building a boat, and finding himself in a great dilemma what to do for a sail, ventured on the bold and original step of taking from the altar of some church or chapel of the island a picture of the Madonna to serve as one; and so well did it answer his purpose that he made an unusually prosperous voyage back to his native shores, and in a fit of generosity offered his holy sail to the worship of his fellow-townsmen. The wonderful of the affair does not stop here. A place was chosen by universal acclamation, two gunshots in advance of the present sanctuary, and a chapel erected, in which the gift was deposited with all due honour. But the Madonna, as it would seem, had an insurmountable objection to the spot selected, for, every morning that God made, the picture was found at the exact place where the actual church now stands. Sentinels were posted at the door of the chapel, the entire village remained on foot for nights, mounting guard at the entrance—no precaution, however, availed. In spite of the strictest watch, the picture, now undeniably a miraculous one, found means to make its way to the spot it preferred. At length the Castellini came to understand that it was the Madonna's express will, that her headquarters should be shifted to where her resemblance betook itself every night; and though it had pleased her to make choice of the most abrupt and the steepest spot on the whole mountain, just where it was requisite to raise arches in order to lay a sure foundation for her sanctuary, the Castellini set themselves *con amore* to the task so clearly revealed to them, and this widely-renowned chapel was completed. This took place in 1619. In the course of time some rooms were annexed for the accomodation of visitors and pilgrims, and a terrace built, and many other additions and embellishments are even now in contemplation, and no doubt will be accomplished some day; for, although the Castellini have but a small purse, theirs is the grand lever which can remove all impediments—the faith that brought about the Crusades."

As Antonio ceased speaking, John and Miss Hutchins, two personages of whom we have been lately strangely forgetful, were at Lucy's stirrup, who playfully asked the Doctor, if the taboo were raised, and she might now look behind her. "As if you had not been doing so for the last hour," said Antonio, shaking his head at her. Lucy turned sharply round, and embraced at one glance the wonderfully varied scene before her.

To the north a long, long vista of deep, dark, frowning gorges, closed in the distance by a gigantic screen of snow-clad Alps—the glorious expanse of the Mediterranean to the south—east and west, range upon range of gently undulating hills, softly inclining towards the sea—in the plain below, the fresh, cozy valley of Taggia, with its sparkling track of waters, and rich belt of gardens, looking like a perfect mosaic of every gradation of green, chequered with winding silver arabesques. Ever and anon a tardy pomegranate in full blossom spread out its oriflamme of tulip-shaped dazzling red flowers. From the rising ground opposite frowned mediæval Taggia, like a discontented guest at a splendid banquet. A little farther off, westwards, the eye took in the Campanile of the Dominican Church, emerging from a group of cypresses; and further still, on the extreme verge of the western cliff, the sanctuary of our lady of the *Guardia* shewed its white silhouette against the dark blue sky.

A half fretful, half plaintive, "Now, Lucy, my dear, if you would only put off your enthusiasm till after dinner," from Sir John, interrupted Miss Davenne's silent but delighted survey, and brought her at once to her father's side. They sat down to a succulent dinner, of which Sir John partook with an alacrity and zest highly complimentary to the hygienic qualities of the mountain air. The repast being over, Lucy proposed that they should take coffee on the terrace, which being agreed to by her father, they immediately went thither, and Sir John, after sipping his Mocha, and paying an ample tribute of admiration to the loveliness of the view, took the *Times* from his pocket, and plunged into its columns. Lucy and Antonio thus left to themselves sat watching in silent wonder the glories of the evening hour.

The sky was bright and limpid as polished steel, save where three lovely cloudlets, like long scarfs of orange gauze, hovered in the west. The sun, half hidden behind the brow of the western mountain range, shot, through the breaks of the lower hills in front, some of its rays in fiery columns aslant the valley. As the dazzling orb sunk slowly, the zone of shade on the mountain opposite rose with corresponding progress, and like a tide of dark waters, chasing before it the broad sheets of light, narrowed them by degrees to a purple line, which lingered for a while on the topmost ridges, the last farewell then vanished with a quiver. Now the foremost range of the chain resumes at once the rigidity of its outlines, while those in the background, behind which the sun has gone down, float in a transparent mist of lapis-lazzuli and pink. The sky in the west is a glorious furnace, the warm reflections from which befleck with crimson the distant snow of the Alps, and light up the horizon of the sea. Another moment the reddish glare pales and gives way, the shadows thicken in the valley beneath, and the gorges to the north darken and darken apace. The fiery coruscations in the west have softened into subdued rosy tints, and these in their turn, by a harmoniously graduated scale, fade into a greenish mother-of-pearl transparency, which passes from grey to azure, until west and east merge into a uniform deep blue, spangled here and there with a trembling star.

"And our beautiful clouds?" said Lucy.

"Gone!" replied Antonio, sadly; "emblem of many a bright hope, vanishing even as you watch them."

"But they will come again to-morrow," said Lucy naïvely, and as in so saying she bent her head a little towards Antonio, the evening breeze carried some of her golden curls over his lips, as if offering them to his kiss.

"Who can tell," said he, "but that black clouds pregnant with thunder will envelop those summits to-morrow!"

The wonderful evolutions of light and shade which, out of respect for our reader's patience, we have unceremoniously despatched in a few lines, had in reality occupied a full hour, the first quarter of which had been consecrated by Sir John to his newspaper, the second to find a commodious posture, and the last half to a glorious doze. This was the reason why the young lady and the gentleman spoke in whispers, and speaking in whispers chanced now and then to lean towards each other.

The impressive stillness of the evening was suddenly broken by the bells of the six churches of Castellaro ringing the Ave Maria, echoed in quick succession by those of the far more numerous churches of Taggia, and of the far away Capuchin and Dominican convents. It was the sweetest and most melancholy concert imaginable. Sir John changed his position, but did not wake; and Antonio began reciting, almost in Lucy's ear, the so often quoted, yet most excellent to quote, incomparable lines of Dante,—

> "Era già l'ora che volge il disio
> A' naviganti, e 'ntenerisce il cuore
> Lo dì c'han detto a dolci amici: a Dio;
> E che lo nuovo peregrin d'amore
> Punge, se ode squilla di lontano
> Che paja il giorno pianger che si muore."

TRANSLATION.

"Now was the hour that wakens fond desire
In men at sea, and melts their thoughtful heart,
Who in the morning have bid sweet friends farewell;
And pilgrim newly on his road with love
Thrills, if he hear the vesper bell from far,
That seems to mourn for the expiring day."—CARY.

"I never entirely felt till now," said Lucy, with glistening eyes, "the full pathos of those beautiful verses. The regret for the distant fatherland which informs them strikes home to the heart. They must have been written in such an hour as this."

"And by an exile," added Antonio. "Probably the eyes of the great Ghibelline were gazing on a chain of mountains such as that rising before us, which stood between him, and 'Il *bello ovile ov' ei dormì agnello. Nimico a' lupi che gli danno guerra.'" *

"But while we are talking," he went on, "night has dropped her veil in earnest, and the fire-flies begin to light their tiny lanterns—a signal that it is time for me to go home."

"Home!" repeated Lucy, surprised; "you are surely not going back to Bordighera to-night?"

"Oh no," said Antonio; "you do not suppose I am such a fickle cavalier. Do you see that mass of white there to the left of Taggia, with lights in it?"

"I remarked that house before," returned Lucy; "it looks mysterious."

"That is what I call my home when I come to Taggia."

"It is rather far off," said Lucy, "can you not stay here?"

"There is no room."

"Have you no friends at Castellaro?"

"None half so dear as the one who expects me at Taggia."

* . . . The fair sheep-fold, where a sleeping lamb
The wolves set on, and fain had worried *him*.—CARY.

"You are, then, much attached to that friend?"

"I love and revere her with all my heart," was the answer.

Lucy was silent.

"You recollect," Antonio went on, "my telling you once that of all my fellow-creatures the one who ranked highest in my eyes was of your sex. I am now going to that lady. Good-bye till to-morrow, and pleasant dreams.—Bless me, how cold your hands are! You had better go into the house. Yet the air is so soft and mild. Do go in immediately, and have a cup of hot tea, pray do.—You will not? Well, good-bye, I must not stay longer."

Notwithstanding that Sir John, now thoroughly awake, repeatedly urged her to go in, Lucy lingered on the terrace till she saw a tall, dark figure cross the bridge beneath, amid a shower of fire-flies,—the valley by this time looked like a sea of dancing stars. Then, and then only, she rose and joined her father, who had himself gone in to order tea.

Two hours later the same tall figure which had crossed the bridge, was at one of the casements of the mysterious house, standing out in bold relief against the light within. Now, had you whispered in the ear of that figure, as it stood at the window in silent contemplation, "There is sleeplessness somewhere in the neighbourhood on your account," what a start it would have given. So true is it, that even the most thoughtful and tender of men cannot think of everything that the sensitiveness of a woman will suggest to plague herself with.

The figure at last withdraws, shuts the window with a sigh, and an earnest "God bless her!"—a wish in which we join with all our heart.

CHAPTER XVI.
New Characters and Incidents.

IN the place of honour, viz., at the foot of the balustrade which separates the main altar from the body of the neat little church of the sanctuary, we find, at eight o'clock next morning, Speranza and Battista on their knees, most devoutly hearing the mass performing on their behalf. The altar, on which the miraculous image stands, but hidden from profane view by a curtain, is richly ornamented, and the walls around it, as well as those of the two minor chapels to the right and left of the nave, are covered with ex-votos, most of them consisting of silver hearts, occasionally interspersed by a silver leg or arm, with even a silver baby swaddled according to inviolable Italian fashion. There are also many primitive little pictures, nine out of ten of which are intended to represent vessels sinking in horrid seas, with preternatural waves, and the Madonna seated on a cloud, looking placidly on.

Mass being over, the balustrade is flung open by the old Sacristan, who beckons forward Speranza and her betrothed. This is the signal for the congregation, composed chiefly of women, to rush towards the altar. The four tapers in front are lighted, and then the curtain slowly rises amid a jingling of little bells, and there appears a picture of small dimensions—something less than a yard high, and about two feet in breadth—containing three figures, our Lady and the Divine Infant, with round each head a golden glory, and a St. Catherine by their side. A general murmur of satisfaction is sighed forth by the worshippers, whose eyes brighten and glisten as they are raised in contemplation. The Sacristan looks radiant. Speranza on her knees, crimson with blushes, makes her offering, a huge silver heart; Battista slyly and awkwardly tenders his, a picture representing a carriage just upsetting, with the Madonna as usual on a cloud. A short prayer from the priest, a short response from the congregation, and then the priest retires. The Sacristan, while slowly extinguishing the tapers, carries on a little ex-official conversation with some of the bystanders, in the course of which he remarks that it is wonderful to see how much more beautiful the picture grows every day; there is a jingling once more, the curtain falls, and the devout drop away one by one.

"How can these people," said Lucy to the Doctor, as they descended the stairs of a small gallery over the door of the chapel, from which they had witnessed the whole ceremony; "how can these people believe that so small a picture could have served as a sail?"

"Your observation, my dear Miss Davenne, smacks horribly of the heretic," returned the Doctor, gravely; "had the picture been of a proper size, where would have been the miracle?"

And leading the way to the left of the chapel, through a vault supporting the terrace, where they had sat the previous evening, watching the sunset, Antonio added, "Now, if you will trust yourself to my guidance, I will take you where an agreeable surprise awaits you."

"As you please," said Lucy.

This cold way of receiving a proposal sportively made, so different from her habitual, rather buoyant manner, on similar occasions, caused Antonio to look first in her face, then say, "I fear you did not sleep well last night."

"On the contrary," was the abrupt reply, "I never slept better in my life." (Oh! Miss Davenne, Miss Davenne, were it not for that crimson blush staining and burning your cheek, how properly we should scold you for telling such a fib in the very teeth of the Madonna!) Antonio looked at her again, but said nothing, did not even offer her his arm; indeed, she kept sufficiently far from him to justify his thinking, that just then she did not wish for his support. And thus they walked on in silence, till after a sharp turn round a rock they came to a small table-land, covered with a thick jungle of wild roses. Lucy, even in her present mood, could not help brightening up at the sight. "This is where the original chapel stood," said Antonio; "you can perceive the remains of the old walls among the bushes; keep back a little, or you will never get free from the brambles," he added, as he himself plunged into the very thick of them, and began cutting away right and left; then carefully stripping off the thorns, he made a splendid bouquet, and handed it, without speaking, to Lucy, who received it also without speaking.

"Is that a Capuchin?" she asked at last, pointing to a man dressed in a long loose gown, with a rope round his waist, coming along the road at a short distance from them.

"That is the Sacristan who played so conspicuous a part in the chapel this morning. He has laid aside his robes and put on his hermit's gown, for you must know he is the Hermit of Lampedusa, and goes by no other name. He is one of the fixtures of the chapel, and guards it day and night. The Madonna and he are in fact one."

Lucy and the Doctor on their way back to the sanctuary came upon the Hermit, (he probably had been waiting for them,) who made a low obeisance to the lady, and exchanged some words with the gentleman.

"This man," said Antonio, in Italian, tapping the Hermit good-naturedly on the shoulder, "has the Madonna in his sleeve; deny it if you dare." The Hermit, evidently much pleased at this somewhat profane compliment, acknowledged his sense of it with a little toss of the head, and a deprecatory motion of both hands, as much as to say, "Pray, spare my modesty," and passed on. Lucy had eyed him with some curiosity during this halt. He was a thin, dry, ruddy-complexioned man, about sixty, with a pair of small grey eyes, as restless and piercing as those of a ferret,— tell-tale witnesses to his being of a choleric disposition.

"That poor old fellow," said Antonio, "carries on a little trade in common prints of the Madonna, and he told me he was going to call on you presently to show you his collection. He will expect you to make some purchases, which you can bestow on Speranza and Battista, who will be delighted to accept of them. This sort of tribute, which he levies on all visitors to the shrine, with some other trifling perquisites, constitute the Hermit's income, for he has no salary. He is an original worth studying; his fanaticism in all that concerns the Madonna is most ferocious. Compared to him, Torquemada was a pattern of toleration."

They found Battista and Speranza on the terrace. Thus taken by surprise, poor Battista, who had not yet conquered his awe of Lucy, coloured prodigiously, and tried to conceal himself behind Speranza—a manœuvre perceived by every one, but of which, out of compassion to the poor young man, no one took notice. Antonio went to fetch a table for Miss Davenne, and she sat down to sketch. As good as his word, the Hermit shortly after made his appearance, bringing with him a large bundle of prints, admired and praised by all present, and of which Lucy, as just agreed, became the purchaser.

"Have you plenty of visitors?" asked Antonio.

"*Santi chiodi!* I should think so," cried the irascible old man, whose abrupt manner of speaking and habitual jerk of the head caused him to seem in a permanent passion; "I should think so, indeed. It is the same all the year round. People come from Turin, from Genoa, from Nice, from all the parts of the world. And those who cannot come, the Madonna hearkens to just as well if they pray to her; it is faith which saves. Why, only last week, the Marquis of Papparilla, one of the greatest nobles of Genoa, fell ill; the physicians had given him up. But his mother, a really holy woman, do you know what she does?—gives up the physicians as they had given up her son, and sits down and writes a letter to the Curé, begging him to have a Triduo at the shrine. And what happens?—*the very first day* of the Triduo the Marquis was out of danger."

"And what is a Triduo?" asked Lucy.

"A Triduo!" (with the characteristic toss of the head more marked than ever,) "*Santi chiodi!* three days of prayer, and the benediction with the holy sacrament, the bells of the parish ringing all the while. You can have a Triduo for seven francs and twelve sous; three francs for the parish, three for the Madonna, and four-and-twenty sous for the ringing of the bells; eight sous come to me. If you pay three francs twelve sous more, you may have a mass performed each of the three days. Each mass twenty sous, and four additional sous for the walk from Castellaro hither. Why, it is a mere nothing."

"Certainly," said Antonio, "it is not dear. Pray, is the sanctuary of the Madonna *della Guardia*"—pointing to it in the distance—"at all like this?"

"Like this!" exclaimed the old man, reddening, and making a grimace of supreme contempt. "Sanctuaries like this, my good gentleman," he continued with great severity of tone, "are rare, though you hunt through all Christendom for them; a sanctuary like this, my good gentleman, is not to be found elsewhere in all Christendom—but go in to the vestry, I beg, and read the Papal Brief hanging there; it will teach you that this sanctuary of Lampedusa is equal to Rome—yes, sir, the same in point of privileges and indulgences, whether during life or *in articulo mortis*. All that can be got at Rome, where his Holiness the Pope dwells, can all be got here without any exception. When the shrine of our Lady of the *Guardia* can say so much for itself," he concluded with a look of offended dignity, "then, and then only, shall I place it on a footing with this."

"Still," persisted Antonio, with much gravity, "though I am far from wishing to make comparisons, which are always odious things, still I have it from competent authority, that at the intercession of that Madonna of the *Guardia*, some miraculous cures have lately taken place."

"May be so," said the Hermit with cool condescension. "Far be it from me to disparage the Madonna *della Guardia*; may be that she has cured some poor old gouty man or rheumatic old woman. But has she ever restored speech and hearing to those born deaf and dumb, cured paralytics bedridden for twenty-five years, and made rain to fall at a day's notice?"

"You have then yourself witnessed real miracles?" inquired Antonio.

"*Santi chiodi!* have I witnessed miracles? I hope I have," burst out the old man eagerly. "Do you remember the spring of 1835? No, you don't, for you were not yet come to these parts. Not a drop of rain, I give you my solemn word, had fallen for three whole months, and the crop of olives that promised so well that year, was fast going to destruction. There was nothing but lamentation throughout the Riviera. Triduos had been performed; the sacrament had been exhibited for weeks in every parish round; *Novenas* had been going on at the Madonna *della Guardia*, (with a slight sneer,) the relics of San Benedetto had been shown; the miraculous crucifix in the oratory of San Sebastian, at Taggia, had been carried in procession,—still not a drop of rain. All hands were now raised in supplication to Castellaro. 'What are the Castellini waiting for?' was asked on every side. 'They who possess such a miraculous image, why do they not bring it forth? Do they mean to delay till every hope of saving the olives is lost?' Well, sir, what does our Curé do? He writes a beautiful letter to the Bishop of Ventimiglia, which made every one weep who read or heard it; now or never, he writes, is the time for having the Madonna of Lampedusa carried to the parish church, and shown to the faithful. The Bishop, like a holy man, as he is, sends back a beautiful letter in answer to the Curé's, saying, that the time in fact was come to give the Madonna of Lampedusa a fair trial. On the first of May, then, we set off in procession—such a crowd as you can have no conception of:—there were all the Confraternities from Taggia, from Riva, from Pompejana, from Boscomara, indeed, where did they not come from?—so we set off, the Curé in his white surplice heading the procession, the Confraternities following behind with big tapers in their hands —real wax tapers—and we carry the blessed picture under a baldaquin, just as if it had been the sacrament—we carry it, I say, to the parish church. Well, what do you think was the consequence? On the evening of that same day,—mind, of that same day,—rumble, rumble, rumble, flash, flash, flash, a terrific thunderstorm came on, and then down poured rain, rain, rain, in bucketsful, as though it had never rained before. To finish my story, our picture remained in the parish church for fifteen days, and for fifteen days the rain never ceased pouring in torrents; till, at last, fearing there might be a second deluge, we brought the Madonna back in a hurry, and lo! as soon as we had done that, there was an end of rain, and the sun shone out splendidly, and we had a plentiful harvest. Do you call this a miracle or not?" asked the Hermit, looking round on his audience with beaming eyes.

Speranza and Battista, who had listened open-mouthed to the story, in a sort of trance of ecstasy, immediately sent forth a volley of inarticulate sounds, meant to express enthusiastic acquiescence and wonder.

"But this is not all," resumed the Hermit, after a silence of a minute or two, the better to enjoy the renewed surprise of his listeners. "One evening, while the picture was in the parish church, another attendant and I had just replaced the fourteen big wax-tapers that burned before it all day, by the fourteen oil lamps which, for the sake of economy, were lighted at night, and we were going away, when all of a sudden the lamps began to dance up and down. 'Do you see that?' said I to the other man. 'Yes,' answered he all of a tremble; the word was scarcely spoken, when up and down went the lamps again."

"Did the picture also dance up and down?" asked Antonio, with the most perfect composure.

"Not the least," answered the Hermit, earnestly; "the picture did not move in the least. 'The Madonna gives us a sign,' says I to my comrade, 'there is something wrong here.' And so we began rummaging about, poking under the benches, looking into the confessionals, and searching every hole and corner. For my part, to tell you the truth, I thought that there might be thieves in the church, for you must know we have ten beautiful silver lamps there. We looked, and looked, without finding anything, and we had made up our minds to go away, when all at once the lamps began dancing more violently than ever. We set to work to search all over again, and guess what we found at last?—(A tantalizing stop; Speranza and Battista's eyes were ready to start out of their heads with thrilling expectation)—We found a little boy of six years old, quietly sleeping under the shelter of one of the minor altars. Now fancy, if the poor child had awakened in the dead of the night there all alone, he would certainly have died of fright. This is what the Madonna would not permit, so she gave us a sign, and through her holy interference, the innocent little creature was saved from certain death."

This conclusion not being contradicted by anybody, while it was most emphatically agreed to by Speranza and Battista, who knows how many more miracles the old man would have narrated, had it not been for Antonio, who, announcing that he must go to visit some patients, both at Castellaro and Taggia, playfully drew the Hermit's arm under his own, and carried him off, on the plea of having some important communication to make respecting our Lady of the *Guardia*. Lucy recommenced drawing, Battista crept farther and farther away, then vanished altogether; and Speranza, seating herself by the side of her young benefactress, began to work at some of her wedding garments. We ought to have said before, that, among the contrivances provided by Doctor Antonio's foresight for the convenience of his fellow-travellers, there figured a wide awning, which had been by his orders put up over the terrace that morning, and it is under its shade we leave Miss Davenne for a while.

Among the numerous loungers who were the constant ornament of the Boulevard de Gand of Taggia, and consequently one of those who had marked the progress of our little party through the *Pantano*, was Signor Orlando

Pistacchini, manager and chief actor of the dramatic company bearing his euphonious name, and forming the delight of the respectable public of Taggia. When we make this last affirmation, we avail ourselves of a rather hyperbolical phrase, copied literally from the manuscript bills placarded at the four corners of the *Pantano*. If we were to state facts in their genuine historical nakedness, we ought to say, that as nobody went to the theatre, so the company in question formed the delight or horror of nobody; and we are free also to declare, that the honourable *corps dramatique* were *bona fide* starving. A very unpleasant predicament, and one which caused the unlucky manager, who was fasting from all food, to lean rather dejectedly against a stone pillar, ruminating as to how or where he was likely to find a dinner. Roused from his sad reflections by the advent of the strangers, Orlando Pistacchini languidly raised his hat, speculated for one moment on what they might have had for breakfast, and then relapsed into his painful meditations. But when fame with her hundred trumpets, or to speak less poetically, but more truly, when a tall, fair-haired cabinet-maker spread far and wide the intelligence that Doctor Antonio's two companions were none other than the Milordo Inglese of Bordighera and his daughter, on their way to Lampedusa, where they were to stay a couple of days—when the manager, we say, heard this, a sudden flash of light revealed to him an endless succession of breakfasts and dinners; he ran home at full speed, sat down at his table, and wrote as follows:—

"MOST ILLUSTRIOUS MILORDO,

"When a friend and protector of the fine arts of your rank and generosity, comes within the reach of such humble but sincere votaries and worshippers of Melpomene and Thalia as we profess to be, we should be unworthy indeed of that name of artists in which we pride ourselves, did we not reverently tender to the noble representative of ART and GREAT BRITAIN such public testimony of respectful

sympathy and deference as in our power lies. To that effect the Pistacchini Dramatic Company are making preparations for an extra performance on the evening of to-morrow, the 22d June, to consist of the fifth act of the celebrated Tragedy
ARISTODEMO,
FOLLOWED BY THE HIGHLY ENTERTAINING COMEDY
L'AJO NELL' IMBARAZZO,
(*The Tutor in a Puzzle,*)
in which Orlando Pistacchini will have the honour to appear as Aristodemo and l'Ajo. Such is the entertainment for which we solicit the patronage of the English Mecænas, and at which we humbly crave the favour of his presence, and that of his unparalleled daughter. All Taggia will flock to the theatre to do honour to such distinguished guests. We hope you will come. Alas! the muse is too often unheeded now-a-days, and if noble and generous hands are not raised in her support, what is to become of her? We therefore entreat you most humbly to come. This is the ardent prayer of your Lordship's most humble and obedient servant,
"ORLANDO PISTACCHINI,
"*Manager and Chief Actor.*

"*N. B.*—No pains or expense will be spared to give the performance the splendour befitting so glorious an occasion. The house will be lighted *a giorno*, and a flight of pigeons will take place between the Tragedy and Comedy. We trust to your noble heart too entirely to apprehend the disappointment of a refusal."

Orlando made two copies of this sort of last lay of a manager on the brink of destruction; the second, with slight variations, being intended for Miss Davenne, and then went to bed, "perchance to sleep." The next morning saw him and his spouse Signora Rosalinda, (a little round body, choking with fat, and something asthmatic,) both dressed in their best attire, blowing and panting in the hot sun, on the road to Lampedusa.

Sir John Davenne, much about the same time, after a comfortable breakfast, had taken a fancy to go and enjoy his morning's paper in the shade of one of the two evergreen oaks that spread their dome of verdure at a little distance in front of the sanctuary. The shade being very thick, and a little breeze blowing from the north, Sir John, after an hour or so, felt rather chilly, so he got up, and began, with eyes still riveted on the paper, walking slowly forward in the sun, and, as his evil star would have it, in the direction of Castellaro. The Baronet was in the keen enjoyment of a very sharp attack on the Whig leader of the House by a member of the opposition, when all of a sudden a shadow fell on his paper, and raising his eyes, he found himself confronted by a very short apoplectic-looking woman, in a faded pink bonnet, and a tall, lanky yellow man, all skin and bones, both of whom, with outstretched arms and frantic gesticulations, proceeded forthwith to apostrophize him in a violently theatrical manner. Sir John hurried on with an oath; the man and woman, gasping and panting, but keeping their place on either side of the astounded Baronet, most gallantly maintained their fire. Sir John in despair wheeled round again, and quickened his walk almost to a run; the dramatic pair wheeled also, quickening their pace in the same proportion, the lady in particular skipping after him in hot chase.

"Gracious me!" said Speranza, happening at the moment to look in that direction; "what can Milor, your papa, be running so for?"

"Don't you see a man and woman pursuing him?" exclaimed Lucy in dismay; "they are thieves, perhaps."

"Oh, no! no danger of that," replied Speranza. "I see now who they are; it is the manager of the Taggia theatre, Signor Pistacchini, with his wife. I'll run down and see what it is they want."

In another moment, Sir John stepped on the terrace, quite out of breath and temper. "What is the matter, papa?" cried Lucy.

"How can I tell you, child?" grunted Sir John. "A couple of vagabonds, who stick to me like my shadow, bellowing all the while as if they were possessed. I don't understand a word they are saying. No privacy to be had in this country, not even at the top of a mountain."

"Speranza knows these people," said Lucy, soothingly; "they are actors belonging to the theatre of Taggia; they mean no harm, I am sure."

"What is it to me whether they mean harm or not, when they do me actual harm?" replied the Baronet, sullenly. "Confound the—a—pair of impudent strollers."

Lucy was silent. Speranza came back presently with the two famous addresses, and said that Signor and Signora Pistacchini having heard of Miss Davenne and Sir John's being in the neighbourhood, (it was worth something to hear Speranza say *Sir John*,) had settled to give a grand performance in their honour, and had come up on foot all the way from Taggia to entreat that father and daughter would honour the theatre with their presence. "The poor creatures are steaming like horses, and are so worn out and faint," continued the girl, her voice dying into a whisper, meant only for Lucy's ear.

"Are faint with hunger!" cried out Lucy, quite shocked, and her voice vibrated with painful surprise. "Papa, these poor people have walked all the way from Taggia, and have had no breakfast."

"Well, what of that?" returned papa, peevishly; "if they have had no breakfast, why, let them have one, that's all."

Acting upon this hint, Speranza was despatched with orders to see that Signor Pistacchini and his wife were treated to a good meal, and to say that afterwards Miss Davenne would be happy to receive them. Lucy then looked over the addresses, and not without some peals of laughter did she translate to her father the one intended for him. Sir John could not help smiling at what he properly named the hungry style of the address. Shall we add that the incense it exhaled, however gross, rather agreeably tickled the worthy Baronet's senses, and that the statement about the advent of the British Mecænas found favour in his sight?

"Suppose we go, papa!" said Lucy, seeing her father restored to serenity.

"And come back past midnight, up that break-neck road!" asked Sir John. "Nonsense, my dear. Signor Pastaccani, or whatever you call him, and his wife, do not care a fig for our presence; it is money they want. Give them some, and get rid of them."

"We had better ask Doctor Antonio what to do," said Lucy. "Though it is clear enough that these people are sadly in want, yet" (she went on with some hesitation) "it is difficult to offer money to people who ask for none, and, for what we know, may have seen better days."—Kind, sensible, considerate Lucy!

"Pooh!" said Sir John, rising to go, "try and you will see whether they take it or not."

Agreed, Sir John, ten to one they would take it. Hunger, *malesuada fames*, as you have read at school, is a beast hard to manage, and most of those who are in the saddle will dismount on any terms. Still the method you propose has objections. Might not that handful of coins you bid your gentle daughter tender in the shape of alms, bring a blush on those two wrinkled brows, which had better be spared them; or rend away one more shred of that last safeguard of honesty, self-respect, which had better be left untouched? While, if you wait till to-morrow, and send your large or small donation—through the benevolent Doctor, for instance —send it as an equivalent for the pleasure that was prepared for you, the odds are ninety to a hundred that you wound no feeling, bow down no head in shame, and are blessed all the same as a generous benefactor.

These reflections, that for the sake of effect, we have put under the form of an apostrophe to our friend the Baronet, rose spontaneously in the mind of our sweet heroine, and prompted her behaviour during her subsequent interview with Signor Pistacchini, and Signora Rosalinda. Far from offering money, Miss Davenne did not make even a remote allusion of the sort. She said how sorry she was that they had had such a hot and fatiguing walk, and how grateful she and her father were for their flattering invitation; she was not sure whether she could avail herself of it, but some of her friends would be sure to go to the theatre, and consequently she begged that two boxes, at all events, might be retained for their party in the name of Sir John Davenne. Upon this Signor Pistacchini and his wife took their leave, if not quite satisfied with the result of their expedition, yet highly enchanted with their reception, and so entirely conquered by Lucy's grace and kindness, that they emphatically declared to Speranza, as she faithfully reported, that the young lady was an angel, and as such, they still hoped, would condescend to honour them with her presence on the ensuing evening.

"And why should you not go, dear lady?" said Speranza, her great eyes sparkling—"only think what a splendid performance it will be, with illuminations as bright as day, and a flight of pigeons!"

"Should you like to see it?" asked Lucy, smiling at the peasant girl's enthusiasm.

"Oh yes!—of all things in the world—and Battista too," was the naïve reply. "Signor Pistacchini is such a beautiful actor, they say."

"Indeed!" said Lucy; "well, Speranza, you shall go."

"Not unless you do," answered Speranza, resolutely.

"And why not?" returned Lucy. Speranza silently shook her head. "We shall see what Doctor Antonio says about the matter; at all events, you shall stay here till to-morrow. Hutchins, I daresay, will find a corner for you in her room, and Battista must do the best he can for himself."

"Oh! never mind him, he can sleep anywhere," said Speranza; and away she ran in high glee to communicate this unexpected arrangement to her lover.

When Doctor Antonio returned, Lucy gave him Signor Pistacchini's fine piece of eloquence to read.

"What do you think of doing?" he asked.

"What should you advise?" inquired Lucy in her turn.

"I should advise you to go," said the Doctor; "here a little bit of human nature offers to your observation, why should you not profit by the opportunity? So my advice is, Go."

"I would fain do so," returned Lucy, "chiefly on Speranza's account, who has set her heart on going. But papa objects, as it would be difficult to come back to Lampedusa at night."

"I don't see why you should absolutely come back to Lampedusa for the night," observed Antonio.

"Have you not told me yourself many a time that there is no decent hotel at Taggia?"

"True," said the Italian; "but you and your father could sleep at Signora Eleonora's."

"You mean at the house you call your home?"

"Just so. Signora Eleonora wishes very much to make your acquaintance."

"I am much obliged both to her and you, but it is not my habit to put to any inconvenience persons whom I don't know. We shall not go."

This brief sentence was delivered curtly, haughtily, almost scornfully, in the best style of Sir John Davenne himself, when on his high horse. Antonio coloured deeply, but said nothing. He went to a chair at some distance, took up the paper that was lying on it, sat down, and seemed absorbed by its contents. We cannot vouch that he did actually read, unless he read the same word over and over again, as his eyes did not move. Lucy went on with her drawing, seemingly in a great hurry to finish and get rid of it.

Presently Speranza came in singing merrily, "*Ma l'amor della Rosina, Dove mai lo trove,*"—but the song died on her lips the moment she saw the couple on the terrace, sitting so far apart from one another, with every appearance of indifference to each other's society. She went on tiptoe to

Doctor Antonio, and asked in an under tone, "Are we to go to the theatre?"

"I am afraid not, my poor Speranza; Miss Davenne refuses to sleep at Signora Eleonora's."

"Oh! what a pity!" cried Speranza, very crest-fallen, "and why does she refuse?"

"I do not know—you can ask herself."

Speranza went to Lucy, and bending down at her side, said something to her in a whisper, overheard by the Doctor. Lucy rose instantly, went up to Doctor Antonio, and leaning on the back of his chair, said, with some little confusion, "Is the kindest of doctors still inclined to introduce the crossest of girls to Signora Eleonora?"

"To be sure!" said Antonio, looking up at her with a queer mixture of amazement and pleasure; "how can you doubt it?"

"Then," said Lucy, all smiles and blushes, "I shall be most happy to make your friend's acquaintance."

Now or never would have been the time for the Doctor's exclaiming with Figaro:—"*Donne, Donne, eterni Dei chi v' arriva a indovinar?*" Who, indeed, can fathom the depths of a woman's heart? Here was a girl, just now all pepper and vinegar, who suddenly becomes as sweet as sugar-candy; she, who scornfully refused, but a moment ago, to accept a civility from a person she *did not know*, now begs as a favour to be introduced to that very person! Where is the criterion, we would like to know, whereby to account for such flagrant contradictions? We had a faint hope of finding a clue to this riddle in the few words whispered by Speranza to the young lady, but the more we reflect on those words, the less can we see how they could have occasioned that sudden change in Miss Davenne's disposition; however, let the judicious reader judge for himself, and make what he can of them; we transcribe them literally. "Why," had said Speranza, "why, dear lady, will you not go to Signora Eleonora? She is the nicest and sweetest old lady in all the Riviera."

Another thing that puzzles us is this, how a man of sense and feeling as we take Antonio to be, should not have called on Lucy to explain the why of her unreasonable crossness, or how it was that he should not have thought proper, at least, to put on a look expressive of some displeasure at the wilful ways of the dear spoiled child. But quite the contrary. Antonio gazed on her more fondly than ever, and addressed her with a thrill in his voice, as if Miss Lucy's whim had still more endeared her to him.

"And Sir John?" asked the Doctor.

"We must try and coax papa to agree to go," said Lucy. The negotiation with Sir John was long and difficult, lasting all dinner-time. Lucy brought all her feminine diplomacy to bear against papa, and was admirably seconded by that rogue of a Doctor Antonio, who, from time to time, threw out mysterious hints about Signora Eleonora's ancestors, and talked in such a way about the loop-holes and casemates of that lady's dwelling, as invested it with the prestige of a castle. What could Sir John, thus attacked in every weak point, do but yield? Lucy was in the most amiable and cheerful mood all the rest of the day, she had taken such a fancy to the *old lady*, that she could speak of nothing else, and during the quiet walk she took after dinner, with her father and Doctor Antonio, to the jungle of wild roses, Lucy insisted on hearing the Signora's story, which did not take long telling. Signora Eleonora was a widow, of whose numerous family only two sons survived, and both of these sons were political exiles. The lady had left Genoa, the former residence of the family, for the environs of Taggia, where all that remained of the bulk of her property was situated, and where she lived in great retirement. A short story, concluded Antonio, which might easily be made a long and impressive one, could only the hundredth part of the sorrow, fortitude, and active charity, comprised in it, be related. How warmly Lucy sympathized now with Doctor Antonio's admiration for Signora Eleonora; how keenly she felt for her, and for another poor bereaved mother whose only son was also an exile!

CHAPTER XVII.
The Theatre.

ON coming to the Sanctuary next morning, Antonio found Lucy very busy making a sketch of Signora Eleonora's house, which she intended as a present to the old lady. Lucy had not discovered till that morning how picturesque the old building looked, and how nicely the dark-vaulted gallery along its front contrasted with the open terrace above, all verdant with a trellis of vine. Antonio sat down by Lucy, and began telling her how on the previous evening he had paid a visit to the Pistacchinis, whom he had found supping on a salad—to give them the longed-for news that Sir John Davenne and his daughter would honour the play with their company on the morrow; and how the intelligence had been received with such frantic demonstrations of joy, such hurrahing, such dancing about the room, such a throwing of the poor salad out of the window, that he, the Doctor, had for a moment hesitated whether he ought not to have recourse to his lancet as a sedative. "To see the manager," pursued the Doctor, "as I have seen him this morning, parading through the *Pantano* in all his glory, receiving and answering with a royal condescension suited to Aristodemo, applications for tickets pouring in on him from all sides —to hear the thrilling inflections of his voice, as he confidentially stated to me that places were at a premium, and that he relied on the receipt of a hundred francs—to see and hear this was better than any comedy ever acted. You are going to make the fortune of the company. All Taggia will assemble in the theatre to see the English family."

"But how do they know that we shall be there?" asked Lucy.

"Everything is known in small places like this, and then Pistacchini has taken good care that the public shall be circumstantially informed. There is even now hanging over the *Cartellone* (huge play-bill) in the *Pantano*, this announcement in letters half-a-foot high, *Under the Patronage of the English Family;* besides which, all the manuscript bills placarded at every corner have a significant N. B. in large text, *The presence of the English Family is certain!*"

Lucy was excessively diverted by the notion of thus forming the great attraction of the evening's performance, and Antonio went on to tell her of the arrangements he had made. There was, as far as he could judge, but one possibility of anything going wrong. Signora Eleonora had done wonders already in providing for the reception not only of Sir John and his daughter, but also in finding a room for Speranza and Hutchins; that, however, was all she could do. Now, Doctor Antonio had his misgivings how English John would stand the delights and comforts of the Taggia *Locanda*, whither he was to go under Battista's charge. John had, to be sure, been seen to smile when told at what cost he must enjoy the theatre; "but his ignorance," stated Doctor Antonio, "is a bliss from which I dread *his* awaking. And tomorrow, at two o'clock," ended the Doctor, "I have settled with Sir John that the whole party shall be at the cross-way, where the Taggia road joins that of Nice, to return to Bordighera."

"I shall be glad to see that old ugly Osteria again," said Lucy, smiling; "what transports Rosa will be in to have us back!"

At a little past seven in the evening, Sir John and Lucy mounted the mules that were to take them down the mountain. Sir John was as trim and precise in his dress as if he had been going to Her Majesty's Theatre on a drawing-room night; Lucy was in her blue muslin, and broad straw-hat, which Speranza had adorned with blue cornflowers and red poppies, and vastly lovely she looked, the little flutter of her spirits giving unusual brightness to her complexion. It being still broad daylight, the descent though steep had no danger; Antonio, however, had his hand all the way on the young lady's bridle-rein. They left the mules at the entrance of the bridge, and joined by the two English servants and the Italian lovers, they crossed over in military order, turned to the left, and after a five minutes' walk by the river-side, came all at once on an enormous palace. "It is curious, is it not," remarked Antonio, "to find in a small town like Taggia, a building belonging to a private family, of such magnificence and taste as this, having a theatre to boot, like another Versailles?" A crowd was assembled here, evidently gaping with curiosity, but a passage was at once made for the English visitors, who where piloted by Antonio, through a gate to the left, into a peristyle swarming with people on tiptoe also, to get a peep of the illustrious strangers.

To the left of the entrance-door was a table covered with a red cloth, and on the table, between two lighted wax-candles, was a silver basin, containing a fair average of coins, some modestly enveloped in paper, others boldly uncovered, and before that table, like the Dragon of Hesperides, was seated our newly made acquaintance, Orlando Pistacchini, in the royal robes, and on his head the royal bandeau of Aristodemus, king of Messenia. As soon as he caught a glimpse of Sir John, he rose up, laid his two palms on his heart, and in that attitude made a low obeisance to the new comers. Sir John, who had been previously instructed by Antonio of the custom on such occasions, dropped a very neat compact little packet of white paper into the basin, which, as it fell, gave forth a most exhilarating jingle. Expectation was at its highest pitch, every neck lengthened and strained towards the table. Aristodemus bowed once again, had one wild passing thought of snatching at the packet; but conquering the temptation, led the way up a flight of wooden stairs to the two reserved boxes. Here he again crossed his palms over his heart, bowed low, and retreated without turning his back, as though in the presence of royalty. Lucy put off her hat, and leaning over the front of the box, with her beautiful rich ringlets flowing in profusion down her cheeks and neck, elicited a general murmur of admiration from every part of the house.

It was a pretty little theatre, brilliantly illuminated with wax-candles, and pit and boxes crammed to suffocation. "All the *ban* and *arrière ban* of the local aristocracy are at their post," whispered Antonio to Lucy.

"Aristocracy at Taggia!" said Lucy, smiling.

"Yes, indeed, and among the most stiff-necked of aristocracies," remarked Antonio, slyly. "The list is headed by a marchioness, that elderly lady there with the Genoese *pezzotto* on her head, and who looks—mark that I only say *looks*—so unpretending. This palace and theatre belong to her, and her family have been lords of the soil from time immemorial. The marchioness has paid you the compliment of giving up her box to you this evening."

"How kind! exclaimed Lucy; "I should like to be able to thank her."

"You can adopt our Italian custom, if you like, and pay her a visit in her box. That pinched nose and yellow face, shadowed by white feathers on the left, belong to a baroness, and the old gentleman with the powdered head, whispering in her ear, and who looks so full of importance, is the mayor of the town. That grey-haired, grey-eyed, lusty countenance beyond, which looks so innocent"—Antonio's descriptions were suddenly cut short by a sharp whistle, and the curtain rising discovered to view Aristodemo in that peculiar brown study, which seems the normal condition of all tragedy heroes. But not all Orlando's efforts at official despondency could subdue the joyous twinkle which the certainty of a monster-receipt had kindled in his eyes. Aristodemus went through his part with spirit, and met his death in gallant style, his fall being pronounced capital by connoisseurs. Lucy had all the while the benefit of a double performance, of which the one on the stage was not the most interesting. Through a chink in the wooden partition between the boxes, she and Antonio could see Battista's countenance, and watch all the *crescendo* of terror depicted in the young man's features, when he saw the king feel for his poniard and try its point. "Is he going to kill himself?" he asked of Speranza in great alarm; and what a start he gave, and how his hair literally stood on end when the steps of the spectre, who is supposed to inhabit the royal tomb, were heard approaching, and Aristodemus, driven to madness by the sound, actually plunged his poniard into his breast!

The flight of pigeons which came after the tragedy gave rise to an incident which still farther increased the excitement always attendant on this pretty sight. Inventive Signor Pistacchini had arranged, as he hoped, an agreeable surprise for the English visitors and the public, in the shape of a pigeon, which, fastened by some contrivance of his own to two packthreads thrown across from a sort of *œil de bœuf* in the drop-scene to the front of the box occupied by the strangers, was to appear to glide of its own accord within their reach. Now, from some impediment or other, the bird thus launched only achieved half of its aerial course, and stopping midway, hung head downwards, fluttering its wings most piteously. This mischance caused an immoderate uproar; the whole pit rose at once, the most enthusiastic standing on the benches with uplifted arms, vainly striving to reach the pigeon, while a universal shout for the manager was raised. Pistacchini quickly made his appearance, armed with a pole, and getting down from the stage into the pit, he managed to push the unlucky bird sufficiently near to Lucy to allow Antonio to release and deliver it into the English girl's hands, amid a thunder of applause.

This little addition to the entertainment, which was not in the evening's programme, being over, Lucy went and paid a visit to the marchioness to thank that noble lady for having given up her box. "So very kind," said Miss Lucy, "as it undoubtedly afforded the best view of the stage;" and then she spoke so nicely about the beauty of the palace and the prettiness of the theatre, that she left the old dowager highly prepossessed in her favour.

After having endured the protracted terrors of the tragedy,

Battista might be held entitled to some indemnification at the manager's hands, and if so, he certainly received an ample one from the comedy which followed. Who could depict his transports at seeing the "Puzzled Tutor" listening thunderstruck to his eldest pupil's confession that he is married, yes, positively married to the young lady of the house opposite! Unhappy tutor, what is he to say to his pupil's father, who has ordained and decreed that his sons are never to exchange a word with one of the other sex! Not only married, but, Heaven help us! the papa of a baby who is actually heard crying and screaming! The tutor is ready to tear his hair. His pupil a familyman, his misogamist employer a grandfather! Into what fits of irresistible laughter was Battista thrown when the youngest son of this terrible count is surprised by his father, on his knees, making a declaration to Martha the old cook! and then, when the "Puzzled Dominie" is persuaded to go and fetch the baby, and is confronted on the way back by the count, who flings open the poor man's scanty cloak and discovers the infant Bernardino topsy-turvy, like the poor pigeon, what ecstasy of glee could be compared to that of Battista! And, indeed, who could help laughing at the drollery of this comedy? Even to Sir John Davenne, who understood but little of what was going on, the laughter was contagious, while, as for Lucy, she laughed almost as much as Battista.

Before the end of the evening the marchioness returned Lucy's visit, and the mayor, as the representative of the town, came partly to pay his respects to Sir John and Miss Davenne, and partly to indulge his own curiosity and that of the baroness, whose compliments he was charged to deliver. Lucy was really pleased with all this attention, and the proud Baronet not a little gratified, particularly as that wag of a doctor minutely detailed with becoming gravity all the titles and qualifications of these personages.

It was past midnight when the curtain fell for good and all, and our party made their exit from the theatre, Antonio confiding to Lucy as he saw John—rendered more than

usually solemn by the reflected honours of the evening—
marching away with Battista, that he respected John as a
martyr. As for the English lady's-maid, who, arm-in-arm
with Speranza, followed in the rear of Sir John, Lucy, and
Antonio, she was in a great state of flutter; and when she
discovered that the party of young men—the cabinet-maker
very conspicuous—before and behind them, carrying blazing
torches, and singing Rossini's "Buona Sera," were there to
do them honour, she fell to crying and laughing, it was so
dreadfully affecting, she declared. This escort was quite a
spontaneous compliment, Doctor Antonio asserted, with
which he had nothing to do. Thus accompanied they reached
Signora Eleonora's house, where they were received by a
smart young woman and man, it having been made one of
the conditions of the acceptance of the old lady's hospitality,
that she should not sit up for them; and after taking tea,
which was all ready, the Baronet and his daughter were
shewn to their rooms, Speranza and Miss Hutchins to theirs,
and the Doctor departed to find a bed at some other friend's
house.

It was rather late in the morning when Lucy, after a night
of sound sleep, got up, and going to open the window to let
in the fresh air, caught sight of a comely lady, dressed in
black, walking in the garden below, who appeared to be im-
pressing directions in a cautious whisper on the smart young
woman, Lucy's acquaintance of the previous evening, now
busy gathering flowers to add to the large nosegay she
already held in her hand. The noise of the window opening
caused Signora Eleonora to look up. "Ah! good morning,
Miss Davenne," said the lady in a tone of hearty welcome,
"it does my heart good to see you; I hope we have not disturbed your sleep?"

"Oh! not at all, thank you," said Lucy, blushing, "I have
slept so well."

"So much the better," returned the kind old lady; "young
people need a good deal of rest. You must let me know when

you are ready to receive me. I long to kiss that sweet face of yours."

When, shortly after, the Italian lady, carrying the flowers with her, went to visit her young guest, there was in her voice and smile so much softness, something so touching in the slight melancholy that fell, like a veil, over her whole person, something so truly motherly in the manner with which, taking Lucy's hands in her own, she parted the ringlets from the fair brow, and kissed her the while, and called her "my child," that Lucy felt a tightening of her throat, which prevented her giving an answer to the kind inquiries after her health, and leant her lovely head on the bosom of her newly-found friend. Poor Lucy could not help thinking all the time of her own dear mother.

While the two ladies were thus making acquaintance with one another, Sir John had been on a tour of inspection, and was receiving impressions from all he saw much to the advantage of the dwelling and its owner. Though not looking half so grand as they had done on the night before, when seen by torch-light, still the gloomy archway and avenue of stone pillars that led up to the house, and the dingy, strong-built house itself, all had a solemn, stern appearance of their own, which pleased and interested the Englishman. The half-effaced frescoes on the time-worn walls, the mutilated statue of the marble fountain, facing the entrance, the coat of arms, carved in black stone over the doors and over the mantel-pieces of the huge fireplaces within, all such vestiges of ancient splendour had been noticed and chronicled in favour of Signora Eleonora, and had set working the bump of veneration for old things and old times, which was among the most prominent on the Baronet's skull. Doctor Antonio, bent on obtaining his breakfast, came suddenly upon the Baronet, who was standing with head thrown back, apparently meditating on a species of old funnel, with a double opening over the great door, which Doctor Antonio said was an appendage of most houses near the coast, being meant to enable those within to pour down heated liquids on the assailants. The appearance of the Châtelaine, just coming from the garden, hand in hand with Lucy, completed the series of agreeable impressions received by the Baronet, who, unable to express his feelings otherwise, hastened forward to hand the old lady to the house with all due deference. Signora Eleonora was not only ladylike, as he subsequently whispered to Antonio, but had all the dignity of manner belonging to a court.

The table was laid on the terrace, of which we have already had occasion to speak, and Signora Eleonora and her guests sat down to breakfast in the pleasant shade of a vine, which, trained over a trellis, hung down in festoons, forming a verdant wall on all sides, except to the south, from whence there was a glorious view of the sea. Signora Eleonora did the honours of the table with that easy grace of manner, under which a true lady of the old school knows so well how to hide her unremitting attention to the comfort of each guest. To see her smile so pleasantly, to hear her talk so cheerfully, you would never surmise that the dear old lady had wounds in her heart which bled without intermission. Signora Eleonora did not make one of that numerous sisterhood who use their own sorrows as a club with which to knock down other people's spirits. Indeed, during the two hours she had spent with Lucy the kind soul had not so much as made the most covert allusion to her trials; and Lucy, though ardently wishing to show her sympathy, had not dared to broach a subject so kept in the background. Encouraged, however, by the Doctor's presence, our sweet English girl now made bold to ask Signora Eleonora how her sons were. They were very well when last she heard, was the answer.

"I hope," went on Lucy, after a little hesitation, "that you hear regularly from them?"

"Pretty regularly," said the old lady, "hitherto, thank God; a little sooner or a little later, letters from my sons have always found their way to me."

Lucy's eyes turned to Antonio.

"Signora Eleonora means to say," explained the Doctor, "that hitherto the person or persons deputed to open and scan all letters from the Signora's sons to her, or hers to them, have been generous enough to let them reach their destination."

"It is too bad," exclaimed the warm-hearted Lucy, "to interfere in that way between a mother and her sons."

"Bad as the case is," observed the Signora, meekly, "it might be still worse. I have heard of poor Polish refugees who were pitilessly cut off for years and years from all epistolary intercourse with their mothers and wives."

Honest Sir John, on being made cognizant of the topic they were discussing, declared that he considered the charge thus laid at the door of the Government of so serious and odious a nature, that—that—that—

"That you can scarcely believe it," prompted Antonio, "unless clearly proved by facts. This is but just. Will Signora Eleonora allow me to tell Sir John the story of the French marshal?"

Signora Eleanora having smiled assent, Antonio proceeded thus:—"One of Signora Eleanora's sons, at that time a child of eight years old, while living here, took a great liking to a boy of his own age, a native of Taggia, and they became great play-fellows and friends. In the course of years this boy was drawn for the army, and rose to the rank of serjeant. Two years ago this young man happened to come here on a visit to his parents, and Signora Eleonora, naturally enough, in writing to her son, mentioned that his former play-fellow, now a good-looking soldier of eight-and-twenty, had risen to be a non-commissioned officer. The Signora's son wrote back how glad he was to hear of the good fortune of the 'marshal,' as he jokingly called his former playmate. Well and good. A few days after receiving this letter, who should call upon Signora Eleonora but that same powder-headed old gentleman who paid you a visit in your box last evening, no other, in fact, than the Mayor of Taggia, who required of her to let him see without delay the French marshal she harboured in her house, or it would be his unpleasant duty—such being the precise orders he had received from Turin—to proceed to search the house. Signora Eleonora at first could scarcely believe her own ears. A French marshal!—where had she ever known one? At last she recollected her son's letter, and so laughed at the worthy magistrate as quite to put him out of countenance. Explanations were given, the letter shown, and here the matter ended."

Sir John had heard before of permanent courts-martial for trying, shooting, or hanging Italian patriots by the score, of thousands languishing in prison, or wandering homeless through the world, yet none of these collective misfortunes had awakened his sympathies or aroused his indignation half so much as this little anecdote. There was something so puerile, so mean in such surveillance, he said. Thus, a homœopathic dose of medicine has sometimes been known to act powerfully on constitutions which had resisted allopathic doses ten thousand times as strong. It may be, too, that the sight of the gentle-looking person to whom such indignities had been offered, had roused all the man in Sir John's breast. We suppose that he knew nothing at that time of a certain English statute which made it legal in certain circumstances, and under certain regulations, to break the seal of private letters and pry into their contents, even in his constitutional and free country; ten to one but that, when he did become aware of such a provision, though loathing the very name of reform, he wished for a reform in that respect, and did his best to bring one about.

After breakfast Lucy went to her room to fetch the sketch which she had made of Signora Eleonora's house. The old lady was as much pleased with it as though it had not been the work of a beginner, and fastening it to the wall in her sitting-room, said that she should never see it without thinking of her young English friend. It was now time to go. The Signora insisted upon accompanying them to the end of the avenue. Sir John offered her his arm, and it was a pleasure to see with what a courtly and deferential air he supported his hostess, and the care he took to suit his step to hers. The parting between the two ladies was touching; they separated more like friends than acquaintances of a few hours' standing. Big tears trembled in Lucy's eyes as she fondly kissed the withered cheeks of the old lady, and said, "I pray that one day you may be consoled by your dear ones being restored to you." Big tears trembled in Signora Eleonora's eyes, as, kissing the fresh beautiful girl, she answered, "May it please God to listen to your prayer. I live in hope; but if the Almighty has willed it otherwise, I have faith that we shall all meet there," and she raised her eyes to heaven. "God bless you! Farewell!"—and they were gone.

Signora Eleonora stood still, giving a last wave of her hand ere they disappeared at the turn of the road, then, with slow steps and brow bent to the ground, the lonely soul walked back to her lonely house.

CHAPTER XVIII.
Antonio pledges himself.

EARLY and quietly on the next day but one after the return to the Osteria, Battista and Speranza were married in the parish church, and by ten o'clock, the usual breakfast hour of the English family, every trace of such little festivity as could not be dispensed with, viz., the modest repast, and a very limited number of guests, had all disappeared. Much as Battista had set his heart on parading the fair prize he had won, through the main street of Bordighera, and on the being serenaded in the evening—much as Speranza would have liked to display to the whole town her complete bridal attire, a gift from Lucy, which had arrived from Genoa the day before, and last, not least, to exhibit the bridegroom's comely figure, killing locks of hair, and new suit of velveteen, yet, upon consideration, they thought it wiser to deny themselves such indulgences. The fine gauze dress, rich veil, orange-flower wreath, and white satin shoes, were therefore laid by with an effort so heroic, that we can conceive none greater, unless we compare it to that which Battista made when he thanked the musical band of Bordighera, and begged them not to come.

"So that we are happy, what does it signify whether we appear so or not to other people?" said Speranza in explanation to Miss Davenne. "Were we to make a smart show, or did I put on the beautiful things you have given me, there would be a gossip and outcry about the bride, and her finery, and the wedding, and this and that, ten miles round. And what would be the consequence? Why, that we should be recalled to mind in a quarter where it is safest for us to be forgotten. The less Battista's name is mentioned the better for us." *Non destar can che dorme,*—Don't rouse sleeping dogs,—an Italian proverb of much import and frequent application in a country where everybody's fortune and liberty are at the mercy of irresponsible powers; where, for instance, a poor woman can be despoiled, *ipso facto*, of her hard-earned savings, and hear them adjudged to the denouncing party by a commandant in his cups; and where a legal adviser for suggesting legal means of redress, can be sent to a fortress, and kept there for months to learn to hold his tongue another time. No wonder if, with such flagrant examples before their eyes, people grew prudent in self-defence. Were you aware that you were walking over mined ground, would you not do so with cautious steps? Similar cases to the one above quoted had been, and were of public notoriety. We have picked one out of a hundred as peculiarly illustrative of a system which meddled with everything and everybody on any and every occasion. Travellers describe a tree in the island of Java, whose pestiferous exhalations blight every tiny blade of grass within the compass of its shade. So is it with despotism. No detail of life, however purely personal or trivial, is safe from the subtle, all-pervading action of this accursed upas-tree.

As soon as the hot weather had regularly set in, which was by the middle of July, it was decided that Miss Davenne should begin her course of sea-baths. Her wish was to bathe in the dusk of the evening, but Antonio put in his *veto* against this, and was not to be coaxed into consenting, his fear being that the bath, acting as a stimulant, might interfere with her night's sleep. "We will build a bathing-machine for you," said the considerate Doctor, "in which you may be as private as in your room." And this was no boast as the sequel proved, for a few hours afterwards, there rose on the beach of the Gulf of *Spedaletti*, as trim and commodious a machine as ever graced the shores of fashionable Brighton or Dieppe. "What a turn for mechanics this man must have had, he is always contriving," I fancy I hear some reader exclaim on reading this. I beg your pardon, sir or madam —Antonio had no more turn for mechanics than you or I, but he had what I wish you and I had, a great will to serve and oblige his fellow-creatures; and there is nothing like that, I am told, for rendering a man ingenious. Set to it in a proper spirit, gentle reader, and you will yourself be the first to wonder at the result.

Antonio's bathing-machine was nothing more nor less than the body of an old cart with an awning and curtains, fastened by ropes which could be shortened or lengthened at will, to stout piles driven into the beach. A short ladder gave access to it from the land side, and a longer one on the sea side. A contrivance, you see, not likely to have cost its inventor much effort of imagination. Four red streamers floated gracefully from the four poles supporting the awning, and gave a smart look to the whole. But in this and other embellishments Antonio had no share whatever, they were Battista's exclusive fancying and making.—*Suum cuique.*

Every morning at peep of day, Lucy, attended by Speranza as bathing-woman—Speranza who could swim like a shark —went to enjoy her bath and the wonders of the sunrise. Though a part of her childhood had been spent in the country, yet, owing to her indifferent health, Lucy had never been an early riser; consequently, that marvellous *crescendo* of light, and sound, and life, with which Nature seems to hail the advent of her Great Luminary, was quite a novelty to her, and a delicious one. After the bath, which was to last at first a quarter of an hour and no longer—such being the precise orders of the Bordighera Esculapius – and which Speranza was not the woman to see infringed, Lucy was to have a cup of hot tea, and return to her bed till seven, when she got up. The rest of the morning till ten, when she joined her father for breakfast, Miss Davenne employed first in watering and tending her flowers—she had quite a garden of her own now—then with her pencils and brushes in the balcony. Doctor Antonio always made his appearance about eleven, remaining an hour with her, talking or reading. The hours between mid-day and dinner were occupied by a siesta, by strolls in the garden, by a book enjoyed in the shade, by painting again, or the piano. We have omitted, we believe, to say that an excellent piano had been procured from Nice. Occasionally, there were duets with the Doctor, who never failed to make a second call in the afternoon. Her day generally closed with a short walk up the hill, or a visit to the Count's casino, with sometimes a drive to a neighbouring town or hamlet. But this last became daily of rarer occurrence, for the gentle-natured girl had observed poor Battista's disappointment and mortification whenever he saw the carriage at the gate, and the crest-fallen looks with which he vanished into the gloomiest recesses of the garden; and she had no heart to inflict on any one unnecessary trials. Battista's first excessive terror of Lucy had given place to a reverential adoration as excessive. Whenever she went out to walk, he would watch her from a respectful distance, or, if he thought himself unobserved, follow at her heels; and many a time had his quickness and cleverness in getting out of sight, on the walkers turning suddenly round, and then once more re-appearing in their rear, been a source of amusement and astonishment to Lucy and Doctor Antonio. There was a good deal of the dog in

Battista's nature; which remark is not meant in disparagement, but quite the contrary, considering that the canine race are remarkable for fidelity, devotion, and sagacity, all qualities in which few other animals of the creation excel.

Our sweet Lucy benefited much by the sea-baths, and more still, it is allowable to conjecture, from such a tenor of life as we have depicted, one equally free from ennui or excitement. Sir John was in raptures at her glowing cheeks and dawning *embonpoint*, and would jocosely observe to the Doctor, that she was certainly about to rival Signora Pistacchini in size. If country life be healthful to the body, it is no less so to the mind. Few have sought to become intimate with Nature, interesting themselves in her wonderful proceedings, without bearing witness to the enlargement of ideas, and the awakening of wholesome sympathies consequent upon such communion. At all events this was the case with Lucy. Perhaps — we hope we shall not be charged with presumption in behalf of our hero, when we hint, that, perhaps, her constant intercourse with a man of some experience, practical good sense, and genuine simplicity of heart, like Antonio, might have contributed in some degree to such a result. Be this as it may, one thing was certain, Lucy felt and was quite another being, with new powers, both physical and mental.

Antonio, in the meanwhile, was stroking his beard violently. Ever since the trip to Lampedusa, or to be more particular, ever since that afternoon when Lucy proved so whimsical and inconsistent, a change had come over our dear friend. That evenness of spirit and temper, which might have been compared to the gentle, measured flow of transparent waters, was now somewhat disturbed, and subject to fits of intermission. Antonio was less talkative than he used to be, and would sit by Lucy's side for half an hour together without uttering a word; evidently abstracted even to absence of mind. One day on being suddenly aroused from one of these reveries by the question, "What are you thinking of?" — he reddened prodigiously, and — curious enough—Lucy caught the infection, and blushed also. There was, too, at times, something formal and ceremonious in his manner of addressing Lucy, as of one desirous to retrace some of those steps which, circumstances aiding and abetting, had led to that gentle familiarity which existed between himself and Miss Davenne. But Lucy would not submit to these manœuvres; she took the bull by the horns, as the saying is, and with the pettishness of a spoiled child, would exclaim on any such occasion, "What have I done to you that you look so cold and distant to-day? Do you wish to show me that, now I am quite well, you do not care about me,—that I am a bore to you?" or some such remonstrance. As there was no resisting the spell of her voice, and of the feelings that prompted her words, the upshot of the matter was, that any attempts at formality, if there were any intention of the kind on Antonio's part, ended in creating still more friendly feelings and interest in the heart of each for the other.

The symptoms exhibited by our Doctor were such as to give intimation of some inward struggle; a struggle about the definite nature and object of which, we regret that we cannot be as explicit as we would—nay, can offer nothing more than mere conjecture. A human heart is a skein of such imperceptible and subtly interwoven threads, that even the owner of it is often himself at a loss how to unravel it, and, in all likelihood, this was the case with Antonio. That a man of his discretion and temperate habits of mind, and withal a dealer in realities, as we have known him to be, should willingly and consciously give himself up to rash castle-building, is an hypothesis which we cannot for a moment admit. That Fancy—insidious fairy as she is—might not have succeeded in catching him now and then off his guard, and practising some of her conjuring tricks on him, we would not certify. Antonio was but a man after all, and labouring, to all appearance, under an indisposition common to mankind, and which is said to affect the organs of mental vision. Besides, there are hours in life—we denounce among others twilight's treacherous hour—when the best constituted mind is not proof against the spell of fond imaginings, and most impossible things appear possible, nay, easy. When a man, the paroxysm once over, does his best to aid reason to re-assert her predominance, he does all that, in our judgment, can reasonably be expected of him; and who can tell but that Antonio's fits of taciturnity and thoughtfulness were the silent workings of a mind bent on banishing the deceitful phantoms evoked by Fancy in an evil hour!

But it is time for us to resume our narrative.

"Do you know Lord Carnifex?" asked Antonio of Sir John one evening, after Miss Davenne had retired to her bedroom. The query was put in a would-be unconcerned tone, which was evidently assumed.

"Very well," replied Sir John; "he is a distant relation of my wife's family. What of him?"

"I read a paragraph about him and his youngest daughter in your paper this afternoon. Here it is," continued Antonio, taking the paper from a table behind him, and handing it to Sir John, who read aloud:—

"*Romance in high life.*—We entertained our readers not long ago with the account of a silly scene enacted at Florence, and in which Miss Fanny Carnifex, youngest daughter of the noble Lord of that name, and a young Roman painter, played the principal parts. The scene we related has lengthened into a two-act comedy, and just as Lydia Languish would have wished, in this case there has been an elopement after all. As the matter is now one of public notoriety, we have no hesitation in giving all the names concerned at full length. According to our informant, the hero, Marini, a handsome young fellow, scarcely two-and-twenty, is of a respectable bourgeois family, and considered a rising artist. It seems that he was Miss Fanny's drawing-master, and took advantage of the opportunity thus afforded him to win his pupil's affections."

("The impudent scoundrel!" parenthesized Sir John.)

"One morning the love-stricken pair burst in on the

young lady's noble parent while in his dressing-room, and kneeling down before him, implored his consent to their union. The upshot of this step may be foreseen. Marini was *sans façon* turned out of doors, and Miss Fanny consigned at once to the care of her maternal aunt, Lady Biribi, who carried the fair culprit off to Rome. Here closes that first act of which we gave an account already. The sequel may be told in a few words. Eluding the strictest vigilance, Miss Fanny succeeded in joining her rash young lover, who had followed her to Rome. This deplorable *dénouement* has created a painful excitement throughout the English colony at Rome and Florence. The noble Lord, we are assured, has taken no steps whatever with regard to the fugitives, and is fully determined to leave his daughter to her fate."

"Serve her right!" exclaimed Sir John, crumpling the paper with hands that trembled with emotion. "If I were her father she would never see a shilling of mine. Let them starve. I know him well. By God! I would never speak to him if he were to have anything to do with the"— The last word was inaudible, as the Baronet rose, and began angrily striding up and down the room.

"What good purpose can all such anger answer now?" said Antonio, quietly.

"Give a warning to all silly minxes, sir, disposed to disgrace their family," retorted Sir John, impetuously.

The Doctor ventured to observe, in a conciliating voice, "Luckily the young man seems respectably connected."

"D— such respectability!" roared Sir John. "A fellow little better than a beggar, living on his pencils and wits."

"Michael Angelo and Raphael lived on their pencils and wits," remonstrated Antonio, beginning to feel chafed.

"Welcome to do so," replied the Englishman. "I would have given my daughter to neither of them for all that."

A sharp repartee quivered on Antonio's lips, but he gulped it down.

"The consummate rascal!" went on the Baronet, with renewed fury. "And to think that not one Englishman among the whole set had spirit enough to blow the fellow's brains out. It's enough to make one disown one's country!"

"Come, come, Sir John," said Antonio, good-naturedly, "you must not be so severe. Love and two-and-twenty is a terribly intoxicating draught."

"Love!" laughed the Baronet, contemptuously. "Nonsense: it was the girl's pounds, shillings, and pence, that the cold-blooded villain wanted. They only marry for money, these,—a—confounded Italian adventurers."

The Italian grew scarlet, and bit his lip. Perhaps the Englishman noticed this, or perhaps it was only the sound of his own words that sobered him. He paused for a second in front of Antonio, who, his arms folded over his breast, stood leaning against the piano; then, moved by a sudden impulse, Sir John stretched out his hand and said, with noble simplicity, "Very wrong of me to wound your feelings. Pray forgive me. I did not mean it. That odious story quite got the better of me. I confess I have an unconquerable aversion to marriages with foreigners. Don't let us speak any more on the subject. And now, are you for a game?"

Antonio *was* for a game, and they sat down to it; but Sir John was so *distrait* that his opponent had to take all imaginable pains to make him win. It was near midnight when the Doctor issued from the little garden-gate: instead of turning to the right to gain the highroad to Bordighera, he took to the left, down the lane towards the sea, and began walking up and down the beach. His step, though slower than usual, gave no evidence of overwrought feelings, nor did his countenance, to which the pale moonshine, that fell on it, imparted an expression of calm solemnity. He walked thus for a considerable time, then lay down at full length, his face upturned to the heavens. The grey light of breaking day found him in the same posture. He then rose, and, as if summing up the result of his long reverie, said aloud, "What matters it, after all, whether a man is happy or unhappy, so that he sees his duty and abides by it? So now,

Viva l'Italia! my first and my last love!" and he bent his way homewards.

From that day all fits of moodiness or taciturnity were at an end, and the gentle current of serene good sense and quiet humour, which gave such a charm to the Italian's manner, flowed on rich and equable as when we first made his acquaintance. Had that night of solemn thought conquered the struggle within, or only ministered to the combatant sufficient strength to control and keep down its outward manifestation? Was Antonio in the solitude of his own dwelling as much master of himself, as composed, even cheerful, as he was at the Osteria in Lucy's presence? We leave it a secret between the well-meaning creature and his Creator.

CHAPTER XIX.
The Idyl at a Close.

IT was one of those hot sultry days in the month of August, so trying to the nerves of sensitive people, and during which, Nature, as it were, herself exhausted, seems to come to a stand-still. Shooting through a thin veil of white clouds, as through a burning glass, the rays of the sun poured down upon the earth volumes of heavy malignant heat. No leaf stirred, no bird was singing, the very cicadas had suspended their shrill chirp. The only sound that occasionally broke the ominous stillness, was the plaintive cry of the cuckoo calling to its mate.

Lucy had tried drawing, gardening, practising, sleeping, all with no success, and now lay panting on a sofa. "Here you are at last!" said she, as Doctor Antonio walked in; "I have been longing for you these two hours. I feel so ill."

"Indeed!" exclaimed Antonio, turning white; "what is the matter with you? I met Sir John on his way to the Count's not an hour ago, and he never breathed a syllable about your being unwell."

"I said nothing about the matter to papa," answered Lucy, "he is uneasy enough already at not having heard from Aubrey."

"You mean your brother?"

"Yes; Aubrey was to write by the Indian mail which we see has arrived, and without bringing any letter from him."

"I am very sorry for that," said Antonio. "But tell me all about yourself. You have not been coughing, have you?"

"No; but I feel very uncomfortable—so faint—so oppressed—so hot."

"No wonder. Everbody suffers more or less from this weather. Let me feel your pulse—there is no fever. It is this confounded sirocco that tells on your nerves. Now, just lie down again quietly," and he arranged the pillows under her head, "and I will try to make you more comfortable. Miss Hutchins," he added, walking away, "will you make a glass of strong lemonade for Miss Davenne? the juice of two lemons in half a tumbler of water—lukewarm water, if you please."

"Yes, sir," answered the lady's-maid, in the most mellifluous voice at her command. Miss Hutchins, be it known, was quite conquered; a hard conquest, but Antonio had achieved it. The once stiff abigail now courted his notice, and prided herself on carrying out his directions.

Presently Antonio re-appeared, followed by Speranza, both of them looking like Jacks in the green on a May morning, or like a bit of Birnam-wood, from the quantity of cut boughs they were carrying. They spread them all over the floor, then Rosa bringing in a watering-pot, the Doctor watered the branches several times, saying, "This will soon cool us, provided we let in no air from the furnace without." He shut up the glass-door, and let down the green curtain over it so as to create a twilight. "Do you like your lemonade?" he asked, as Lucy put down her glass.

"Very much, it is so refreshing."

"Do you feel inclined to go to sleep?"

"No," said Lucy; "are you going?"

"Not unless you feel sleepy.—You do not? Very well. Shall I read to you?" continued Antonio, going to the bookshelves near the piano, and coming back with a book—"shall I read something from your favourite poet, Giusti?"

"What a clever man you are!" said Lucy, instead of answering the question. "I feel better already. What is to become of me when you are no long"—The rest of the phrase was lost in a burst of tears.

Poor Antonio stood still with the book in his hand, and large tears in his eyes, within an ace of crying also. Fortunately for him, something stuck in his throat at this moment, and necessitated his clearing it violently. Having by this means recovered his voice, he said, "See how nervous you are—you weep without the least cause, as if you were going away to-morrow. Don't you know the Italian proverb:—'*Prendi tempo e camperai?*'" His tone was that of a mother chiding her pet-child. There ensued a pause, during which Lucy by degrees recovered from her emotion.

"Doctor," said she, all at once, "do you believe in presentiments?"

"Not a bit," replied Antonio, briskly; "I believe in the sirocco."

"You are wrong then," said Lucy, gravely. "Did you not tell me once of sensitive plants which foretold storm? Well, I am one of them. I am sure that some misfortune is about to happen to me. I feel it in the air."

"You feel the treacherous south wind, that is what you feel. A shower of rain will put your discomfort and presentiments all to flight."

Lucy shook her head incredulously, then said, "Will you read to me? Anything you choose."

"Let us try 'Il Brindisi di Don Girella.' It is so droll, it will make you laugh;" and carrying a chair close to the glass-door, in order to profit by the little light that stole in through it, he began reading.

We have reasons of our own for particularizing as minutely as possible the details of this domestic scene, and the position, with regard to each other, of reader and listener. A little to the right of the glass-door, at some five or six paces from it, stood sidewise the sofa on which Lucy was lying, her face towards the light. She had on a white muslin gown with a blue sash; her broad-brimmed straw-hat was hanging by its blue ribbons on a corner of the back of the sofa, just over her head. Miss Hutchins, her arms crossed before her, sat at the large table in the centre of the room, busily engaged in trying to swallow a series of obstinate yawns, that would not be suppressed. Opposite to Lucy, that is, to the left of the glass-door, but so close to it that the green curtain touched his book, was seated Antonio.

Well, the reading had been going on for some time, and more than once had the condensed *vis comica* of the inimitable poet brought a faint smile on Lucy's pale face. By degrees, however, her perception of the author's meaning became fainter and fainter, and the rich melodious voice of the reader, soothing her like the murmuring of a brook, lulled the sweet girl into that state, which is not yet sleep, yet neither is it waking, but a voluptuous compound of the two. All on a sudden a heavy footstep is heard coming up the stairs—Lucy started up—"Who can that be?" faltered she with a shudder. At the same instant the glass-door is flung open with a crash, a colossal figure stalks in noisily, and, "Halloa, Lucy, my girl," roars out a voice like thunder, as the living tower stoops down to kiss the prostrate form. "Here you are at last! Heyday! what is all this! By Jove! with your green boughs and watering-pots, you look as pastoral as one of the shepherdesses in a ballet. *Une chaumière et ton cœur.* Ah! ah! nothing is wanting to the Idyl, as they used to say at Eton; d—it, not even the shepherd!"

"Aubrey!" cried Lucy, in a tone of reproach, but could say no more. The oath and witty sally, we need scarcely remark, were aimed at our friend the Doctor. Antonio had received such a violent slap from the door, when Aubrey entered, as to be nearly felled to the ground, and in the effort to recover his balance his chair was upset. The new comer turned round at the noise, saw Antonio, and uttered the silly vapid joke about the shepherd.

The eyes of the two men met in no friendly way. Aubrey's haughty scowl, curled lip, and somewhat aggressive demeanour, evinced little good-will to the object of his present scrutiny. Antonio's firm-set lips, ashy-pale countenance, and collected look of self-defence, gave evidence of his scenting the near approach of a foe. Thus they stood, confronting each other, types of two fine races, two such as even Greece and Rome had seldom seen the like; the one, fair, rosy, blue-eyed, (Lucy's very eyes!) the other, dark as a tempest; the Englishman taller by nearly a head than his tall antagonist, square-chested, broad-shouldered in proportion, the very *ne plus ultra* of muscular development and strength; the Italian less bulky, but as firmly knit, springy and supple as a tiger, with iron nerves and sinews, ready servants of the indomitable will betrayed in the sombre fire of his eyes. God grant that they may never meet in anger, for theirs will be like the meeting of two thunder-clouds!

This mutual survey did not last ten seconds, but even that time sufficed to develop between the two a strong feeling of antipathy. Lucy, woman-like, divined it, and her increasing terror loosened her tongue. "My brother, Captain Davenne.—Doctor Antonio, my doctor—papa's best friend." The words broke the spell. Captain Davenne bowed slightly, as did Doctor Antonio. A parting recommendation to Lucy to keep quiet, and to go to bed early if she did not feel better in the evening, and the Doctor withdrew.

Aubrey began kicking about in the most uproarious manner all the chairs and arm-chairs that were in the room, —every fresh kick eliciting a fresh start from Lucy,—till, at last, having disposed them somewhat symmetrically by the side of the sofa, he stretched his ponderous limbs on this extempore couch, talking loudly all the while. Lucy was thus made aware, between one kick and the other, of the string of lucky circumstances which had procured for her so unexpectedly the blessing of her brother's company. They were briefly these. The invalid brother officer, whose duties had devolved upon Aubrey, recovering more rapidly than had been anticipated, Captain Davenne had, in consequence, been enabled to sail by the very Indian mail, the arrival of which, without a letter from him, had caused Sir John's uneasiness in the morning. What was the use of writing, when he should reach England at the same time as his letter? In London he had met Tom Carnifex—eldest son of Lord Carnifex—who had just received a hasty summons from his father to join him at Florence as quickly as he could. Tom had offered Aubrey a place in his britschka; Aubrey had accepted it, and here he was. Of the stranger he had found in his sister's company, of the pleasant or unpleasant impression made on him by the sight, not a single word.

Who so surprised and happy and elated as Sir John, when, on entering the room soon after, the first thing his eyes fell upon was his long-missed treasure, Aubrey, seated by the side of his sister? Sir John would, had his sense of decorum permitted, have done foolish things. How proudly and fondly he gazed on the "boy," as he called him! Truth to say, Aubrey's Herculean proportions and handsome features must have excited the admiration of a more impartial judge than his father. The Baronet's eager inquiries immediately brought forth a second edition of Aubrey's statements just related, and then began between father and son a brisk fire of queries and answers, like hammers plying in quick succession on an anvil. No wonder they had much to say to one another, considering their ten years' separation. They rattled on uninterruptedly, until John Ducket's advent to lay the cloth for dinner put an end to their effusions. Captain Davenne complimented John on his good looks, an honour which spread on John's grave face a grin of intense complacency. The two gentlemen then adjourned to Sir John's own room, from whence they were shortly after

summoned forth by the announcement that dinner was on
the table. Aubrey ate and drank enough for two, and as he
ate and drank, his praises of the fare, the wines, the situation, rendered still more impressive by sundry oaths and
tremendous peals of laughter, which made plates, glasses,
decanters, and very glass-door, ring again, grew louder and
louder.

"By the by, my dear boy," said the Baronet, "at what
inn did Carnifex leave you?"

"At none," was the answer. "I left my portmanteau at
a kind of pot-house, where he changed horses. I say, John,
you must go there after dinner and have my pormanteau
brought here."

"I am afraid," said Sir John, "that there is no room for
you here; it is a mere nut-shell; there is not a hole to spare,
I know."

"Never mind," retorted Aubrey, "*à la guerre comme à la
guerre*, I can sleep on the sofa, or on the ground, anywhere.
Here I am, and here I mean to stay, for I suppose you won't
turn me out by force."

This being Aubrey's ultimatum, from which it was clear
that no reasons, however good, would divert him, a short
consultation ensued between Sir John and John Ducket, the
upshot of which was that John should manage to find a
resting-place for himself where he could, and that his room
should be made as comfortable as possible for his young
master. To be of service to Aubrey, John would have
willingly slept in the fields.

Dinner over, Captain Davenne, to Sir John's great
amazement and consternation, lighted an enormous cigar.
"First-rate cigars," said he, puffing away; "I hope you
don't dislike the smell, Lucy; I know my father doesn't."
Lucy protested she had no objection to it—she-rather liked
it than not. Now, the truth was that she could not bear it.
What was it that forced from her an assertion so little consonant with the truth? Lucy, almost unconsciously, felt a
sort of necessity to humour her brother. Poor, timid, weak

Lucy! How many of thy sisters have I seen, as candid and artless as thou art, sin in a like and worse way, to propitiate such bears as this brother of thine! For all which sins, let us hope, not the weak sensitive things will be called to account some day, but the blustering, overbearing rulers, in whose violence the sins originated.

Sir John neither openly admitted nor contradicted Aubrey's declaration as to himself; it might be he did not feel sure how a flat denial on his part would be received, or it might be that he chose, on that first day of re-union, to be indulgent. He only prudently proposed a *levée en masse* to the garden, where they would have coffee. The usual hour for Antonio's evening call was now past, and no Antonio had appeared. "I hope the Doctor is not going to give us the slip," said Sir John, after he had consulted his watch two or three times. "My son's company is no good reason why I should not have my friend's also. I wish you very much to make his acquaintance, Aubrey — as nice a man this Doctor Antonio as you could meet anywhere — quite a gentleman: we are under infinite obligations to him." And then Sir John told his son all over again the story of the overturn, and the Italian's timely help, already related in sundry letters to India; and, warming with the subject, the Baronet went on to enlarge on all the unremitting attention Antonio had paid to Lucy, and how ingeniously he had contrived to amuse her during her confinement to the house. The lending of books, the lectures on botany, the lessons on the guitar, were all set forth, the catalogue winding up with that stupendous masterstroke, the easy-chair invented by the Doctor. To all of which discourse, Aubrey listened with an attention quite edifying, and an appearance of great gratification — a gratification made more evident as he watched the pleasure the details afforded to his darling sister, on whose glowing countenance the sympathizing brother's eyes rested all the while.

"I long to shake hands with this Phœnix of doctors,"

said Aubrey, "and apologize for my rudeness. I suppose it was he I found here this morning?"

"Yes," said Lucy.

"What do you say," continued Aubrey, speaking to Sir John, but looking at his sister, "to our going and laying violent hands on this forgetful friend of yours, and dragging him captive here!—ha! ha! ha!"

"Ah, do!" said Lucy, with sparkling eyes, and inwardly calling herself all sorts of names for having so unkindly misjudged her brother. Sir John agreeing immediately to the proposal, Captain Davenne lit a fresh cigar, and out they sallied. As they passed through the garden-gate, Aubrey was seized by a violent fit of laughing. "What are you laughing at?" asked Sir John, perplexed.

"Why, this is such a devilish queer house—such a wrong-sided look about it. I would give something to carry it bodily to London and show it at a shilling a-head. I bet something no one would credit that Sir John and Miss Davenne had lived contentedly weeks in it. I verily believe Hutchins and John have forgotten what a decent room is like."

Sir John felt his son's words as a personal reproach. He hung his head.

"*A propos de bottes*," (Aubrey had been in love with a French actress at Madras, and spoke French fluently, and liked to show that he did,) "the old Duke of B— asked after you."

"Very kind of him," said the Baronet, his features expanding. "How is the old gentleman?"

"As fresh as ever," said Aubrey; "he wondered what had become of you. Indeed, everybody does; Lady Deloraine most of all, at whose house I met the—ian ambassadress and her daughter-in-law, Lady Charlotte Tuicy, both of them full of suspicions about your absence, and willing to join in any conspiracy for carrying you off by force from your mysterious hiding-place."

"God forbid they should put their threat in execution!"

said the Baronet, chuckling. "But, talking of carrying off, have you heard of that pretty business of Fanny Carnifex's elop—"

"Blast the cowardly Italian beggar!" yelled out Aubrey. "I have heard all about it."

"Are they—married at least?" asked Sir John, with an effort.

"They are; but it is a matrimonial alliance that won't last long. Fanny will soon be a jolly widow, I can tell her."

"How do you mean?" inquired Sir John, surprised. Aubrey stopped short, slowly raised his right arm, held it out as if taking aim, and, with a clack of his tongue, imitated the report of a pistol. "Tom Carnifex is one of the best shots in England, my dear sir," said he, carelessly, by way of explanation.

The acting of this little scene was so splendidly natural, there was in the look of the performer something so savage, that Sir John could not help a shudder. However desirable it might have once seemed to him that the offender should be made an example of, it was no part of Sir John's programme of to-day to be present at the execution.

Engrossed by such pleasant converse and anticipations, the chief of the Davenne dynasty, and his heir, had come in sight of Doctor Antonio's poor dwelling, just as its tenant, in no very pleasant mood, was issuing from the door. Antonio was little prepared for the present warm greeting from the surly stranger of a few hours back, who now, shaking him heartily by the hand, made a sort of laughing apology for having been so unceremonious in the morning. Though rather taken by surprise, the Italian returned Aubrey's advances in as kindly a spirit as he could summon on such short notice; and the three, Antonio in the middle, walked back to the Osteria, where they found the Count, between whom and young Davenne an introduction in due form took place. The evening passed, if not as quietly as usual, not the less agreeably, perhaps, for being rather noisy. Captain Davenne was in the most communicative of humours, and rattled away famously, laughing a good deal at his own jokes and stories, drinking freely all the while of what he called lemonade; and so it was, only with a strong infusion of old Jamaica rum. Some of his tiger-hunting adventures, which he told with great spirit, were listened to with thrilling interest,—Antonio translating for the Count, who had learnt about as much English as Sir John had Italian. Lucy retired early, but not before she had seen a real good-will and friendship springing up between her brother and her doctor and friend. Let us hope that she slept well, poor girl. As ten struck, Sir John and Antonio, according to habit, sat down to their game of chess, which was on the Baronet's part a series of continual blunders. His thoughts were otherwise engaged.

When Lucy, about eight next morning, after her early bath, and one or two hours of additional rest, crossed the ante-room on her way out, she found her brother already installed on the sofa, and yawning violently. "Where are you going?" asked Aubrey. "To water my flowers. I have a nice little garden of my own; come and look at it." Aubrey raised his long length, went, looked at it, and admired it. The garden was not her own making, was it? Oh, no! Speranza had made it. Speranza, the landlady's daughter, a very nice girl. Doctor Antonio had given Lucy most of the plants. "Are they not beautiful?"—"Very," said Aubrey, adding, "Do you know, Lucy, I am quite in love with that Doctor of yours?"

"Are you?" said Lucy, looking up at him with such beaming eyes.

"I have seldom seen a more commanding figure than his, and he is very gentlemanlike, certainly. I wish he were an English Duke."

"Why?" said Lucy. "I assure you he is quite contented with his lot."

"Because if he were, young lady, you would make a handsome couple." Lucy grew scarlet. "As it is," pursued Aubrey slowly, in a clear, cruel, stern voice, "As it is, I would rather see you dead and buried than married to that man."

The little watering-pot slipt out of her hand, and her knees gave way.

"D— it!" cried Aubrey, raising her from the ground, "you needn't take fright at a mere supposition!" And, without another word, he passed his powerful arm round his sister's waist and led her up the stairs to the sofa. This was the first and the last time that Antonio's name was mentioned between them.

The Doctor called, as was his wont, during the morning, but instead of his usual warm recognition from Lucy he received a silent bow. Her cheeks were dreadfully pale, her eyes red. He inquired about her health, and got a hurried answer that she was very well. He would have felt her pulse,—there was no need, she assured him, she was very comfortable. When he stooped over her shoulder to examine her drawing she recollected that she had left a brush in her room, which was indispensable at that moment, and got up to fetch it. There was a constraint about poor Lucy which Antonio had never seen. His heart contracted painfully. That Aubrey was the cause of the sweet girl's altered looks and manner, Antonio had not the least doubt; but how and why? Was he, Antonio, in any way connected with this new state of things? To solve the mystery he would have willingly shed his blood. Oh! for ten seconds alone with her, but ten, to ask one question, receive one answer. He loitered longer than he generally did, to take advantage of a possible chance. In vain. There stood between him and her a moving Chinese wall.

Four days passed without the situation mending. Aubrey had taken such a fancy to the wretched Osteria that neither the Count's pressing invitations, nor his father's exhortations to take his horse and go and enjoy the fine scenery, could prevail upon the colossal dragoon to leave its precincts for a moment, unless Lucy did, which was commonly the case in the evening, when he would put her arm under his and fondly support her steps. All the rest of the day, from seven in the morning to eleven at night, Aubrey would spend in-doors, most of the time stretched at full length, smoking and indulging in his favourite beverage, or shaking the poor inn with his ponderous strides. His most gracious smile and heartiest squeeze of the hand was for Antonio, to whom he had taken such a liking, that for nothing in the world would Aubrey have missed a minute of his new friend's company. A boisterous, rather vulgar, lively, good-tempered, companionable fellow, this young Davenne, easily satisfied with everything and everybody, making light of the inconveniences of his far from comfortable room down stairs, never hinting by word or look at any the least wish on his part to leave his present quarters. His conversation with Sir John turned almost exclusively, it is true, on London, (the London, we mean, whose existence is acknowledged by people of rank and fashion,) London gaieties, the illustrious relatives and acquaintances of the Davenne family, on the general regret at the Baronet's prolonged absence, and so on. But nine times out of ten it was Sir John himself who broached the subject; and then, was it not natural and proper for a dutiful son to dwell on such topics as were palpably the most agreeable to his father?

Meanwhile the healthy bloom was fading fast from Lucy's cheek, and her head drooped like a lily deprived of sunshine. It was not enough that poor Lucy was to be weaned all at once from the joys and benefits of the friendly intercourse which habit had made a sweet necessity to her. But she had to wear a mask and act a part too cruelly at variance with her feelings. Why she was compelled to do so she scarcely knew, but a mysterious warning from within told her that only at such a cost might something awful be averted. Her heart was full of strange misgivings and fears. Aubrey's show of friendship to Antonio, far from reassuring her, added to her uneasiness. It was clear, even to her inexperienced eye, that all that extreme good-will was assumed, a mere display, and being so, what could be

Aubrey's motive? And the saddened girl brooded, till her head grew giddy, over the hostility of the two young men's first meeting, the significant hint given to her on the morrow, and Aubrey's sudden change of manner.

No pleasant early associations connected with the boy came to counteract the painful impressions aroused by the full-grown man. Aubrey, be it remembered, had spent his boyhood at Eton, and of his holidays Lucy recalled little, excepting her terrors for her doll, and for a favourite kitten it had been his delight to torment. But there was no want of clearness in her perceptions with regard to his six months' stay at home, previous to his entering the army. The almost daily quarrels between father and son, her mother all in tears, the gloom that pervaded the family, Aubrey's angry scowl, and something worse, in return for her childish attempts at conciliation, (she was scarcely ten years old at the time,) and the fear in which she stood of him; such were Lucy's sole recollections, such the images and feelings linked in her memory with that brother of hers. Intervening years had softened, but not obliterated, these impressions, and the Aubrey that, to the day of his arrival, figured in his sister's mind, was anything but the type of youthful dutifulness and affection. What she had now seen of him brought the conviction home to her, that the man had kept the promise of the boy. Lucy, from the first, had felt afraid of him. His boisterous ways and overbearing manners, his frequent oaths and coarse mirth, told cruelly on her nerves, and wounded all the sympathies of her refined nature. Delicate, sensitive organizations, like Lucy's, have an inborn horror of violence in any shape; it is with them a dissolving element, something incompatible with their being, from which they shrink as instinctively as those plants to which Miss Davenne had likened herself in her last conversation with Doctor Antonio,—shrink from the touch of a hand. On these grounds alone would the pressure of Aubrey's presence have been too much for Lucy. How incomparably more so when fancy obscurely hinted at the possible bursting of that violence, of which she stood in such awe, in a direction where much of her grateful affection and reverence lay!

On the fourth day from his son's arrival, Sir John gave a farewell dinner, and announced to the small but select party, the Count, the Mayor, Doctor Antonio, &c., that his departure was fixed for the day after the next. Aubrey might watch his sister as much as he pleased, Lucy did not wince. Indeed her misery was such that she felt almost relieved by the announcement.

So that she may but say, "Thank you, Doctor Antonio, God bless you and your country,"— so that she may but say this to him freely, as her heart prompts, without restraint, with no eye upon her, Lucy will depart in peace. This thought is ever uppermost in her mind; nay, she has no thought but this one, which presses on her temples like a crown of thorns, to thank and bless him. It would look so unfeeling not to do so. This man has been all forbearance, all gentleness, all kindness to her. What could a friend, a brother, a father, do more than he has done for her! "Bless you and your country." She murmurs the words to herself, she would fain write them down for him, but that they look so cold on paper. He has no idea, she is sure, of the depth of her gratitude, of all that she is feeling. Fool that she was, not to have let him know when time was her own,— when no dark cloud cast its shadow between them, on one of those bright mornings frittered away in general conversation on the balcony,—on one of those moonlit evenings spent by the water's edge, so near that the silvery wave came creeping lovingly to their very feet. Oh, those sweet strolls in the garden,—those boatings on the blue sea,— that blessed trip to Lampedusa! O that she could recall one minute, only one, of that past!

Vain yearnings, vain imaginings! Unrelenting time rolls on, the day is come, the very hour of departure is at hand, and Lucy has found no opportunity of unburdening her heart. She sits on her invalid chair looking vacantly before her, as though in a dream; Aubrey and Antonio stand in the balcony and discuss the English policy in India, Antonio with a very pale face, and unwonted animation of manner; Sir John paces the room, meditating a farewell speech, casting now and then a disconsolate glance at his daughter; Hutchins is bustling up and down, in and out, in a state of flurry and excitement; John Ducket left for Nice in the morning to make room for the Captain in the rumble; and poor Hutchins has been working for two. She announces that the horses are to the carriage. "Now, Lucy," says the Baronet, encouragingly. Aubrey is already at his sister's side, and helps her to rise; Hutchins has noticed a small basket hanging on Lucy's arm, and offers to carry it for her; Lucy draws it back hurriedly, and frowns on her maid;—a handful of poor withered, almost colourless flowers, once so blue,—such is the treasure she clings to so closely.

As Sir John and the Doctor go down the steps, followed by Aubrey and Miss Davenne, a number of persons assembled in the garden, take off their hats and caps, and wave them in the air. Sir John's tongue cleaves to his palate, and he gives up his speech. He even thinks it prudent to proceed to the shaking of hands in silence. Those who choose to kiss his hand, Prospero, his younger brother, their aged mother, all are free to do so now. Sir John offers no resistance. Meanwhile, Aubrey hurries Lucy on to the little gate, where the carriage is waiting. Rosa and Speranza, and a little in the rear, Battista, are crying like fountains. Lucy returns half-unconsciously the warm caresses of the two women, who kiss her hands and clothes, and cling desperately to their young benefactress, until Aubrey, with an oath, jerks her into the carriage. Antonio helps the Baronet in. "Pleasant journey, Sir John; *buon viaggio, Signorina*, take care of yourself." The Signorina does not say a word—does not smile, does not bow, but stares at the kind face—the kind face that dares not even smile, alas! for it feels the evil eye resting on it. A clack from the postilion, a shout from the assembled by-standers, "*Buon viaggio, il*

Signore gli accompagni," the ponderous machine rolls up the lane, and the kind face disappears. Lucy arouses from her trance,—"Papa, are we going?" and she bursts into a passion of tears. It was like the giving way of a dam in a river. Papa fairly gives way, too, hugs the suffering child to his bosom, and father and daughter mingle their tears. While this passes within, Aubrey, in the rumble, lights a fresh cigar from the one he had been smoking.

Those left behind stood on the highway watching the fast-diminishing carriage. They watched till it disappeared. Poor Antonio was sick at heart, and would fain throw off his mask. But no;—he must listen to the idle verbiage of the Count and the Mayor, who insisted on accompanying him home. He reached it at last, threw himself upon his bed, and—man is but man after all—wept like a child.

CHAPTER XX.
Absence.

WHEN two persons dearly attached to one another separate, how much more to be pitied is the one who remains than the one who goes! Every old familiar place and object becomes to the former a cruel remembrancer, out of which rises the image with which it is associated. Every hour that passes brings back the recollection of some sweet corresponding habit, now, alas! broken, and with it fresh yearnings and regrets; while every hour that flies, every object that fleets by, the excitement of the motion, the incidents, the very annoyances of travelling, create for the latter a thousand little diversions, the effect of which cannot but be to divide and lessen the concentration of thought and feeling on one given point.

Lucy was no exception to the rule. It was not her fault if the scenery between Bordighera and Nice united to its character of loveliness one of grandeur,—if the road often climbed to aerial heights,—if the towns below were so picturesquely grouped,—if the indentations of the coast proved so capricious, and opened at every turn new and bold prospects. It was not her fault if she had eyes, and through them received impressions. We do not mean to say by this that the agony of separation did not continue to throb in her bosom; that her thoughts did not impetuously rush back, clinging round the friend she had left; that she did not feel desolate and miserable. We only mean to say, that the novelty and variety of external things and incidents forced themselves upon her notice, and mingled with the main current of her thoughts and feelings.

At Nice, which was their first halting-place, the Davennes met a family,—one of the elect few whom Sir John could condescend to acknowledge,—such as England only can send forth, consisting of a father and mother, young still, with a train of from twelve to fifteen sons and daughters. The female members of this family, seven in number, pounced upon Lucy, and took possession of her. She had to visit, under their guidance, all the remarkable places in the town and its environs,—to join in picnics ostensibly got up for her,—to go to a *dilettanti* French play, a professional concert, and to hear a celebrated *improvvisatore*,—all of which occupations and amusements, compressed within the three days she spent at Nice, left our poor heroine but little leisure time to devote to tender regrets.

At Paris, where, according to his old programme, Sir John made a sojourn of a month, what with official sight-seeing of the Louvre, the Luxembourg, the Palais-Royal, Versailles, St. Cloud, Fontainebleau, &c. &c., the indispensable daily drive in the Champs Elysées and the Bois de Boulogne,—the trying on of innumerable new dresses and bonnets,—the theatres, soirées at the Embassy, going to parties, and giving parties,—and last, not least, morning visits among the English in Paris, life was a race indeed,—without taking into account a formal presentation at the Tuileries, and the honour of a seat along with her father and brother at the royal dinner-table at Neuilly. Though little partial to the chief of the Orleans dynasty, whom he could not forgive for being the son of Philippe Egalité of revolutionary memory, and making no mystery of his feeling on the subject, Sir John, to use his own words, thought proper to yield to the policy of the day, and considered it a part of his duty as an Englishman to help on the "*entente cordiale*," even at some cost to his personal sympathies. Only fancy a man of Sir John Davenne's importance going through Paris without visiting the chief of the State! One's hair stands on end to think of the consequences.

But her Paris dissipations were rest and peace compared to the vortex of visits, breakfasts, dinners, fêtes, and balls, in which Lucy found herself whirling as soon as she set foot in England. Not one of the most distant, in point of situation or connexion, of her numerous relations, or of the numerous circle of friends and acquaintances of the family, but insisted on a day at least from the fair traveller. Sir John, on his part, once at Davenne, made up for lost time by filling his splendid mansion to the very unknown garrets, and with Lucy—the cynosure of all eyes—doing the honours, had open days, and gave entertainment after entertainment to half the county. For weeks and months Lucy had not a spare moment to herself; dressing and visiting, visiting and dressing, those two great duties and occupations of a young lady of high station everywhere, and more especially in England, was the order of the day. Unable to resist the current that bore her down, what could she do but let herself drift along, half-pleased, half-worried?

Antonio, in the meantime, do what he would, could think of nothing but Lucy. The bright star that had for a moment shone above his horizon had long set for ever, while still his eyes gazed on, riveted on the halo of light it had left behind. It was all the same whether he remained brooding in his own dwelling, seated on that very easy-chair he had contrived for his cherished patient, or whether he went abroad on his usual avocations, there was the dear face looking at him out of every corner, haunting him at every turn. The little library out of which he had lent her books still warm with the touch of her hand, the flute and guitar he had so willingly played for her amusement, the map of Sicily he had taken to her when her interest in his country was first awakened, the flowers she had given him religiously preserved,—all around him was full of her. All seemed to ask, "Where is she?" If tired of poring over a volume, on which he had uselessly tried to fix his attention, Antonio got up and looked out of the window, the first thing his eye met was the Count's casino, to which he had accompanied her many and many a time,—there the rich Italian pine expanded its green canopy under which she had sat, when she tried the sketch of the coast towards France,—there, glancing in the sun, was the large yellow stone, from under which, to Lucy's great terror, they had seen creep out a snake, as big as her little finger,—further on, at that turning, she had stooped to pick up a stray, tiny, white shell, and given it to him.

It was worse still when his profession called him to the other side of the promontory. What a crowd of memories rose at the sight of the old, weather-beaten, dingy-red Osteria, with its cumbrous balcony, the little garden, and the pebbly shore! Not a foot of ground but was hallowed by some recollection of her. There, past that sharp descent of the road, he had seen her for the first time, pale as death, but so lovely in her paleness that he wondered how such a peerless creature could exist on earth. There she had smiled on him so sweetly, when he had ordered the litter to be turned round; there, on the first fold of the hill behind the house, one day, at dusk, she had discovered the first fire-flies of the season, and screamed with delight. Not a path but they had trodden it together, not a flower but they had examined it together, not one of Nature's mysterious sounds—from the voice of the ocean to the chirp of a grasshopper—that they had not listened to together, not one of the thousand hues of sea, or earth, or sky, that they had not admired together! Then everybody spoke of her; Rosa,

Speranza, Battista, the Count, the drawing-master, Prospero, his mother, knew of no other topic. His very patients would inquire of him whether the "*bella Signorina*" was ever likely to come back again. Even the urchins playing in the streets would stop in their game to ask him where the "*Inglesina*" was. It seemed so strange, so unnatural, so impossible, that she should have passed away from a place so full of her, that Antonio would sit for hours, in sight of the Osteria, expecting to see her white dress fluttering in the balcony, or to hear her birdlike voice singing one of the Sicilian airs he had taught her. At times he got almost angry with himself, and determined to shake off this sort of continual obsession; he tried long expeditions on foot under a scorching sun, but to little purpose. The song of the nightingale in the valley, the scent of thyme on a mountain pass, the white outline of some distant village, the tolling of a far-away church-bell, awoke old associations, and out of them stole the fairy form, and kept alongside of him. Do what he would, struggle as manfully as he might, there was no way of ridding himself of it. Antonio was sick at heart.

Sir John's acknowledgment of the Doctor's services was at once delicate and munificent. On the day after the departure of the English family, Prospero, according to the previous instructions he had received, presented himself at Antonio's dwelling with a letter and Buffy. The Baronet, in a few lines, full of feeling, begged Antonio to accept of the cob as a remembrance from one he had laid under many an obligation, and not to forget, if ever he made up his mind to go to England, that he had there an old friend, who relied on a visit from him, and on being allowed to do the honours of his country to the Doctor. The letter contained a small packet of English bank-notes to the amount of a hundred pounds, but to these the writer made no allusion. Dr. Antonio took from the sum what he considered a handsome fee for his services—ten pounds, and handed over the rest to the mayor as a gift to the parish from Sir John, to be applied as the town-council might deem proper.

The mayor convoked the town-council at once, who instantly passed a vote of thanks to the Baronet, and delegated to the mayor the business of penning and sending to the generous donor an address expressive of the grateful feelings of both parish and council, with a copy of the minutes of the meeting annexed. To this address and minute Antonio joined a letter of thanks from himself for the present of the cob. Two months after there came to the mayor a note in answer, of most Spartan laconism. Sir John stated most distinctly, that, as he had left no funds for the purposes indicated in the mayor's letter, he could accept of no thanks, but that, as he was anxious to deserve the good opinion expressed, he begged to enclose a draft for a hundred pounds, to be devoted to the benefit of the parish. This note, curiously enough, brought a wasp's nest about our friend's ears. The town-council met in a hurry, and summoned Antonio to their presence to explain the matter. This the Doctor did with the ready straightforwardness that was his characteristic. He said, that on receiving from Sir John Davenne a sum ten times larger than what he considered a sufficient remuneration for his attendance on that gentleman's daughter, without any direction or hint as to what was to be done with the surplus, the only interpretation left him, and one, too, which he believed in keeping with the generous nature of the sender, was that the balance had been intended to be used by Doctor Antonio for the benefit of the parish, and he himself had judged that through the town-council he would be most sure of obtaining that end.

This explanation was not considered satisfactory, and loud complaints were made against the Doctor for having compromised the dignity of the council. Then followed a long and stormy deliberation as to what was to be done. Three members, known as the creatures of the curé, and evidently instigated by him, urged a vote of censure against Antonio, which motion, however, was negatived. A fourth moved that Antonio should be compelled to explain and

apologize to the English gentleman, which Antonio flatly
refused to do. A fifth proposed that the money should be
sent back to Sir John, but this proposal was unsupported by
any one. At last, upon the motion of some one more
reasonable than the rest, it was unanimously agreed upon,
that the question should be put off till that day six months
—a decent manner of burying it for ever. From that day a
party—headed by the curé's three friends above alluded to
—was formed against Antonio; in course of time it was
joined by the majority of the priests in the town, and by
many of the pious women among their penitents. The
animosity went so far that, a little after, the curé falling ill
of an indigestion, sent for the doctor of Ventimiglia, and
placed himself under his care. But not all this display of
hostility, not all the underhand propaganda of the Church
party, and the charge of imposture laid against Antonio,
had power to shake his popularity among the peasantry,
who, in spite of all the efforts made to entangle the question,
held fast in their homely good sense to the one plain fact,
that for their benefit Doctor Antonio had given up a good
round sum of money, which he might, without blame from
any one, have quietly kept in his pocket.

CHAPTER XXI.
Eight Years after.

WE beg at this place to use our privilege of novelist,
and to leap over a period of no less than eight years at
once. If the gentle reader will but take into consideration
the amount of matter, bearing or not upon the subject, with
which we might have filled up this gap, and the saving of
time and patience attendant on our expeditious way of
getting over the ground, we trust he will not grudge us the
effort of imagination we impose upon him, and even give us
some credit for discretion. Henceforth no sweet allure-
ments will delay us on our road. Farewell cool shades

and bright hills!—Farewell quiet paths strewn with flowers, clear rivulets gurgling merrily by the way-side! The sunny portion of our course is past, and lurid clouds darken that which remains. Let us hurry over it as fast as we can.

The time is the middle of March 1848, the scene that same road, on which, eight years ago, we first met Lucy and her father, and, as then, the principal object on it a travelling carriage, wending its way from the heights of Turbia to the sea-girt Mentone far below. An overcast sky, a sea of a leaden colour, a narrow grey horizon bounded both on land and water by a hazy sheet of falling rain,— such is for the time being the dull aspect of the country through which this equipage is passing. The olive plantations of hill and valley shiver and shudder under the keen gusts of wind that sweep over them, changing in quick succession from white to dark, from dark to white, according as the swaying breeze turns up the silvery or the deep-green side of their leaves. Well may the middle-aged English man-servant in the rumble—his nationality is unmistakably written in his florid complexion, and in the elaborate curve of his grey-reddish whiskers towards the point of his nose—well may he button up his great-coat and wink half-maliciously, half good-humouredly, at the starched female colleague seated by his side, as much as to say, "This then is the fine country you told me such wonders about!"

Certainly the poor beautiful Riviera looked sadly unlike itself in this ungenial day; and a lover of fine scenery would have had nothing better to do than shut his eyes and go to sleep. Yet a traveller alive to other phenomena than those arising from combinations of form and colour, might have discovered, even through this murky atmosphere, something to win his interest, and rouse his sympathies into active play. More than once had the carriage come up with groups of soldiers gaily plodding through mud and mire, and singing songs such as the surrounding mountains had rarely echoed. The once proscribed name of Italy resounded in the choruses, coupled with another—one for a moment so full of bright promises, and then so pregnant with long disappointment to Italian ears and hearts—the name of Pius the Ninth. An unusual air of animation prevailed throughout the many small towns and villages scattered along the road, or perched above it. In the main streets stood knots of citizens of all classes, warmly discussing, in spite of wind and rain, the topics of the day; streamers of every dimension waved over roofs, or floated from windows, all alike displaying the Italian colours,—white, red, and green; improvised national guards, with nothing of the soldier but the musket, mounted guard before the flag-decorated town-halls. No doubt of it, the thrice sweet goddess, Liberty, had breathed over this land, and, with her warm breath, stirred up to life the long-dormant populations of the Riviera.

None of these signs of altered times were lost upon the lady inside the carriage, who watched them with an eagerness that heightened the hectic spot on each pale cheek, and added to the ominous lustre of her sunken eyes. With every step of the fast-going horses, her interest in everything seemed to increase, and, as the carriage drove past Ventimiglia, and the first of a series of promontories, projecting in a crescent-shaped cerulean line into the sea, began to loom out of the rainy mist, the fair traveller was so overcome by her feelings, that, laying her hand on her side, as if striving to repress the bounding of her heart, she fell back on the seat and gasped for breath. The reader has scarcely needed this last circumstance to guess who the lady was.—Who, but our sweet heroine, would betray such emotion at the sight of Bordighera? It was indeed Lucy, sadly altered but still beautiful,—her rich auburn hair hanging as profusely as ever over a forehead as pure and smooth as eight years ago. But what sorrow or care, gentle daughter of Albion, has worked that net of small horizontal lines between thy temples and eyes? What invidious hand has cut those two deep lines that form an angle with each of the corners of thy mouth?

Lucy had done what nine hundred and ninety-nine young ladies out of a thousand would have done in her case.—She had married. When Sir John, half in joke, half in earnest, had first mooted the question as to who, among the numerous retinue of suitors thronging round the rich young beauty, had found grace in her eyes, Lucy, colouring deeply, had declared that she had never thought of any such thing, and that her only wish was to continue to live as she had done with dear papa. On hearing which, dear papa had laughingly retorted, that what she said was sheer nonsense; —young ladies were born to marry and be married. Aubrey, who happened to be present at this conversation, made no remark at the time, but a day or so after took an opportunity of asking his sister what objection she could possibly have to Lord Cleverton. She had no particular objection to the Viscount, or anybody else, only she was not inclined to marry. But he, Aubrey, was strongly inclined that she should do so, and, if within two months from that day she had not made a choice—well, it was for him to guess where the obstacle lay, and to take good care to remove it. This was said with the gentleness of speech and manner peculiar to Lucy's brother,—that is, with flashing eyes and stamping feet. Lucy was not, as the reader knows, of that coriaceous stuff of which heroines are made, who beard their tyrants and shake their fetters at them—in books or on the stage. She was a poor, weakly, nervous creature, with more in her nature of the reed that bends, than of the oak which makes head bravely against the blast. Besides, Captain Davenne's threat was two-edged. Women, when they fear for others, are soon disarmed; so Miss Davenne made her choice within the allotted time, and four months afterwards was married, —married without love, but without repugnance,—on the contrary, with a degree of sympathy, which, properly nurtured and cultivated, might, and ought to have ripened into a steady and lasting affection.

Lord Cleverton was a man whose attentions and preference could not but flatter a girl of Lucy's warm feelings,

even had he not been what he professed to be, an
enthusiastic admirer of Italy. It was, in fact, in Italy that
the Honourable Mr. Tyrrel, a wild young attaché at Florence,
had made his *début* in life, and, if fame reported truly, had
sown then and there a plentiful crop of wild oats. In the
midst of a career of thoughtless extravagance, unexpectedly
called upon, by his father's death, to assume the paternal
title and a seat in the Upper House, the dashing attaché,
like another Prince Hal, had turned aside from his follies,
and astonished the world by his steady application and uncommon aptitude for business. Handsome still and young-
looking, though fully five-and-twenty years older than his
bride, and quoted as a model of elegance and good taste,
Lord Cleverton united to all the brilliant accomplishments
of the man of the world the more solid attainments of the
statesman. No one could utter with a better grace those
amiable nothings which are the current coin of drawing-
rooms; no one, with more cogent logic, attack the ministry
amid the enthusiastic cheering of the opposition benches,
on which he sat. Unfortunately, the qualities that command
success in fashionable coteries, or oratorical triumphs in
political assemblies, do not always secure domestic happiness,—not, at least, as our Lucy understood it. She was
some little time before she found this out, but she did find
it out at last.

What did the young Viscountess want or miss? She was
like a little queen in her new household, her husband her
first subject,—wherever she went both old and young did
her homage,—grave statesmen put aside their speculations
to entertain her with those lighter topics proper to interest
her age and sex,—celebrated poets sang her beauty, and
first-rate painters disputed the honour of portraying her
lovely features on canvas,—and yet she was not happy!
What did she care for having her womanly vanity fed to
satiety, while her heart had cravings which remained un-
satisfied!

Lord Cleverton was one of those men whose existence

lies principally in the head. Ambition was the great passion
of his nature; deep, exclusive, all-engrossing attachments,
if such things were, he regarded in the light of bars to the
attainment of power,—according to him, the only noble, the
only legitimate, the only aim worthy of being pursued by
man. His respect for his young wife was really unbounded,
as was his deference to her every wish that did not interfere
with his ruling passion. He looked on her always with infinite complacency, and when he saw her doing the honours
of his house to a crowd of distinguished guests, with that
grace and dignified ease of manner, which won her all hearts,
gratified pride was his predominant feeling. But no warmer
sentiment animated his admiration. His great interest in
life lay elsewhere. Politics occupied most of his time.
What with schemes, meetings, deputations, acting as president to societies of every denomination, besides attending
the House, he was so taken up that Lady Cleverton scarcely
saw him for weeks together, and then only in company.
The world stood for ever between him and her. No possible privacy with such a man, none of those sweet out-
pourings of the heart, none of those refreshing *causeries* by
the fireside, which rouse sympathy into affection, and are to
affection like the fresh dew of the morning to flowers. His
cares were not her cares. In vain, at the beginning, had
she repeatedly sought, on noticing a cloud on his brow, to
know what caused it, that she might try to dispel it. All her
attempts to win his confidence had been gently, and with
much kindness, but not the less pertinaciously frustrated.
His motive for this was, he said, his unwillingness to disturb
the serenity of her life. This reason, she thought, might
have held good with a stranger; but was she not his wife,
and as such entitled to her share of his joys and sorrows?
And so it came about that poor Lucy's heart shrunk and
withered, and felt more lonely every day. This was not the
work of a few days, or weeks, or months—the drop must
fall long ere it wears a hole. Nor was the dissolving process
continuous. No; there were ups and downs, halts, hopings

against hope. But the day came at last, and a sad day it was, when the Viscountess realized her situation, when she saw her dream of love and happiness vanish like a brilliant soap-bubble, and cold *ennui* began to coil itself, like a snake, round her heart.

Had the joys of maternity been granted to Lucy—had she possessed a dear infant, on whom to bestow the overflowing riches of her soul, all had been well with her. But Providence willed it otherwise. Lord Cleverton had longed for an heir with all the ardour of the chief of a new dynasty, but he was too well bred and generous not to conceal, as well as he could, the bitter disappointment under which he smarted. Her ladyship's acuteness, however, soon led her to perceive that something besides political preoccupations weighed upon her husband's mind; and by dint of searching for the cause she found it. It is inconceivable how quick we are to guess at that which will pain us. This discovery completed Lucy's misery, and few were the nights that she did not moisten her pillow with bitter tears. How many of the great, with rank and riches—envy of the vulgar who look up to them as suns and stars shining overhead,—how many show, when brought close to the eye, some mysterious canker, some unsightly excrescence, that renders them objects of pity! Just like that beautiful rose so eagerly plucked, and which lets drop its gorgeous corolla, giving to view a hideous worm in its calix. Lord Cleverton came to remark his wife's altered looks and frequent fits of absence, not only with pain, but with displeasure. That admirable grace, that rich flow of conversation so natural and animated, which had drawn around her the wisest and gayest of society, leaders in politics as well as leaders of fashion, were gradually being replaced by mere formal monotonous courtesy. Lord Cleverton, who liked to hear his house talked of as one of the most agreeable in London,—for he looked on such a reputation as one of the aids of his ambition,—watched with a growing discontent, legible enough in his countenance, his wife's alternations of gaiety and gloom. Lucy, aware that his scrutinizing eye was on her, strove to mask, by perpetual smiles, the real dejection that preyed on her. Constraint arose on both sides; time, as usual, widened the breach, and the husband and wife became every day more estranged from each other. We do not pretend to develop, we only indicate the situation.

Meanwhile, as Lady Cleverton's health and spirits drooped, so did her duties, as mistress of one of the most splendid and hospitable mansions of the metropolis, become more burdensome, and never more so than in the spring of 1847. The Administration *in esse* was tottering, and a new Ministry spoken of, in which public opinion assigned to Lord Cleverton an important post. Ambitions, high and low, were up at an incandescent point, and none was higher than that of Lucy's husband. One more desperate push, one more defeat of the Cabinet, and power, that long-desired goal, would be reached. Lord Cleverton's house became the headquarters of his party, where, amidst the glare of the ballroom, and the din of Italian and German singers, wavering voices were secured, places assigned, and the plan of a new campaign determined on. Now was the time when the young Viscountess's fascination of manner, and the persuasive charm of her conversation, was to accomplish all that which Lord Cleverton had counted on when he first thought of her as a wife. He required of her to be assiduous at Court, to accept all invitations, no matter whether from his Grace or Excellency, or only from some of the Manchester school. She must shew herself everywhere, where fashion commands ladies of high degree to be, and, in order to triumph, look at all times as if triumph were already secured. All this Lady Cleverton did, unostentatiously, calmly. Her husband admired and wondered, then felt grateful to her. The way in which she conformed to all his wishes, and adopted his views, caused a doubt, even in the heat of the chase, to enter his mind, as to whether he had been all he ought to have been to this fair creature; and he resolved that, once the present crisis was over, the future should make amends for the past. But it was too late. Lord Cleverton, in the midst of his worldly plots and plans, took a fever, and died in a few days. He died with sad misgivings of having mistaken his road to happiness, and blessing the angel who tended, nursed, and consoled him unremittingly and tenderly to the last.

The young widow, sadly shattered in health and spirits, repaired to Davenne, where growing age and severe fits of gout had kept Sir John a prisoner for the last two years. The tender father was frightened at the altered looks of his child, and was still more alarmed at the state of profound discouragement in which he saw her plunged. Lucy, in fact, felt as if she were dying, and nothing could shake her firm conviction that her days were numbered. Sir John did his best to reason her out of this gloomy fancy all in vain, until the idea of her going abroad suggested itself to him.—"Why should not what had succeeded once do so again? She only required fresh air, change of scene, and quiet. Why not go for a little while to Bordighera, and consult Doctor Antonio? She was certainly far more delicate when they were there eight years ago than now, and how soon he had set her to rights. Probably the Count would let them his Casino, or they might induce the Doctor to go with them to Rome. He, Sir John, was sure that Doctor Antonio would do anything for her." The worthy Baronet had struck the right chord, and, perceiving his advantage, he reiterated his arguments. And now Doctor Antonio and Bordighera, Bordighera and Doctor Antonio, and the old Osteria, and Speranza, and Battista—those long unspoken names—became the daily themes of conversation at Davenne Hall. Buried recollections rose again to life, old associations asserted their power, refreshing and vivifying Lucy's heart. A dawn of hope gleamed on her downcast spirit. Yes, if anything could save her, it was the attendance of that kind Doctor of hers—it was the soft-perfumed air of the sweet Riviera. It came to be settled accordingly, that as soon as her first year of mourning was over, Lucy and her father should set out for the

Riviera. Lucy waited with a sort of nostalgia, longing for the arrival of that moment, which, when it came at last, found poor Sir John nailed fast by a fit of the gout, severer than usual. He would not, however, consent to any delay on Lucy's part, and was peremptory as to her going, for friends and doctors had long agreed that the Viscountess must leave England before the March winds began to blow. Sir John would join her at Bordighera, at Rome, at Naples, anywhere, but go she must, and at once. Lucy, not liking to go so far from home with only servants, engaged a middle-aged lady to travel with her as a companion; and thus *chaperoned*, she set out for Paris in the middle of February 1848. Too anxious to reach Italy to find any temptations for delay in the French capital, Lady Cleverton resumed her journey, luckily, previous to the appearance of the Republican barricades on the Boulevards. Once at Nice, her impatience knew no bounds. She would not even allow herself a few days to recover from her fatigues; but her sensitive nature shrinking from the idea of exposing to a stranger the emotions she knew must be roused by the scenes she was about to revisit, she left her companion at the hotel, and, attended only by the faithful Hutchins and a man-servant, went on to Bordighera with the feverish eagerness of one whose life is staked on the throw of a die. She wished to live now; and no doctor, save Doctor Antonio, could make her live. Lucy had a sort of superstition on this point.

At last the carriage passed the promontory of Bordighera, and the little valley beneath opened to view. Lucy strained her eager eyes to take in at one gaze all the details of the once familiar scene, and her heart sank within her. What was it that gave the poor Osteria, the garden, the very sea-side, such a desolate, deserted look? In the growing flutter of her spirits she could see nothing distinctly; still she discerned enough to feel that, whatever the cause, a change had come over the spot. She stops the carriage, hurries with trembling limbs down the lane. The little gate hangs from one rusty hinge, as if no human being had passed through it for ages; the garden is a perfect wilderness of weeds and brambles; the once luxuriant grove of lemon and orange trees has dwindled into a scanty assemblage of shivered, scattered, skeleton-looking trunks,—the few dry reddish leaves, still hanging on the branches, look as if they had been scorched by lightning; the house, all cracks, splits, and holes, is fast tumbling and crumbling to pieces. The only part entire is the massive flight of stairs. Such of the shutters as are not swinging to the wind, or lying on the ground, are hermetically closed. Everything around bears the marks of utter neglect, decay, and desolation.

While knocking at the glass-door, which is fastened from within, and calling Speranza and Battista, Lucy is startled by a voice at the foot of the stone-steps. It is a young villager, who informs her that there is no one in the house to answer her knocks or calls; the house is uninhabited, and has been so ever since the death of the last proprietor.

"What! Speranza dead?—Battista dead?"

"No, no; Speranza and Battista are both alive, thank God, and in good health. They keep the post-house at Mentone. They had sold the Osteria to an old man, who had since died."

Lucy breathes more freely.

"And—the parish doctor of Bordighera," she falters. "What of him?"

"Doctor Gabriele, you mean? He is very well, thank you."

"Not Doctor Gabriele—I mean Doctor Antonio—a tall gentleman with a long beard—a Sicilian."

"Ah, yes! I know now who you mean. I beg your pardon, but I do not belong to this place. The Doctor you speak of went away long ago; at least so I have heard."

Lucy leant against the balustrade—her knees were giving way.

"And you don't know of course," said she, trembling from head to foot, "where he is?"

"No, I do not, and I fear that nobody hereabouts knows."

The young peasant had all this time been examining his fair questioner with much curiosity and interest. "Perhaps," added he, with some hesitation,—"perhaps you are the *Signora Inglese* who lived long in this house, and did so much good to the country?"

It was a cordial to Lucy to find how well she was remembered. The interest felt for her by those left behind had not then died out. The young man's words somewhat soothed the smart of this bitter disappointment.

"You have guessed right," she answered. "I am that *Inglese*. Take this for the sake of one who loves Bordighera well;" and, hurrying to the carriage, she bid the servant order the postilion back to the Post Inn at Mentone.

The rain had been dropping fast during Lucy's halt, and she was now wet and shivering. Hutchins suggested the expediency of her stopping somewhere to have her clothes dried, and to get something warm to drink; but Lucy would not hear of stopping before she reached Mentone. The promise of a fabulous *pourboire* inspiring the postilion with fresh courage, he whirled his long whip round his head with such violent smacks, as set his horses off into a gallop, and away they went, plashing furiously through mud and mire. The day was on the wane as the bespattered carriage stopped in front of the Inn of the Post.

The sky had partially cleared to the west, and the rosy tints of the sun setting amidst a mass of huge black clouds, streamed down on a group at the side of the inn-door,—one of those homely domestic pictures of which Teniers or Mieris would have made a little wonder. On a wooden bench sat a black-eyed, black-haired, handsome young woman, and, a little way from her, a dark-complexioned, dark-whiskered man of thirty, with a pipe in his mouth, was squatting on his heels, with arms outstretched towards a rosy, curly-headed cherub,—both parents encouraging, by act and word, the little fellow's first attempts at walking, while he, with screams of infantine delight, tottered from the one to the other. Lucy gazed earnestly on the trio. Speranza turns and catches sight of the sweet face. "Madonna Santa! Mother, mother, it is la Signora." In an instant she is on her feet, and, thrusting the infant into the crouching Battista's arms with an impetuosity that lays her husband flat on his back, with the child sprawling over him, she springs up the carriage steps, and falls on Lucy's neck. "Oh, my dear lady!—my dear lady!" is all Speranza can say. Rosa rushes out, with but one thought of course, that of some mortal injury having happened to the screaming hope of the family. Battista scrambles to his legs, and a general recognition takes place amid such blessings, blubberings, clapping of hands, and invocations of the Virgin, as would be highly comical, were it not very touching.

"Bless me! how cold your hands are, Signora. How wearied you look! If only Doctor Antonio was here." Speranza bites her tongue; Lucy is rather carried than shown up stairs to the best room of the house. A bright fire soon crackles on the hearth, a sofa is wheeled forward, and Lucy, her wet shawl and dress taken off, is comfortably wrapped up and laid upon it to warm and rest herself. Speranza leans fondly over her lovely charge, strokes and kisses by turns her cold hands and feet, dries and smoothes and kisses the fair, damp curls, smiling all the while, and chatting and blessing the day and the hour, and the Madonna, yet, even in her excitement, forgetting nothing that can in the least minister to the comfort of her *cara cara padrona*, as she calls Lucy; least of all, the toast and the hot tea,— not the everyday tea, but that kept in the green canister for extraordinary occasions. Miss Hutchins is completely set aside for the time being, and takes it good-humouredly. Speranza will yield to no one, not even to her mother, the right to place the little feet in warm slippers, or to put the "monk" to air the bed, or to do the slightest service for this adored *padrona* of hers.

Lucy felt herself revived in this genial atmosphere of devotion, and, as she sat sipping her tea, which seemed like nectar to her, a glow of comfort spread itself over her weary frame and heart. It was long indeed since she had enjoyed such a banquet, for eight long years she had been famishing. Not all the prestige of station and fortune, not all the pleasures of gratified vanity, had given her an hour like this. Of all the homage that had been pressed on her, of all the smiles that had beamed on the noble lady, be it even those from royal lips, none had so gladdened, none had so flattered her, as the smile of this peasant woman, as the homage of these simple folks. There are blessings, thank God, that rank does not command, nor riches buy.

Lucy told Speranza of her visit to Bordighera, and of the shock she had received on seeing the altered state of things there, and of her disappointment at finding Doctor Antonio gone. "We will speak of all that to-morrow, dear lady," said Speranza, who had remarked Lucy's dropping eye-lids, "and after you have had the good night's rest I expect you to have. I will only just tell you that Doctor Antonio went back to his own country, and is there still, at least was there two months ago. Signora Eleonora has had a letter from him, and she can tell you everything about our dear friend. We heard there was a great revolution in Sicily, and that he fought like a lion. There has been a famous revolution in Sardinia too, and one here at Mentone, and at Roccabruna. Battista was at the head of it,—upon my word he was!—and he is to be an officer in the National Guard. The Commandant of San Remo has run away, and there are to be no more commandants, at least so they say; and the carabineers are to count as nothing more than other people. Has there been a revolution in your country also?" asked Speranza, with very much the air of a person who takes for granted the thing inquired about.

"No, thank God!" said Lucy, smiling.

"No revolution!" repeated Speranza, rather disappointed. "But then you have no commandants in your country," she added, as if that settled the matter. Thus, while addressing Lucy, Speranza, notwithstanding her wise resolution to put off all conversation till the morrow, told what was most interesting to her hearer. It was something to know that all trace of the Doctor was not lost; so, after receiving Speranza's blessing, Lucy fell asleep, and dreamed all night of blue seas, perfumed orange-trees, and that she was walking in the little garden of the Osteria with Doctor Antonio.

Early in the morning Speranza brought her children to Lucy,—two healthy, beautiful girls, as dark as night,—Lucia Maria and Rosa Lucia, and the little curly-headed Lucio. "Did you know before that there was such a name as Lucio?" asked the proud young mother.

"I believe I did," replied Lucy.

"Well, I am sure, for my part, I did not," said Speranza; "and I was sorely puzzled, as he was a boy, how to name the little one after you, for I was determined to do so, even if I had had to make a name on purpose. Battista wanted me to call him John, after your father, but that would not have done half so well; and so what do you think I did? I took an Almanac and looked through all the Saints, and at last I found a Lucio—bless him;" and Speranza showed all her white teeth in the delight of relating her discovery.

Lucy Mary and Rose Lucy being dismissed in good time, and Lucio given over to his grandmother's spoiling care, Speranza turned to Lucy and said, "Ah! dear lady, you can never know how we felt when you were carried away from us so suddenly. Do not be angry with me for saying so, but it was downright cruel of your brother to come here just to take you from a place where you were so well and happy, and where every one, old and young, doted on you. I shall never forget the feeling I had when I lost sight of the carriage. We were all as miserable as could be, and did not know what to do. Mother pined and sighed all day long and every day, Battista was like a fish out of water, and grew quite cross, and as for the poor Doctor," (here Speranza shook her head ominously,) "how he wandered up and down, here and there, like a soul in purgatory, finding no peace nor rest go where he would! It made one's heart ache to watch him sitting for hours together where he could get a sight of the Osteria. Who would ever have thought matters were to end so, when we used to see you and him walking side by side, both so young and handsome, and so pleased to be together, that it seemed as if God had made you on purpose for one another. But what is the use of repining now?" continued Speranza, noticing Lucy's changing cheek. "No doubt it was the will of God that things should go wrong in the way they did, only the poor Doctor never recovered the shock of your going away—he was never like the same man again. I do not mean to say that he was not as good, and kind, and charitable as before,—it would be a lie to say he was not all that; but he had grown grave, and never had anything droll to say to make a poor body laugh. The priests, too, with the curé at their head, had taken a dislike to him,—and then there was always the same story of the communion-ticket at Easter. Can you believe that the curé one day asked, from the pulpit, what business foreigners had amongst us?—as if foreigners were not Christians! Altogether, Doctor Antonio had a sorry life of it, and he had a great mind to go away. Well, one day, —it was in the year 1842, he received a letter from his home with the news of his mother's death. The kind, good soul took it so much to heart that he fell ill, and if it had not been for that fat little English doctor from Nice, you remember, Signora, who came and nursed him like a brother, I do believe Doctor Antonio would have died. He did recover at last, but, oh, dear me! he looked like the shadow of himself. The English doctor took him away to Nice, and soon after Doctor Antonio sent to tell the town-council that he gave up his appointment as parish doctor, and from that time we never saw him again. Once, when the English doctor stopped here a night, he told us that Doctor Antonio's mother had managed some way,—I did not rightly understand how, but she had done something which prevented the Government in her country from taking away the fortune she had bequeathed to her son; and then we heard by chance that our good friend had left Nice, and was away travelling, no one knew where.

"Your going had made Bordighera sad enough and dull enough to us, but now that Doctor Antonio was gone too we began to hate it, and we made up our minds that we would go also as soon as we could. Everything had thriven well with us, and we had saved a good sum of money. A blessing was on all you had done for us. People came from far and near to look at the old Osteria, where the great English Milor and his beautiful daughter had stayed so long. Almost all the travellers on this road from your country stopped at our house, and liked to hear us talk of you and all you did; and they paid us handsomely for what they had, and would often stay over the night, because, they said, we had learnt from you how to make English people comfortable. We liked them all for your sake, Signora, though none of them seemed to know you. So we were as well off as heart could wish. The landlord of the Post Inn at Mentone wanted to retire from business, and had offered to sell us the whole concern, but we were afraid to say yes before we had found a purchaser for the Osteria. We had good luck in that also. An old sailor, whom every one had given up for lost, all of a sudden returned to Bordighera, after having been away for forty years. He was a man who liked to live alone, and as he found all his people dead, it made him more unwilling to stay in the town. He took a fancy to the Osteria, because, he said, it was out of the way, and he should not be troubled with seeing many faces. So we made the two bargains at the same time, and then we came here, where we have been for six years, with only one wish,—that the day might come when we should see again the Heaven-sent angel, to whom, after God, we owe everything we possess, and that we are as we are;" and grateful Speranza took within her own hard hands Lucy's soft small ones, and covered them with hearty kisses.

"But how has the poor Osteria come to be such a ruin?" asked Lucy.

"It was the earthquake of 1844,—a tremendous one, that did that; it nearly threw it quite down," returned Speranza. "Almost all the houses in or round Bordighera suffered more or less, but none so severely as the poor old Osteria del Mattone. Some persons say it was because the foundations were bad. As to the garden, there has been no one to look after it for years, so no wonder it has run all to waste. The old sailor died the year after the earthquake, and as he left no will, and seemed to have no relations, the house was shut up, and it and the garden left to take care of one another. Battista says he saw in the Gazette, the other day, that notice was given, that if no relations of the late owner came forward to claim the property by such a time, it was to go to the king."

Lucy spent that day and the following night at the Inn of the Post, determining to go the morning after to Taggia, to ascertain from Signora Eleonora, if possible, where Doctor Antonio was likely to be found. She made no attempt to conceal from her humble friend her earnest desire to place herself under his medical care, nor her superstitious feeling that no one but Doctor Antonio could restore her shattered health. The affectionate Speranza, who had not failed to notice Lucy's emaciated appearance and her frequent fits of coughing, but had given no other sign of the anxiety she felt than by clinging more fondly than ever to her benefactress; Speranza gave her hearty approval to this plan, convinced, like the lady, of Antonio's powers; nor, for anything that Lucy could say to the contrary, was Speranza to be dissuaded from going to Taggia with her. "Mother and Battista can take care of the children and mind the business," said Speranza; "now that I have you once more, let me make the most of the Godsend."

Signora Eleonora was not at Taggia, she had just left for Genoa, with her two sons, both of whom had returned from banishment. Lucy was delighted at this news, and only longed the more to see and congratulate her old acquaintance. Speranza pleaded a similar wish so earnestly that she got leave to accompany her English friend to Genoa. The little journey was charming, the sky cloudless, the sun bright and warm, the sea deep blue; and Lucy felt rekindle within her that passion for the beautiful which had shaped so many of her pleasures in past days; she inhaled with delight the genial air, and at the sight of that privileged Nature, went over in her mind all her former sensations and emotions, with a keenness of enjoyment only to be compared to that of a miser who tells over and over again all the coins of a long lost, newly regained treasure.

On reaching Genoa, Lady Cleverton found no difficulty in tracing out Signora Eleonora; the good old lady held out her arms to her unexpected visitor, without any words of articulate welcome. What a myriad of thoughts rushed through the mind of each as they held one another in a close embrace! Lucy was the first to speak. "Did not I tell you that, one day or other, you would receive back your dear ones?"

"God bless your kind heart," returned the Italian lady; "the Almighty has indeed listened to our prayers, and made me one of the proudest and happiest of mothers."

Speranza came in for no small share of the Signora's caresses and kindness; and if angels ever weep for tenderness, we take it for granted that they did so as they watched this meeting.

Signora Eleonora had little to add to the information about Doctor Antonio, already given by Speranza, and that little was ill suited to raise Lucy's spirits. Only once had the kind old lady heard from her Sicilian friend since his return to his own country. She showed the letter to Lucy; it was dated Palermo, the 1st Februar 1848, and gave a short account of the struggle that had just taken place between the king's troops and the popular party. The Doctor had evidently written in the first moments of excitement, after a dearly bought victory. The letter had this postscript. "I have God, be thanked! been so fortunate as to shed some of my blood in my country's cause. A half-spent Neapolitan ball wounded me in the right shoulder; it is a mere scratch, and does not prevent my using my arm, as you see. I only tell you of it lest you might see my name among the casualties, and be uneasy. I will write again soon."

"And you have not heard from him since?" exclaimed Lucy, turning cold. Signora Eleonora shook her head. "His wound, then, must have proved more serious than he thought, otherwise he would have kept his promise. He must be ill, I am afraid, that"—and her fancy getting the upper hand of reason, she at once pictured to herself this dear friend alone, sick, helpless, perhaps even dying. Lucy made up her mind on the instant she would go to Naples, cross to Palermo, and, *coûte que coûte*, find him. She accordingly wrote, by that same day's post, to her father to come and join her at Naples, adding, that if, by chance, she were not there on his arrival, he would, at all events, find further directions as to her movements at the British Embassy. She wrote also to her companion, who was still waiting at Nice, to come post-haste to Genoa; and three days after, our delicate, fragile Lucy was on board a steamer bound for Naples.

Signora Eleonora and Speranza saw her on board, and remained with her to the last, uttering words of hope and comfort. The parting was a sad affair, particularly with Speranza, who would not let go her hold of her dear *padrona's* dress till she forced a promise from her that if, at any time, Lucy wanted her she would send for her. "I know that I am only a poor, ignorant, peasant woman, and you a high-born, rich lady," said the poor creature, the tears running down her cheeks, "still they say a mouse once helped a lion; so, pray, my dear, dear mistress, never forget that I am all yours, and if the poor peasant can be of any service call her to you;—oh! promise you will, and I will abide by you and serve you to my last day;—I will! indeed I will, so help me the Madonna!"

CHAPTER XXII.
Naples.

THE tide of national feeling, which, ever since the accession of Pius the Ninth, and the first reforms granted by him, had been swelling slowly but uninterruptedly throughout Italy, had nowhere risen higher than in Naples and Sicily. But while the daily increasing demands for reform met with no hostility from the ruling powers in Rome, Tuscany, or Piedmont, nay, were in some degree yielded to, the case was very different in Naples and in Sicily. There, on the contrary, a determined opposition to all progress was arrayed in panoply of battle, and more than once had the loyal cries of "Long live Pius the Ninth!—Long live Ferdinand the Second, and Reform!" been responded to by volleys of musketry, and been followed by severe incarcerations. Sicily, her patience worn out, her moderation, her long-suffering, her fidelity, all alike disregarded, at last resolved to snatch by main force what her petitions and remonstrances had hitherto failed in obtaining. Chivalrous in her misery, she named a day to her King, until when she would wait the issue of her last prayer for redress. If it were overlooked, she would then take to the *ultima ratio* of peoples as well as of kings. As might be anticipated, this appeal was treated with the usual cruel indifference, and Sicily, true to her word, rose in arms. Palermo took the lead, and, on the appointed day, was in full insurrection.

The news set all Naples in a blaze. It was like a lighted match thrown into a smouldering fire. Thousands poured into Via Toledo, thousands crowded the square before the Royal Palace. They were, it is true, unarmed, and their cries were the pacific ones of "Viva il Re, Vive la Costituzione," but the attitude was that of menace. If we may judge from all appearances, the King was well inclined to look on this effervescence of popular feeling as a personal challenge, which he was nothing loath to accept. A huge red flag, never hoisted but as a signal of war, was seen to float from the towers of the Castle of St. Elmo. The multitude kept the position they had taken up, in no way scared by the ugly emblem, whose sanguinary appearance they answered by cries, the sound of which was becoming fiercer. Tricolor cockades seemed to spring from the pavement below their feet, and, eagerly distributed, soon decorated every hat and coat.

There comes a moment in which bayonet and cannon are powerless against what appears unarmed, defenceless numbers. Once the blood of the people is up, hands and arms of flesh tear down stone-walls and mock at artillery. Modern history, from the destruction of the Bastile downwards, is full of examples. Such a crisis was now at hand; that it passed without bloodshed, may be attributed to the courageous refusal of General Roberti, the brave and honest commandant of the Castle, to bombard the town. Rather than do so, he tendered his resignation. All this occurred on the damp and gloomy morning of the 27th January 1848.

The King finding himself in an awkward dilemma, called around him most of the eminent men in whom he had confidence. Count Statella, commander-in-chief of Naples, and General Filangieri, were among the number. With one voice they answered Ferdinand by advising him to change his Ministers without delay, and to grant the Constitution. The Cabinet was accordingly dissolved, and its moving spirit, the hero of Bosco and Catania, Del Carretto, unceremoniously put on board a Government steamer. The disgraced minister, followed by the curses of his countrymen, and met by the execrations of Genoa and Leghorn, where the vessel had to stop, made the best of his way to Marseilles. The banishment of Del Carretto was an act of tardy justice, and mild, too, when compared to his crimes, but it was not the less an act of black ingratitude on the part of the King. The moment Ferdinand began to fear for himself, he behaved like any common villain, sacrificing, without hesitation, one whom he ought to have supported, as his active, unscrupulous accomplice and faithful servant.

The universal prayer of the people was at last to be listened to, a Constitution was promised, and a few days after publicly proclaimed. The King used the following words in its solemn preamble:—"Concurring in the unanimous desire of our most beloved subjects, we have promised, of our own full, free, and spontaneous will, to establish in this kingdom a Constitution, and, in the awful name of the Most Holy and Almighty God, the Trinity in Unity, to whom alone it appertains to read the depths of the heart, and whom we loudly invoke as the Judge of the simplicity of our intentions, and of the unreserved sincerity with which we have determined to enter upon the paths of the new political order, we have decided upon proclaiming, and we do proclaim, as irrevocably ratified by us, the following Constitution."

On the 24th of February, with every pomp and circumstance of solemnity, this Constitution was sworn to by the King, the Princes of the Royal Family, the new Ministers, the chief officers of the army, the magistracy, and all the other high functionaries of the kingdom. A few days after the Electoral law was promulgated, and the convocation of Parliament fixed for the 1st May.

It is in the nature of things, that those who are at the head of affairs, in any time of great excitement, should give little satisfaction to any party. What has been is overthrown—what is to be is yet unsubstantial hope. Expectation is strained to such a pitch, that no wonder the men at the helm fail in coming up to it—indeed, necessarily fall far short. Nor were the new Ministers any exception to the rule. Fault was found with them on every side for not at once discovering a solution for the Sicilian question, the Gordian knot of the situation—for not giving to their politics a more decided Italian character—for not adopting the three national colours, and so on. In short, the Cabinet could do nothing right, and became so avowedly unpopular, that its only course was to resign. The accession to power of the new Administration—called, from the date of its formation, the Ministry of the 6th March—was hailed by an unbounded and general cry of joy. This was the state of things when Lucy, towards the end of the month of March, reached Naples.

The great bustle and animation of the city, the demonstrative joy of all classes, especially that of the lower order, (the very lazzaroni were adorers of liberty at that moment, and all that can be argued from after events is, that Machiavellian arts can pervert man's most natural feelings,) would have afforded our heroine ample scope for observation and interest, had not other thoughts and other cares exclusively absorbed her. The people of the hotel in Via Toledo, where Lady Cleverton stopped, opened their eyes, and pursed up their lips, when told to have the noble lady's passport, and that of her suite, *viséd* for Palermo. "Perhaps miladi did not know that Palermo was in open rebellion, and all Sicily in an uproar." Miladi knew it perfectly well, but miladi was determined on going, and they must do as they were desired. Presently, in hot haste, came Mr. X——, a young attaché from the British embassy, where the passports had been presented for signature. This gentleman was a cousin of Lord Cleverton, to whom he owed his diplomatic post, and waited on her ladyship to dissuade her from attempting what he styled a mad expedition. The two countries were positively at open war,—the sea was not safe,—Neapolitan cruisers were out expressly to prevent any strangers from landing on the island,—without any actual danger, Lady Cleverton might be placed in some very unpleasant predicament. Lady Cleverton looked very obstinate. "Her Britannic Majesty's ambassador," continued the attaché, "was unwilling to authorize her ladyship's running such risks. There was a talk of Lord Minto's being the bearer of terms to the Sicilians in a few days. If Lady Cleverton really persisted in her present determination, a passage might be obtained for her at the same time in the royal steamer." Lucy was not to be persuaded that all these precautions were necessary for an English lady travelling for her health. His Excellency came himself in the evening to talk to his refractory countrywoman, and so seriously urged her adoption of the plan he had proposed, that there was nothing else for it than to yield, particularly as she dared not be explicit as to why she so preferred the air of Palermo to that of Naples; not indeed that she felt in the least ashamed of what she was doing, for never had Sister of Charity been actuated by purer motives, but Lucy had now sufficient experience of the world to know, that it rarely puts the best construction on actions susceptible of two interpretations, and so out of self-respect she kept her own secret.

Our Viscountess found the days that followed dreadfully long. Nothing more difficult than to wait. Mr. X——, the attaché, who, in virtue of his cousinship, claimed the right of amusing her, was most assiduous in his attentions, proposing all the usual excursions and sight-seeing. Lucy would accept of no amusement; she could not bear to have her thoughts disturbed, though her gentle, graceful nature prevented her telling her visitor that his efforts rather increased than allayed the fever of her impatience.

One day the young diplomatist came in a greater bustle than usual. He always appeared, even in his idleness, as if he bore the weight of the world on his shoulders. Well, this day he was full of the news, that on the ensuing evening there was to be a great reception at Court, the first since the establishing of a Constitutional Government. It would be worth going to, if only for the fun of the thing.

"What do you mean?" asked Lady Cleverton.

"*Per San Gennaro*, as they say here," returned the attaché, laughing, "we are to have all the veterans of Carbonarism, all the celebrities of the Progress party. A batch of musty *avvocati* and doctors are to play first fiddles at Court now. Lord, how Ferdinand will mystify them!"

"I do not understand why you, who, being an Englishman, ought to know better, should ridicule the learned professions," remarked Lady Cleverton, dryly.

"But who on earth, my sweet lady cousin, ever thinks of putting Neapolitan doctors and lawyers on the same footing as English ones?"

"And why not?" asked the lady, in the same dry voice.

"Don't look so fierce," answered the fine gentleman, laughing, but not pleased, "for really I only echo the opinion of every one. I know none of the gentry you seem so interested in, save by sight. His Excellency has luckily put your name on the list of strangers to be presented to-morrow. You had better go and judge for yourself."

"I think I shall," returned Lady Cleverton; "it will be worth while to see men whose name will figure in a page of history."

The attaché was regularly puzzled by the widow of his illustrious relative. "After all," thought he, "the best of her sex will say no to Pompeii, Vesuvius, and the San Carlo, on the plea of health and want of spirits, but she'll go to Court though she were dying."

The knowing attaché's prognostications were not to be verified. When Lady Cleverton joined the royal circle, she found every one and everything looking much as they generally look on such distinguished occasions; it was even impossible to tell that there was any want of blazonry in the assembly. Perhaps, owing to the new elements introduced, there was more animation, certainly less dulness, than usual. If there were any deviations from Court etiquette, the example was set by the king himself, who went from group to group, shaking hands and speaking courteously to everybody, acting the citizen-king to' the life. He was simply dressed in black, and, but for the Grand Cross of San Gennaro, the ribbon of which he wore saltier-wise, and the deference shown him, might have been taken for one of the guests, and not one of the best-looking either. Tall, long-legged, small-headed, grey-haired, and short-sighted, with little of the prepossessing or commanding about him, save what he owed to his erect carriage and deliberate gait, Ferdinand the Second had rather the appearance of an elderly cavalry officer on half pay than of a king eight-and-thirty years of age.

But Lady Cleverton gazed at him with unmixed admiration. All that she had heard from Doctor Antonio of Ferdinand himself, or of his race, was at that moment forgotten, and the shades cast on his brow by untoward precedents disappeared in the *auréole* of popularity which encircled, in her eyes, the Prince of reform,—the Prince who, like a philosopher, had yielded to the voice of public opinion,—the Prince who, like a father, had granted the prayers of his people. Did not he, who had diffused happiness throughout a whole kingdom, deserve blessing and affection?

But the young attaché, who was resolved on being her cicerone, would not leave her to her reflections. "Look at those two gentlemen," said he, "between whom his Majesty is walking; the one on the King's left is Bozzelli, minister of the interior, a refugee of yesterday; and the other, big-headed, shaggy-haired, and middle-sized, is Carlo Poerio, minister of public instruction. All that one knows about them is that they are both advocates, with lots to say for themselves, and have often been imprisoned on political charges, which, however, could never be proved against them. And now, you see, for all that, here they are, quite the rage in Naples, and looked upon as the two great pillars of the cabinet."

The gentleman the attaché called Poerio, forcibly attracted Lucy's attention. His was the vast powerful forehead, which she had so admired in Doctor Antonio, his the clear unsparkling, hazel eye, and thin, firmly-set lip, which bore evidence to an unconquerable will.

"That thin, fair-haired, meditative-looking young man," continued the attaché, who, so that he might talk, did not care much whether he was listened to or not, "is Professor Settembrini, editor of a leading paper, an out-and-out Utopist. He was to have had a place in the ministry, but some one, I believe, objected to him on account of his looking so young. However, you may be sure he is booked to be one of the future legislators of this country. And so is that tall old fellow in gold spectacles, passing close to us— some mushroom magistrate; I forget his name. Paron— —something. Ah! Pironti, that is it; an intriguant of the first water; they are every one of them people of yesterday. Heaven only knows where they spring from! The tall portly gentleman in the embrasure of that window opposite," said the Englishman, lowering his voice to a respectful whisper, "is the King's own brother, his Royal Highness the Count of Syracuse, formerly Viceroy of Sicily. I wonder who he is speaking to? It is a face I don't know—some other *parvenu*, I suppose."

Lucy could not help giving a great start; the blood rushed to her face, and thick drops of moisture rose on her brow. "What is the matter?" cried the unfledged diplomatist. "Are you ill?"

"It is nothing;—a sudden giddiness."

"Would you like to go away?—it must be from the heat of the room."

"Very likely," answered Lucy, in an unsteady voice.

Fortunately for her, the English ambassador himself came up to her, and the attaché made his bow without further comment. His Excellency was very sorry, but he had reason to believe that Lord Minto's mission to Sicily would be put off for another fortnight at least. New complications had arisen. The Viscountess received this piece of news very coolly. She did not mind a little delay; it was just possible she might give up her plan altogether. His Excellency was too well-bred to do more than raise his eyelids at this unexpected announcement; he, who had really been taking no little trouble in the matter, was thrown overboard without so much as "thank you." After a little desultory talk the ambassador went to make his usual round of bows, and Lucy was at length left to herself.

The companion of the Count of Syracuse was a tall,

black-haired, black-eyed man, who, at first sight, looked
scarcely past thirty; his countenance was thoughtful but
serene, his smile most winning, his carriage noble and erect;
the countenance, the smile, the figure, in one word, of
Doctor Antonio. Instead of his long beard he had now a
thick moustache on his upper lip. Save this slight difference, and a shade of pallor, greater perhaps than of old,
there was nothing changed about him; he looked as young
and handsome in his way as he had done eight years ago.

The King coming near them, the Count and Antonio left
the window and approached his Majesty, who, stopping to
exchange a few words with his brother, suddenly took the
Doctor's arm, and, drawing it through his own, continued
his walk. Lucy had not lost one of the details of this little
scene, least of all had she missed the sudden flash of those
well-known black eyes as they met hers, or the colour that
set the pale countenance all in a glow. What was the feeling that made the Viscountess turn her head away, and try
to get behind some ladies? Was it fear of an august
presence, or was it a misgiving that she was sadly changed
from what she had been? Lucy scarcely knew. The motion
had been instantaneous, mechanical, irresistible, and she
was in far too great a flutter of spirits to scan or analyze the
secret springs of the action.

Half an hour passed, in the course of which Lucy's eyes
turned more than once in the direction of the door, through
which she had seen the King and Doctor Antonio disappear. More than once had the advent of some score of
tall, black-haired, and moustached gentlemen through that
door made her heart beat loud and fast. Here *he* comes at
last—not in a hurry, but with his usual long quiet strides,
as gentle and unpretending amid his changed fortunes as
when, a poor village doctor, he went his rounds among his
humble patients of Bordighera. Here he comes, and, with
beaming eyes, makes straight for her.

 "You here!" he exclaimed, as she placed her hand in
his. "What an unlooked-for happiness! Who would ever

have dreamt, eight years ago, of our meeting at Naples, and, of all places in the world, at Court?"

"Who indeed!" was all that Lucy could say. Her soul was entranced by the sweet magic of his voice falling once more on her ear.

"How are you, and how is my good friend Sir John?" asked Antonio, after a short pause.

"Papa, when I left England, was laid up with a fit of the gout. He is soon to join me here. By the by, he gave me a letter for you, thinking I should find you at Bordighera. You shall have it the first thing to-morrow morning."

"Thank you," said the Doctor. "How glad I shall be to shake hands again with kind Sir John!"

"How do you happen to be in Naples?" inquired Lucy. "I thought you were at Palermo, and badly wounded, too."

"How do you know anything about my wound?" said Antonio, briskly.

"I saw Signora Eleonora at Genoa, and she told me. She is so happy now—both her sons are with her. She let me read your letter to her. She was very uneasy about you, and so was I."

"Were you? Bless her kind heart!" said Antonio. "What have I done to deserve two such friends?—Two such form an oasis for me in this vile wilderness of a world."

"I won't hear you speak ill of the world," returned Lucy, with something of her old childlike manner.

"Very well, I will not—now," said Antonio.

"Tell me about your wound;—how is it?"

"Perfectly healed. It was a mere scratch."

"And what made you delay so long writing to Signora Eleonora? What excuse have you for leaving your friends in anxiety?"

"'Constant occupation and worries of every kind. It was very wrong of me, nevertheless. To-morrow, I promise, I I will send a letter to Genoa," said the Doctor.

"Mind you don't forget, and give the dear old lady my best love. Now, then, tell me all about yourself since we parted,—about the Revolution, and Sicily, and everything. You have not forgotten, have you, my old love for asking questions?" added she, smiling.

"It is as welcome as of old," he replied. "You shall hear everything about myself and Sicily, but first I must know everything about you and your health, fair lady," continued Antonio, who had been eyeing his long-lost friend with some anxiety. Lucy told him at once all about her health, just as she used to do; and he listened to her with that same interest and attention with which he had been wont to listen to her in the wretched Osteria *del Mattone*.

"We will put all that to rights again, with God's help," said Antonio, cheerfully, when she had finished. "Fresh air, quiet habits and method—you know of old, my love of method—and a proper obedience to your doctor's directions," (he smiled, and Lucy's eyes assured him there should be no want of this desideratum,) "will do wonders for you, as they did at Bordighera."

It was now Antonio's turn to give an account of himself, which he did very succinctly. We shall follow the good example, only taking up the subject a little farther back, and touching upon one or two points he omitted, just as much as is indispensable for the clear understanding of our story.

When awakened from his fond dream of an hour at Bordighera, Antonio, as we have said, had sworn in his heart to have no other mistress than his country, and to devote to her, and her alone, all the energies of his soul and mind; and when we say his country, we mean of course Italy, for Antonio's patriotism was not confined to the isle in which he was born, but embraced the whole of the motherland. In pursuance of this idea, he had not delayed putting himself in communication with the leading men of the Italian emigration, less with the intention of becoming a propagandist, and winning over new elements to the Liberal cause, than of combining those already existing, and giving them that unity of purpose and direction, which could alone secure success in the day of trial. The fortune he had inherited from his mother gave our doctor a modest independence, and consequently the means of pursuing more interruptedly, and furthering more efficiently, the object he had set before himself. A pedestrian tour in Switzerland, undertaken for his health in the spring of 1843, afforded him an opportunity of knowing, and being known to, a good many of the influential Italian exiles; and as their views and hopes were identical with his, it was a very easy matter to establish an understanding with them. Antonio spent most of his time, from 1843 to 1847, at Turin, where, by his gratuitous attendance on the poor, he earned a well-deserved reputation for charity and skill, and by several medical pamphlets the name of a profound and elegant writer. About that time, we mean the spring of 1847, the news of Sicily began to be of serious importance. The Neapolitan Government, as before remarked, far from yielding any satisfaction to the popular feeling, roused to the highest pitch by the reforms granted at Turin, Florence, and Rome, was combating against it in the most brutal manner. An outbreak was imminent at Palermo, so said private letters. Antonio, with a few friends, embarked for Malta, and from thence, in the beginning of January 1848, crossed to Palermo, where he and his companions remained concealed till the 12th of January, when, a tricolor-flag in hand, hey made their appearance on the Piazza of the Fieravecchia. The cry of "*all' armi*" was responded to from all parts, and the rising began in earnest. The struggle was long and obstinate, lasting from the 12th to the 29th of January; but in spite of a reinforcement of fresh troops, landed by the Neapolitan fleet on the 15th, and a brisk bombardment of the city by the fortress of Castellamare, the popular impetus proved irresistible. Stronghold after stronghold was carried as if by enchantment, the fortified royal palace was attacked with such spirit, (it was there that Antonio was wounded,) that its garrison abandoned it on the 25th, and the troops, driven out of the town on every side, were hotly and triumphantly pursued.

The fire of insurrection spread all over the face of the island; Girgenti, Catania, Messina, Caltanisetta, Trapani, Syracuse, one and all in rapid succession, followed the example set by Palermo. Some garrisons laid down arms, some were utterly defeated, others retreated into the forts, as did that of Messina, which, from the citadel, where it was intrenched, kept firing against the city. The last town of any importance which joined the movement was Noto. Her adhesion took place on the 4th of February, and on the same day the tricolor-flag waved from the ramparts of the fortress of Castellamare. It was then that the General Committee of Palermo, which had been constituted to organize and give proper direction to the insurrection, assumed the powers and title of Provisional Government of Sicily, with the venerable Ruggero Settimo as its president.

In the meantime, as we have before stated, a new political order of things had been inaugurated at Naples, a circumstance which gave fair hopes of a speedy arrangement between the two countries. In fact, shortly after negotiations were entered into—under the auspices of Lord Minto—between the Neapolitan Government and that of Sicily; about which it is only necessary to remark here that they were far from being handled and conducted, on the part of Naples, in that spirit of straightforwardness and conciliation which could alone, if not entirely dispel, at least diminish the distrust, deplorable precedents had deeply rooted in the minds of the Sicilians. The justice of this assertion will be clear to any one who will take the trouble of going over Lord Minto's official correspondence at that time with Viscount Palmerston. "I begin," writes Lord Minto to Lord Mount Edgecumbe at Palermo, "I begin very seriously to believe that there is no intention here (Naples) to come to a friendly understanding, and that all that has been done, or is doing, has no other object than to gain time to prepare for hostility, or to secure foreign aid." Such is the sense of his lordship's letter, dated February 22d.

Tired of being kept at bay to no purpose, and aware of

the expediency of relieving the country and themselves from the dangers of their provisional position, the General Committee of Palermo published at last a declaration, in which was distinctly set forth that it would not continue to treat as to terms of peace unless the *sine qua non* condition that none but a Sicilian army should garrison the island, was agreed to. At the same time the Electoral Colleges were convoked for the 15th of March, and the 25th fixed for the opening of Parliament.

The Neapolitan ministry, on their side, in utter despair of being able to surmount the difficulties of the situation, resigned, and were succeeded by the administration of the 6th March. The accession to power of such men as Carlo Poerio, Saliceti, and Savarese, bid fair to bring the arduous Sicilian question to a final settlement. A cabinet council was held on the 7th of March, the King present—Lord Minto was there also by invitation—and a series of measures was concocted and a number of decrees signed, which were thought likely to give satisfaction to the Sicilians. The Convocation of Parliament, already fixed by the Committee of Palermo, was legalized by an act of Convocation emanating from the King for the same day; the Neapolitan Government granted to Sicily its separate Parliament, its own separate ministers, with the exception of the minister for foreign affairs; and the most popular man of his day, the incarnation, as it were, of the Sicilian revolution, Ruggero Settimo, was nominated Lieutenant-Governor of the island, in the name of Ferdinand the Second. The office of a special minister for Sicily, who was to reside at Naples, and be a medium of communication between the island Government and the King, was created, and Commendatore Scovazzo, a Sicilian, appointed to this dignity. But the ticklish and most important point, of none but a Sicilian army being quartered in Sicily without the consent of the Sicilian Parliament, was completely overlooked. Truly, it does seem strange that Lord Minto, in whose presence all these measures were decided upon, should not have broached this vital question, he who, but a few days before, on the 1st of March, had written to Lord Palmerston—"The Sicilians, in seeking to place their liberties under the safeguard of their fellow-countrymen, are justified by their experience, and, indeed, there is nothing in the character or conduct of the existing Government (Naples) that merits their confidence."

This unaccountable silence about the army—the great point at issue, was considered by the mass of Sicilians to be full of dark augury, and obliterated all the good effects the above-named concessions might have produced. Such, indeed, was the prevalent distrust of the Neapolitan Government and the fear of its treachery, that the only chance of tranquillizing the irritated minds was the removal of an army which had for thirty-three years held Sicily enslaved, and against which Messina was still fighting. Popular feeling declared itself so strongly averse to the conditions of the 7th March, that the General Committee pronounced them "unacceptable, on the ground that they were contrary to the Constitution of 1812." Lord Minto then insisted on the Committee proposing their own terms, which they did, but the Government of Naples pleaded the impossibility of discussing the conditions proposed, without the concurrence of the Neapolitan Parliament, which had not yet met. On the day previous to the assembling of the Sicilian Legislature there came a protest from the King, charging the Sicilians with "endangering the resurrection of Italy, and risking the independence and glorious destinies of the common country." This protest declared null and void, beforehand, all acts that might be accomplished in Sicily. There was nothing left for the two countries but to try the fortune of arms.

The direful prospect of a fratricidal war filled many a noble heart on both sides of the Faro with horror and dismay. "What!" cried our friend the Doctor, "while the ancient rallying cry of *Fuori il barbaro* is ringing throughout the Peninsula—while war with Austria is rendered inevitable by the heroic insurrection of Milan—is it possible that there

are here two noble Italian States bent, not on exerting their
utmost energies against the common foe, but against each
other?" And, as he said this, Antonio buried his hand in
his hair. Was there no means of averting this most hideous
of calamities? Perhaps there was. It would not do to sit
down and despair. Could the Neapolitan Government be
prevailed upon to accede to the one condition, that no army
but a Sicilian one should garrison the island, no doubt that
the terms of the 7th March would be accepted, and peace
restored between the two countries. Such was at least the
firm belief of Antonio, and of many of his friends of the
Moderate party, with whom he was debating the point. They
determined accordingly to make a strenuous effort to bring
about this most desirable result. Antonio drew up a memorial, in which he exposed, with great stringency of logic,
the reasons which ought to persuade the Neapolitan Government to yield on the army question, and expatiated at full
length on the benefits certain to accrue to that common cause,
invoked by the King himself in his protest, from a renewed
understanding between Naples and Sicily. This memorial
he read to his friends, with whose complete approbation he
sent it to Naples. It was placed in the hands of one of
the Ministers, between whom and Antonio a mutual esteem
and good-will existed—the fruit of a former long and important correspondence. A few days after, there came a
brief note in answer, the purport of which was as follows:—
"Could the writer of the memorial come to Naples, and
urge *viva voce* the arguments he had so admirably expressed
on paper, ten to one but he would succeed. Never was his
Majesty better disposed to make concessions than at the
present moment. Not a day to be lost!"

And Antonio did not lose a day, but went to Naples. He
knew very well to what this step laid him open. He knew
very well that his intentions would be misconstrued by
party spirit; that his name would be torn to pieces; that he
would be branded as a runaway, a renegade, a traitor, but
he did not care. So long as he had a hope of doing good

to his country, he was not the man to be deterred by personal considerations. So to Naples he went, saw the Ministers, saw his Majesty, and warmly pleaded the cause he had taken up—if to some or no purpose we shall see hereafter.

CHAPTER XXIII.
The 15th of May 1848.

THE next day, at the same hour which he used to pay his morning visit at the Osteria, Doctor Antonio made his appearance in Lucy's drawing-room. We must not forget to say, that by this time he knew everything about Lucy's marriage and widowhood—knew it from Sir John's letter, which Lady Cleverton, true to her word, had sent him early in the morning. He greeted his fair friend as cordially as ever, and, with the freedom of old times, began at once to find fault with her quarters. "A magnificent and stately suite of rooms," observed the Doctor; "but they will not do for you. You must have fresh air to breathe, and something better to look at in beautiful Naples than fine houses. There is an hotel not far off, at Santa Lucia, that will suit you exactly; not so fashionable, to be sure," adds our Doctor, slyly, "as Toledo or Chiaja, but less noisy, and that is no slight advantage. I know the master of the hotel which I am recommending to you. He is a most obliging and respectable person." Lucy was ready to make the change. "Come and judge for yourself," says the Doctor; and away they went. The lady was delighted with the situation, commanding, as it did, a view of the Bay and Mount Vesuvius, and went into raptures about a wide-projecting marble balcony into which the rooms opened. "We shall fancy we are at Bordighera again," she said, flushing and looking at Antonio. "To be sure," he answered. "Suppose we go, while your people are bringing your things here, and lay in a stock of plants and flowers to make something of a garden for you?" And when the carriage was so stuffed with roses, magnolias, and dwarf orange-trees, that our hero and heroine did not know where to find a place for their feet, the dilemma made Lucy laugh as she had not laughed for many a day. Antonio, just as mindful as ever about her, proposed going to buy paper, pencils, and colours—she would soon long to be sketching from her window. "And a piano?" asked he, as they drove past a shop where there were some. "Ah! to be sure," was the ready answer. "You must teach me more Sicilian songs." The piano and the drawing materials ordered, they went back to the new hotel.

Plenty of work now for the busy Doctor.—The plants and flowers to dispose of to their best advantage in the balcony,—the paint-box and pencils to arrange, so that she may find everything she wants under her hand,—the best light and spot to choose for the easel,—the best place for the piano, just coming in,—all of which things he did with that quietness, method, and taste, which made Lucy think of her arrival at the Osteria. And as she now sat at the piano, following his every movement with her eyes, and letting her fingers strike the keys, how busy the while her thoughts with old days,—how vividly memory was painting that first evening, when he put up the curtains and pasted the paper, to her father's horror, over the crevice in the door. How full of gratitude to overflowing her heart! Was it the mysterious power of association that taught the listless fingers to find the notes of that Sicilian air he had first sung to her, and which, from her wedding-day, she had never played?

The days of Bordighera are come back again. The same flowers, the same sky, the same wondrous nature, even to the sweet scents in the air,—all that she had admired and enjoyed there, were hers once more. Better, too, and dearer, was the return to that wholesome alternation of occupation and repose, to the same sweet converse, the same quiet evenings on the balcony; but best and dearest of all, was that same vigilant, unremitting care, she felt as much hers now as then, the proof, if she wanted any, that Antonio, like her, cherished the past. It seemed as though her youthful bloom and gentle gaiety would blossom anew. Happiness was a better physician than even Doctor Antonio. The events of the past eight years faded from Lucy's memory as if they had not been. She could almost have fancied she had fallen asleep on that dreary day when she left Bordighera, to wake again at Naples, after a long, painful dream, and find nothing changed about her.

Antonio prescribed nothing for his patient, but he arranged her life for her hour by hour; so much for walking, driving, reading, drawing, and music—very little pianoforte playing, however, for it fatigued and heated her,—fresh air, short walks, beside the daily drive into the country, no theatres, no crowded places, no heated rooms, and if to Court she must go, let it be as seldom as possible. And yet, with all these restraints and prohibitions time did not hang heavy on Lucy's hands, nor did she ever complain of the monotony of her life; on the contrary, all her letters to her father had this burden, that she was happy and comfortable, and Doctor Antonio the kindest and cleverest of doctors, and that Sir John was not to fret at not being able to join her so soon as they could both have wished.

Antonio, just as he used to do invariably, came to see Lucy twice in the day, once in the morning—the physician's visit, as she laughingly called it, and the other in the evening—the friend's visit. His thoughts seemed continually occupied about her, and his anxiety to comfort and amuse her was unceasing. He brought her views, engravings, his own sketches of the beautiful environs which they were to visit together some day, new books, both Italian and English, the novels most in vogue, and the pamphlets on the interesting topics of the day. Of subjects to arouse the curiosity and fix the attention of one so interested in Italy as Lucy, there was certainly no lack at that time. The late insurrection of Milan and Venice, the entry of the Piedmontese army into Lombardy, the chances of the war, the internal state of the country and of the different parties, Pius the Ninth, Carlo Alberto, and the other leading men of the day, the Court of Naples, the King, and his Ministers, all and each, in turn, afforded scope for Antonio's quick observation, ingenious views, and graphic powers. Lucy had long ago learned to value his even flow of spirits, his earnest feeling, that happy combination of reason, sensibility, and humour, which made his conversation so original, his society so cheering; but now he was laying bare to her all the treasures of his heart, initiating her into all the mysteries of this ardent soul, making her the depositary of his hopes, fears, and disappointments.

He told her how, at the very moment he had fancied all difficulties to the attainment of the object of his self-imposed mission removed, a split took place in the Cabinet, and the identical person on whom he depended left office; and the ground Antonio believed gained had to be re-conquered. Discouraged, but persevering still, he had renewed his efforts, when the news arrived that the Sicilian Parliament had deposed the King and set aside all of his race. Antonio would then have returned to his country, to share her fate, had not the King himself urged him to remain; his Majesty professing, in spite of all that was actually taking place, the most liberal and conciliatory intentions towards the Sicilians. He would send them, some day, such terms as they themselves would be astonished at, and Antonio should be the bearer. But that day had never come. "I believe he wants to bribe me," remarked Antonio, "for he has more than once hinted at his wish of having a *physician of my merit* permanently attached to his person. However, he cannot throw dust in my eyes. There is something crooked about him,—a squint in his looks and dealings; he has a sleepy way of his own, with an occasional twinkle in his eye, that always reminds me of a cat lying in wait for a mouse. I am greatly mistaken if this man does not have all of us hanged one of these days."

Lucy would not listen to such predictions, and shut the

Doctor's mouth very effectually, by laying her hand on his lips; she was ashamed to see how he gave way to such prejudices. "Well, well," he would smilingly answer; for more than once did Antonio recur to the subject,—*vedremo*. If free in his remarks upon the King, Antonio never spared his own party, whenever he saw cause for blame. The Liberals of Naples he sometimes likened to the dog in the fable, who lost the meat by running after its shadow. "For instance," said he, "the Constitution is not come into action, and they are already loud in requiring its enlargement; a Parliament has no existence as yet but on paper, and they are in full cry against the House of Peers. They call on the King to send an army into Lombardy to co-operate with the Piedmontese, and they hint in all their papers that he is at heart an Austrian. Who doubts that he is so? but where is the use of saying it? Is the upbraiding him with being an Austrian likely to make him an Italian patriot?"

It was to this very point, that of inducing Ferdinand to take an active part in the war of Independence, that the new Ministry directed all their efforts. It was in the hope of contributing also in some measure to this desirable result, that Antonio still remained in Naples. Besides the furthering the cause of Italian independence, so dear to the Doctor's heart, another and not less precious advantage would be obtained by the step,—that of rendering for the present hostilities impossible between Naples and Sicily. Time, that great peace-maker, would heal many wounds, soften many excited feelings, and pave the way to some future honourable compromise. The reluctance of the King to part with even a minimum of the army was extreme. Nevertheless the feeling on the subject was so strong in the capital, the Ministers so earnestly averred the impossibility of carrying on any government without some gratification of this feeling, that the King submitted at length to the measure. A corps of troops, fourteen thousand strong, was sent off to the seat of war, and a part of the fleet ordered to the Adriatic, to act in concert with the Sardinian and Venetian naval forces,

There was nothing after this to detain Antonio at Naples, nothing but the sweet spell he was under, unless we add,— Destiny. The meeting of the Neapolitan Parliament was at hand. Might he not as well stay to be present at its opening, and judge for himself of its prevailing spirit, and of what it portended for the future? And he stayed.

The legislative bodies were to assemble on the 15th May: previous to that the Cabinet published a programme of the ceremony which was to take place on that day. One of the articles of this programme said that the Deputies were to swear allegiance to the King and Constitution; but there was no mention of a clause inserted in the Manifesto of the 3d April,—the declaration of the political principles of the Cabinet of that date,—which conferred on the Electoral Chamber the right of modifying and enlarging the Constitution. This omission appeared fraught with danger to many of the Deputies, who assembled in the town-hall of Monte Oliveto, there to deliberate on the matter. We regret to have to note so flagrant an illegality, so gross a usurpation of power. The Chamber of Deputies not being yet legally constituted, the members had no right to assume the character or authority of a deliberative assembly. Well, the Deputies then met; the oath, as inserted in the official programme, was rejected, and negotiations were set on foot with the ministry for the purpose of finding a formula satisfactory to both parties. Deputations kept going up and down from the Chamber to the Ministry, from the Ministry to the Chamber. This happened on the 14th of May. The news of this conflict spread like wildfire over the city, and created a good deal of excitement. Suspicion and alarm were predominant in people's minds. Some attempts at an open outbreak had even to be lamented. These ominous signs made both parties sensible of the urgency of a conciliation, and after many a negotiation and effort, an agreement was entered into that Parliament should be opened without any oath being asked or taken.

It was with a heavy step and downcast heart, that, early

In the morning of the following day, the 15th of May, Antonio bent his way to Lucy's lodgings. Lucy had expressly wished him to call betimes, and report to her about the state of affairs. She knew nothing of the happy settling of the difficulties, it having only taken place far in the night. The streets through which our Doctor had to pass were crowded to an extent very unusual at that early hour, and the looks and bearing of the crowd were anything but agreeable. Knots of persons were forming here and there,—an infallible symptom of impending trouble,—and the Doctor noticed individuals passing from group to group, and addressing them in whispers. It was clear that agitators (instigated by whom?) were busily at work. In spite of the sad foreboding which filled his heart, Antonio approached Lucy with his usual serene composure, and, in reply to her eager inquiries, gave her the assurance that any cause for alarm had disappeared, and that all was going on as well as could be wished.

"And now," said Antonio, smiling, "we will let politics alone; I am thoroughly weary of the subject. Let us talk of old times,—of our peaceful, verdant Bordighera. I wish I was there still, I was so happy there."

"And so was I," replied Lucy, with a deep blush. "I must tell you," she went on, after a little hesitation, "that I have never given up the idea of building myself a pretty cottage in one of its quiet nooks, and going to live there. The woman can now realize the whim of the girl. What do you say to the plan?"

"A very good idea," said Antonio; "but are you sure that you will not get tired of a life of retirement; that you will not some day regret your fine acquaintances, the advantages of rank and wealth, the attractions of London, the Court—"

"I don't care for rank and Court," interrupted Lucy, "so long as papa and—you are with me." Antonio began stroking an imaginary beard, and then suddenly got up and took some strides up and down the room.

"We will speak of this presently," said he, returning and

calmly resuming his seat by her side. "Do you remember this day eight years ago?"

"Do I not? I recollect it as if it were only yesterday. I could even draw you at that moment, when you said to me, 'Now, Miss Davenne, suppose you were to try and walk;'" and she tried to imitate his way of speaking. "The very tone of your voice still rings in my ears."

"Dear noble friend!" exclaimed Antonio; "never—no never was the least show of kindness on my part lost on you. I confess I was dreadfully afraid at that moment, and then in proportion happy."

"Yes, afraid of my being lame," said Lucy, "and happy that I was not so." Antonio looked at her with surprise.

"Now, say it was not so, if you dare," insisted Lucy, playfully.

"I am not going to deny it, indeed,—so far I must render justice to your penetration."

"Young ladies," pursued Lucy, in the same sportive tone, "are not always either so blind or so silly as they choose to appear. I never was taken in with 'nothing but a sprained ankle;' papa was, but not his daughter. I knew from the first that my leg was broken."

Antonio opened his eyes as wide as they would open.

"What depths of dissimulation I discover in you," he said at last, laughing. "It seems now you took *me* in. You positively knew your leg was broken, and said nothing about it, even to me."

"No," returned Lucy; "I was resolved you should have the full benefit of your kind deception. I allowed you to cheat me as much as you pleased."

Antonio answered nothing, but took the small white hand that was hanging over the arm of her chair, took it in his, and slowly and deliberately raised it to his lips.

The sharp, distinct report of a volley of musketry, rent the still air, and made every window and door rattle.

Antonio was on his feet in a moment, as pale as if every one of the bullets fired had gone through his heart.

"What can that be?" asked Lucy, in mortal alarm.

"Nothing of consequence," said Antonio, with a mighty effort to look unconcerned. "Probably only some Government powder expended in saluting the opening of Parliament. By the by, I must not be too late."

As he took his hat, another discharge was heard, almost instantly followed by a brisk running fire.

"There is fighting going on, I am sure of it," cried Lucy, terrified, and shaking all over. "Do not go, for mercy's sake! What is the use of your going? What can one man do, and alone?"

"Satisfy his own conscience that he has done all in his power to prevent civil war," replied Antonio, with tranquil determination. "Let me go, I beseech you."

"You shall not," cried Lucy, now quite beside herself with terror, and interposing her slight form between him and the door. Antonio looked at her.

"I *must* go," he said. It was as if Fate had spoken. Lucy felt at once unequal to struggle with that iron will. She joined her hands like a child about to pray, looked up in his face, and said, "O Antonio!" There was a world of things in this simple appeal.

The Italian drew her to him, pressed her closely to his bosom. "Lucy," said he, solemnly, "this is no moment for many words." (The firing never slackened while he spoke.) "Lucy, I love you—I have loved you dearly all these long eight years—I shall love you to my grave. But my country has claims on me prior to yours. These claims I vowed more solemnly than ever to respect on that day, when prejudice, armed with a pedigree, stood between you and me. On that day, I pledged myself anew to my country. Let me redeem that pledge—let me do my duty—help me to do it, Lucy! Lucy, my noble friend, help me to be worthy of you and myself. In the name of all that is holy, let me depart without a painful struggle!"

The heroic spirit that dictated his self-immolation, in the sweetest moment of his life, shone out in his face and thrilled in his voice. He stood transfigured to more than man in Lucy's eyes. Her more feeble nature raised itself, in this supreme instant, to a height at which every sacrifice of self is possible.

"Noble heart!" she said, with a burst of enthusiasm, "Go! and God be with you and preserve you. I will try to be worthy of you;" and she loosened her hold of him.

"And God bless you for these words!" cried Antonio, almost unmanned, clasping her hands and holding them to his heart. "God bless you!—your love shall be my buckler!" So saying he laid her on a sofa, and whispered, "You shall soon see me again, or hear from me." He stood for a second to look on the now dejected prostrate form before him, passed his hand over his eyes, and went without another word.

In the ante-room he found Miss Hutchins in her usual place. He asked her for some ink and paper, and wrote a few lines, which he handed to her. "Go now at once to your lady," he said; "she is not well. Should she feel worse, send for the physician whose name and address I have just given you."

"Are you going away, sir?" asked Hutchins, in right of her calling, at once understanding the reason of her ladyship's illness.

"No, not going away exactly; but I may be prevented from coming here for some time. See after Lady Cleverton. Good-bye, Hutchins;" and Antonio held out his hand to the faithful waiting-woman. Hutchins' face began to twitch nervously, but, in obedience to his orders, she went to her mistress. Then Antonio, seating himself at the little worktable, hastily wrote a short letter, sealed and addressed it, and, without venturing a glance at the closed door, he put on his hat, and was gone.

During this time, hundreds of people, in a state of distraction, were running through the streets, detachments of soldiers were marching in every direction, the city was covered, as if by magic, with barricades, fighting was going on at many of them, in short, civil war, with all its horrors, was raging in beautiful Naples. Whose sacrilegious hand had kindled the torch of discord? Which side had fired the first shot? The Republican, obstinately bent on destroying the monarchy, as afterwards affirmed by the Court party? or the Court party, which, as pleaded by the Liberals, had in cold blood laid the train, trusting to a chance spark igniting it, and scattering to the four winds of heaven the liberties just snatched from despotism's iron grasp? No one knew then, and to this day it remains a secret.

Contemporaneous events are scarcely ever traceable to their sources, obscured as they are by contemporaneous passions. That the Republicans should deliberately have challenged the Government seems scarcely credible in the teeth of a fact, allowed by all impartial writers, and avouched for by eye-witnesses, viz., the insignificance of the Republican party, if, indeed, any such were to be found in Naples in 1848. The cry of "Republic" never passed the lips of the combatants, and no acknowledged Republican character ever figured among the many prisoners afterwards brought to trial on political charges. If the adage, "he did who gained by it," proved always true, it would go far to back the accusation against the executive power, that of having courted a collision of which it took such advantage and made such profit. But it is not our intention to urge any conjectural evidence, and we will give the executive the full benefit of the absence of direct, substantial, irrefutable proof. We would fain be just even to King Ferdinand the Second of Naples. There were reasons enough for the catastrophe of the 15th May without its being necessary to assume that it was prepared or premeditated on either side.

A political paper of the day styled it, as justly as comprehensively, the loss of equilibrium between two fears, (*lo squilibrio di due paure*,) and this was literally the case. Ever since the 29th January the supporters of divine right and the partisans of constitutional freedom had eyed each other with undisguised feelings of hatred and distrust. The people had not forgotten that shots and thrusts of the bayonet had more than once answered their cries of "*Viva Pio Nono! Viva la Riforma!*" The King had as little forgotten that the Constitution had been wrested from him by force; he, for ever on the *qui vive* for his menaced prerogatives, they equally on the alert for their liberties in jeopardy. The ill-timed encyclical letter of the 29th April, the fatal act by which Pius the Ninth inaugurated his secession from the national movement, was a powerful wedge in widening the breach. The one party hailed it with elation and revived hope, the other openly manifested their resentment at the letter itself, and at the hopes it encouraged. Things were at this pass when there occurred the unlucky misunderstanding between the Executive and the Deputies as to the form of oath. Here, then, we have the spark that fell on the combustible materials so long gathering. The attitude taken by the Deputies seemed to the Executive the harbinger of revolutions; the demeanour of the Executive appeared to the Deputies to denote an impending *coup d'état*. Without taking into account the lawless passions, always abounding in large communities, and which float on the surface in times "that are out of joint," there was no lack of ardent spirits on either side to fan the smouldering fire into a blaze. The conflagration spread far and wide, until the whole city was one flame.

"What is the matter?" asked Antonio, when he reached the street, of a priest who was hurrying past.

"The King is arrested,—the Heir-apparent shut up in a convent,—the Chamber of Deputies has declared itself in permanence."

A young man now came rushing along with frantic gesticulations. Antonio stopped him also with the same query.

"All the Deputies assembled have been massacred,— those on their way to the House are being hunted down like wild beasts,—martial law is proclaimed. Oh! that I could but find a musket!" cried the maddened youth.

Our Doctor believed neither statement, but dreaded the

worst from both. He crossed the *Piazza Reale*, where he found an imposing force of infantry, cavalry, and artillery, drawn up in front of the palace, and hastened on in the direction of the firing; but he had not gone a hundred steps in Via Toledo when his progress was impeded by a barricade, which was erecting. He did not stop to ask questions, but forced his way over the obstruction, and ran as fast as he could to another barricade that he had descried from a distance, and from whence came the continuous sound of firing. The majority of its defendants evidently belonged to the educated class; they were mostly very young men, many scarcely beyond boyhood, and altogether not more than forty in number. The assailants, owing to the height of the barricade, could not be seen from where Antonio stood, but the well-kept up regular fire shewed that it proceeded from a disciplined body of considerable strength.

Antonio hesitated for one second as to the possibility of any words of his being listened to, but seeing the utter hopelessness, under the circumstances, of any attempt at conciliation, he looked around in search of a musket. The sight of a man lying at his feet, seriously wounded, instantaneously changed the current of his thoughts. There were other and more sacred duties for him to perform than killing or being killed. He knelt down by the side of what was a mere lad, drew out his case of instruments, and set about examining and dressing the wound. Another and another of the combatants rolled on the ground, some past all earthly help. Antonio was now in his element. He stripped off his coat, tore it into bandages, and, entirely absorbed by his attendance on the wounded and dying, forgot there were such things as bullets hailing round him. A loud shout from the defenders of the barricade caused him to look up at last; there they stood facing him, waving their hands and gesticulating. He turned his head to see what they were pointing at. A thrust from a bayonet sent him over weltering in his blood.

CHAPTER XXIV.
Tidings.

LUCY'S distraction during the fatal affray, the sickening alternations of hope and despair through which she had to pass during each day of the seemingly endless week that followed the catastrophe,—the gradual sinking of her heart at failure after failure of every fresh attempt to ascertain Antonio's fate,—all this we must leave to the reader's imagination. To describe such a state would be a too heart-rending task, and one to no purpose. Who can paint to the life agonies of suspense and terror such as hers? Words—any words must fall short of the sad reality. While there was anything to do,—while there were fresh channels of information to be sought after,—while there was any call for exertion, Lucy's body and spirit kept up wonderfully. But when all sources within her reach were dried up,—when every inquiry, and every possible research, had been made,—when nothing remained for her but to cross her hands over her bosom and say to herself, "Antonio is dead, else had I seen or heard of him,"—then the fragile frame and enthusiastic spirit alike gave way. Even in this crisis, the lost Antonio's care and love were around Lucy's sick-bed. Hutchins, left to her own responsibility, at once sent for the physician whose address Antonio had left with her, and whose assiduity and skill proved him worthy of Antonio's confidence.

For ten whole days Lucy's life and reason hung on a thread. Then there came an almost imperceptible amelioration, and with it some intervals of consciousness, during which Lucy fancied she saw a form moving noiselessly about the room strangely resembling Speranza. Of course it was not she. How could it be Speranza? It must be fancy. Lucy had seen so many strange things and persons during these last days. Still this vision did not leave her as the others had done—it haunted her with a pertinacity that made her heart beat very fast. She said nothing, but watched it with evident pleasure. She came to see it without any wondering. Perhaps she imagined she was still at the Osteria with her father, or at the Post-house at Mentone. The occasional faint murmur of names on the pale lips, indicated some delusion of the kind. Poor Lucy! her head was so confused and her sight so dim.

Late one night she awoke after some hours of refreshing sleep, with her ideas unusually clear, and, meeting two large black eyes watching her fondly, as in days of yore, she suddenly asked in a whisper,—"Is that you, Speranza?"

"God bless you, my dear, dear mistress, it is your own Speranza," and down went the loving creature on her knees, pressing her lips on the emaciated hand held out to her; "here I am, and here I stay, never again to leave you. But you must not talk, not even one word more," and, arranging the pillows, the kind creature gently turned the pale face away from herself. Lucy silently complied with the injunction; she did not want any explanation; she was soothed and calmed by having her humble Italian friend by her side. Oh, glorious power of affection, blessing and blessed!

But by what mysterious agency had Speranza come to be by Lucy's sick-bed just when she was most needed? By a most simple and natural one. Speranza was the last legacy of kindness Antonio had it in his power to leave Lucy. So thoroughly did he understand her, that he instinctively knew what would best comfort her should any evil befall him. In such an event, would it not be Lucy's consolation to have some one to whom she could talk of him, and be sure of sympathy? So he wrote those hasty lines to Battista's wife, in which he told her, that unless she heard from him again within the course of a week after receiving his letter, she was to embark immediately for Naples, and go to the hotel he named in his date, where she would find Lady Cleverton. Speranza acted up literally to the instructions received, and reached Naples just in time to take her place, as a tender and affectionate nurse, by the bedside of her unconscious mistress. Those who sow in kindness reap also in kindness.

Lucy's convalescence was long and difficult. It was full three weeks before she could sit up in bed, and a month more went by ere she was able to rise for an hour; and double that time was required to gain strength enough to bear a drive in the open air. The first going out had almost produced a relapse,—the sight of the streets, of the military, of smiling women leaning on the arms of friends or husbands, while she felt so desolate and bereaved,—was a trial very hard to bear. Many remarked that ghastly face peering so eagerly into every passing coach. What foolish hope could hers be! Now, indeed, it became evident how well Antonio had done in summoning Speranza to Naples. Who else could have understood or soothed Lucy at this time! Starting out of long fits of silence, Lucy would sometimes talk by the hour of Antonio. Speranza knew, if no one else did, how good, how kind, how noble he had been. Speranza could understand what a friend Lucy had lost. Struggle against her grief! Why should she! Where should she ever find his like again! Who had ever been to her what he had been! She had a right, and ought to mourn for him. Had he not saved her life! Had he not thought of her and her comfort to the last! At other times she would go back to her accident, and begin relating all that passed at the Osteria, at Lampedusa, at Taggia, laughing as she talked—a laugh more painful than weeping—and seeming to have quite forgotten the awful 15th of May, until some chance word silenced her, and made the large tears spring from her eyes. They were not like common tears, swelling and overflowing; Lucy's really started from out of the eyelid.

Lucy always spoke of Antonio as of one who was no more,—occasionally alluding, but faintly and vaguely, as if she could not articulate the necessary words, to finding where he had been buried. But Speranza would in no way agree to considering Antonio's death as certain. No Doctor of Laws could have argued the case more dexterously than this uneducated woman. Her tact, her acuteness, were admirable in themselves, but they were adorable when one knew that all this intelligence was the offspring of a grateful heart.

Taking the worst for granted, would Speranza say, and that Doctor Antonio had not made his escape, as such a clever man would be sure to do, why was he not as likely to be a prisoner as dead? Had not "her *cara, cara padrona*" read in the newspaper that hundreds of persons had been arrested on and after that dreadful 15th May; and where was the wonder if, among such numbers of persons, the name of one should not yet have been found? It was all for the best; for, if he was not mentioned, the greater the chance of his getting out of prison without being tried. Some day or other "the *padrona*" would see that Speranza was right. Doctor Antonio was not the sort of man to be lost in that ridiculous way. The Signora knew very well that he was one of the King's friends, and some day the King would ask what had become of him, and then all the prisons would be searched, and he would be found.

"If he were alive, he would have contrived some way of letting me know," persisted Lucy.

"But, Signora, how can he find messengers if he is in prison, with chains on his hands and feet? But give him time," concluded Speranza, with a most competent air; "and oh, *cara, cara Signora Padrona*, don't you believe that the Holy Virgin will take care of such a good, good man? We must have faith." And Speranza's hint was taken by Lucy. She prayed, poor soul, and tried hard to bear up.

Misery acquaints a man with strange bed-fellows. It does more;—it often acquaints him with unexpected friends. Lady Cleverton had bethought her, that, through Mr. X——, the young attaché, she had some slight chance of getting at information as to any newly-made political prisoners, or some return of the killed,—and with small expectation of any good result,—for she looked with unfavourable eyes on her *soi-disant* cousin, she sent for him on the morning of the 17th of May. Mr. X—— was shocked at the havoc in her appearance; and the kindly tone of his voice in addressing her, led her, instead of making a ceremonious request, to rush into confidence. She told him of the obligations she was under personally to Doctor Antonio,—of how much Sir John also esteemed him. She drew a beautiful little picture of his life as parish doctor of Bordighera, and of how she had met him again at Court, with the King leaning on his arm. She related, with simple pathos, how he had left her on the 15th, not in the fury of party spirit, but to risk his life in striving to prevent brother slaying brother, and, without knowing it, betrayed that she thought this Italian the best, and wisest, and noblest of men. She had requested Mr. X—— to come to her, that she might ask his assistance in tracing out Antonio's fate. She had no other friend in Naples on whom to rely.—Would he help her?

It is a fact honourable to human nature, that this appeal sufficed to make the foppish young man espouse Doctor Antonio's cause as warmly as though it had been that of his own brother; and that he proved to our heroine, throughout this sad period of her history, the most disinterested, discreet, and serviceable of friends. There was in the young gentleman's heart, amidst much conventional alloy surrounding it, a golden mine, which only needed a chance touch to give to view its rich ore. Mr. X—— had worked hard, but vainly, to get some clue to Antonio's fate. He had used every official, and extra official means, which his position afforded him, or the kind hints of his chief pointed out. He had forced all his high and low Neapolitan acquaintances to contribute, knowingly or unknowingly, to his purpose; he had made friends with army officers, police officers, *employés* of every station and colour,—and one and all with a cleverness, perseverance, and prudence, that was never once at fault. He had also, during Lucy's long illness, kept up an almost daily correspondence with Sir John with much diplomatic skill, in order to tranquillize the old man, whose journey to Naples was, by his Doctor's orders, indefinitely postponed.

Late events had much conquered the young gentleman's antipathy for those he had once sneeringly called the "*Avvocati*," and, more wonderful still, transferred a great portion of it to the party which had formerly engrossed the whole of his sympathy. As chance would have it, the outbreak of the 15th May had caught and forcibly detained Mr. X—— at a house close to the barricade of St. Ferdinand, the spot at which the most desperate struggle of the day had occurred. Here he had witnessed the savage acts committed by the soldiery; he had seen men who had laid down their arms, and were crying for quarter, shot by the score—he had seen fathers, mothers, wives, and children, on their knees, pitilessly butchered—he had seen brutal cruelty that made his hair stand on end. All of generous and manly in his nature rose up in arms at the spectacle, and nothing but the certainty that such execrable conduct would meet with exemplary punishment kept his indignation within bounds. But when he saw, by the official Gazette, the perpetrators of these horrors praised and rewarded, when he had it from unimpeachable authority, that the King in person, from the lobby of the Royal Palace, had never ceased, by word and gesture, to instigate the troops to the slaughter, urging the artillery below, whom humane and excellent officers were seeking to restrain, to use their field-pieces—when he heard and saw all this, his whole soul revolted from the party who had so lately monopolized his partiality. A cause thus defended was not the cause he had upheld.

Six months had elapsed, and poor Speranza was at her wit's end how to inspire with new hopes (hopes, alas! that she no longer felt herself) her unhappy mistress, whose gloom deepened more and more, when a few lines in an unknown hand suddenly changed this gloom into unspeakable joy. A letter had been left at Lady Cleverton's door, the contents of which were as follows:—"Your friend is

alive, but a prisoner. If you have any person, of whose
fidelity you are sure—mind I say *sure*—send him to me for
further particulars. He will find me, the day after to-
morrow, at dusk, at the entrance from Rome by the barrier
Capo di Chino. Let him hold a white handkerchief in his
hand. Not even the air you breathe must suspect that there
is any communication between you and me. It is only by
strictly observing this precaution that you have a chance of
being of any use to your friend in the future. My every
step and act is watched by the police."

He was alive!—Oh, God be thanked, he was alive! What
mattered it that he was a prisoner?—he was alive! She
would force open his prison doors—she had interest and
influence—she would write to England,—the ministers there
would do something for Lord Cleverton's widow—she would
so pray and entreat, no one would have the heart to refuse
her; her father, too, had powerful friends—he would get
the English Government to interfere. Yes, she would find
a way to wrench Antonio from the tyrant's grasp. Alas!
poor, warm-hearted Lucy!

Her faithful ally, the attaché, went, at her request, to the
place of rendezvous, and found an elderly gentleman waiting there, who began by telling him what we already know,
that a party of soldiers had surprised from behind, and
placed between two fires, the barricade where Antonio was
attending to the wounded. The gentleman went on to say
how the soldiers gave no quarter, and how Antonio, felled
by a thrust of the bayonet, owed his life to the presence of
mind with which he had counterfeited death. The corpses,
and among them the Doctor, had been thrown in a heap
into a cart, and then conveyed to a guard-house close by, to
be kept there till evening. So infuriated were the soldiery
that Antonio had had no choice but to continue his feint of
death, and it was only when, late in the night, he was being
carried with the dead to the burial-ground, that he had no
other alternative but to show some signs of life. Part of
the escort were for qualifying him at once for the destina-

tion of the other bodies, but there were some more humane present, whose opinion prevailed, and, accordingly, our wounded hero was lodged in the prison of Santa Maria Apparente, which, luckily for him, was on the road of the lugubrious convoy. He was left for a week in the company of common felons, and then transferred to the Castello dell' Uovo, and put *au secret*. While in his first place of confinement, Antonio had never ceased moaning and complaining of his wound—fortunately a slight one—begging, for God's sake, that he might have a surgeon to dress it, if only once; but he spoke to the winds. Nor were his piteous appeals to his new jailer in the castle more successful; he might as well, indeed, have addressed the stone walls of his dungeon. One day he asked, in a faltering voice, for a confessor, declaring that he felt as if he were dying, and the turnkey gave him for answer that he was quite at liberty to do so, when and how he pleased, but no confessor should he have. The explanation of all these groans, lamentations, and prayers, was Antonio's all-absorbing thought of how to let Lucy know that he was still alive. He hoped to find in the surgeon or confessor one Christian enough to take a message to her, apprehension and anxiety for whom swallowed up all fear for self.

The strict severance from all human intercourse, except that of the jailer, inflicted on the political prisoners, was not merely for the security of their persons, but with the aim and intention, successful in many cases, of impairing their mental faculties, and weakening their powers of resistance. But Antonio's equanimity never failed him; and his wound, with no other medicament than cold water, healed fast. Six weeks after his removal to the castle the prisoner was taken before a Judge Inquisitor for examination. Here, as always, pre-occupied by the recollection of Lucy, he had recourse to the expedient of firmly declining to answer any question unless previously allowed to communicate with a legal adviser. Remanded and re-remanded, threatened or cajoled, still Antonio persisted in his silence. The struggle between

judge and prisoner lasted four full months, but at last
Antonio carried his point. A counsel was assigned to him,
one and the same with the writer of the anonymous letter to
Lady Cleverton, and the person now giving these details to
the attaché. Antonio had been fortunate, for this lawyer,
though timid by nature, and rendered more so by the difficulty of the times and the pressure of a large family, was
yet an honest, liberal man, and with a sense of his professional duty high enough to postpone to the interest and
safety of a client all personal considerations.

The attaché, as it had been agreed upon between him
and Lady Cleverton, alluded to a possibility of obtaining
foreign diplomatic interference, and hinted also, that no sum
of money would be thought too great if an escape could be
brought about. "Beware of trying anything of the sort,"
whispered the barrister, in great alarm. "An attempt at
flight would infallibly fail, and only serve to aggravate the
situation of your friend, dangerous enough already, I assure
you. You would easily find jailers or understrappers of the
prison to accept your bribe, who, within half an hour, would
have denounced the briber to the police. No such thing, for
God's sake! You have no idea of the corruption which
prevails in this unhappy country. The noisome, filthy dens
that serve for prisons are infected by a set of fiends in human
shape, the outscourings of jails, who pride themselves in
being spies and traitors. As for diplomatic interference,
unless backed by broadsides from your ships, worse than
useless, as it would only heighten animosity, by making the
prisoner a disputed prey. We have but one safe auxiliary
—time. Time will mature events, and these may force a
change in the policy of this country. Much depends on the
issue of the new campaign said to be at hand between
Sardinia and Austria,—much on the attitude of England and
France. A considerable period will elapse before the trial
of your friend and his co-accused can take place. The
Istruzione, by which I mean the preliminary proceedings on
the affair of the 15th of May, is scarcely begun, and bids fair

not to be soon terminated. In the meantime we have the chances of life for us; what is uppermost to-day may not be so to-morrow, and something may occur to put an end to all State prosecutions. At all events, by patience we shall gain one point, that passions which, at this moment, are boiling, will be cooled down. My best advice to you and Lady Cleverton, and to all who wish well to Dr. Antonio, is to keep quiet, and to wear a mask of indifference. I hear that many of the English have left off going to the Court since the fatal 15th of May. You must not do the same. Let none suspect your disapprobation of the Government. Go to Court, frequent all official circles, hear the prisoners abused and calumniated without so much as wincing. See and listen to all that is going on. You may thus be able to give me some useful information. This is the only way in which, at present, you can serve your friend. On my part nothing shall be wanting, and I shall let you hear of any circumstance worthy your attention."

The account brought back by the attaché of this interview was a great damp to Lucy's elation. The dictates of prudence and experience jarred too much with her feverish impatience to have Antonio free, and the man who could preach about time and patience, while a dear friend was in prison under a capital charge, could not but be taxed with lukewarmness. She took the advice, however, about appearing at Court and mixing in society. When thus enabled to judge for herself of the general tone of feeling towards the unhappy prisoners, —when she daily heard men of honour and education reviled as assassins,—when she daily heard it more than hinted that it was high time to have done, once for all, with such *canaille*, —when the representative of a great power, sounded on the subject, answered, that, having no influence whatever on the resolutions of the Neapolitan Cabinet, he could not make a demand, which, in all probability, would be unheeded,— when Lucy became aware of all this, then, and then alone, she was willing to admit the wisdom of the man who had recommended patience and reliance on the action of time.

Not long after there came new tidings to the attaché, the essence of which was this:—A paper in Antonio's handwriting had been seized at the house of a co-accused,—the memorial we saw him write at Palermo,—and in which he had said "that the hour had come for all the honest friends of liberty and independence to unite and form a holy phalanx." The Doctor had been accordingly examined, and, from the tenor of the queries put to him, it seemed but too probable that an accusation would be levelled at him, as being one of the founders of that secret sect whose preparatory process was in actual progress.

The next communication received from Antonio's counsel, and the last which we think necessary to record, was merely to confirm the preceding supposition. Antonio was to be prosecuted as one of the originators of the Secret Society of the Italian Unity. The epoch of the trial would depend much on the turn of political affairs in Italy and abroad.

Time went on, and did mature events,—none, alas! calculated to better the prospects of political prisoners anywhere. The defeat of the Piedmontese at Novara, the subjugation of Sicily, effected by a Neapolitan army, the restoration of Pius the Ninth to despotism and the Vatican by French bayonets, the occupation of the Roman Legations and Tuscany by the Austrians, and, lastly, the fall of heroic Venice, are the salient points of the Iliad of evils which the space of a few months had heaped on the unfortunate Peninsula. Reaction rode rampant everywhere but in Piedmont. That country was, indeed, a bright exception; there the loyalty and good sense of the young sovereign, and the loyalty and good sense of the people, had succeeded in maintaining public liberty and private security. For Naples we have the reverse of the medal. There the hour had come for the Government to reap the harvest of the bloody seed sown on the 15th of May.

CHAPTER XXV.
Væ Victis.

BEAUTIFUL Parthenope looks coquettishly at herself in her lovely bay, pure as crystal. The sun pours down on the city luminous torrents, that carry light and heat into the remotest recesses; an unceasing human tide rolls over the sunny quays and lava-paved streets, in hot pursuit of business, amusement, and pleasure. Everything is bright, everybody smiling, as though Liberty had not been bled to death but yesterday—as though the Constitutional Parliament had not been sent to hold its sittings in State prisons,—as though, at that very moment, Procurator-General Angelillo was not asking for two-and-forty heads!

Only forty-two to begin with! The rest will come in course of time. The scales of Neapolitan Themis run no danger of becoming rusty for lack of use. No one need be uneasy on that score. The number of the imprisoned, for political offences, in the happy kingdom of the Two Sicilies, in this year of grace 1850, is said, on good authority,[*] to be somewhere between fifteen and thirty thousand. Assuming the lowest number as the one nearest to probability,—assuming, that out of these fifteen thousand, two-thirds will be disposed of in a summary paternal way, (*economico*, they style it most elegantly,)—that is, without any form of trial whatever, there remains a balance of five thousand human beings amenable to justice;—enough, it must be allowed, to afford occupation and sport to all the High Courts and lower Courts of the kingdom, and to the habitual frequenters of all those Courts, for some years to come. There are, among others, from four to five hundred individuals imprisoned for the affair of the 15th of May alone, which promises a monster batch.

The one with which we have at present to do is more remarkable for the great variety of the social elements of which

[*] Gladstone. Two Letters, &c.

it is composed, than for its number. All stations, from the loftiest to the humblest calling, have contributed their contingent to the formation of this group. We count among the accused an ex-Secretary for the Home Department, an ex-Magistrate, an ex-Chief of Division in the Ministry of Public Instruction,—all three of them Deputies; two former Captains in the army, the representative of a ducal family, two private gentlemen of education and fortune, one of whom has declined a diplomatic post; several barristers and physicians, four priests, an arch-priest, and sundry small tradesmen, shopkeepers, and artisans; a former gendarme, a porter, and a domestic servant. They all stand charged with belonging to an anarchical secret society, some of them subsidiarily with having fought at the barricades in May 1848,— an excellent precaution for detaining them for another trial, in case of their being acquitted in this one. A particular charge is brought against a few of having attempted to destroy the existing Ministers, and other persons, by means of terrible explosive agents,—a single bottle, which has exploded in the breast-pocket of one of the accused, without injury to himself or any one else. A blacker set of villains never disgraced the dock of a Court, if we are to believe Procurator Angelillo. A more wronged, more ill-used party of honourable citizens, never cried to Heaven for vengeance, if precedents and presumptive evidence go for anything in this world. Is it among men of such public and private character as Carlo Poerio, Settembrini, and Pironti,—among such historical names as that of Carafa,—or among such gentlemen of education and fortune as Nisco, Gualtieri, Braico, &c., —such dignitaries of the Church as the arch-priest Miele, that anarchy recruits its supporters, and crime its abettors? What would you say, O English reader, to a charge of treason brought against some of your most eminent and respected statesmen, leading Members of your Houses of Parliament, —judges, nobles, churchmen, and gentlemen? Well, the men whose names I have just written down, and whom you see introduced into this gloomy hall of the Palace of the

Vicaria, manacled and escorted by gendarmes, these men stand as high in the social scale of their country, rank as high as to character and position, as any of your English statesmen, Members of Parliament, magistrates, nobles, and gentry.

This is the famous State prosecution of the sect of the Italian Unity, which wrung from a noble-souled English stateman a cry of indignation soon re-echoed by all Europe. The Court that sits is the Grand Criminal Court of Justice, the highest tribunal in the kingdom. It sits not as an ordinary, but as a special Court, with a view to despatch—by which is meant, that any of the forms, invaluable for the defence, may be dispensed with at the pleasure of its President, Navarro,—"the delicate, scrupulous, impartial, and generous Navarro."* The lugubrious drama is about to begin. The scanty space allotted to the public is crowded, and so is the hemicycle, reserved for privileged spectators, among whom we perceive a closely-veiled lady. The Judges are in their seats; in front of them, on a raised platform, sit the accused. They look pale and worn. The place they have been brought from, truth to say, is none of the healthiest, especially at this time of the year, in Naples, the month of June. No less than one thousand three hundred and eighty human beings are cooped up, one upon another, without air or light, amidst beastly filth, in the contiguous prison of the Vicaria, where our forty-two are confined. We must also take into account a previous detention, for none less than ten months,—for many much longer,—which they have already undergone. Nor must we forget the proper degree of wholesome discipline applied to body and mind, with which imprisonment on a political charge is invariably seasoned at Naples,—a double treatment, for the praiseworthy purpose of eliciting truth, whereof we may hear enough by and by for our edification. Evil-minded people might call it "torture," but torture is abolished, we know,—at any rate the name is. No wonder, then, if the accused

* Gladstone.

look worn and sickly. But if the flesh be infirm, the spirit that dwells within is full of strength and energy;—at least the air of quiet determination about them—the quiet determination of a garrison who are aware they have no quarter to expect, and prepare to sell their lives dearly—would seem to intimate as much.

On the names of the prisoners being called over, one of them, Margherita, (a custom-house officer,) rises to retract his former declaration, extorted, he says, through physical and moral coercion, and suggested by the Judge *Inquisitore* himself. Another, Pitterà, (a writing-master,) declares, that when taken out of a *criminale* (an underground cell, almost or wholly without light) to be examined in the Castello (dell' Uovo,) he was, in consequence of constant privations and repeated menaces, overcome by mental stupor. A third, Antonietti, (a custom-house agent,) follows, saying that, when interrogated, he was so exhausted in mind and body he would willingly have signed his own sentence of death. If any wish to know more distinctly what kind of pressure it was that could thus unnerve and unman far from sensitive weakly persons, Pironti, and many besides him, will tell us the particulars. Pironti, a late deputy and magistrate, relates having been in solitary confinement in a dungeon, where he had to lie on the naked ground, amid every sort of vermin, for forty-two days. His hair and beard, by special orders, were shaved by a galley-slave. He then underwent an insidious examination from the commandant of the castle, who tried first threats, then wheedling, promising him the royal clemency, to induce him to make revelations, *i. e.*, turn king's evidence. De Simone, a perfumer, was threatened with two hundred blows of sticks, soaked in water. Faucitano (a contract-builder, he of the explosive-bottle) was dragged to the Prefecture of Police by twenty Swiss guards, six police-inspectors, and twelve *sbirri*, who beat him, spat on him, tore his clothes, hair, and beard. He was kept for two hours at the police-office bound with wet ropes, then conducted to the castle, thrust down into a dark, damp *criminale*, without even a handful of straw to lie on, and detained there for nine days with no food but musty bread, no drink but fetid water. His first deposition was forced from him by the alternative of receiving two hundred blows. Muro (a servant) was kept for five days in complete darkness, and when on his way to be examined, a lieutenant in the army, who knew him, told him, as if out of compassion, that unless he put his name to whatever the Commissary desired him to sign, he would be ruined for life. On being asked how it happens that he now maintains that he does not know Pironti, after having, when first confronted with that gentleman, at first recognised his person, Muro replies that the Commissary had told him beforehand to lay his finger on the one of the four individuals standing in a row who had no moustache; and he had obeyed. Sersale, a merchant, underwent such prolonged fasting, that his health is incurably undermined.—(The voice of the prisoner is faint, and he can scarcely stand.) His wife was kept in prison for five days on bread and water, in order to frighten her into deposing to the truth of the charge against him. Cocozza, a solicitor, signed his interrogatory without reading it over,—that being the condition of his release from a horrible *criminale*. The Commissary required him to depose to Nisco (one of his co-accused) being the cashier of the sect of the Italian Unity. Caprio, a carpenter, was urged by the Commissary, in the presence of the head jailer, and of the turnkey, Carmine Bisogni, to denounce Nisco, and to declare on oath that he (Caprio) had received from that gentleman six thousand ducats, for the purpose of bribing the troops, and was promised his liberty if he did so. Errichiello, the master of a café, had been offered an employment worth twelve ducats a month, if he would second the views of the Commissary. Dono, a chemist, was not once examined during the ten months of his incarceration.

Carafa, of the Dukes d'Andria, rises to tell a sad tale. When first arrested, his mother was seriously ill. From that time he had received no news of her. He had even been given to understand that all his relations had renounced him. Signor Beccheneda, a Cabinet Minister and Director of Police, had come to visit him in prison, and assured him that his matter could be easily arranged, if he would only give testimony against his co-accused, Poerio, on a certain point. On Carafa's refusal, the Minister had taken leave of him with these words—"Very well, sir, you wish to destroy yourself—I leave you to your fate!" One night the unfortunate young man had fainted away, and in falling to the ground, had injured his right eye. He called for help, but no one came to his assistance. It was whispered about that he was to be transferred to a *criminale*, full of most filthy vermin, and that his doom was irrevocable. After a month's imprisonment, under the combined influence of moral torture and of feverish impatience to hear of his mother, his heart failed him, and he wrote a letter, wherein he deposed against some of his co-accused—wrote it at the suggestion of the Judge *Inquisitore* in the house of the commandant of the castle, under the eye of the Commissary. He now retracts all he had written in that letter; nor does this public recantation suffice to set his conscience at rest. He feels the desire and necessity of making further amends for his fault. He wishes to ask for forgiveness, which he now does, in the presence of the Judges and the public,—of his dear friends, pointing to the other prisoners. His voice thrills with an emotion that touches the heart of all present.

So much for the fair and humane treatment of prisoners, accused of political offences, *before* their trial. Now for a single illustration of the humane manner they are dealt with *during* their trial.

The Court has resumed its sittings, which had been suspended for a fortnight on account of the serious illness of one of the accused, Leipnecher, late a captain in the army. The President, Navarro, impatient to go on with the cause, had early that morning, 17th June, summoned the seven medical men attending Leipnecher, and made known to them that the Government had come to the determination that the trial should go on at any rate. All he required of them was an answer to one single question:—Could Leipnecher be brought into Court without danger of immediate death? After having timidly stammered some observations, the doctors answered that Leipnecher had not any fever, and though certainly suffering from nervous irritation, this need not prevent his being present at the sitting, provided he was carried in a chair to the hall, and properly taken care of when there. The President then assumes his seat in Court, and, upon a sign from him, a sedan-chair, surrounded by numerous gendarmes, is brought into the hall; the prison attendants lift out of it a sick man, who is utterly unable to support himself; they carry him in their arms like a child, and place him on a chair, arranging two pillows to support his head. The names of the prisoners are called over, Leipnecher's among the number, but he does not answer. He cannot—he hears nothing. At last, urged by his companions, who succeed in rousing him from his torpor, he exclaims, wandering in his mind, "The physicians will not cure me!" Pretending that these words are meant as an accusation against the medical men, the President, Navarro, desires them to be written down in the minutes, and decrees that Leipnecher shall be the first called up for examination. During the reading over of the notes of his previous answers before the *Inquisitore* and the Grand Criminal Court, the unfortunate man gives no other sign of life than some mechanical motions. The reading ended, the President asks the accused if he has anything to add, retract, or modify. The prisoner utters no sound. The President desires Leipnecher's counsel to answer for his client. This the counsel declines to do, alleging the character of the examination to be one entirely personal to the accused. Navarro insists on the counsel going close to his client, communicating the questions, and transmitting to the Court whatever answers he may receive. The counsel, evidently in great emotion, approaches Leipnecher, and immediately perceives that it is impossible to attempt any oral communication with him. The poor creature's forehead is covered with a cold sweat, and the panting of internal agony alone shows that he is not already a corpse. The Procurator-General, coming to the assistance of the puzzled President, observes that the physicians' report having been made early in the morning, fever might have come on since then, and suggests the expediency of having the medical men sent for to give their opinion again. In the meanwhile the cause can go on. After a considerable delay, two out of the seven physicians of the morning's report appear in the hall, accompanied by five strange medical practitioners. They are sworn, and, after examining the patient, answer, "That he has fever, and that it is on the increase." The Procurator-General wishes to know whether the sick man could not remain in Court for another hour without positive danger. The reply is, "That there would be no instant danger, but that the state of the patient is such as not to allow of his remaining longer where he is without serious injury." Upon receiving this opinion, the President declares the sitting closed. This took place on the 17th of June 1850; on the 22d of the same month Leipnecher was dead.

Let us now gather at random a few instances of the impartiality of the Court, and of its religious respect for the liberty of defence.

The subsidiary charge against Poerio is, that he fought furiously at the barricades on the 15th of May 1848. He asked permission to prove, that during the *whole* of that day he was detained by the duties of office at the Council of Ministers, whence he accompanied the actual Minister of War, Brigadier Carascosa, to his (Carascosa's) house. He proposed also to prove, by unexceptionable witnesses, and by a document of certain date, viz., a report against himself, all written in Iervolino's hand, that he, Poerio, knew Iervolino to be a paid instigator at the time when he (Poerio) was alleged to make Iervolino his political confidant. The court refused both requests.

Pironti is charged with having received, towards the end of October 1848, a letter full of high treason, at his own residence, *Vico Ecce Homo*, *No.* 9. He demands to prove that he had not returned to Naples from Santa Maria of Capua before the 2d of November, and that it was not before the 4th that he had taken up his residence in the house, where, according to the accusation, the letter had been given to him towards the end of October. He is ready to make good his assertion by the testimony of those who moved his furniture, by that of his fellow-lodgers, and by that of his landlord. The Court rejects the demand.

Bocchino, a grenadier in the Royal Guard, a witness for the prosecution against Cocozza, is heard. Though he has been decorated by the Pope, Bocchino's moral character is none of the highest. It results from certificates, signed by the colonel of his regiment, that the witness has suffered punishment for various causes eleven times—for having left his post, for thefts, for insubordination, and for attempted rape; he has been twice sentenced to be bastinadoed, once to thirty, the second time to sixty blows. This man deposes to having taken a letter from Mazza to Cocozza—both of them among the accused. He went to Cocozza, gave the letter into his hands, heard nothing about revolutions or sects, and remembers nothing more. The President exhorts him to tell the whole truth, but Bocchino persists in saying that he knows nothing more. Then the President orders the witness's long and circumstantial written declaration to be read. This Cocozza's counsel opposes, and with great energy claims the observance of the law. Navarro desires him not to interrupt the Court, but to sit down. At this point Settembrini, boiling with indignation, rises and asks to be reconducted to his prison. Since even this mere sham defence is to be thwarted, he will not, he says, legitimate by his presence such a continual trampling under foot of all laws, both human and divine.

Navarro growls some inarticulate words, and, with the snarl of a mastiff, orders Settembrini to hold his tongue. Settembrini, however, replies with warmth. Navarro repeats his threats of having him punished for his temerity. All the accused rise to their feet with one accord. The general emotion is at its height.

When calm is restored, Poerio gets up and says, that public discussion is the crucible in which truth is tried; through it all the facts gathered in the preparatory written process, whether incomplete, altered, or exaggerated, are re-integrated in their purity; through it all the spurious elements are eliminated. It is, therefore, logically indispensable that any witness called into a public court should himself relate and arrange the facts that are within his cognizance, and when his oral declaration be not in the whole conformable with his written deposition, it is an absolute necessity that the witness's retractations, variations, reticences, and hesitations—in a word, all the circumstances capable of affording a criterion of his sincerity, should be clearly registered. If witnesses were only brought forward to give a dry confirmation of their written declaration, then the end and aim of the law would be missed, and public debates would amount to nothing more than to a faint rehearsal of previous private examinations.

Cocozza's counsel quotes Articles 248, 249, and 251 of the Code of Penal Procedure, and submits to the Court that a witness called into a public court must give his oral testimony without assistance from his written one, that every addition, retractation, or modification of his former sayings, must be registered in the verbal process, and that only after this being done the President may refer him—if the President judge it opportune so to do—to his written declaration. The public prosecutor opposes these demands as unfounded. The Grand Criminal Court retires, and after an hour returns with a deliberation, which, admitting that all the additions, retractations, and modifications, of witnesses, are to be exactly set down, declares, at the same time, that the President alone is the best judge of the opportune application of the rule. The Court, in consequence rejects the demands. Thereupon the examination of the witness Bocchino is resumed, his written declaration is read over to him, and he repeats and confirms it, sentence by sentence.

Malacarne,—also a grenadier of the Guard,—another witness for the prosecution, deposes against two of the accused, Cocozza and Brancaccio. Cocozza, rising, protests that he never saw the witness in his life, and desires that the witness should look at him and say whether he recognises him, Cocozza. President Navarro makes a sign to the witness to turn round, and asks him whether the one of the prisoners now standing be Cocozza or not. The witness, turning round, and pointing to Cocozza, exclaims, "That is the man." The other accused, Brancaccio, calls upon the witness to identify him also, but uses the precaution of remaining seated. Navarro, before allowing the request to be complied with, orders Brancaccio to stand up. Upon which the latter observes, that if he stand up there is not the least doubt as to the witness singling him out from among his fellow-prisoners. Navarro replies that no one can be permitted to keep their seat while speaking in presence of the Court, and that, therefore, he cannot admit the identification unless the prisoner rises.

Colanero, another grenadier and witness for the prosecution, deposes to having spent a whole day with the accused Colombo. Mazza, one of the prisoners, rises, and, in behalf of Colombo, who remains seated, demands that the witness should identify Colombo's person. Navarro remarks to Mazza that he is not Colombo's mouthpiece, and that, if Colombo has any request to put forward, he must stand up himself. Mazza retorts, that if Colombo, who is to be identified, were to rise, how could any doubt exist as to the identity of his person? Colombo's counsel demands, on behalf of his client, that the confrontation should take place without his client's rising. The Procurator-General maintains, that the witness having indicated the accused by his surname and Christian name, to wit, Salvatore Colombo, the demand of the said prisoner's counsel could not be admitted, since, according to the law, the act of confrontation was to take place only when the person was vaguely indicated. Poerio remarks that the opposite system had been acted upon on the preceding day,—*vide* the case above quoted,—when a witness had designated Francesco Cocozza by both his names, and yet the President had, nevertheless, authorized his identification. The Grand Criminal Court withdraws, and, after an hour's deliberation, rejects the demand of Colombo's counsel.

Now for the morality of some of the most important witnesses for the prosecution.

Among them stands conspicuous Mauro Colella, one of the witnesses against Poerio. It results from the deposition of a priest named Mingione, that this Mauro Colella, while at dinner, last year, in Easter week, at deponent's house, confided to him that a *denunzia*—a false charge—was being concocted against Imbriani's brother-in-law, explaining that he alluded to Carlo Poerio. Some time after that, Colella, who lives opposite to deponent Mingione, called to him from one of his windows; and putting one hand across the top of the middle finger of the other,—a significant gesture,—said to Mingione, "The bird is limed," (*l'amico c'è capitato.*) "Who?" asked Mingione; and Colella answered, "Poerio," adding, "I'll just come over and tell you all about it." In fact, he did go to Mingione's house, and after relating Poerio's arrest, said that they had entangled that gentleman in such a net that he would infallibly lose his head. And on Mingione's asking what could have induced him (Colella) to denounce Poerio on such false grounds, Colella replied that it was because Poerio had been a deputy and a defender of the nation, (*sic*,) and would kill everybody if not killed himself; and also because he, Colella, had been promised for so doing a place in the police worth twelve ducats a month. These statements of Priest Mingione, given on oath before the Great Criminal Court, are confirmed and corroborated by the evidence of Mingione's mother and sister. Colella, according to his *fede di perquisizione*,—a certificate referring to the judicial antecedents of a person is thus called,—has been prosecuted for thefts committed in his convent, while he was a Friar, for perjuries, cheating at play, blasphemy, and he is now in prison under a charge for violent rape.

Francesco Paladino,—since dead,—witness for the prosecution against Nisco, is noted in his *fede di perquisizione* for thirty-two offences,—coining false money, forgery of banknotes, cheating at play, extortions of money on false pretences, swindling, &c.

Gennaro Fiorentino, another witness for the prosecution, comes in for eight charges of thefts, perjuries, and frauds.

Antonio Marotta, witness against Priest Nardi, is noted in his *fede di perquisizione* for false testimony, and perjury in a state prosecution against Canon Colamella, and is actually under warrant of arrest from the Great Criminal Court of Potenza, in spite of which he remains free. This man is the very Brutus of informers. To denounce Priest Nardi, his cousin, was such a mere trifle for him, that he had followed it up by the heroism of denouncing his own two brothers. He glories in having done so, as it was in the King's service. The fact is, that Marotta's two unfortunate brothers, unable any longer to bear the disgrace brought on an honourable family by his infamous conduct, had turned him out of their house, and he, out of revenge, had become the accuser of his own blood.

Remains Iervolino, the keystone of the accusation against Poerio, Settembrini, and Nisco. We will devote a separate chapter to the evidence of this consummate rascal, and to the various incidents to which it gave rise. They occupied the whole of the fourteenth sitting of the Court, than which none gives a more comprehensive idea of the whole proceedings, none brings out in stronger relief the wickedness and gorundlessness of the accusation, the noble attitude of the defence, the cool predetermination to condemn on the part of the judges.*

CHAPTER XXVI.
Continuation.

THE phœnix of informers, the spoiled child of the Prefecture of Police, a smartly attired, middle-sized, pale-looking man, upwards of thirty, is introduced. A long visage, slightly pitted with the small-pox, a pair of little unexpressive eyes, that seem to look nowhere, a low narrow forehead, make him anything but prepossessing. In he comes with an air of assumed innocence and timidity, highly creditable to his powers as an actor. Iervolino is incontestably the one of all his worthy associates in infamy and degradation, who best earns the meagre pittance of twelve ducats, or about two pounds a month, allowed him by the police. Unlike Gennaro or Marotta, who declaim their calumnies, Iervolino lets his drop from his lips modestly, hesitatingly, like one who recollects with difficulty; but once put on the right track by a frown or word from the President, he goes on coolly and methodically, but with decision and fluency.

He deposes, that finding himself in great want, and without work, the goldsmith who usually employed him having none to give him, he went to Baron Poerio, then a Minister of the Crown, to procure from him what he calls *un pane sicuro*—a certainty of bread. Seeing that, in spite of the promises made him, there was no office forthcoming, he drew the conclusion that his failure must be owing to his not be-

* The particulars contained in this and the following chapter are abridged from a correspondence, published at the time by a moderate and ably conducted periodical of Turin, the *Risorgimento*, the only newspaper, that we know of, which warmly took up the cause of conculcated innocence and humanity, and gave all the publicity at its disposal to the prosecution against Poerio and consorts. The veracity of the correspondent, a conscientious eye-witness, may be relied on.

longing to any sect; whereupon he urged Poerio to enrol him, the deponent, in the sect to which Poerio belonged. The Minister received his overtures with pleasure, and sent him with Attanasio, a friend of Poerio, to Nisco, who, in his turn, sent him to Pacifico, at a café situated near Santa Brigida. Pacifico introduced Iervolino to a person named D'Ambrosio, who took him to his own house, and there initiated him into the sect of the Italian Unity. But of the oath and signs imparted to him then and there, Iervolino has no longer any recollection. In this way he became intimate with Poerio, and knew all Poerio's familiar friends—Nisco, Attanasio, the Reverend Father Grillo, Cassinensis, and a jailer called the *Carlonajo*—all of them Sectarians. Poerio made him acquainted with Settembrini also, but of the latter's friends, he, deponent, knows nothing, as Settembrini never spoke of them to him. Iervolino, moreover, went frequently to Nisco's house, and saw those intimate there. Poerio and Settembrini intrusted him with several affairs, or commissions; thus, Settembrini gave him, for distribution, twenty printed copies of an invitation, or address to the public, not to smoke, or put into the lottery, or pay the taxes; and Poerio one day desired him to go and verify whether the flag in front of the royal palace was white or tricolor. Poerio told him also on another occasion, that the members of the Sect were to have medals whereby to recognise one another, and that many of these were being struck; and that he, Iervolino, should have a good number to distribute among his proselytes. Settembrini also told him that a movement was at hand; that Garibaldi was expected, and asked him how many associates, and what number of muskets, he could muster; and, on hearing that Iervolino had five or six muskets, and thirty associates on whom he could depend, Settembrini showed great satisfaction. This was of course mere boasting, and only said by way of winning the confidence of the Sectarians; for Iervolino, far from seeking to collect people to fight against the King, had repented having ever figured among his Majesty's enemies; and used, for two months previous, to make his report at the police-office, where he had also deposited four incendiary proclamations, handed to him by Settembrini some days before this latter's arrest. He recollects nothing else.

The President bids him recall to mind his written deposition, and exhorts him to tell the whole truth. Iervolino declares that he has said all he recollected, but that he is ready to ratify all he has written, because it is the truth. Iervolino's first declaration, subsequent ratification, delation, (*denunzia*,) and three secret reports, are then read. He cannot say what was the tenor of the oath he took, or what were the signs taught him, having forgotten both. He recollects the signs being changed every now and then. He always received them from Settembrini, who was continually recommending him to mix among the men of the people (*popolani*) belonging to the Sect. Who these "men of the people" were, he could not say, no one in particular was pointed out to him. To the question, "What rank he held in the Sect?" he answers that he was only a common member. But on being made to remark that his reply is in contradiction with his statement on the subject in his written declaration, he recollects that in fact he was promoted by Nisco to the rank of Unitarian. Questioned again as to the oath he took, all he remembers, he says, is, that the oath was for the Constitution. Questioned again if this was all, and if a change of the form of Government was not implied by the oath, he replies, that at first the oath was to support the Constitution, but that afterwards, as he learned from other associates, it aimed at the establishment of a Republic.—(Here, as usual, when that longed-for word is pronounced, the President shows marked approbation and satisfaction.) Iervolino does not recollect the signs of recognition first imparted to him, but, among those communicated to him later by Settembrini, he remembers the words,—"We are all children, the mother is Rome," and a sign, which consisted in touching the nose and the left eyelid with the index of the right hand. —(These are the signs given in the printed indictment.) He was never present at any meeting of the Sect, nor does he know whether there ever were such meetings.

Poerio's counsel demands the insertion in the minutes of Iervolino's statement, that the oath required of him was for the Constitution. Both the President and the public prosecutor oppose the demand. The counsel insists on the point. Then the President asks Iervolino again about the form of the oath, and Iervolino repeats that the Constitution was sworn to, but he heard it said that later they must come to a Republic; and in these terms the answer is registered in the minutes.

The accused Poerio rises, and begs the President to ask Iervolino whether all his secret reports to the police be inserted in the process. The query is put, and answered in the affirmative by Iervolino.

"This man lies," rejoins Poerio; "for I here present to the Court a report entirely written in his hand, and directed to a functionary of the police named Gennaro,—a report full of the most disgusting calumnies against Settembrini and myself. I call on the delator (*denunziante*) to say if this report be his, and, in the case of his denying it, I demand that the identity of his handwriting may be legally ascertained."

Navarro expresses his astonishment at hearing that a written report against the accused Poerio should be in that person's hands. To which Poerio answers, "I am not bound to say how I obtained this document. It is a secret confided to my honour, and one that will remain buried in my bosom as long as I live. The document is of use for my defence, and I here exhibit it on my own responsibility, and in the exercise of a right bestowed on me by the law. This must suffice for your watchful justice, Mr. President, as well as to make you aware that, even in these most disastrous times, oppressed virtue has more friends than the wicked can believe."

Iervolino is desired to examine the document. He comes forward with an unsteady step and blanched cheek, looks at the paper, carefully scans the address, then says, "It ought to be directed to Don Gennaro Cioffi," thus supplying the missing family name on the address, the paper having been torn away in that place. Iervolino reads, and turns and returns it several times, then falters out that he does not recollect having written it, but thinks it is his. At last, after being pressed by question on question, he says, "That paper is mine, but the address does not seem to me in my handwriting." The paper is read aloud by the Secretary.

Poerio rises again and speaks. "Among the grounds of defence—*posizioni a discarico*—that I submitted to the Court, there figured one, by which I propose to prove, that, so far back as the month of May 1849, I was perfectly aware that this man was a secret agent of that impious faction which is set upon ruining me, let it cost what it will. I then offered to show to the Court a report against me, written and signed by this man, and I requested that two highly honourable persons, and most excellent friends of mine, to whom I had given that nauseous paper to read as soon as it reached me, might be examined. But the Court thought proper to reject this particular request, together with the others I had made. When called up for examination I did not fail again most respectfully to urge the admission of my previously rejected grounds of defence, in particular of this last one. I was again refused; yet the Court, in its high wisdom and justice, reserved to me the right of asking for the hearing of the two witnesses indicated by me, whenever the use or necessity of their being heard should be made manifest in the course of the public debates. I demand that this right be now made good. If Divine justice has permitted me to be a target for the arrows of calumny, it has also brought forth from the womb of calumny itself the means of my justification. Ye, high priests of human justice, ye cannot grudge me, ye will not take from me this benefit bestowed by Providence."

Poerio's counsel backs his client's demand with legal arguments. The public prosecutor opposes it. Poerio rising, says, "It is with a most grieved spirit that I am forced to remind the honourable magistrate, that when I first produced this identical ground of defence, the public prosecutor opined for its admission. How, then, can the public prosecutor now urge the rejection of that same *posizione a discarico* which he admitted at a former period—urge its rejection now that the document is proved authentic?"

The President here sharply admonishes the speaker, and reminds him that he is not entitled to censure the Court. The Procurator-General was in the exercise of his right when he admitted, as now when he rejects, an identical ground of discharge, for his opinions are always conscientious and conformable to law.

The accused answers, "The Honourable Procurator-General cannot belie me when I state a positive fact, an undeniable fact, when I show him to be in flagrant contradiction with himself. This I do not assume to censure, for I know my duty, but I may be allowed to deplore it, for I know my right also, and how to exercise it, subject to and under the control of your impartial justice."

The Court reserves its deliberation on this point.

The President asks Poerio if he has any remark to offer touching Iervolino's declaration, and the accused answers thus:—"Most Honourable President, the *denunzia* (delation) is audaciously calumnious, and the very police judged it to be so. This wretch, urged on by spite, by misery, and wickedness, elaborates a false charge, and presents it on the 19th April 1849. It is read at the police-office, and no heed is taken of it. Iervolino renews his attack, and is not listened to. Not before the 16th of May, that is, after the lapse of nearly a month, is this informer called on to ratify his affirmations. He is asked for corroborating witnesses; he has none. Commissary Maddaloni dismisses him, begins no process, has no thought of arresting me; and this at the moment when the police unhesitatingly imprisoned, not only the pretended chiefs, but even the simple pretended members of the pretended Sect. When I was arrested, two months after, it was not in consequence of Iervolino's delation, but, as it appears from a certificate inserted in the process, on the ground of some one at Archpriest Miele's house having said he had heard that Baron Poerio and Duke Proto were the chiefs of the Sect. But even then Commissary Maddaloni did not institute any investigation relative to Iervolino's *denunzia*, for Nisco, who had been eight months in prison, was not once examined about the Sect, and all the persons named in that *denunzia*, and put forward as my accomplices and Sectarians, Attanasio, D'Ambrosio, Pacifico, and Father Grillo, continued to live unmolested in Naples. Nor does the police believe in Iervolino's envenomed accusation at this moment, since but lately it granted a free passport to one of the denounced parties, the honourable Father Grillo, now at Rome. Iervolino's calumnious charges were only disinterred at a later season, to serve that evil inclination of police commissaries, who like to give themselves the airs of judges-inquisitor, and to swell the processes with the secret information of their spies. But it is not my present purpose to confute the falsehoods gathered together in that wretch's infamous reports. I shall only, with your leave, most honourable President, put some questions to him. Where had I first the honour of making his precious acquaintance? Was he introduced to me by any friend? Did he come alone or in company?"

Iervolino replies that he sought Poerio, when he was secretary for the home-department, at his private house, to present a petition to him. He was neither introduced nor recommended by any one.

Poerio again:—"This man equivocates on one point. He did not come to my house, but to my office; however, this matters little. He asserts that he urged me, while I was a constitutional minister of the Crown, to enrol him in a certain Sect. How did he know one of the King's ministers to be a Sectarian? How did he dare make a request to a high functionary of the State which might cost him dear?"

Iervolino answers, that it was a fact publicly known that

Poerio was member of a Sect. He further recollects *now*, that his solicitations about entering the Sect did not take place immediately after his introduction to Poerio, as perhaps appears from his first delation, but at a later period, and when Poerio was no longer minister; certainly not before the 16th May 1848.

"But how, then, could Poerio, if out of office, be of use to the *denunziante?*"

Answer.—By recommending him to the other ministers.

Poerio.—"The *denunziante* affirms that he was a daily visitor at my house. Where did he wait? At the street door, in the hall, the antechamber, or in my own room?"

Answer.—In the beginning, sometimes at the street door, or in the hall, or anteroom, but, as he became more intimate, he used to sit in Poerio's bedroom.

Poerio.—"Such being the case, the deponent will certainly be able to name some among the deputies, peers, magistrates, ministers, who honoured me with visits."

Answer.—Iervolino took no trouble to know the name of Poerio's visitors, excepting those of the four he wrote down in his *denunzia*.

Poerio.—"But if he was accustomed to spend all his mornings in the hall, he must have come to know some of the heads of the different bureaux who called daily for my signature."

Answer.—Iervolino saw numbers of persons, but never made inquiries as to their names.

The President asks the accused Nisco if he has anything to say. Nisco answers, "I have to observe, in the first place, that it seems strange, to say the very least, that I should not once have been examined as to this pretended Sect. I solemnly declared that I never was a Sectarian; a villain starts up, and charges me, behind my back, with being so; of this heinous charge a mystery is made to me during the whole of the preparatory process, that is, during fourteen long months, and now I am suddenly required to answer, in a public Court, the vile calumniator."

The President interrupts the accused, and warns him not to insult the witness, who is entitled to respect.

Nisco rejoins,—"This man is no witness, he is a *denunziante*,—a delator. If you will not allow me to call him a calumniator, I shall call him by his name, and that will be enough, nay, quite the same thing. I shall say he is an Iervolino; that name is the impersonation of all human wickedness. Well, this Iervolino confesses himself a Sectarian, confesses having taken the oath to a Sect, having, during the course of a whole year, received and executed commissions connected with that Sect. This man then, is amenable to justice, and cannot be heard as a witness. Let Iervolino come up and take his place on these benches, let him stake his own head, and then his wonderful revelations may be, I will not say credited, but listened to without offence to the law." Here Nisco enters at length into details and statements in order to prove, that during Poerio's administration, that is, from the 6th of March to the 3d of April 1848, he, Nisco, was never in Naples, and, consequently, cannot, out of physical impossibility, have held any communication with Iervolino, as asserted by the latter, in a place where he, Nisco, was not. "I know very well," continues the accused, "that Iervolino has retracted his former saying in one respect, and assumed just now that his solicitations to Poerio to be enrolled in a Sect were made at a later period, and when Poerio was no longer in office. But when did this informer change his tactics? When the incredibility of his first affirmation stared him and every one else in the face. But Iervolino's new declaration surpasses in absurdity, if possible, the old one. His object, he declares, was to be recommended by Poerio to some of the new ministers. To the ministers, forsooth, of the 16th May! —that same administration to which Poerio, as a deputy, never ceased to offer from the tribune a loyal, conscientious, but unflinching opposition." Nisco concludes by demanding to prove, by unexceptionable witnesses, the exactness of his allegations as to his *alibi* from Naples, at a time when

Iervolino alleges to have held personal intercourse with him in the capital.

Settembrini, on being asked by the President if he has anything to say, rises and answers, "After the questions put to the informer by my friend and co-accused Poerio, I have nothing to ask him with regard to myself. All I can say is, that I never knew Iervolino before, and that I wish I had not known him now. That man is in the pay of the police, he receives twelve ducats per month, besides perquisites, depending on the services he renders. See how he has cleaned and furbished himself up; he looks anything but poor now. He confided all this himself to his friends, Nicola Rubinacci, Luigi Mazzola, Ferdinando Lanzetta, and Giovanni Luigi Pellegrino; these confidences he made on an occasion when Rubinacci, complaining to him of the hardness of the times, Iervolino exhorted him to do as he did, and he would soon be out of want. I demand that the persons I have named may be heard as witnesses, and I hope the Court will grant me at least this request. I take this opportunity of reminding the Court that I stand here in a solitary and unprecedented position, namely, that I am the only one in this cause whose grounds of defence have been *all* rejected in a lump. If the necessity of hearing some witness in my behalf does not arise from this man's deposition, it will arise no more, for, with the exception of this single *denunziante*, there is no other witness to the charge against me in the public debates."

The Court prepares to withdraw. Poerio rises and requests to speak. Navarro looks much annoyed, and shows signs of impatience, but Poerio maintains his right, and claims from the well-known "justice of the President the full exercise of the liberty of defence." After some hesitation, the President, who had already risen, sits down again, and the accused speaks as follows:—

"Gentlemen,—In the interest of my defence I feel called upon to submit to you a few demands, which naturally arise from the declaration of the delator. Iervolino has acknowledged as his own the infamous document I presented to the Court, but, unable to divest himself entirely of the sad habit of lying, has pretended to doubt whether the address was in his own handwriting. This doubt ought to be removed, and I therefore request the Court to appoint some persons skilled in such matters, and to commit to them the care of legally ascertaining whether or not the handwriting of that paper be the same with that of the address on the cover. Iervolino denies that, towards the end of May 1849, —the time at which I learned that he was a paid spy and informer,—I ordered him out of my house; he even asserts that he continued to frequent it at a posterior date. I affirm, on the contrary, that precisely at that same date I read the nauseous paper I have exhibited here to two honourable friends of mine, and that in their presence I forbade him my house. It is the examination of these two witnesses I now demand, the necessity of their testimony having arisen from the public debates. I must also urge the admission of two other demands, of which I leave you in your wisdom to weigh the strict legality and high importance."

The President interrupts the accused, reminds him that Iervolino's deposition alone has already taken up six hours, and desires him to be short, and leave out useless things.

Poerio answers,—"It certainly is no fault of mine if Iervolino's complicated falsehoods have lengthened this discussion. As to the method of my defence, and the choice of my arguments, I beg to be allowed to follow the dictates of my judgment, and nevertheless to anticipate that benevolent attention which your noble eagerness after truth, most honourable President, and never-failing respect for the liberty of defence, (Navarro winces and fidgets on his seat,) secure beforehand to a man in my situation. When the Court rejected my grounds of defence, it left me the right of asking for the hearing of the witnesses produced in support of those same rejected grounds, whensoever the necessity or expediency of their being heard should arise in the public trial. Of that right allow me now to make use.

When the Court rejected my special demand for the reintegration in the process of a document relating to a pretended letter of the Marquis Dragonetti, the Court reserved to me the right of orally repeating the deductions contained in the unproduced document. Let me now benefit by that reservation, to show you the pertinency of a last request of mine."

Navarro observes to the accused, that these means have been already amply developed in his printed defence, and that their repetition will only cause a useless loss of time to the Court.

Poerio.—"The time you devote to the hearing of the defence, is time put to its noblest purpose; nor will you regret it, honourable President, if it serves to satisfy you of my innocence, and of the wicked animosity of my enemies. Gentlemen, in my grounds of defence, I have appealed to the testimony of eminent persons, Cardinals, Ambassadors, Ministers, Generals, &c. I have called on them to depose, both to my opinions and my acts as a public man. This Iervolino, a man who has sold his soul to the faction bent on my destruction,—this type of all vice dares, with the most insensate and vilest calumnies, to sully five-and-forty years of a modest but fearless and virtuous life. Can you, after listening to him, deny me the means of justification? If the list of witnesses I have produced be too long, curtail it in your wisdom, but do not reject them *all* on the plea of their being *many*. Do not thus deprive me of the means of vindicating that which is most vital to me,—I mean my honour.

"And now I come to my last request. On the 24th July 1849, six days after my arrest, I was summoned, for the first time, to the presence of the Commissary Inquisitor, and desired to open a sealed letter forwarded through the post to my address, and which was attributed to the Marquis Dragonetti. No sooner had I cast my eyes on it, than I perceived at once the vile imitation of Dragonetti's handwriting. There were among my sequestrated papers some of Dragonetti's genuine letters which I produced. The Commissary Inquisitor and his attendants compared them with the one they had just given me, and, even to their eyes, the forgery stood confessed. Nor did I rest contented with this material proof of the calumny, but I went on to corroborate it by the demonstration of a moral impossibility. How could Dragonetti, one of the purest and most elegant writers in Italy, he whose letters were models of polished style—how could he have penned a paper full of gross blunders, not only of grammar, but of spelling? How could a man in Dragonetti's affluent circumstances, with a large circle of relations, friends, and acquaintances at his service, be supposed to have employed the post in so treasonable a matter,—he who had always forwarded his letters on the most indifferent subjects by a private hand? How could it be possible, that a man of mature age, and brought up in the school of misfortune, should ever dream of writing openly in his own hand, without a shadow of disguise, a letter which must send him to the scaffold, authenticating it with his signature, and the title of Marquis to boot?

"These, and suchlike unanswerable arguments, as I immediately set forth and indited, were entered on a minute, which was drawn up at the time; but this minute does not figure among the documents of the present process, and has been kept back from malignant motives. The forged letter was to inform me that Mazzini, one of the triumvirs at Rome, gave me a rendezvous at Malta; it spoke of a universal rising throughout Italy being at hand; it alluded to a correspondence of Lord Palmerston, engaging the people of this country to proclaim a republic, and offering assistance of every kind; (all eyes here turn towards the representative of Great Britain, Sir William Temple, Lord Palmerston's brother, who is present in the gallery with the Princes Colonna;) finally, that stupid paper announced the imminent arrival of Garibaldi. I formally demand that the missing minute be reinstated among the documents of the cause; and I have no doubt but that you will comply with my demand, for the condemnation of the innocent is a public calamity, and, to remove any such danger, you must concede to me the free use of all such means as tend to establish my being the victim of dark and calumnious machinations. And please to remark, that the entry of Garibaldi is spoken of in Iervolino's *denunzia* against me of the 20th May 1849; that the entry of Garibaldi was mentioned by the witnesses of Pomigliano examined in the preparatory process; and that the entry of Garibaldi is touched upon by the author of the forged letter, attributed to Dragonetti. Here, then, you have the watchword of my persecutors,—here, then, you have the thread to unravel the web woven for my destruction. Gentlemen of the Court, I adjure you to let light shine in upon you. Surely you will not, by shutting your eyes, wilfully remain in darkness."

The Grand Criminal Court withdraws to deliberate; and comes back two hours afterwards with a decision to the following effect:—Of the demands of the accused Nisco, the Court admits, by a majority of six votes to two, the one relating to the proof of his sojourn at San Giorgio by means of witnesses,—rejects the proof, through witnesses, of the precise epoch of his journey to and from Rome, reserving to the accused the right of establishing the date by the exhibition of his passport.

Settembrini's request to prove Iervolino to be a paid agent of the police, by oral evidence, the Court rejects—reserves the right to the accused of proving his assertion by documents.

All Poerio's demands are rejected in a lump.

This trial lasted eight months, from June 1850 up to January (inclusive) of 1851. Procurator Angelillo's speech in support of the accusation took up three days. The advocates on the side of the defence fought like lions for their clients, but with little success. Out of forty-two accused, reduced to forty-one by the death of Leipnecher, eight were acquitted, thirty-three condemned; (we record only the severe sentences;) three, among whom Settembrini, to death; two to the galleys; three to thirty-five years of irons; one, Nisco, to thirty years of irons; three, Poerio, Pironti, and Romeo, to four-and-twenty years of irons; one to twenty years of irons; eight to nineteen years of irons.

As one of the names included in this last category fell from the lips of the clerk of the Court, a shriek came from the reserved gallery-seats, and a great bustle ensued. At the same instant one of the prisoners, a tall, commanding figure, ghastly pale, rose and stretched both hands towards the gallery. It was whispered among the crowd that a lady, the veiled lady who had not missed a single sitting of the Court—some said the sister, some the wife of the prisoner who had stood up—some an English lady, whose life he had saved, had fainted, and been carried away by her friends.

CHAPTER XXVII.
Ischia.

THIS last Chapter finds all the prominent characters of our story (excepting Sir John, who is still confined by his gout at Davenne) in the Isle of Ischia.

Doctor Antonio, in the dress of a common felon, drags his heavy chains in yonder frowning Castle.

Lady Cleverton, ever since last February, has been residing in one of the best situated and most beautiful villas of the island. Owing to ill health her habits are extremely secluded, and she generally leaves it to her cousin, the attaché, and her companion, a lady of most agreeable manners, to do the honours of her splendid mansion to the distinguished visitors, who flock from Naples and the adjacent islands to admire Lady Cleverton's beautiful yacht. Her ladyship's physicians, it is said, have advised her to live as much as possible at sea, and, to enable her to conform to their advice, this paragon of yachts has been sent from England. The *Perseverante*—thus has Lady Cleverton christened her fairy vessel—is better known for twenty miles around than any of his Neapolitan Majesty's ships—goes in and out of the neighbouring little bays at all hours of the day or night—is seen tacking and cruising along the coast, without ever disturbing the siesta of custom-house officer or coast-guard;—the *Perseverante*, in short, is quite at home in these waters of the lovely gulf of Naples.

Speranza, it is scarcely necessary to say, is by the side of her dear mistress.

Battista has given up his inn and his epaulettes to come and settle as a fisherman at Ischia, where he lives in a poor quarter of the town close to the port. He brings, almost daily, to Lady Cleverton's villa, large loads of fish, which are always received by Speranza. As nobody in the house understands Battista's *patois* but Speranza, it is she who makes the bargains; but in all other respects she treats him like a perfect stranger, as indeed do Hutchins and the English man-servant, the only members of the household who have known him before. Battista's custom in the town is not large. Save now and then some chance purchaser, it appears limited to a thin elderly man in a shabby suit of black, undoubtedly an inmate of the Castle, as he is invariably seen to pass the bridge that joins the Castle to the island, when he comes, which he regularly does every second day, to buy his provision of fish at Battista's house. Battista shows great attention to his single customer, terms him "his dear Doctor,"—a diploma of Battista's own conferring,—has a glass of lachryma Christi always ready for him,—loads him with fish, and with mysterious little bundles into the bargain, which last the visitor twists, with the utmost care, round his body under his clothes. These bundles are skeins of strong silk, carefully prepared by Lady Cleverton and Speranza. One hour would be sufficient to loop hundreds of these skeins into one another, and make them into a solid rope or chain, by which a person might descend from any height.

Well, we are in the month of May,—that fatal month of
May! The night is as dark as lovers and smugglers could
wish, and the black outlines of yonder towering Castle are
scarcely discernible on the gloomy background of an overcast sky. A boat, in which are the attaché and Battista, advances cautiously with muffled oars to the foot of the huge
pile, and takes up its station just where the rock plunges
perpendicularly into the sea. A short mile off the little har-
bour of Ischia, the *Perseverante* lies at anchor. In a cabin
on the deck are Lady Cleverton and Speranza, mute as
shadows. Their anxiety is too great for utterance. Speranza
on her knees by the side of her beloved mistress, bathes her
temples. Lucy's life hangs on the issue of this hour.

Every clock of the town strikes twelve—the two women
in the yacht strain their eyes in the direction of the fortress
—the two men in the boat strain their eyes upwards—not a
stir—not a sound. Another hour—an age—is gone, and the
same dead stillness prevails. What can this delay portend?
Midnight was the hour appointed; the filing of the prisoner's
chains, and the iron-bars of the window, through which he
must make his escape, was only to occupy twenty minutes.
Could it be that a discovery had taken place? But if so,
some alarm would have been given, muskets fired, voices
heard,—at least lights would have been seen,—and everything remains as still and dark as death. Or could it be,
that, at the decisive moment, face to face with the abyss
below, the captive's courage had failed him? Three years
of physical and mental torture, as practised in Neapolitan
jails, had been known to unman hearts as noble and fearless
as Antonio's.

While on board the yacht, and in the boat, such conjec-
tures were being discussed in thrilling whispers, the vast
mass of the Castle was becoming every moment more distinct against the gradually whitening horizon. Another ten
minutes, and it would be too late for the boat to withdraw
without arousing suspicion, so the attaché and Battista took
once more to their oars, and, cautiously leaving their

perilous situation, made for the yacht; and in a little more than an hour afterwards, a sedan-chair deposited Lady Cleverton in the hall of her villa. Battista by this time was pacing up and down his poor dwelling, near the port, waiting, with the keenest impatience, for the hour that should bring his mysterious customer from the Castle, and with him the solution of last night's riddle.

He came at last, and with such intelligence as sent his eager listener reeling back like a drunken man. Battista flew to the villa, and was immediately ushered by the terrified Speranza into Lady Cleverton's presence. "*He* won't come out!" groaned the poor fellow, tearing his hair and biting his hands; "he won't come out!" Such was the fact. Antonio had refused to escape, and last night's failure was his own doing.

"This is downright madness!" exclaimed the attaché. The glance that passed at these words between Lucy and Speranza was full of a new terror. At this instant Battista handed to Lady Cleverton a dirty scrap of paper. O joy! it was from him, though it could scarcely be said to be in his handwriting. The letters were formed by little holes pierced in the paper. These few words, traced in complete darkness, had cost the writer a whole night's labour. The contents were as follows:—

"There are five here besides myself, all noble fellows, the least of them worth ten of me. I cannot desert them. You cannot save us all; leave me to my fate. Providence has assigned me my place among the sufferers. Perhaps our trials will be reckoned to our country. Pray that it may be so. Pray for Italy. God bless you! Your own A—."

Lucy buried her face in her hands, and hot tears trickled through her fingers. The other three were scarcely less moved.

"We will save them all," cried she suddenly, raising her head with the look of one inspired.

"We will, so help us God!" said the attaché and Speranza. Battista said nothing, but lifted up his hand in solemn attestation.

In the afternoon Baron Mitraglia called on Lady Cleverton. She had met him at the Court assemblies. Far too important a personage was this baron, general, chamberlain —"three great men rolled into one," far too high in the King's favour was this grand-cross of innumerable orders to be denied admittance. The conversation could not be otherwise than desultory, the Court, the weather, the fine prospect, Lady Cleverton's beautiful yacht which the baron had admired at a distance.—Would he like to go on board? The baron regretted very much he could not avail himself at this moment of her ladyship's kind invitation; the fact was he had come to Ischia on official business, and must return at once to Naples. He had not come, hopes Lady Cleverton, with a forced laugh, to put Ischia in a state of siege? The "official business" had rather startled her.

"I could almost wish I had," retorted the baron, with a chuckle, "were it only to make sure that you do not give us the slip one of these days." There was a twinkle in his grey eye as he said this, quite inexplicable to his listener. "My present mission," continued the baron, gravely—"I may confide it to a lady of your discretion—relates to some political prisoners—I daresay you had no idea of having such neighbours—who are detained in yonder castle;" and he pointed with his finger to the huge fortress, which was distinctly visible from the sofa on which he was sitting.

"Indeed!" was all Lady Cleverton could say, as a cloud passed before her eyes.

"Yes; information reached his Majesty's Government but a few days ago that underhand practices had been carrying on for some time in this island,—something like a plot for the escape of the prisoners I was speaking of. Do not look alarmed, milady, there is no fear of such dangerous characters being again let loose on society. His Royal Highness Prince Luigi, who, as admiral of the kingdom, has charge of this island, sent me here to inquire into the matter. Nothing worth mentioning, after all; mere child's play. However, I thought it best, chiefly in the interest of the prisoners themselves, to order their immediate removal."

Lady Cleverton had listened to this disclosure with the feelings of a criminal with his head on the block; but she commanded sufficient external calmness to ask, in a careless way, "And where are you going to send them?"

"That is my secret, milady," returned the baron, with a smile as sharp as the point of a dagger; "that is my secret," and away he went.

When Speranza, shortly after, came to her mistress, she found her in a swoon. This unhappily, was no uncommon occurrence; for many months past Lady Cleverton had been subject to fainting fits. "It was that horrible man," she whispered. "I will tell you by and by; I cannot think just now, I feel so sleepy." Speranza laid her down on the sofa to sleep. Lucy lay very quietly. Now and then some broken words, evidently connected with a dream, would pass her lips; some one she had long expected was coming, and she must have her blue gown. Once she tried the first notes of an air, which Speranza took up, and hummed gently. It was the first Sicilian song Antonio had taught Lucy. The silence after this was unbroken for hours.

The day was on the wane. Speranza, who had scarcely dared to breathe for fear of disturbing the sleeper, began to be scared, she knew not why, by the stillness around. Unable to stand it any longer, she went on tiptoe to her mistress, and leaned over her. There was a change in the fair face which struck Speranza. She called her by name—no answer; she took one of Lucy's hands—it was cold. Lucy had ceased to suffer.

She looked like a sleeping child. The angel of death had smoothed away the premature lines about her eyes and mouth. Her lips were slightly parted with a smile. She lay with her head turned towards the castle. Her last look had been for Antonio.

Sir John could not stand the shock of the fatal news; he lingered on for some months, then died.

The young attaché solicited and obtained a change of residence. Naples had become unbearable to him.

Battista's mysterious customer was never seen or heard of more.

Battista and Speranza went back to their own country, and bought a fine country house near Nice, where they live to this day in affluent circumstances; Lady Cleverton, who must have had a presentiment of her approaching end, having bequeathed Speranza a large sum of money. But the loss of their benefactress, and the hopeless doom of Doctor Antonio, cast a gloom over their lives. Speranza's looks are sadly altered; her hair is all grey.

Captain, now Sir Aubrey Davenne, made a rich marriage, and never went back to India. He has been for the last few years one of the most respected members of the House of Commons, where he seldom speaks but on what has become his speciality,—religious and philanthropic subjects. The Peace Society counts him as one of its most influential and zealous promoters.

Doctor Antonio still suffers, prays, and hopes for his country.

THE END.

www.ingramcontent.com/pod-product-compliance
Lightning Source LLC
Chambersburg PA
CBHW031414230426
43668CB00007B/304